IMAGES OF
AMERICAN
LIFE

SUNY Series, Education and Culture: Critical Factors in the Formation of Character and Community in American Life
Eugene F. Provenzo, Jr. and Paul Farber, editors

IMAGES OF
AMERICAN
LIFE

A History of Ideological Management in
Schools, Movies, Radio, and Television

JOEL SPRING

State University of New York Press

Published by
State University of New York Press, Albany

© 1992   State University of New York

For information, address State University of New York
Press, State University Plaza, Albany, N.Y. 12246

Production by Marilyn P. Semerad
Marketing by Bernadette LaManna

Library of Congress Cataloging-in-Publication Data

Spring, Joel H.
    Images of American life : a history of ideological management in
schools, movies, radio, and television / Joel Spring.
        p.   cm. — (SUNY series, education and culture)
    Includes bibliographical references and index.
    ISBN 0-7914-1069-2. — ISBN 0-7914-1070-6 (pbk.)
    1. Mass media—United States—Influence. 2. United States-
-Intellectual life—20th century. 3. Education—United States-
-History—20th century. I. Title. II. Series.
P92.U5S625   1992
302.23'0973—dc20
                                                                91-33521
                                                                      CIP

10 9 8 7 6 5 4 3 2 1

CONTENTS

ACKNOWLEDGMENTS

I WOULD LIKE to thank Dawn P. Spring for help in researching major sections of the book. In addition, Danny Silverman did extensive research on the history of the comic book code and Felecia Briscoe did research on the images of women during World War II. John Tryneski and Naomi Silverman used their editorial skills to make suggestions on the organization and writing of the book. I am also indebted to student comments in seminars I conducted at the University of Cincinnati and Teachers College, Columbia University. And, of course, I want to thank the editors at SUNY Press, Lois Patton and Marilyn Semerad, for their help in producing the book. Marilyn Semerad needs to be especially acknowledged for her superior work as a production editor.

___

IDEOLOGICAL MANAGEMENT

IN THIS BOOK I analyze the effect of political and economic forces on the ideas and values disseminated to the general population by public schools, movies, radio, and television. In the twentieth century, I consider these sources to be the most important conveyors of ideas, information, and values to the public. In a broader sense, these are the major sources of public education in the twentieth century. While the tone of my analysis is often critical, I do not intend to present a tale of good against evil. My goal is to achieve an understanding of how ideas are shaped in American society by the interplay between government power, private enterprise, and organized advocacy groups.

The story I plan to tell is complex, with many different and conflicting strands. In a broad sense, I am describing the public education of the American people from the 1920s to the 1980s. Of course, we have no way of knowing the actual influence of schools, movies, radio, and television on the average American. But we can speculate on what people may have learned. For instance, consider the child of the early 1930s who during after-school hours attended movies with particular moral messages and listened to radio programs where superheroes did battle against evil. And consider what it may have meant to the political education of the average American when the major source of news shifted from politically oriented newspapers to the bland and supposedly neutral radio. While one cannot measure the actual effect of these media, one can show what was intended for the education of the public mind by forces that shaped and continue to shape the content of schools, movies, and broadcasting.

My interpretative framework for this analysis is *ideological management*. I first encountered this concept during the summer of 1988 while conducting a seminar on the topic "What is the best political structure for the control of knowledge in a democratic society?" One student in the seminar was a political refugee who had been trained in what was called ideological management in Bulgaria. He explained that ideological management in Bulgaria meant the control of ideas disseminated by public schools, movies, radio, television, libraries, museums, and cultural events. I questioned him about the training required to assume the role of "ideological manager." Interestingly, his studies, except for courses on

1

dialectical materialism, encompassed some of the standard courses in American teacher training programs. For instance, an important part of his program focused on educational psychology and the sociology of education.

The concept of ideological management highlights an important phenomenon in the modern world. Particularly since the nineteenth century, the control of ideas is considered a source of power. What people know, what they believe in, and how they interpret the world have an important effect on their choices and consequently their actions. In totalitarian societies, ideological management usually takes place through a centralized bureaucracy charged with coordinating the ideological messages conveyed to the public by the different media and the schools. In societies with less centralized control, such as the United States, struggles often occur between different political and economic interest groups over the ideas and values to be conveyed to the public, and there is a lack of coordination between the media and the schools. But even with conflict and lack of coordination, efforts are made, as I will argue throughout this book, to manage the ideology disseminated to the public.

In the Western world of the nineteenth century, various political and economic groups believed that government-operated schools could be a mechanism for assuring the distribution of their particular ideology to the population. In this sense, public schools were the first mass medium* designed to reach an entire generation. In modern times, particularly in the United States, different groups battle to assure that their concepts of politics, morality, and society are taught by the schools. In these situations, ideological management does not result from the action of a single individual or group, but is itself the result of conflict. Of course, victory in this contest often goes to the most powerful and the most active groups.[1]

The first competition to public schools as the predominant mass medium came in the form of movies. As discussed in more detail in later chapters, educators in the United States recognized movies, and later radio and television, as a threat to schooling as the primary distributor of ideas. In fact, the reaction of educators to movies, and then to radio and television, was an important influence on their content. Like the public schools, movies quickly became a contested arena. Many political and religious groups feared that movies would undermine the social order. Consequently, there were demands for censorship to assure the removal of objectionable content from films and to give them a role in mass education. The reaction of the movie industry in the United States, which was concerned that censorship and public protests would reduce profits, was to adopt in the 1930s a self-regulatory code to govern the content of films. As I describe later in the book, the stated goal of this code was to make movie entertainment into a form of public education in moral, social, and political values.

---

*For the purposes of my discussion, I include public schools in the term "mass media."

A similar pattern occurred with the development of radio and television. However, in addition to dealing with political, religious, and other groups fighting over the content of programming, the radio and television industries also worried about the power of government licensing. Educators saw radio and television as their competitors. Their reactions to radio and television influenced the content of these media, in ways I describe in detail in later chapters. Eventually, like the movie industry, the broadcasting industry adopted codes in the 1930s to control the content of its programming.

A major influence on schools, movies, and the broadcast industry was the combined forces of the social purity and anti-Communist movements. Beginning in the later part of the nineteenth century the social purity movement attempted to impose on public schools, movies, and broadcasting a particular standard of sexual morality. Composed of a variety of advocacy groups, particularly from conservative religious organizations, the social purity movement was responsible for the censorship of sexual material in movies and broadcasting, and for the content (or in some cases the elimination) of sex education courses in the public schools. The anti-Communist movement in the United States, launched at the end of World War I, had an important influence on the ideas disseminated by the schools, movies, radio, and television. During the Cold War period after World War II, the anti-Communist movement joined forces with the social purity crusade in an effort to censor movies, school materials, and radio and television programs. The influences of these two movements on schools and the media are documented throughout the book.

Therefore, within the United States, ideological management is a hotly contested arena. Outside forces not only influence the ideological content of schooling, movies, and broadcasting, but also the struggles among these different forms of mass media. Out of these conflicts, I argue in this book, emerge certain moral, social, and political ideas that are distributed to the public. To some extent, because of the similarity of forces working on each of these institutions, the ideas disseminated by all of them are very similar. On the other hand, however, there are sometimes important differences between the messages conveyed by these media. For instance, one interesting situation explored later in the book is the tension that existed in the 1920s between the movie industry and schools over sexual values. Movies played an important role in 1920s in teaching sexual techniques and fostering an image of aggressive female sexuality. But during this same period, in opposition to the messages conveyed by movies, public schools advocated sex education as a means of stopping the sexual revolution and controlling female sexuality.

Against the background of this discussion, ideological management can be more specifically defined as the conscious exclusion or addition of information and ideas conveyed to the public by mass media. The purpose of this conscious exclusion or inclusion of material was, in the case just discussed, to shield the population from certain ideas and information or to teach particular moral, political, and social values. In later chapters, I discuss how the debate in the early twentieth century over the censorship of movies made a clear distinction between the exclusion from movies of material that might cause social disorder and the addition of material for the purpose of public education. Often this debate touched on the social role of art. Some advocates of censorship of art believed in the free development of art as long as it did not endanger social stability; others argued that artists had an obligation to convey social lessons to the public.

Another dimension of the term "ideological management," as used in this book, is to convey a concept that is more complex and more inclusive than is ordinarily associated with the idea of propaganda. Often, we think of propaganda as the actions of government officials in manipulating information for the purpose of ideological control. Ideological management as I define it includes this concept of propaganda, but in addition, it includes attempts by a variety of public and private groups to influence ideas and information conveyed to the public. Also, propaganda suggests that there is an agreed upon ideological message to be distributed to the public. While ideological management does not exclude that possibility, I use the term to suggest competition and conflict between groups over what ideas and information should be disseminated. This aspect of ideological management, as I use the term, encompasses the possibility of the distribution of conflicting information and ideas by schools, movies, and broadcasting.

INTERPRETING IDEOLOGICAL MANAGEMENT IN THE UNITED STATES

A variety of approaches can be used to analyze the different forms of ideological management in the United States. In *Conflict of Interests: The Politics of American Education,* I argue that the ideological content of public schooling is shaped by the desire of different groups to have the public schools serve their interests.[2] For instance, a variety of advocacy groups outside the educational establishment, such as environmentalists, civil rights advocates, and religious groups, try to insure the inclusion of their points of view in the public school curriculum. In addition, throughout the twentieth century business groups have tried to make the schools serve their needs.

Conflict exists among members of the educational establishment. School administrators and teachers unions have long struggled over power and money. Political conflict over the content of textbooks influences the decisions of major publishing industries. The knowledge industry, including publishing and testing companies and the educational research community, is also influenced by competition for profits and income.

In *Conflict of Interests*, I conclude that the two major problems plaguing the political organization of American public schools are lack of freedom of thought and expression, and the influence of special interest groups, particularly the business community. The political structure of schooling in the United States makes it impossible to protect freedom of expression. Because of vocal public groups' monitoring the content of schooling, administrators and teachers feel that their jobs will be threatened if controversial political and economic ideas are taught in the classroom. Therefore, we have the ironic situation that the supposed protectors of democracy, the public schools, do little to promote a political culture that would help a democratic society survive.

In addition, *Conflict of Interests* argues that the current political structure of public schooling allows for the domination of powerful special interest groups, particularly the business community. Business influence now ranges from "adopt-a-school" programs and school-business compacts to business domination of the educational policy network. Besides creating an atmosphere that favors the teaching of conservative political and economic doctrines, business has increasingly demanded that education serve their labor market needs. Given these problems, *Conflict of Interests* concludes by calling for a public debate about how to organize the political structure of public schooling in a democratic society.

The interpretative model in *Conflict of Interests* can be used to explain the political and economic forces that determine the information and ideas distributed by the public schools. Edward Herman and Noam Chomsky in *Manufacturing Consent: The Political Economy of the Mass Media* develop a useful model for describing the effect of these same forces on the broadcast media.[3] Their model is based on five "filters" that shape the content of news broadcasts in the United States. The model is applicable to countries like the United States where the news media are privately owned, in contrast to a countries where a state bureaucracy exerts monopolistic control. In their model, the content of newscasts goes through a series of filters before reaching the public. Although there are claims to objectivity by news broadcasters, these filters, the authors argue, have a determining effect on news content. Herman and Chomsky's model, I believe, is useful in analyzing the political and economic forces shaping the content of broadcasting and it has a certain applicability to movies and public schools.

The first filter in their model is the economic structure of broadcasting, which in their analysis is concentrated in the United States in a few companies. These major corporations, they argue, are interlocked and share common interests. These common interests affect the selection of news and programs. The second filter is advertisers who are reluctant to sponsor programs that might generate public controversy or convey a message to the public that is contrary to their interests. These first two filters reflect the structure of American broadcasting, which is built on two realities: It is privately owned and it is dependent on commercial advertising.

The third filter in their model is news sources. Herman and Chomsky argue that broadcasters tend to rely on powerful corporate and government news sources because they are easily accessible and inexpensive. Major broadcasters very seldom contact marginal political and economic groups. In addition, broadcasters fear offending their major sources. This results, Herman and Chomsky argue, in a bias in the content and selection of news.

The fourth filter affects public schools as well as the broadcasting industries. This filter, which Herman and Chomsky call "flak," is the letters, speeches, phone calls, and other forms of group and individual complaints broadcasters receive. Advertisers and broadcasters avoid programming content that might generate large amounts of flak. Advertisers are concerned that flak will hurt the sales of their products, while broadcast owners fear that flak will threaten their government-granted licenses. The result is bland and noncontroversial programs. When the concept is applied to public schools, this filter represents the fear of school administrators that flak might threaten their jobs and/or cause a loss of public funding. Consequently, as previously discussed, educators avoid teaching anything that might cause community controversy.

Herman and Chomsky consider the ideology of anti-Communism to be the fifth filter in news broadcasting. Of course, since the writing of their book world events have reduced the importance of anti-Communism as a filter. But from the 1920s to the 1980s, anti-Communism played a major role in shaping American thought. The ideology of anti-Communism, Herman and Chomsky argue, tends to paint world events as a struggle between good and evil. In their words, this "ideology helps mobilize the populace against an enemy, and because the concept is fuzzy it can be used against anybody advocating policies that threaten property interests or support accommodation with Communist states and radicalism."[4] Therefore, they argue, under the fuzzy ideology of anti-Communism, leftist and labor movements can be cast in the role of enemy, while fascist dictatorships can be considered on the side of good. As I note earlier in this Introduction, the ideology of anti-Communism played an important role in American schools. Often the goals of history and social studies instruction in American public schools have been to build patriotism and to portray the evils of Communism. Of course, as the Cold War continues to thaw this fifth filter might be replaced by some other struggle between "good and evil."

Clearly, Herman and Chomsky's propaganda model can be applied to other conveyors of ideas and values to American society. For instance, during their most influential period of the 1930s to 1950s the ideas and values in movies were influenced by the economic organization of the industry, the fear of "flak," and by the conservative political philosophy of studio owners. In fact, as I discuss in this book, fear of flak played an extremely important role in determining the value content of American-made movies. Obviously, however, the "flak" model cannot be applied unmodified to films, as the role of advertisers and news sources is not directly applicable to the movie industry.

The role of flak in molding the content of media is an important part of Kathryn Montgomery's study, *Target: Prime Time—Advocacy Groups and the Struggle over Entertainment Television.*[5] She traces the role of advocacy groups in influencing the content of television from the 1950s to the 1980s. Four major advocacy groups are identified that in varying degrees affected the content of television. As I shall show, these same groups also affected the content of the public school curriculum during the same period. The first advocacy group identified by Montgomery is organizations representing minorities, women, seniors, and the disabled. All of these groups have campaigned for the presentation of more positive images on television programs. In a similar manner, organizations representing minorities, women, and the disabled work for the presentation of more positive images in the public school curriculum and in textbooks. And, as I shall discuss in later chapters, the role of minorities in films is an important part of the history of movies.

The second group identified by Montgomery is conservative religious organizations—the same groups that played an important part in the social purity movement. Conservative religious groups consistently act as self-appointed moral guardians of American culture. As Montgomery indicates, these groups have a significant impact on television programming. They also played a major role in the early censorship of movies and in the adoption of the movie code in the 1930s. The intent of this code, which was applauded by conservative religious leaders, was to turn entertainment into public moral lessons. Conservative religious groups act as guardians over the moral content of schooling. Without a doubt, conservative religious organizations play a major role in ideological management in the United States.

Social issue groups form the third set of advocacy organizations identified by Montgomery. These groups range from environmentalist organizations to those concerned with drug abuse. With regard to media, these organizations pressure television broadcasters to use entertainment to teach social lessons. For instance, entertainment programs might include anti-drug statements. These groups apply similar pressures to public schools. Public schools are called on to solve a whole host of social problems ranging from drug abuse to saving the environment.

Of particular importance for broadcasting are what Montgomery calls anti-violence groups. She includes in these groups organizations such as the Parent-Teachers Association and the American Medical Association. These groups are particularly vocal regarding children's programming. As I discuss in later chapters, these groups had a major impact on shaping children's radio programs in the 1930s and 1940s, and in the development of the first censorship codes in the broadcast industry.

An important argument of this book is that the similarity of pressure groups affecting the different media resulted in a certain similarity of ideas and values disseminated to the American public. Public schools, movies, radio, and television were pressured by similar organizations. Therefore, while there is no coordinated or centralized effort at ideological management in the United States, there is to a certain degree a common ideology presented to the public as a result of the activities of similar advocacy groups.

Of course, as Montgomery argues, there is no one-to-one correspondence between the demands of advocacy groups and the response of broadcasters. In reality, the final outcome is the result of negotiation between advocacy groups and broadcasters, but also of the organizational and economic needs of the broadcast industry. For instance, while some advocacy groups might condemn sex and violence in television programming and movies, the industries might find exploitation of these themes profitable. Also, as Todd Gitlin demonstrates in *Inside Prime Time: How the Networks Decide About the Shows That Rise and Fall in the Real World Behind the TV Screen,* network executives must negotiate their way through cross-pressures from politicians, advocacy groups, the artistic concerns of producers, the desires of advertisers, and the quest for profits.[6]

I would add the role of government intervention to the list of factors so far discussed as influences on the content of ideas and values distributed to the public. While affecting media in different ways, government intervention plays an important role in shaping the ideas and values disseminated to the public. This book will document the specific ways the government has influenced and continues to influence the ideas distributed by schools, movies, radio, and television. For example, textbooks and public school curricula are directly influenced by politicians at the federal, state, and local levels. This influence can range, for instance, from legislating the teaching of patriotism and morality to regulating the content of textbooks. In the film industry, censorship by local and state governments began during the early days of movies. And, of course, the licensing procedures of the federal government have a direct impact on the organization of the broadcasting industry and on the content of radio and television programs.

In addition, both World War I and World War II resulted in attempts by the federal government to use the media to build pro-war feelings among citizens. Later in this book I discuss how, during World War I, the federal government established the Committee on Public Information to initiate a massive propaganda campaign in the United States, using the public schools and other public relations forums. The federal government did the same thing during World War II, with the creation of the Office of War Information.

Government intervention, economic factors, pressure from advocacy groups, and the ideology of anti-Communism have been the major factors determining ideological management in the United States. Information and ideas are consciously added or excluded in public schools, movies, and the broadcast industry as a result of these factors. It should be stressed that this conscious inclusion or exclusion of information and ideas is often *not* unilaterally determined by a centralized agency, but is a product of conflict and negotiation among these differing elements. It is in this arena of conflict and negotiation that decisions are made about the ideas and values to be disseminated to the American public.

PLAN FOR THE BOOK

These arguments are developed by examining in Chapter 1 the debate over censorship of movies and the work of the Committee on Public Information during World War I. Chapter 2 explores the political and social values that public schools and textbooks disseminated during the 1920s. Of particular importance in this chapter is the discussion of the rise of anti-Communism and the activities of the American Legion. Chapter 3 examines the criticism by educators of the effect of movies on children, and the belief by educators that movies were rivals to public schools for control of the minds of children. Throughout Chapters 2 and 3 document the working relationship between educators and movie makers during the 1920s and 1930s.

Chapter 4 examines the fears during the 1920s that women's suffrage and aggressive female sexual behavior were undermining traditional family structure. Movies were criticized as being a major cause of the sexual revolution of the 1920s. The social purity movement of this period not only criticized the moral content of movies but also advocated sex education in public schools as a means of controlling female sexuality and protecting the traditional family. Chapter 5 shows how the social purity movement and criticism from educators resulted in the 1930s in the movie industry's adopting a self-regulatory code to govern the content of films.

Chapter 6 explores the debate in the late 1920s and early 1930s over whether radio should be controlled by commercial interests or by educators. At the heart of this debate was the issue of who should control the shaping of national culture. During the same period, as I discuss in Chapter 7, radio networks adopted a similar code because of criticism of children's radio programs. These censorship codes stressed the importance of using heroes in children's programming as a method of forming moral values. The stress on superheroes in radio programming, as discussed in Chapter 7, was paralleled by the development of comic books.

Chapter 8 shows how images of America and world conflict disseminated by public schools and textbooks changed amidst the economic ruin of the Depression and the rise of fascism. Chapter 9, documents how, during World War II, explicit ideological management of schools, movies, and radio was justified as part of "the war effort." After World War II, during the development of television as a mass medium, the anti-Communist atmosphere of the Cold War had a dramatic effect on broadcasting, movies, and the schools; this is the topic of Chapter 10.

Chapter 11 shows how, during the 1950s, concern about alienated and delinquent youth resulted in pressure on the television industry and in the adoption of a comic book code. Chapters 12 documents the effect of the civil rights and anti-war movements on public schools, textbooks, and television, and the efforts by the Nixon administration to counter the effects on public schools and television of these two movements. Chapter 13, traces the interconnections between government officials and foundations in the development of the Corporation for Public Broadcasting and the Children's Television Workshop. Of particular importance in Chapter 13 is the creation of "Sesame Street" and the argument that television is "the third educator," along with the family and school.

Chapter 14 brings the story of ideological management up to the 1990s. This final chapter contains a summary statement on the formation of images disseminated to the public. In general, ideological management in the United States involves the interaction of government, private enterprise, and advocacy groups. The interaction of these forces exposes the public to a steady stream of changing images of morality and democracy. It is in this contested arena that ideological management occurs in the United States.

CHAPTER ONE

CENSORING MOVIES AND TEACHING KIDS
TO LOVE WORLD WAR I

ONE OF THE agencies most prone to promote the war spirit is the sandtable," declared a *National School Service* bulletin issued by the federal government's Committee on Public Information during World War I. Using the descriptive title "Natural War Interests of Children," the bulletin urged teachers to encourage children to play war games. The bulletin claimed, "Children are no longer satisfied to build peaceful ditches, pleasant farms or high mountains.... Now trenches appear fortified by whatever accessible material may serve as cannon."[1]

World War I set the stage for a continuing debate about the role of censorship and propaganda in shaping public opinion in American society. These events heralded the sharpening of the conflict over control of *ideological management,* a framework of analysis that I develop in the Introduction to this book. The major struggle on the home front during the war was, in David Kennedy's words, "the war for the American mind."[2] Concerned about the possible lack of national unity and the unclear objectives regarding the United States' entry into the war, the federal government launched a massive propaganda campaign designed to create national unity and justify the war as a war for democracy. The campaign was led by the Committee on Public Information (CPI), which was primarily composed of reformers and educators who believed that the war provided the opportunity to transform America into their vision of a democracy. The CPI used all the major means at its disposal for influencing public opinion, including public schools, movies, advertising, a speakers' bureau, pamphlets, and magazines.[3] From the perspective of the members of the CPI, they were engaged on a major effort at educating the public in the meaning of democracy and nationalism. As will be clear later, they primarily defined democracy in social, not political, terms and they wanted their vision of democracy to become the new religion of American life.[4]

Immediately prior to America's entry into World War I, an extensive debate took place over the effect of movies on public morality. Some reformers believed that censorship should be used to make movies a form of public instruction in moral and social values. Others advocated censorship only of those parts of films which could cause social disorder. This debate continued after World War I with the argument for turning movies into a form of public education winning out in the 1930s. In addition, the movies represented a direct challenge to the role of public schools as the major source of public instruction. Many educators considered films to be in direct competition with the public schools for molding the minds of children (see Chapter 3).

Out of the debate over censorship of movies there developed a relationship between the public schools and the film industry. They needed each other for political and economic reasons. For example, in 1922, Will Hays, president of the newly formed Motion Picture Producers and Distributors of America (M.P.P.D.A.), tried to win educators to his side in the battle against government censorship by appealing for support to the gathered delegates at the annual meeting of the National Education Association (NEA). At the time, the NEA was the largest and most important organization for creating educational policy for the public schools. Hays quoted to the NEA delegates his organization's pledge to the goals of "establishing and maintaining the highest possible moral and artistic standards in motion picture production, and developing the educational as well as the entertainment value and the general usefulness of the motion picture." He concluded his speech with the promise, "We accept the challenge in the righteous demand of the American mother that the entertainment and amusement of...youth shall be worthy of their value as a potent factor in the country's future."[5]

Hays argued for censorship of movies by the industry, not by the government. In other words, the movie industry took the position that self-censorship would permit the industry to *include* material in movies for the purpose of public education in desirable social, political, and moral attitudes and behavior, whereas government censorship would only serve to *exclude* material for the purpose of shielding the population from certain ideas and information that might cause social disorder. Also, the movie industry preferred self-censorship because it was cheaper than making constant revisions required by government censors.

The M.P.P.D.A. was formed to counter demands for increased government censorship of movies. In fact, Hays devoted part of his speech to warning educators about the evils of government censorship of movies. He told the delegates to the NEA convention, "I am against political censorship, of course, because political censorship will not do what is hoped for it in the last analysis." What Hays offered the educators as an alternative to political censorship was censorship by the industry. In his words, "there is one place and one place only where the evils can be eliminated...and that is at the point where and when pictures are made." Hays promised his audience that, "Right is right and wrong is wrong, and men know right from wrong. The corrections can be made, real evil can and must be kept out, the highest standards of art, taste, and morals can be achieved, and it is primarily the duty of the producers to do it."[6]

Besides indicating the position of the movie industry on the issue of censorship, Hays's appearance before the NEA also illustrates the combination of political and economic pressures that created complex relationships between educators and the entertainment world. As the largest and most influential educational organization, the NEA was considered by the M.P.P.D.A. as essential in its public relations campaign against government censorship.[7] At the same time, educators were placing pressure on the movie industry to change the moral content of films. The movie industry's public relations campaign convinced educators to support the self-regulatory censorship code. Equally important, educators created new markets for films by introducing high school courses in movie appreciation. All of these events had a direct impact on the moral and political content of both American movies and public schools. As explained in later chapters, by the 1930s youngsters might attend school during weekday hours, listen to the radio in the evening, and attend movies on the weekends. Whether sitting by the radio at home or in rows in schools or movie houses, children received a consciously constructed vision of the workings of the world.

THE EARLY CENSORSHIP OF MOVIES

Advocates of government censorship wanted the removal of scenes and words that might teach audiences how to commit crimes, or cause them to participate in some form of social disturbance. In addition, there was concern about the influence of movies on moral and sexual behavior. On the other hand, those advocating self-censorship wanted films to be controlled for the purpose of teaching social lessons. In other words, these latter censors wanted movie scripts changed at the time of production so that explicit lessons could be taught to audiences.

Calls for censorship of movies occurred almost immediately after Thomas Edison's commercial introduction of a projection machine in 1894. Two weeks after the introduction of Edison's machine, protests were heard about the showing of the film *Dolorita in the Passion Dance* on the Boardwalk in Atlantic City.[8] In addition to the content of films, concerns were voiced about the social and moral environment of early movie theaters, and their primarily immigrant and working class audiences. Beginning around 1900, immigrant entrepreneurs rented small stores and refurbished them as nickelodeons, where for a nickel or dime a customer could watch short films. As discussed by historian Lary May, the popularity of nickelodeons spread rapidly through working class and immigrant neighborhoods. Those in New York City increased from 50 in 1900 to 400 by 1908, and attendance reached 200,000 daily. By the 1920s, studio owners were trying to overcome the negative image of movie houses in an attempt to attract middle class families.[9]

Typical of attitudes about nickelodeons was the warning by the Chicago Vice Commission in 1911: "Investigations by individuals interested in the welfare of children have pointed out many instances where children have been influenced by the conditions surrounding some of these shows. Vicious men and boys mix with the crowd...and take liberties with very young girls." Examples given by the Chicago Vice Commission included a nickelodeon owner who assaulted 14 young girls, and a 76-year-old man who enticed young girls to attend movies. One unnamed student of the effect of movies cited by the Chicago Vice Commission declared, "I think the nickel theater is a recruiting station for vice. In the first place from the type of pictures often shown there; in the second place from the association."[10]

The fact that early movies audiences were primarily composed of immigrants and blue collar workers gave an added dimension to concerns about censorship. A fear of some groups was that the content of movies would cause riots and social disruption. The fear of mass social unrest reflected the belief, as The Nation magazine declared in 1913, that movies were the "first democratic art." The journal declared that movies were free of upper class pretensions and that they reflected the ideas of the common people. The magazine also pointed out that the price of movies, when compared with other forms of entertainment, made them accessible to the general population. Five cents was a small sum compared with the cost at the time of $1.20 for a Broadway play or sixty cents for an off-Broadway melodrama. Also, silent films were attractive to immigrants because they did not require a knowledge of spoken English.[11]

The concern about movies as the "first democratic art" extended to arguments that movies were developing a class consciousness. For example, an article in The Atlantic magazine in 1915 stressed the social class differences between audiences for spoken drama and audiences for film. The author, Richard Eaton, warned that "the line of demarcation between theatrical audiences and movie audiences will grow sharper, the one representing entirely the bourgeoisie and upper classes, and the other the proletariat." Eaton went on to state, "The movies will become ever more powerfully a factor in the growth of class consciousness."[12]

In addition to fears about the working class composition of movie audiences, there were concerns in some circles about the political content of early movies. For example in The Candidate (1907), workers throw dirt at an affluent politician after a speech and he is later beaten by his discontented wife. In Down with Women (1907), an upper class male declares women incompetent and condemns women's suffrage. Later in the movie, he encounters women in a variety of occupations, from musician to lawyer to taxi and truck driver. Eventually, he is saved by one woman and defended in court by another. Greedy landlords were condemned in The Eviction (1907) and workers in labor-management struggles were treated sympathetically in films like The Iconoclast (1910).[13]

Bankers and factory owners were also frequently criticized in early silent films.[14]These favorable attitudes toward the working class and criticisms of the upper class had disappeared from most films made in the United States by the 1930s. According to film historian Terry Christensen, "One movie maker, however, remained sympathetic with workers, immigrants, and the downtrodden in general as they struggled to withstand the pressures of an urban, industrial society. He was, of course, Charlie Chaplin."[15]

The first government censorship law for movies was passed by the City of Chicago in 1907, which required police review and licensing of movies. In 1909, the law was challenged when Chicago police refused to license *The James Boys* and *Night Riders*. The Illinois Supreme Court accepted the argument of the police that censorship of films was necessary to maintain social order. In the words of the Court, the two films "represent nothing but malicious mischief, arson, and murder. They are both immoral, and their exhibition would necessarily be attended with evil effects upon youthful spectators."[16]

Most government censorship boards operated according to a licensing procedure by which officials would review the films and then decide whether to license them for distribution. Obviously, the film industry resented the process of government censorship because it delayed distribution and created the possibility that each municipality or state would require different changes in a particular film. The delays and constant editing could cost the movie producer a great deal of money. Will Hays, as president of the M.P.P.D.A., argued against government censorship on the grounds that there was lack of agreement on standards among the different censorship boards. Hays argued that this situation was exemplified by particular states' laws prohibiting the showing of a woman smoking a cigarette. According to Hays, these laws "might eliminate any scene of a social gathering happening in another State." In another instance, a lawyer on one censorship board would not allow any scenes that depicted lawyers as unethical or crooked. Of importance for political censorship of movies, Hays wrote, "Scenes of strike riots were ordered eliminated from news reels in one State at the same time newspapers were using photographs of the exact incidents recorded in the films."[17]

The United States Supreme Court supported government censorship of movies as necessary for maintaining social order. A challenge to state censorship occurred in 1915 when the Mutual Film Corporation appealed to the United States Supreme Court a decision regarding the Ohio censorship board. The Mutual Film Corporation was engaged in the distribution of films in Ohio. The company complained that the Ohio requirement that all films be submitted to a state censorship board delayed distribution and was injurious to business. The lawyers for the company argued that the requirement that films be censored before their distribution was a violation of the Free Speech Clause of the First Amendment.

In a decision that was not overturned until the 1950s, the U.S. Supreme Court refused to extend the protection of the First and the Fourteenth Amendments to movies. The court reasoned that films were a business enterprise and, consequently, its decision argues, "We immediately feel that the argument is wrong or strained which extends the guarantee of free speech to the multitudinous shows which are advertised on the billboards of our cities and towns, and which regards them as emblems of public safety...." The U.S. Supreme Court decision argued that censorship of movies is necessary for maintaining social order. In the words of the Court, movies represent a major threat to public safety. Its decision expressed concern about the role of movies in educating the general public. The Court decision argues, "Their [the movies'] power of amusement, and, it may be, education, the audiences they assemble, not of women alone nor of men alone, but together, not only adults only but of children, make them the more insidious in corruption by pretense of worth...."[18]

In 1921, Ellis Oberholtzer, Secretary of the Pennsylvania State Board of Motion Picture Censors, compared state censorship to government control of public schools: "The efforts which are made to convert the unlikeliest of young human beings at school into useful citizens are many. From the care of their teeth and the public feeding of them when they are hungry up to the old purely educational processes developed to the nth degree, our social efficiency has been tried and proved. I for one fail to see, therefore, how by any fair system of reasoning we can be held to be without some duty to inquire into the course of the film man with his 15,000 or more picture houses set in every nook and corner of the land at the door of each inhabitant." Oberholtzer placed censorship in the general category of government responsibility for the actions of citizens. "The misbehavior of this citizen [influenced by movies]...," Oberholtzer concluded, "is not beyond our concern."[19]

In an earlier article, Oberholtzer rejected the argument made by advocates of self-regulation that movies should teach social and moral lessons. The role of government censorship was to remove from films any scenes that might contribute to lawlessness or moral decay. This is an important distinction, as noted earlier, because it made government censorship of movies primarily a negative act of removing offensive scenes, whereas proponents of self-regulation argued that they wanted to transform movies into positive educational lessons.

Oberholtzer claimed that the film maker used the argument that movies could teach morals as justification for including material "to enliven his theme and lend zest, or 'punch,' as he calls it, to his product...." Oberholtzer illustrated his argument with a report from the British Board of Film Censors on movies containing scenes depicting the use of drugs. He quoted from the report, "It is said for such films that they serve to warn the public against the dangers of the abuse of drugs, but the Board decided that there being no reason to suppose that this habit was prevalent in this country..., the evils of arousing curiosity in the minds of those to who it was a novel idea far outweighed the possible good that might accrue by warning the small minority who indulged in the practice." Declared Oberholtzer, "I am, therefore, not to be beguiled by the protestations of such a picture man. I have met him and he resembles a teacher less than any one I have ever seen." In rejecting the whole argument that self-regulation would create movies that taught lessons, Oberholtzer stated, "It is clear that a theater is not a proper place for the inculcation of such lessons, or the theater man a proper person to bear such delicate messages to the young. We have the church, the school, the home and our social organizations...."[20]

Sometimes public protests caused government censors to remove socially controversial scenes. For instance, race relations became a major concern of censors after protests by the National Association for the Advancement of Colored People (NAACP) over the film *Birth of a Nation*. The film was released in 1915 and received wide public attention because of its innovative film techniques and its endorsement by national political and social leaders, including President Woodrow Wilson. In addition, the film's distribution was timed for the fiftieth anniversary celebration of the ending of the Civil War. The NAACP and the African-American community in general objected to the negative portrayal of emancipated slaves and to the depiction of the Ku Kux Klan as the savior of Southern society after the Civil War.[21]

The membership rolls of the NAACP swelled as it led national protests against the film. Ironically, the protests of the NAACP caused government censors to eliminate scenes from later movies that might, as determined by the censors, lead to race riots. On the other hand, however, film makers feared a loss of profits if movies were banned by Southern censors. Consequently, movies made by major companies in the 1920s and 1930s avoided any meaningful depiction of problems in race relations, and primarily presented African-Americans in stereotyped roles as servants.[22]

In some cases, government censors banned movies and scenes depicting organized labor in a favorable manner. The most extreme incident was reported in 1915 when the Ohio censors banned the entire movie titled *The Strike of Coaldale*. According to a contemporary report, the movie's "sole offense was that it dramatized the victory of labor and mildly sided with the cause of labor."[23]

The advocates of self-regulation, as opposed to government censorship, explicitly argued that the role of self-regulation should be to assure that movie audiences were taught moral and social lessons. They criticized government censorship because it only removed negative scenes without controlling the general theme of a film. One of the earliest arguments for self-censorship was given by John Collier, a co-founder of the National Board of Review or, as it was sometimes called, the National Board of Censorship.

The National Board of Review was organized after New York City police, under orders from the mayor and chief of police, closed 550 movie houses on Christmas Day, 1908, for violating Sunday closing laws. The closings were part of a larger crusade against vice. In reaction to police actions, theater owners organized the National Board of Review in hopes that self-censorship would stop future vice raids. Officially organized in March 1909, in conjunction with the People's Institute, a reform organization located in the immigrant section of lower Manhattan, the work of the Board was supported by movie producers, and also by police and city government officials.

The National Board of Review received financial support from the film industry. From the standpoint of movie producers, they hoped that Board approval of a movie would mean its nationwide acceptance and, consequently, avoidance of problems with government censors. It was believed that the illustrious membership of the Board would aid in national acceptance of its standards. At the same time, board members hoped that reforming movies would contribute, like the settlement house, to the reform of urban life. The majority of members of the executive committee of the National Board of Review were wealthy Protestant males, including Andrew Carnegie, Samuel Gompers, presidents of major universities, and "representatives from the Federal Council of Churches, the YMCA, the New York School Board, the Society for the Prevention of Crime headed by the most powerful vice crusader in the city, the Rev. Charles Parkhurst, and the moralistic Postal Inspector, Anthony Comstock."[24]

Collier presented the guiding philosophy of the organization in a series of magazine articles in *The Survey*. As Collier explained, the Board's censorship code emphasized the important role of movies in teaching morality. In this sense, the censors wanted the movies to teach the public uplifting moral lessons, like schools. The code stressed the importance of movies' depicting good winning out over evil: "The results of the crime [shown in movies] should be in the long run disastrous to the criminal so that the impression is that crime will inevitably find one out. The result [punishment] should always take a reasonable proportion of the film." In addition, the code stressed the role of government in maintaining a moral society. "As a general rule," the code argues, "it is preferable to have retribution come through the hands of authorized officers of the law, rather than through revenge or other unlawful or extra-legal means." Of course, the Board also expressed a great deal of interest in the portrayal of sexual relationships. The Board's standards would "not allow the extended display of personal allurements, the exposure of alleged physical charms and passionate, protracted embraces" and it would "also disapprove the showing of men turning lightly from woman to woman, or women turning lightly from man to man in intimate sexual relationships."[25]

Collier argued that government censorship impedes the traditional role of art as a source of social change. "The challenge of the old and the institution of the new," Collier wrote, "are a responsibility of the drama, no less than is the inculcation of accepted virtues...."[26] The heavy hand of government censorship, Collier insisted, undermined the social role of art by the application of absolute standards. He maintained that one of the values of voluntary censorship was inconsistency. "Until censorship can discriminate, can limit the audience, can prescribe the destination of the censored product," he wrote, "it is nothing but a bludgeon-like imposition, by some element momentarily in power, of its prejudices on the mass of the people." The important thing about the Board of Review, was "that being without legal power it is without legal responsibility and can be inconsistent...."[27]

It was inconsistency in the application of standards that allowed the National Board of Review, according to Collier, to support films that taught moral and social lessons. For instance, one of Collier's articles included pictures from a film of a boy torturing a cat. Even though the board prohibited depiction of brutality, these scenes were approved because they were "essential in a plot dealing with the relation of defective mentality to juvenile crime. The boy who is here shown torturing a cat is later restored by medical treatment to normality."[28]

Collier's arguments reflected some reformers' belief in the importance of shaping public opinion as an element in social change. It was this belief that attracted many reformers to the work of the Committee on Public Information (CPI) during World War I. Both the war and the formation of the CPI seemed to many reformers a golden opportunity to reform American society and spread the doctrines of social democracy.

THE COMMITTEE FOR PUBLIC INFORMATION (CPI) AND THE MOLDING OF PUBLIC OPINION

On April 13, 1917, within two weeks after President Woodrow Wilson asked Congress to declare war, the CPI was established to create a national spirit to support the war effort. The Wilson administration organized the CPI to deal with the potential threats of strong opposition to entry into the war, the large German-American population, and the presence of great numbers of immigrants. The 1910 census estimated that one out of every three Americans either was foreign born or had a foreign-born parent. Ten million of those falling into these categories had ties with the Central Powers.[29]

President Wilson justified the war as a war for democracy. This was the theme the CPI tried to sell to the American people. In its campaign, the CPI linked nationalism with democracy and presented democracy as the secular religion of America. Reflecting this belief, the chair of the Committee, George Creel, stated in 1918, "Democracy is a religion with me, and throughout my whole adult life I have preached America as the hope of the world."[30]

Of the many means used by the CPI to influence public opinion, one of the most important from the perspective of this book was the public schools. The CPI's Division of Civic and Educational Cooperation was lead by Guy Stanton Ford. Ford was a professor of European history, who just prior to working for the CPI was Dean of the University of Minnesota's graduate school. As head of the Division, he hired large numbers of muckraking writers to produce pamphlets to support the war effort. In addition, he selected educator William Bagley to edit the *National School Service* (*NSS*), a bulletin designed to create favorable attitudes about nationalism and democratic citizenship among students in the public schools. In 1918, Ford told the delegates to the annual meeting of the NEA, "The Committee on Public Information and the schools have a great common war task to make an Americanized, nationalized American nation."[31]

In education circles, Bagley was known as a leading proponent of education for social efficiency. This particular educational doctrine dominated the goals of public schooling in the early twentieth century. Beginning in the 1890s, educators, business people, labor leaders, social reformers, religious leaders, and social scientists argued that the modern world of urban living and large industries required a new concept of morality and good character. The term that began to appear in educational discussions was "social efficiency."[32] The phrase was applied to school curriculum, organization, and goals. When educators of the period spoke of a "socially efficient character" they meant an individual who knew a particular skill needed by modern society and who knew how to cooperate with fellow workers. Expertise and cooperation were the goals of social efficiency educators, goals shared by many others in the U.S. A cooperative person was desired by both business and labor. In business, cooperation was essential for the operation of modern corporations. Expert and specialized employees needed to know how to cooperate. For labor, cooperation was essential for the organization of unions. Urban reformers argued that cooperation was necessary for people to be able to live in a reasonable manner in modern cities. Many educators and social scientists argued that the modern world required that the school become the new social center of urban life.[33]

Bagley believed that the schools should take on the goal of social efficiency because the World War meant the United States assuming economic and political supremacy in the world. He linked the goals of social efficiency and American economic and political superiority in a speech he gave to the Harvard Teachers Association in 1916, prior to America's entry into the war. The speech was in honor of the newly established chair of education at Harvard. Bagley told his audience that the World War was causing the financial collapse of Europe and would make the United States preeminent in power and wealth.

The assumption of this role of world leadership would require, he argued, "the formulation of educational policies primarily in terms of national life rather than in terms of sectional, local, class and individual demands and interests." In speaking of these national educational policies, Bagley peppered his address with references to "collective strength" and the "collective intelligence of the democratic group." He also told his audience, in the spirit of social efficiency, that "public interest is more readily aroused by, and public funds more readily available for educational plans that promote economic betterment...."[34]

This belief in the necessity of a national educational policy guided Bagley's editorship of the *National School Service* (*NSS*). Bagley joined other members of the CPI and other educators in believing that the public schools should be a vehicle for spreading the doctrines of democracy. And, as indicated already, democracy in this context was primarily defined as a form of social organization.

The formation of the *NSS* was prompted, in part, by a resolution passed at the April 1918 meeting of the NEA calling for the creation of a clearinghouse for propaganda directed at the schools. In addition, the United States Commissioner of Education, Philander P. Claxton, had recommended that the CPI prepare a bulletin to be distributed to the schools. Under the guidance of Guy Stanton Ford, the *NSS* was created in the fall of 1918 with William Bagley as editor. The historian of the CPI, Stephen Vaughn, argues that the general attitude of the members of the CPI toward public schools was best expressed by one member, Carl Becker, when he wrote that the "chief purpose of free education in a democratic society is to make good citizens rather than good scholars."[35]

At the same NEA meeting in 1918 where a clearinghouse for propaganda for the schools was proposed, Bagley outlined his beliefs on the place of education in the war effort. Like many associated with the CPI, he seemed to welcome the war as an opportunity for implementing reforms in American schools. The two major opportunities brought by the war, from Bagley's perspective, were the development of a "new nationalism" and the "growth and development of a new and persuasive and comprehensive meaning for the word 'democracy'." The new nationalism, he argued, was giving "birth...[to] a new, fresh, and vigorous sense of national unity." This new nationalism provided the opportunity to spread the concept of democracy.[36]

Bagley believed that local control of educational policy was a major hindrance in adapting the public schools to the needs of the United States as a world leader. In his 1918 speech before the NEA, he presented the new nationalism as a means of overcoming the localism of educational policy. The combination of the war and the new national spirit opened the door for the federal government to exercise leadership in a national educational policy. Included in Bagley's proposals was a call for federal financing of the public school system. Bagley told the educators, "But now with this new national awakening we find that state boundaries can be easily and quickly transcended. The golden hour of American education has struck."[37]

Bagley placed his arguments for social efficiency within a particular definition of democracy. Bagley and the Progressives associated with the CPI identified two major components of democracy: cooperation and equality of opportunity. This concept of democracy was included in the long-awaited report on the organization of the American high school issued by the NEA in 1918. Issued in the midst of the fervor over the war effort, the document reflects concerns about national unity and cooperation. As elaborated in Chapter 2, the document defined the goals, organization, and social structure of the American comprehensive high school. It became a guiding document for the development of the high school for at least the first half of the twentieth century. In addition, the report gave clear support to the goals of social efficiency as defined by educators like Bagley.

The report, *The Cardinal Principles of Secondary Education,* states that the goals of the comprehensive high school should contain the two components of democracy specified within the framework of social efficiency—specialization and unification, that is cooperation. According to the report, character education, within the social organization of a democracy, is to be linked to one's contribution to society. This is what is meant by the term "specialization" in *The Cardinal Principles of Secondary Education.* Reflecting the concept of equality of opportunity, the report announces that, "The purpose of democracy is so to organize society that each member may develop his personality primarily through activities designed for the well-being of his fellow members and of society as a whole."[38] It was this democratic organization of society that was to provide all citizens with equality of opportunity. In this context, equality of opportunity meant giving everyone an equal chance to find a job best suited to her or his individual talents. And, of course, if everyone found a job suited to his or her talents, then the industrial efficiency of society would be increased. In the rhetoric of the times, equality of opportunity meant an efficient use of human resources.

The report declares that the specialized and differentiated curriculum of the comprehensive high school would train each student to perform a specific task benefiting society. Within the linkage of schooling and equality of opportunity, the report proposes (in bold type) that **"education in a democracy... should develop in each individual the knowledge, interests, ideals, habits, and powers whereby he will find his place and use that place to shape both himself and society toward ever-nobler ends."**[39]

The report also stresses what it calls "the democratic ideal of unification"—the second component of democracy in *The Cardinal Principles of Secondary Education.* This concept of unification, of course, reflected the nationalism advocated by supporters of the war effort. The report defines unification as that part of the ideal of democracy that brings people together and gives them "common ideas, common ideals, and common modes of thought, feeling, and action that make for cooperation, social cohesion, and social solidarity."[40]

The leaders of the CPI combined this social definition of democracy with spiritual and religious qualities. Chairman Creel not only portrayed democracy as a religion but also as a continuous religious struggle. Creel wrote, "Democracy has never been, and never can be, other than a theory of spiritual progress.... Democracy is not an automatic device but the struggle everlasting."[41] Stuart P. Sherman, a professor of English at the University of Illinois and an editor of the *Cambridge History of American Literature,* also emphasized the religious qualities of democracy in an essay he wrote for the CPI. Even after the war, he continued preaching on what he referred to as the "religion of democracy."[42]

Sherman's essay for the CPI, "American and Allied Ideals," was originally given as a lecture in 1917 to the National Council of Teachers of English. For Sherman, the concept of democracy included what he considered to be the basic values of American civilization. These values were embodied in American literature, the intellectual heritage of the founders of the nation, and our shared cultural ideals. Within the context of this definition, democracy was threatened by the culture of Germany and the culture of immigrants who had recently arrived on America's shores. Thus the war effort had to be both external, against German arms and internal, against anti-democratic values. Therefore, he argued, since anyone not believing in democratic values was a threat to the nation, it was necessary for people in the United States to be indoctrinated with democratic values.[43]

The members of the CPI considered themselves on a mission to spread the religion of democracy. In fact, the head of the CPI's Division of Civic and Educational Cooperation, Guy Stanton Ford, actually lamented the end of the war because it curtailed the efforts to educate the public on the meaning of democracy. In his words, "the Germans spoiled some perfectly good enterprises by ending the war when they did."[44]

When Bagley assumed charge of the *National School Service (NSS)* in the fall of 1918, he was faced with the problem of distributing propaganda to a school system that had multiple layers of control, from state governments through county superintendents to local school boards. These multiple layers of control also posed a problem in achieving another of Bagley's goals, namely, a national educational policy. To overcome this problem, the decision was made to distribute the *NSS* directly to individual schools, using a national school building address list compiled by the federal Bureau of Education.

In general, the *NSS* bulletin stressed the patriotic duties of citizens and the necessity of unswerving loyalty to the country. Democracy was equated with Americanism, and the *NSS* bulletin, like other publications of the CPI, defined democracy primarily by what the CPI believed to be the culture and ideals of the United States. Good citizenship was presented as the fulfillment of duties and responsibilities to society, as opposed to active individual participation in political activities. This concept of passive rather than active citizenship persisted in the schools after the war.

Notably absent from the literature of the CPI and the *NSS* were discussions of democracy involving the exercise by individuals of political power. In fact, Bagley rejected ideas of democracy that included direct control of the government by the people. Like other social efficiency educators, he believed that government should be operated by experts with the consent of the people. Thus, in addition to teaching loyalty, duties, and service to the country, the role of education according to social efficiency educators was to educate students to want to be governed by experts.[45]

The major part of each issue of the *NSS* was devoted to detailed lessons for elementary and high school classes designed to teach patriotism, the evils of the enemy, and the principles of "democracy." In addition, the lessons were planned to increase students' interest in and acceptance of modern warfare. For instance, the *NSS* bulletins recommended turning children's games into war games. As already indicated, one bulletin was titled "Natural War Interests of Children." Besides applauding the use of the sand table as a means of sustaining the interest of children in war, the bulletin states:

> No form of occupation material can claim exemption from war service. Drawings of ponies and friendly cows are supplanted by galloping cavalry horses. Crayoned ships sail the ocean bringing supplies to our soldiers, while bits of folded paper floating through the air become miniature air ships. Clay cannon, bullets, and soldiers are a common sight on the modeling table. Soldier games and marching songs are called for. 'Over There' seems to be known to all and is more popular than the most tuneful childish melody.[46]

The bulletin goes on to encourage teachers to promote war games in the classroom. "The primary teacher," the bulletin states, "who is awake to her opportunities will allow this natural war interest of the children to run its course. More than that, she will follow the lead thus given her by the children themselves and will provide the mediums for its full play."[47]

An important wartime pamphlet for high school students was prepared by one of Bagley's assistants, Samuel Harding. The CPI distributed enough copies of the pamphlet to reach every senior high school student in the United States. Enitled "Study of the Great War," it was first published in the January 1918 issue of *The History Teacher's Magazine*. Because of teacher demand for the article, the CPI decided to sell it as a pamphlet for five cents a copy. By the end of the war, 700,000 copies of the pamphlet had been sold and 40,000 additional copies of the January 1918 issue of *The History Teacher's Magazine* had been reprinted and sold by the publisher.[48]

The pamphlet primarily attempts to drum up hatred of the Germans with statements such as, "Germany does not really wage war. She assassinates, massacres, poisons, tortures, intrigues; she commits every crime in the calendar, such as arson, pillage, murder, and rape...." After seven chapters of building up high school students' hatred of Germany, the pamphlet concludes with the promise that an allied victory would probably result in the end of warfare on earth.

Patriotic lessons for elementary grades were delayed until August 1918 because the first version written for the CPI took a negative view of the role of nationalism in the world. The final version recommended the integration of war themes into all subjects. The pamphlet suggested focusing on "Stories of War Incidents," "Celebrations of Special Holidays," and "Talks on the War and the Children's Relation to It." In addition, it recommended systematic instruction in patriotism, beginning with two 15-minute periods each week for the first and second grades of elementary school and increasing amounts of time for students in higher grades.[49]

One of the themes that runs throughout the pamphlet for the elementary school grades is the need for educators to work on the emotions of children and to avoid creating emotions that would lead children to a rejection of war. In other words, emotions were to be whipped up in support of the Allied war effort and for the United States, but the emotions related to the horror of war were to be avoided. The pamphlet states, "In teaching the war to young pupils, the appeal should be directed primarily to the imagination and to the emotions. It is not enough that our pupils shall be informed of the events of the war.... Their imaginations must be awakened and their feelings aroused to an appreciation of the significance of the great happenings of the time."[50]

In contrast to the enthusiasm the teacher was to display for patriotism and support of the Allied cause, the teacher is cautioned not to dwell on the "horrors inseparable from war and peculiarly characteristic of the present struggle." The pamphlet warns that focusing on the horror of war might cause "Permanent injury...to young children through emphasis on the terrible and repulsive."[51]

One might speculate on the effect on young children of the promotion of war games, the creation of emotional attachment to the war cause, and the avoidance of discussions of the horrors of war. It is certainly possible that this combination of instruction would teach children to love war and to glorify the life of the American combatant. Much of the rhetoric of the CPI promised that the war would end all wars. But, in reality, the effect of the material actually distributed to the public schools might have been to prepare students to accept a world that was permanently at war.

The issue of teaching about war in public schools continued as an issue through the 1920s. Efforts were made to require compulsory participation of high school students in the Reserve Officers Training Corp (ROTC) as part of a general campaign against teaching radical ideas in schools. General Pershing declared in the 1920s, "I firmly believe that a sane program of military training for every young man is a great immunity against idle, insidious and foolish propaganda of the I.W.W., the parlor Bolsheviks and all other shades of Reds of which there are too many right now." In 1925, the Inspector General of the Army warned that liberals and church workers opposed to compulsory ROTC in the schools were acting as agents of Communism. "Revolutionary forces," he said, "are at work...in our schools."[52]

Howard Beales, selected during the 1930s by the American Historical Association's Commission on Social Studies in the Schools to investigate intellectual freedom in public schools, found that in the 1920s teachers advocating militarism were favored over those who were pacifist. Beales described cases of teachers fired in the 1920s for being pacifists: "Trouble has not been made for teachers who advocate military training, or urge boys to join cadet corps, or propagandize for armament programs of the D.A.R., the American Legion, or the National Security League." Beales believed advocates of peace were at a disadvantage in influencing schools because of their lack of organization and relative weakness compared with the power and money of the federal government.[53]

The campaign in the public schools during World War I was only part of the massive effort by the CPI to build support for the war. A bureau was organized to blanket the nation with four-minute speeches drafted by the CPI. Speakers were given careful instructions for their presentations in movie houses, at public meetings, at meetings of service clubs, and at any other gatherings that were considered appropriate. This was certainly one of the most ambitious public speaking projects ever initiated in the United States. These messages were written to build nationalism and win support for the war effort. In September 1918 alone, forty thousand speeches were given across the country. In Illinois, by the end of the war, Four-Minute Men were speaking weekly to some 800,000 people. By the end of the project, an estimated one million four-minute speeches had been given to 400 million people.[54]

The CPI also launched what its Chair, Creel, called the "greatest adventure in advertising." The country was blanketed with posters carrying a variety of pro-war messages. Posters depicting menacing German soldiers were used to sell Liberty Bonds. Others showed soldiers rushing from their loved ones back to camp with the message "He Must Not Overstay His Leave!" One of the more grotesque posters is titled "This is Kultur," showing German soldiers cutting off the hands of a victim while in the background another German soldier is strangling a woman. One series of posters told readers how to write cheerful letters to their loved ones and another series warned against the spread of rumors that would aid the enemy.[55]

The CPI also organized a War Cooperating Committee, to use the talents of the film industry to produce training and propaganda movies. The committee included movie greats D.W. Griffith, Cecil B. DeMille, and William Fox. The short duration of American participation in the war—from April 1917 to

November 1918—did not allow enough time to produce a large number of films. The major ones were *Pershing's Crusaders, America's Answer,* and *Official War Review.* Under the auspices of the CPI, a film starring Douglas Fairbanks was produced with the descriptive title, *Swat the Kaiser.*[56]

The war also affected the content of public school textbooks. Since the United States was allied with Great Britain, it was considered necessary to down play the tension between the two nations during the American Revolution. Bagley, as former head of the National School Service, recalled in an interview in 1932, "There was a tendency to change textbooks during the War to soft-pedal the American Revolutionary War." In keeping with the desire for removal from textbooks of all suggestions of a basic conflict between the two nations, publisher George Putnam told an English audience in 1918, "Textbooks are now being prepared which will present a juster account of the events of 1775-1783, 1812-1815 and 1861-1865."[57] As discussed in Chapter 2, the pro-British bias in textbooks during World War I became a major issue in the 1920s.

In summary the brief period of America's direct engagement in World War I, from 1917 to 1918, saw the Committee on Public Information launch one of the most massive attempts at ideological management in the history of the United States. From the standpoint of the public schools, it was the first major attempt to bring the goals of locally controlled schools into line with the policy objectives of the federal government. This pattern was repeated during and after World War II.[58] Thus, the end of World War I, as pointed out in the next chapter, did not mean the end of national attempts to use the public schools to mold children according to a particular concept of good citizenship. Nor did it end attempts to influence other means for molding public opinion.

CONCLUSION

In 1921 Walter Lippmann wrote in *Public Opinion,* in reference to the work of the Creel Committee on Public Information, "The Administration was trying, and while the war continued it very largely succeeded, I believe, in creating something that might almost be called one public opinion all over America."[59] As a leading progressive journalist and a co-editor along with Walter Weyl and Herbert Croly of the journal *The New Republic,* Lippmann was disillusioned by the reactionary political mood that gripped the United States after the war. One of the issues the war created for Lippmann was the role of public opinion in a democracy. Interspersing his book with examples of censorship and propaganda methods used during the war, Lippmann cynically states, "the manufacture of consent is capable of great refinements…and the opportunities for manipulation [are] open to anyone who understands the process."[60]

The major problem for a modern democratic government, Lippmann maintains, is the inability of the average voter to understand the workings of a complex economic and political system. The idea of a rational and knowledge-able voter, Lippmann argues, is a product of a time when the United States was primarily composed of geographically small and simple communities. In these conditions, it was easy for voters to know and understand the workings of their immediate society. But as American society became more complex during the nineteenth and twentieth centuries, it became more difficult for the voter to understand political and economic issues. The modern voter, Lippmann maintains, is often reduced to voting yes or no without fully understanding the issues involved. Very often, he contends, voting is based on pictures or symbols in the voter's mind and not on an understanding of the issues. Thus, different events and issues can have different meanings for particular individuals depending on the pictures in their minds. An apparently unified public opinion might be, according to Lippmann, a result of general acceptance of a symbol that actually means different things to different people.

For instance, public opinion might support the idea of Americanism. But Americanism can mean to one person "preservation of isolationism..., [to] the second...rejection of a politician who clashes with his idea of what an American president should be, [and to] the third...a call to resist revolution." In using this example, Lippmann was undoubtedly thinking of the Americanism campaign that swept through the United States at the end of World War I. "The symbol [Americanism]," he stated, "in itself signifies literally no one thing in particular, but it can be associated with almost anything. And because of that it can become the common bond of common feelings, even though those feelings were originally attached to disparate ideas."[61]

While Lippmann does present methods for manipulating public opinion, his primary concern is the role of knowledge in a modern democracy. He dismissed the idea that newspapers could be an unbiased source of information for the voter, and urged the establishment of government bureaus that would present the public with factual information. These bureaus would be operated by intellectuals who would work in an environment free from political bias and pressure. He proposed ways of structuring the bureaus so that they could operate independently and be protected from pressure from special interest groups. In this manner, knowledge dispensed by the bureaus would inform and not manipulate voters.

The solution offered by Lippmann reflects the progressive faith in the role of the expert and the social scientist. Certainly, a number of issues can be raised about the possibility of expert intellectuals dispensing unbiased information to the public. However, the important thing is not Lippmann's solution, but his recognition of the problem of the politics of knowledge in a modern democratic society.

Lippmann's book touches on a real set of problems that emerged after World War I. Various groups began to compete for influence over the mechanisms for molding public opinion. As discussed in the next chapter, advocacy groups struggled to have the public schools teach their particular version of Americanism and citizenship. And, as described in Chapter 3, the influence of movies on the general public continued to be a concern throughout the 1920s.

AMERICANISM AND CORPORATE SPIRIT IN THE 1920s: BUILDING CHARACTER IN THE PUBLIC SCHOOLS

"THIS IS WHY 'live wires' and 'go-getters' are such heroes to the bulk of the people; in and of itself all this is quite legitimate, and indeed moral," states the report of the 1926 Committee on Character Education of the National Education Association (NEA) in reference to the American public worship of success.[1] In the 1920s, public school leaders wanted schools to produce "live wires" and "go-getters" as workers in the developing corporate world. The social environment of the school, particularly the high school, was organized to produce employees imbued with a spirit of cooperation and a desire to work for the good of the corporation. The high school world of football, basketball, cheerleaders, student government, assemblies, clubs, and rallies to promote school spirit were suppose to form the new corporate personality.

School spirit and corporate spirit were accompanied by a spirit of Americanism. Leading the Americanism campaign in public schools was the American Legion. Topping the list of resolutions at the American Legion's first convention in 1919 was a resolution against "Bolshevism, I.W.W., radicalism...[and] all anti-Americanism tendencies, activities, and propaganda." Targeting its Americanism campaign at the public schools, the American Legion eventually joined arms with the NEA in a campaign for citizenship training in the schools.[2]

Reflecting the same fears, the U.S. Commissioner of Education, John Tigert, declared in 1921 his "determination to crush out of the schools communism, bolshevism, socialism, and all persons who did not recognize the sanctity of private property and 'the right of genius to its just rewards'."[3] Teachers and administrators were called upon to purge schools of all subversive idea. Writing in the 1930s, historian Howard Beales expressed his belief that the reason a War Facts Test was given to New York high school teachers in 1919, which asked about Russian Communism and the sources for such information, was to identify teachers with radical views.[4]

In another study by Beales published in 1941, he ranked the relative influence of various organizations interested in purging schools of subversive ideas. "On the whole," he wrote, "the American Legion seems to be the most important. Next come benefactors of the school, the D.A.R., the Chamber of Commerce, and 'other patriotic organizations,' including in the South the United Daughters of the Confederacy."[5]

Rather than spawning the Progressive dream of political reform, the aftermath of World War I sent a wave of political reaction through American society. At the heart of this reaction was a fear that the 1917 Russian Revolution would spread Bolshevik ideas. These fears were fed by a series of events in 1919. In February 1919, in the midst of a general strike in Seattle, a bomb was mailed to the city's Mayor, Ole Hanson. Shortly afterward, mail inspectors intercepted thirty-four other letter bombs sent to national political leaders. Another letter bomb blew off the hands of the maid of a Georgia senator. In May 1919, battles broke out between "radicals" and "patriots" in Boston, Cleveland, and New York. In June a bomb blew up part of the residence of U.S. Attorney General A. Mitchell Palmer.[6]

In 1919, supported and aided by "patriotic" organizations such as the American Legion, the Ku Kux Klan, the National Security League, and the American Defense Society, Attorney Palmer launched the Great Red Hunt. Disregarding legal requirements for warrants and due process, Palmer tried to rid America of what he considered to be the evils of Bolshevism and anarchism. While the Great Red Hunt had begun to abate by 1920, many conservative organizations continued thereafter to influence public opinion.

In the context of ideological management, several patterns emerged in the War and its aftermath. First, the War created an impetus for the federal government to try to centralize control over the major influences in the formation of public opinion. This pattern became apparent during World War I and was later repeated during World War II, and to a certain extent during the Korean and Vietnam Wars. Second, periods of reaction and anti-Communist hysteria followed in the wake of both world wars. This hysteria directly affected schools and the media. For instance, after World War I, various organizations, particularly the American Legion, demanded that public school teachers express their loyalty to the United States Constitution. After World War II, in the midst of purging "radicals" from movies and broadcasting, there was another campaign for loyalty oaths for teachers. Third, the period of the 1920s marked the growing importance of right-wing political and religious organizations in determining what was conveyed by the media to the public.

DESIGNING AMERICAN CHARACTER

In the 1920s, there was a flood of plans, codes, and reports on character education issued by professional education associations, and by federal and state governments. In addition to suggesting topics for classroom instruction in character development, a majority of the reports and plans emphasized the development of character through the social activities of the school. These arguments justified the expansion of the social life of the American public school, particularly the high school, into a whirlwind of extra-curricular activities including school clubs, assemblies, student government, school newspapers, dances, and football and basketball games. Most character education plans were based on the idea that democracy was primarily a cooperative social system requiring individuals who would fit into corporate organizations, and work hard for the good of the group.

Most character education plans were prepared by professional educators and social scientists. Typical of the attitude of these experts is a statement by Thomas Galloway, Associate Director of the Department of Educational Measures of the American Social Hygiene Association, in the manual for sex education published and distributed by the American Social Hygiene Association in 1924: "All amusements, shows, theaters, movies, and the like should be socialized, and controlled by expert psychologists and educators just as are our schools at their best."[7] Galloway echoed the sentiments of many professional educators, psychologists, and sociologists of the late nineteenth and early twentieth centuries that the good society could be achieved through scientific management by experts. The key to achieving the good society, according to many such experts of the period, was the scientific molding of character in the public schools. Reflecting this faith in the scientific expert, pioneer sociologist Edward Ross's influential book, *Social Control,* in 1906 declared that education was an inexpensive form of policing and that civilization was at last understanding the effectiveness of education for social control. "To collect little lumps of human dough from private households and shape them on the social kneadingboard," Ross states, "exhibits a faith in the power of suggestion which few peoples ever attain."[8]

Important events in organizing for character education were contests for the best plans for character education, sponsored by the National Institution for Moral Instruction.[9] The contest engaged state departments of education in the planning of character education. The National Institution for Moral Instruction had been incorporated in 1922 as the Character Education Institution founded in 1911 by a long-time advocate of moral education, Milton Fairchild. Its board of trustees and executive board included the U.S. Commissioner of Education, all state superintendents and commissioners of education, and the secretary of the National Congress of Mothers.[10]

A contest for the best character education plan was initiated in 1916 by a $5,000 donation from an anonymous businessman to the National Institution for Moral Instruction. The competition lasted from Washington's Birthday in 1916 to Washington's Birthday in 1917, and involved 70 writers, at least one from each state. The winner of the contest was William Hutchins, President of Berea

College. The code, known as "The Children's Morality Code for Elementary Schools," received wide distribution in the 1920s in both an original and a revised form.[11]

This contest was followed by a contest sponsored by the same anonymous donor for the best public school plan for character education. The prize for this contest was a significant sum for its time, $20,000. This contest was held from October 1, 1919, to Washington's Birthday, 1921. The contest focused the attention of state educational leaders on the issue of character education. In each state, research groups were appointed by a committee composed of the state superintendent of education, the president of a university, and "a person of general influence, usually a woman," to develop a plan for the contest.[12] The state winner of the contest was Iowa. The same "anonymous businessman" paid for the printing and distribution of five thousand copies of the Iowa Plan.[13]The combination of involvement of state educational leaders, the prestige of the membership of the National Institution of Moral Instruction, and free distribution made the Iowa plan an influential document.

In both the Children's Morality Code and the Iowa Plan, citizenship education was a part of character education. In other words, a well-developed character involved being a good citizen. In explaining the contest to educational leaders at the 1918 NEA convention, Milton Fairchild stated that he preferred the use of the term "character education" over "moral education" because it was "a broader term" referring to the "unfolding of the child's better self."[14] In the same speech, Fairchild related character education to America's role as a world power. The future role of the United States, he claimed, depended on character education.[15]

The organization of Uncle Sam's Boys and Girls Clubs in elementary school classrooms was one method used to spread the Children's Morality Code. Membership in the clubs depended on adherence to the Code. All members were given a badge as a symbol of correct conduct. Reflecting the emphasis on Americanism, one description of the clubs written in the mid-1920s states, "When a child becomes 'disloyal to Uncle Sam' he or she is suspended from the club and required to relinquish his badge."[16] The last item in the code is:

XI. The Law of Loyalty: Good Americans Are Loyal

If our America is to become ever greater and better, her citizens must be loyal, devotedly faithful, in every relation of life....[17]

The Iowa Plan combined the goals of good citizenship and social efficiency. In fact, the plan justified the public school's of the role of educating character — in other words, the whole child—by claiming to carry out the will of the state. The Iowa Plan states, "The school as an institution represents the collective will of the state and must command the respect of the teacher and pupil alike. The teacher is the representative of the state as an expert leader." The role of the teacher as a representative of the state, according to the plan, is to be an educator of children who, as a result, shapes the destiny of the state. "The secret of democracy," the plan states, "is that the individual and the collective mind exist for each other bound together in an organism. Unless the state or school is a tender mother toward its children, it is already hardening toward its death."[18]

The majority of the goals for character education in the Iowa Plan were related to good citizenship and social efficiency. The Plan links freedom and individuality to the life of the group. This is necessary, the Plan argues, because there is no room in the modern world for an individual to live independently of others. In the words of the Plan, the individual in the modern world "must find his freedom through the group, rather than independently of it." And, in language used throughout this period of time, this goal can be achieved through the reconstruction of the school into "a natural cooperative community." Making the school into a community was a major theme of the character education movement.

The other side of social efficiency was preparation as a worker in the modern world of specialization. The fourth goal of the Iowa Plan, "Preparation for Industrial and Economic Relations," states: "Children should learn in the school the satisfaction that comes through productive work; the cost in honest effort of a piece of money, and its value in an honest purchase."

"Preparation for Civic Relations" touches on a major theme of educators in the 1920s as they justified the expanding social activities in the school. Of particular importance is the idea that team and school spirit would be transferred with the student from the school to the workplace and the political world. In the words of the Iowa Plan, "Loyalty to the group and the school should ripen naturally into loyalty to truth, to the State, and even into 'loyalty to loyalty'."

Therefore, the ideal character structure as defined by the Iowa Plan was directly related to the needs of the work place and government. In other words, the definition of good character was made a function of the perceived needs of the political and economic order of society. Thus, good character in the Iowa and in other plans is defined as subordination of self to the good of the State and the economy.

Like the Iowa Plan, the famous 1918 report of the NEA, *The Cardinal Principles of Secondary Education,* emphasizes the education of a socially efficient person.[19] *The Cardinal Principles of Secondary Education* defines democracy as a social system that allows all an equal opportunity to find employment suitable to their talents. To function properly, the report argues, democracy requires cooperation and social solidarity. This definition of democracy justified the report's recommendations for the social organization of the comprehensive high school.

The importance of *The Cardinal Principles of Secondary Education* for the structure of American public education is that it resolved some important issues plaguing the development of the American high school. One major issue was whether or not there should be separate high schools with different curricula. In other words, should there be separate schools for those preparing for college, for those receiving a general education, and for students receiving vocational training? The report answered this question by advocating that all students attend a comprehensive high school. In this context, "comprehensive" meant including all three curricula in one school. The comprehensive high school, in which all curricula, extracurricular activities, and athletics were included, was the model for the American secondary school in the first half of the century. It was in the social life of the comprehensive high school that American youth were supposed to develop good character.

The key to achieving the cooperation required in a democracy, the report argued, is the "social mingling of pupils through the organization and administration of the school," and through "participation of pupils in common activities...such as athletic games, social activities, and government of the school."[20] In other words, in the comprehensive high school preparation of student character for a democratic society occurred in school sports, clubs, student government, and school assemblies. In these essential activities, students as future citizens were to learn cooperation and to develop loyalty through school spirit. Through extracurricular education, students would be prepared for cooperation in large-scale organizations (the workplace) and for loyalty to the American government.

In 1921, the NEA again tackled the problem of character education by forming a permanent Committee on Character Education to work in cooperation with the American School Citizenship League and the NEA Committee on The Teaching of Democracy.[21] In 1926, the Committee on Character Education issued its report, which was reprinted and distributed as a bulletin of the U.S. Bureau of Education.[22]

The report stresses the importance of cooperation and group activity. This is similar to the Iowa plan's emphasis on freedom through the group. The report of the Character Education Committee in its opening chapter states, "The most profoundly moral lives are those in which the I is most completely merged into the We." This expansion of personality, the report argues, results in the accomplishment of social purposes, and the forming of communities. Joy is what the report named the inner satisfaction that occurs from the accomplishment of social purposes, as the "I" merges with the "We." Like most discussions of the period, the psychological arguments were placed in the framework of social efficiency. The report considers the most important social purpose to be a unified life career or, in the language of social efficiency, one's contribution to the good of the whole. The report declares that "Purpose expanded arrives in achievement, success, life-career. This is an impressive phase of moral development and furnishes a powerful motive for conduct."[23]

What emerges from the report's discussion of a life career is an image of the businessperson similar to that parodied by Sinclair Lewis in his 1922 novel, *Babbitt*. The character goals advocated in the report are captured in its discussion of the powerful motives engaged by career goals. In discussing the motivational power of the hope of a successful career, the report states, "It [success] has powerful appeal to 'the man on the street,' who loves to hear about 'doing big things,' and probably dreams more or less about doing big things himself." And, in language that captures the "Babbittry" of the 1920s, the report claims that the public worships successful people who are "live wires" and "go-getters."[24]

Within this conceptual framework, joy was something achieved by the "live wire" and "go-getter." It was also achieved, according to the Committee, through community; this was the other aspect of the social efficiency argument. In the language of the report, "Two elements are characteristic of the community experience: The first is cooperation and the resulting efficiency. Each member of the group has his own function, his own part to play...." The second element was joy. Joy, according to the Committee, pervaded cooperative activities and gave spiritual meaning to the community.[25]

Therefore, in the framework of the report, people with a good character structure sought pleasure from doing what they were best able to do for the good of the group or community, and this was linked to their pursuit of success. The height of success, which resulted in joy, came from being a "live wire" or "go-getter." This, I argue, was an expression of the ideal worker in the modern corporation and factory. The "I" of the worker is submerged in the needs of the corporate organization, where the worker tries to be a "live wire" who works to benefit the organization as a whole. Corporate workers were to feel joy as they benefitted the organization.

At the same time the NEA was formulating its national report on character education, state governments, sparked in part by Fairchild's contest, were busy legislating character education. One was Utah. In 1919, the Utah state legislature passed a law requiring compulsory character education. The law gave public schools the power to supervise character education all twelve months of the year. Up to the age of eighteen, males and females were required to be either in school or in an activity approved by the school.[26] Like the Utah law, the 200-page manual issued under a Nebraska law adopted the Children's Morality Code for elementary schools. This code, called in Nebraska the Squires Code, was reissued by Milton Fairchild's Character Education Institution, and was also used in high schools.[27]

Not only states but also city school systems required character training. In *The Teaching of Ideals* published in 1927, W.W. Charters identified Boston as having the "best character development training in the country." Under the

Boston plan, the Children's Morality Code was used to define the ideal citizen. The code was divided into four instructional categories for the classroom and a monthly magazine was issued containing instructional materials on such subjects as "character building by history lessons," "the pageant of the virtues," "reliability club," and "visual training for citizenship."[28]

Practically all the writers on character and citizenship education in the 1920s stressed the importance of student government activities in forming good character and citizenship. The *Cardinal Principles of Secondary Education* declared that socialization in the high school should be through "participation of students in common activities...such as the government of the school."[29] The 1926 report of the NEA's Committee on Character Education claimed that student government worked best in developing the character of secondary school pupils. Caroline Morlay, a counselor at Shaw Junior High School in Philadelphia, wrote to the Committee, "The student council of the Shaw School has received the most satisfactory comment that a thing of this kind can obtain—'it works.' Under the name of student council...students are receiving daily lessons in practical, everyday citizenship." The Central High School of Evansville, Indiana, reported to the Committee that its student government had survived a succession of principals because it inspired confidence and displayed fairness in its actions. Student government in the 1920s and early 1930s was thought of as vocational training in democracy designed to improve the character of students without permitting the exercise of political power.[30]

In the 1920s, the school assembly was another method of character development. With its origins in the chapel exercises in eighteenth- and nineteenth-century schools, the secular assembly programs in American schools of the 1920s were designed to give students a sense of unity and school spirit. The 1918 *Cardinal Principles* report of the NEA expressed concern that placing different groups of students in different curricula in the high school would undermine the historic role of the American school in building a common culture in a diverse population. By bringing all students together in the school auditorium for a common program, the school assembly was to carry on the tradition of cultural homogenization. For example, an Associate Superintendent of Schools in Pittsburgh, Pennsylvania, wrote in 1925, "Students are divided into classes according to their academic advancement, further divided by their curricula.... Blocking the pathway to unity is an almost infinite variety of individual differences. The assembly is the one agency at hand capable of checking these tendencies."[31]

The assembly became a major event in American junior and senior high schools. During the 1920s, the educational market was flooded with books, programs, and articles suggesting different types of assembly programs. Band concerts, vocational talks, drama productions, class projects, and patriotic exercises all became part of the public school paraphernalia. The very opening of the book *Assemblies for Junior and Senior High Schools,* published in 1929, states, "Junior and senior high schools daily accept the challenge to prepare students for life in a democracy.... Specialized organization and complex activities necessitate unification through athletics, the school newspaper, and the assembly. Because of its frequency and provision for universal participation, the assembly may be considered the foremost integrating factor."[32]

Therefore, the local reorganization of the high school, state laws, and the avalanche of reports and codes on character education were providing a design for educating loyal and obedient citizens who would be "go-getters" and "live wires" in the corporate world. The world of football teams, pledges to the flag, student government, and school clubs was to produce the democratic citizen. Underpinning these designs for a democratic citizen was an Americanism campaign led by the American Legion. The "go-getter" and "live wire" were to be "100% Americans."

EDUCATION FOR 100% AMERICANISM AND THE AMERICAN LEGION

Before the delegates to the NEA 1934 convention, Russell Cook, National Director of the Americanism Commission of the American Legion, pledged the resources of his organization to help battle the cutbacks in funding for public schools from the Great Depression. Cook reminded his audience of the fifteen-year relationship between the two organizations. Reciting the folklore of the American Legion, Cook said, "The members of the American Legion were rudely awakened to the necessity of more general education while serving the flag of our country on the battlefields of the World War. At no other period in our national history has the importance of education been more pronounced than during the war when members of the Legion experienced a handicap which a lack of schooling placed upon comrades."[33]

The inability to read orders, he claimed, caused deaths among the troops. Voicing concern about the problem of illiteracy among the foreign-born, he recounted how the Americanism Commission of the American Legion originally sought the aid of the NEA "in establishing an annual program in which the American people might dedicate themselves each year to the ideal of self-government based upon an enlightened citizenry. Out of that thought was born American Education Week." Reminding the NEA of the Legion's dedication to the education of the foreign-born, he told the delegates, we "realized that aliens in this country must have help in fitting themselves to accept the responsibilities of American citizenship and in understanding and solving the problems of everyday life in America."[34]

Cook's speech gave a fairly accurate account of the Legion's concern with education and its attempts to influence policies in local public schools. His speech would probably have been applauded by the twenty American military officers who had gathered in Paris in March 1919 to organize the American Legion. The meeting was called after Theodore Roosevelt Jr. had made a proposal the previous month to organize some form of World War veterans' organization. Concerns among organizers of the American Legion about illiteracy and foreign-born Americans were tied to a general fear that members of the United States military forces in Europe were being exposed to radical political ideas, and also to worries about reports from the United States of the increasing spread of Bolshevism.

As William Gellerman concludes in his study of the American Legion's involvement in education, "Ex-soldiers were restless. Bolshevism had triumphed in Russia. American leaders both at home and abroad were worried. They were afraid that ex-servicemen might organize along Bolshevistic lines, and exercise such power as to threaten the status quo in America. The American Legion was organized to prevent any such catastrophe."[35]

The organizational structure of the American Legion maximized opportunities for influencing both local and national educational policy. While membership was attached to local American Legion posts, policy making was centralized. Legion leaders wanted to present a united front. The membership of the American Legion during the 1920s grew from 845,146 in 1920 to 1,153,909 in 1931. By 1923, the Legion had established 11,129 local posts.[36] Within this organizational structure, the Legion's National Americanism Commission dictated its Americanism campaign to local posts.

The National Americanism commission was created at the Legion's first convention in 1919. The original resolution proposed, "the establishment of a National Americanism Commission of the American Legion to realize in the United States the basic ideal of this Legion of 100% Americanism through the planning, establishment and conduct of a continuous, constructive educational system...."[37] The resolution lists the following goals in the promotion of "100% Americanism":

1. combat all anti-American tendencies, activities and propaganda;
2. work for the education of immigrants, prospective American citizens and alien residents in the principles of Americanism;
3. inculcate the ideals of Americanism in the citizen population, particularly the basic American principle that the interests of all the people are above those of any special interest or any so-called class or section of the people;
4. spread throughout the people of the nation information as to the real nature and principles of American government;
5. foster the teaching of Americanism in all schools.[38]

The National Americanism Commission focused a great deal of its activity on the last goal, "teaching of Americanism in all schools." The Commission defined Americanism as patriotism and as obedience to law and the Constitution. Members were urged to participate actively in community activities to spread the doctrines of Americanism. The Commission's 1924 handbook, *Service—For God and Country,* states, "Real Americanism work means action and not words. We saw a great deal of insincere flag-waving during the World War, a lot of talk.... The National Americanism Commission has worked out a constructive program and it requires hard work...." Members were told to view the preamble to the organization's constitution as a clear statement of "100% Americanism": "For God and country we associate ourselves together for the following purposes: To uphold and defend the Constitution of the United States of America; to maintain law and order; to foster and perpetuate a one hundred per cent Americanism...."[39]

As part of its Americanism campaign, local Legion members were urged to help weed out subversives from local school systems. The 1921 Legion convention passed a resolution calling for state laws to cancel certificates of teachers "found guilty of disloyalty to the government." In addition, Legion members were asked to volunteer the names of subversive teachers to local school boards. In 1919, the National Americanism Commission warned that, "We have those who believe that the red, white and blue presided over by the eagle shall be replaced by the red flag with the black vulture of disloyalty and international unrest perched upon its staff. Through the schools and through the churches the radicals are now seeking to put across their policies."[40]

In 1921, the National Americanism Commission joined with the NEA to sponsor American Education Week. Henry J. Ryan, Chair of the Joint Advisory Committee of the NEA and the American Legion, and National Director of the Americanism Commission for 1921–1922, explained to the delegates to the NEA convention in 1921 the reasons for the Legion's interest in supporting an American Education Week. "America is God's last chance to save the world," he told the delegates. "We can save it only by giving to every boy and girl in America an equal opportunity for education...opportunity to learn of that government [United States]...so that...they will be able to say, 'We learned to love our country at school'."[41]

The American Legion believed that sponsorship of American Education Week gave it the opportunity to win school authorities to the cause of education for 100% Americanism. In this endeavor, the two organizations were aided by the U.S. Office of Education. In 1925, the American Bar Association and the Daughters of the American Revolution (DAR) also joined in sponsoring of American Education Week. In that year, one day of Education Week was called Equal Opportunity Day, devoted to making "Democracy safe for the world through universal education."[42]

In working with the American Legion and the NEA in sponsoring American Education Week, the DAR was expressing its traditional concern with education for Americanism. Chartered as an educational organization by the United States Congress in 1896, the DAR was originally concerned with the civic education of newly arrived immigrants. In addition, the DAR was indirectly connected to the development of student government in public schools as a form of citizenship education. Speaking at the same NEA convention in 1934 where James Cook of the Americanism Commission outlined the history of the Legion's concern with education, Mrs. Russell William Magna, President General of the DAR, told the educators, "The Daughters of the American Revolution stand for all educational measures, for character building, good citizenship, and the assuming of the responsibilities pertinent thereto." She went on to explain that the DAR participated in American Education Week because "reverence for the nation's founders and interest in schools fit in with our conservation of the values of the past, and the constructive growth of the future.[43]

During American Education Week, local educators and representatives from local Legion posts, DAR chapters, and the American Bar Association cooperated in sponsoring a series of activities supporting the public school and projects for education in Americanism. In 1925, American Education Week emphasized instruction on the U.S. Constitution and the building of patriotism. The 1925 program defined patriotism as "a fulfillment of individual obligations to the community, State and Nation in peace or in war; a wholesome respect for the symbols of the commonwealth; and a will to defend the principles of liberty, equality, justice and tolerance...." In 1926, each day in American Education Week was designated by descriptive titles, such as, "For God and Country Day," "Constitutional Rights Day," "Patriotism Day," "Equal Opportunity Day," "Know Your School Day," and "Community Day."[44]

Besides searching for subversive teachers and helping to organize American Education Week, the Legion sponsored school essay contests and issued citizenship awards. The topics for the essay contests reflected the ideological thrust of the Legion's general approach to Americanism. In 1923, the assigned topic in the contest was, "Why America should prohibit immigration for five years," and in 1924 it was, "Why Communism is a menace to Americanism." The Americanism Commission argued that their school awards were an "effective antidote for the teachings of those groups opposed to the patriotic principles embraced by the American Legion." In addition to these activities, local Legion posts promoted flag education and the saying of the Pledge of Allegiance in local public schools.[45]

It would be difficult to determine the impact of these activities by the American Legion on the ideological content of instruction in local public schools. On the surface, it would appear to be quite extensive. Local educators probably welcomed the Legion's support for increased financial support for public schools. Also, educators probably wanted to avoid any criticism from local Legion posts. Certainly, teachers were probably wary of being branded subversive by the Legion. Besides, Legionnaires appear to have been important members of their communities. William Gellerman concluded in his study that the average Legionnaire was a business or professional man."[46]

TEXTBOOKS AND AMERICANISM

At the center of classroom instruction in public schools are textbooks, as one of the most important sources for ideas promulgated by public schools. The American Legion, along with many other groups, was concerned about the content of textbooks. Throughout the twentieth century, many groups have struggled to gain a voice in determining the content of textbooks. In most periods, "patriotic" organizations, such as the American Legion, have been at the forefront of this struggle.

A variety of influences determined the content of textbooks in the 1920s. First, there was the desire of publishers to maximize profits by gaining the widest acceptance for their textbooks. Often publishers trimmed or added material to textbooks to eliminate the possibility of offending groups that might influence textbook purchases by public schools.

In the 1920s and 1930s, the American Legion, the D.A.R., the Women's Christian Temperance Union, and religious organizations monitored the content of public school textbooks. In the 1930s, Howard Beales recorded the feelings of an author of American history texts regarding the impact of these organizations: "In trying to guard against criticism and opposition, authors are driven to sins of omission and commission." After describing how he adds material of little importance to his history texts and deletes other material because of pressure from outside advocacy groups, the textbook author told Beales, "And, if any author tells you he is not influenced by such pressure, that he tells 'the truth, the whole truth and nothing but the truth' as far as he knows it, don't you believe him. He is a conscious or unconscious liar."[47]

Textbooks had to be in tune with the beliefs of local school board members who were responsible for book selection. As discussed at the beginning of this chapter, various studies of school board membership in the 1920s found that their social composition consisted mainly of businessmen and professionals. Radicals throughout this period criticized school boards for being dominated by a conservative political philosophy.

Third, textbooks had to conform to the requirements of state laws. This often meant that a law in one state would affect the content of textbooks in other states because publishers did not want to publish separate editions for each state. Most state laws affecting textbooks in the early twentieth century dealt with building patriotic citizenship. For instance, the Lusk Laws passed by the New York State legislature in 1918 prohibited any statements in textbooks fostering disloyalty to the United States. The law established a state commission to examine books in "civics, economics, English, history, language and literature for the purpose of determining whether such textbooks contain any matter or statements of any kind which are seditious in character, [or] disloyal to the United States." A 1923 Wisconsin law prohibited any textbook "which falsifies the facts regarding the war of independence, or the war of 1812, or which defames our nation's founders or misrepresents the ideals and causes for which they struggled and sacrificed, or which contains propaganda favorable to any foreign government." An Oregon law prohibited any textbook that "speaks slightingly of the founders of the republic, or of the men who preserved the union, or which belittles or undervalues their work."[48]

In addition, textbook publishers depended on the advice and authorship of educators. In the 1920s, the NEA's Committee on the Teaching of Democracy reported that, "Each publisher of school textbooks will be furnished with a copy of the Specification and Analysis [of recommended goals for citizenship education], with two ends in view—the incorporation of contributory material in forthcoming texts and the specification of existing contributions in texts already published."[49] The Committee hoped that this would result in textbooks that reflected the citizenship goals of the character education movement.

As part of his study for the American Historical Association's Commission on Social Studies in the 1930s, Howard Beales conducted a study of the textbook industry. Beales' study focused on the effect of state legislation and outside advocacy groups on textbook publishing in the 1920s and 1930s. As part of the study, he interviewed authors and publishers. One head of a publishing firm described the publisher's dilemma as, "He wants to tell the truth, and have his authors do the same. Yet he must sell books." Beales concludes,

> Therefore even the most honest publishers must modify books to remove "objectionable" features that will hurt sales, yet at the same time save their own and the author's consciences, and withal rationalize their business reasons into scholarly ones and never admit to the public that they change texts for the sake of sales.[50]

Beales catalogued the major pressure groups influencing textbooks following World War I. One important issue in the 1920s was the portrayal of the British in textbooks. As discussed in Chapter 1, textbooks during World War I were changed to present a more favorable portrayal of the British. It should be noted that many Americans did not support the United States' entry into the war on the side of the British. After all, in this war "to make the world safe for democracy," it seemed strange to be fighting on the side of a country with a monarchy and a large colonial empire. Following the war, the Hearst newspapers, Irish-American organizations, and the Catholic Knights of Columbus began a national campaign against what they felt was a pro-British slant to public school textbooks. In response to the post-war criticism of these changes,

Beales quotes a statement made in 1922 by a New York school superintendent: "The publishers of all the books under criticism...have promised to bring out revised versions, [to] correct passages found to be erroneous in fact, inadequate, or in bad taste."[51]

The Women's Christian Temperance Union besieged publishers in the 1920s to assure that hygiene and physiology texts contained sections on the evils of alcohol. Religious groups protested references to evolution in science texts. And even public utility companies tried to fight off attacks on their industry by influencing the content of textbooks. In 1928, it was reported that the utility interests negotiated with Ginn and Company to eliminate a sentence from a social studies text that stated, "As late as 1926 a man then serving as president of a number of electric light companies in the Middle West gave [in] a single primary election over $200,000 to the campaign funds of both parties." At a public hearing in 1928 before the Federal Trade Commission, leaders of the utility industry complained that they were unable to eliminate all references in textbooks "to watered-stock and power-ring political activities."[52]

George Counts, an educator and well-known critic of the schools in the 1920s and 1930s, wrote about the effect of all these forces influencing the content of textbooks, "Since these [publishing] companies are interested in getting their own books adopted as widely as possible, they very commonly bring pressure to bear upon the authors to eliminate everything that might be objectionable to any important body of citizens in the nation." Consequently, he concluded, "Under these conditions the textbook tends to become a perfectly innocuous and colorless compendium of non-controversial knowledge and consequently an instrument of social conformity."[53]

These influences were reflected in a survey conducted in the late 1920s by Bessie Pierce. She concluded that American public school textbooks primarily emphasized obedience, patriotism, service, and cooperation. These values found their way into textbooks mainly as a result of the combination of state laws, pressure from interest groups, the publishing market, decisions by local school board members, and the influence of educators. Pierce's survey included 97 history texts, 67 books on civic, sociological, and economic issues, 45 geography texts, 21 foreign-language books, 109 readers, 50 music books, and 63 courses of study issued by state departments of education and city school systems.

Her survey of courses of study in history found that the teaching of history mainly emphasized patriotism. She wrote, "Most makers of courses of study are united in their belief that the main aim of instruction in American history is the development of a vivid conception of American nationality and a high sense of patriotism and civic religion." As a typical example of this approach to the teaching of history, she cited the study guide for Idaho public schools, which stressed the importance of history instruction so that when students salute the flag they remember that it "stands for democracy, for liberty under the law; it stands for heroic courage and self-reliance, for equality of opportunity, for self-sacrifice, and the cause of humanity. It stands for free public education, and for peace among nations." Eight states called for teaching patriotism through history by stressing the role of national heros. For instance, the 1925 curriculum manual for the State of Georgia, as quoted by Pierce, states, "A study of men and women who have made the present what it is by their deeds in the past offers a splendid opportunity for the development of the fundamentals of Citizenship and Americanization." The manual continues, "Teaching patriotism, a sense of brotherhood, a devotion to law and order, a harmony of all the good elements of citizenship in the 'citizen of the future' should be among the chief aims of the teacher of history."[54]

Pierce concluded that history and civics texts primarily emphasized the duties and responsibilities citizens owed the government because of the protection it provided. She stated that the consciousness of the mature citizen has been moulded by "the instruction of his tender years, which taught him an avalanche of responsibilities and duties as a fair return for the protection given." She argued, "The whole subject of government in the schools is charged with the duties and responsibilities of citizenship."[55]

With regard to America's relationship with foreign countries, Pierce found a definite emphasis on the superiority of the United States. In textbooks, Spaniards were portrayed as harsh and cruel, while the United States was portrayed as generous and helpful to Central and South American people. Germans were charged with greed and militarism, but the United States was shown as generous toward China (this when Chinese and Japanese immigrants to America were being treated negatively).

Thus, the textbooks of the 1920s conveyed to students a patriotic and uncritical view of the United States. Reading these textbooks, students learned that good citizenship primarily involved fulfilling duties to the various levels of government. As was the case for participants in student government, readers of textbooks were kept innocent of the concept of politics as the exercise and pursuit of power. In this regard, the message in textbooks complemented the social world of the school.

CONCLUSION:
LIVE WIRES AND 100% AMERICANISM

Imagine the world that educators planned for children and youth in the 1920s. Children in elementary school learned moral codes and good citizenship through participating in classroom exercises and groups like Uncle Sam Clubs. The message conveyed in textbooks and school activities was that good citizenship is primarily a passive activity of obeying the law and fulfilling one's duties to government. The message of patriotism and the superiority of the United

States rang out from textbooks, assembly exercises, patriotic songs, and the constant recitation of the Pledge of Allegiance. Through classroom activities and school events, students were supposed to learn that democracy is a cooperative social system requiring work and sacrifice for the group.

The final development of citizenship and character were to take place, according to educators of the period, in the busy social world of junior and senior high schools. Just as the NEA Committee on Character Education emphasized a positive image of the "live wire" and "go-getter," the high school honored as its student heroes those who were elected to student government, participated in clubs, and showed school spirit at rallies and athletic events. Admission to the school honor society required both good grades and active participation in extracurricular activities.

Educators hoped that the values students gained from this consciously constructed social world would meet the needs of a socially efficient society. In the language of the 1926 NEA Report on Character Education, students would learn to merge the "I" with the "we," to work for the good of the school and, later, the firm. Patriotism and school spirit were to blend and produce loyalty to the State and the Company.

Contributing to the citizenship education movement was the drum beat for 100% Americanism coming from local posts and chapters of the American Legion and the DAR. Just as one might wonder if student government turned democratic practices into a hollow exercise, one can also ask if local Legion and DAR activities turned the concept of democracy into ritualistic activities and the worship of symbols. Continuing this line of inquiry, one can also ask if, by weeding out "subversion" from teachers and textbooks, these "patriotic" organizations used anti-Communism as what Herman and Chomsky refer to as a "filter" through which the ideas disseminated by public schools were screened and shaped. In the words of Herman and Chomsky, in the Introduction to this book, the ideology of anti-Communism "helps mobilize the populace against an enemy, and because the concept is fuzzy it can be used against anybody advocating policies that threaten property interests or support accommodation with Communist states and radicalism."[56] Within the context of this argument, the public schools became resistant to teaching any ideas that might question the economic and political status quo in the United States.

One wonders if the schools of the 1920s might have bred a certain level of cynicism among students about the political, economic, and social structure of the United States. Certainly the social world of the American high school conveyed mixed messages. When A. B. Hollingshead studied the social life of a small town high school in the 1940s, he discovered that the leaders and most active participants in student government, clubs, and other school activities were primarily from the town's most affluent families. The youth of lower class and poor families were noted by their absence from the social world of the school. The high school live wires and go-getters were not drawn from all social classes. The democratic social world of the American school turned out to be a world that reinforced the social class structure of the community.[57] Indeed, racial segregation, a fact that contradicted the democratic aspirations of American schools from their early beginnings, belied the social concept of democracy that educators hoped to convey through the school. In reality, the existence of social class and racial segregation meant that American schools did not provide the opportunity for all people to contribute their best to the social system.

CHAPTER THREE

EDUCATORS AND THE MOVIES IN THE 1920s AND 1930s

"AS SOON AS the Jews gained control of the 'movies,'" railed Henry Ford's anti-Semitic *Dearborn Independent* in 1921, "we had a movie problem, the consequences of which are not yet visible. It is the genius of that race to create problems of a moral character in whatever business they achieve a majority."[1] Looked down upon by established American wealth, the film industry became an outlet for the entrepreneurial skills of recently arrived immigrants and their children. Working their way out of the tenements of New York, Boston, and other American cities, the founders of the major film studios created an ironic twist to the call for "100% Americanism." As patriotic organizations beat the drum for "Americanism" and the end to immigration, Hollywood, under the domination of Jewish immigrants and their children, was producing films that would shape the consciousness of Americans and create an image of Americanism for the rest of the world.

The founders of Hollywood faced a series of problems that caused them to reach out for alliances with educators and other groups who might give them an appearance of respectability in a world dominated by white Protestant money. One problem was raising money for an industry scorned by the Eastern financial community. Another was the increasing clamor for more government censorship of films. And, as the movie industry became more concentrated in the hands of a few firms, studio owners feared government anti-trust action.

Movie producers also felt the necessity of mounting a public relations campaign because of charges of immorality and decadence. In 1920 a series of scandals rocked the movie world. First, the nude body of screen star Olive Thomas was found on the floor of a Paris hotel, her death due to an apparent drug overdose. Shortly afterward, comedian Fatty Arbuckle was accused of the rape and murder of starlet Virginia Rappe at a party in San Francisco. In the same year, after director William Desmond was murdered, it was discovered he had been leading a double life under two names and had a previously secret wife and children. It was in this atmosphere of scandal that the Motion Picture Producers and Distributors Association (M.P.P.D.A.) was formed in 1922.[2]

49

Studio owners selected William Harrison Hays, an elder of the Presbyterian church from Indiana and former National Chairman of the Republican Party, to act as their front man in heading the Motion Picture Producers and Distributors Association (M.P.P.D.A.). Protestant, Midwestern-born, and politically well-connected, Hays made an ideal public relations leader for the industry. The idea of forming the M.P.P.D.A. and creating a "dictatorship of virtue" over the content of films as a method of improving the industry's public image is supposed to have originated with Louis Selznick, a Ukrainian Jew, who in 1912, after immigrating to Pittsburgh and entering the jewelry business, became a partner in the recently organized Universal Pictures. In forming the M.P.P.D.A., Selznick took his cue from professional baseball, which, in attempting to improve the public image of the sport after it had been racked by numerous bribery scandals, formed an association and hired Judge Kenesaw Mountain Landis to act as a czar over its ethics.[3]

In 1921, Selznick therefore approached Will Hays, then Postmaster General of the United States, to act as leader of the M.P.P.D.A. Hays had been one of the first political strategists to work with the movie industry, while acting as Republican National Chairman during the Harding campaign in 1920. On January 14, 1922, Hays accepted the offer at a salary, extraordinary for the time, of $100,000 a year.[4]

The formation of the M.P.P.D.A. reflected the growing concentration of the movie industry. In the 1920s, the "Big Eight" film companies that formed the M.P.P.D.A. made 90 percent of American films, whereas in 1912 60 firms had been in operation in the United States. The "Big Eight" included Paramount, 20th Century Fox, Loews (M-G-M), Universal, Warner Brothers, Columbia, United Artists, and Radio-Keith-Orpheum (RKO.).[5]

The M.P.P.D.A. can be considered an organization designed to help immigrant entrepreneurs function in an environment that was hostile to both immigrants and Jews. The head of Paramount was Adolph Zukor, a Jew born in Risce, Hungary, who came to the United States at the age of sixteen and began his career doing upholstery work on the Lower East Side of New York City. Louis Mayer, head of M-G-M, the son of a Russian Jewish peddler of scrap metal in Canada, immigrated to Boston to practice his father's trade. Marcus Loew, pioneer developer of movie theaters and also one of the organizers of M-G-M, was born into a German-Jewish family living in poverty in the Lower East Side of New York, and got his start in the garment industry. The head of Columbia was Harry Cohen, whose father was a German-Jewish tailor in New York City and whose mother was a Russian Jew from an area near the Polish border. The Warner brothers were children of a Polish-Jewish cobbler who settled in Baltimore in the 1880s. Carl Laemmle, founder of Universal Pictures, in which Larry Selznick became a partner, was born in Laupheim, Germany, in 1867, the son of a Jewish land speculator and salesman. Coming to the United

States at the age of seventeen, Laemmle began his career as an errand boy for a druggist. William Fox, founder of 20th Century Fox, was born of Jewish parents in Hungary and worked his way up from a street peddler on the Lower East Side. RKO studios was formed in the late 1920s when the Radio Corporation of America (RCA) became interested in sound systems for the new talking pictures. The mastermind behind the organization of RCA was a Russian Jew named David Sarnoff, who was born in southern Russia in 1891 and after immigrating to the United States in 1900 began working as a delivery boy on the Lower East Side.[6]

The concentration of the industry in the M.P.P.D.A. made it possible for the Hays Office, as it was called, to exercise the "dictatorship of virtue" over the content of American films. The exercise of this power occurred when movies were becoming a major leisure time activity for most Americans. Money spent on movies made up the largest portion of the recreation budget for the average American family during the 1920s. Large cities averaged one movie seat for every five to seven people in their population. Furthermore, the composition of movie audiences was changing during the 1920s. In 1912, only 25 percent of the movie audiences were clerical workers and 5 percent were from the business classes. But during the 1920s, the composition of movie audiences changed from being mainly working class and immigrant to include the middle class.[7]

Shortly after taking office, Hays launched a major public relations campaign designed to improve the ability of film studios to gain outside financing; to stop attempts at increased government censorship; to hold off possible antitrust action; and to improve the image of movies for their growing middle class audiences. Gaining loans for the industry was one of Hays' first accomplishments.[8] He organized a public relations office, a public information department, and a title registration bureau. Hays used the public relations department as a vehicle for establishing ties with groups that could potentially attack the industry and could be used instead to improve the industry's moral and social image. At the first meeting of the M.P.P.D.A. in June 1922, Hays appointed Lee Hanmer of the Russell Sage Foundation to chair the Committee on Public Relations, which included representatives from the Camp Fire Girls, the Boy Scouts, the General Federation of Women's Clubs, the International Federation of Catholic Alumnae, the Young Men's Christian Association, and the National Education Association.[9]

A focal point of the public relations campaign was the increasing pressure for government censorship of movies. This pressure contained a certain element of anti-Semitism. Members of Protestant evangelical groups often laced their attacks on the bad effect of movies on morality with statements about the low morality of immigrants. Given that Jews comprised the major immigrant group in the movie industry, this form of nativism was a cloak for anti-Semitism. For instance, Protestant evangelist Billy Sunday campaigned in 1921 for laws that would close movie theaters on Sunday. He preached that, "No foreign bunch can come over here and tell us how we ought to observe the Lord's Day. The United States at heart is a God-fearing and a God-loving nation and most of our laxity on this point I lay at the door of those elements which are a part of our population, but are not assimilated." In 1920, the Rev. Wilbur Crafts crusaded for Sunday closing legislation at the federal level with the claim that movies, despite their production in the United States, were causing a "Europeanization" of America.[10]

Another source of concern for pro-censorship advocates was the apparent increase in public violence and race riots after World War I. As mentioned in the previous chapter, the years immediately following the end of World War I were punctuated with a number of public bombings. In addition, major race riots occurred in Northern cities.[11] Fearful of race riots and social disorder, government codes restricted racial themes and the portrayal of criminal acts. In his study of censorship laws, Richard Randall found that most laws prohibited movie scenes containing "obscenity," "indecency," and "immorality." In addition, many laws banned scenes that would promote "racial, religious, or class prejudice." And, reflecting the concern that movies would teach people how to commit criminal acts, many of the censorship codes called for removal of scenes that involved "incitement to crime," "portrayal of criminal behavior," and "disturbance of the peace." These codes inhibited the production of movies dealing with social issues.[12]

The Nation magazine reported that in 1921 the Kansas State Board of Review banned from movies all scenes of race riots in Tulsa, Oklahoma, even though newspapers carried front page pictures. The Kansas board also prohibited any mention of the Ku Kux Klan. It is important to note that these actions were taken against newsreels. The words, "Probe of murders laid to Klan," were censored from newsreels in Ohio, according to *The Nation*. And in an act of political censorship, Ohio censors trimmed from an International News Service film about Eugene Debs the words, "Leaving the White House after telling President Harding he has not changed his mind." In another newsreel, Pennsylvania forced the substitution of the word "fanatics" for "anarchists."[13]

Richard Randall's survey of litigation found that in most situations, the courts upheld political censorship of movies. During the 1930s, the right to cut mild anti-Fascist statements from a film on the Spanish Civil War was upheld by a Pennsylvania court. And in *Thayer Amusement Corporation v. Moulton,* Randall writes, "allegations by the Providence, Rhode Island, police department that the Soviet film *Professor Mamlock* was 'Communist propaganda' were enough to sustain a ban in the state."[14]

The pressure for increased censorship of movies was reflected in the passage of state laws. Between the enactment of the first municipal censorship law in Chicago in 1907 and the 1930s, a wave of municipal and state laws dealing with the content of movies spread across the country. New York, Ohio, Pennsylvania, Virginia, and Kansas were just a few of the states that adopted licensing laws. It is estimated that between 1922 and 1927, 48 bills dealing with movie censorship were introduced into state legislatures and that prior to the 1950s there existed at one time or another ninety municipal censorship boards. The most important of these municipal boards were located in Chicago, Detroit, Memphis, Atlanta, and Boston.[15]

In addition to government censorship in the United States, movie producers worried about censorship by foreign governments. This was a major issue after World War I, as U.S. movie companies gained domination of world film production. World War I virtually halted European film production, leaving little competition for American films. By 1919 over ninety percent of the films shown in Europe and virtually all films shown in Latin America were made in the United States.[16] Consequently, American film producers had to be very concerned about foreign censorship boards if they wanted the broadest possible distribution of their movies.

A major consequence of concerns about foreign censorship was the tendency in American movies to avoid portraying any foreign nation in a negative manner for fear that the film would be banned from that country. As explained in Chapter 6, the desire to protect foreign markets played a major role in the self-censorship standards adopted by the movie industry in the late 1920s and the 1930s. These standards did not allow a negative portrayal of foreign governments or the people of a foreign nation.

The debate over government censorship versus self-regulation continued through the 1920s. For instance, when the Massachusetts legislature was considering legislation for licensing movies, the film industry campaigned for state reliance on the decisions of the privately controlled National Board of Review. Under what was called the "Boston Plan," licenses were to be granted to movies approved by the National Board of Review. But Amy Woods, a member of the executive committee of a Massachusetts organization in favor of government censorship, reported that, after months of studying the work of the National Board of Review, "the conclusion reached was that state control is the most effective method yet found to prevent the showing of many of the objectionable features which are now being produced in photo plays." She argued that the findings of a study of movies approved by the National Board of Review and shown in Boston during the week of February 20, 1920, showed that a majority of these films depicted "indecent, immoral or obscene conditions." She also cited a study that compared the work of the Pennsylvania State Board of Censorship to that of the National Board of Review. It was found that in 178 films, the Pennsylvania State Board of Censorship eliminated 1,108 scenes, while the National Board of Review eliminated only 41.[17]

In response to Amy Woods's article, the Executive Secretary of the

National Board of Review, W. D. McGuire, argued that his organization cut fewer scenes because "the National Board did not delete the pictures from the news weeklies showing the actual conditions in the coal regions during the strike, nor condemn Brieux's play, *Damaged Goods,* nor make over forty eliminations in *The Miracle Worker.*"[18]

The major defense of a voluntary self-censorship code was the argument that movies were an art form that had the responsibility to teach the public moral and social lessons. Since it was in the economic interests of the movie industry to support self-censorship, as opposed to government censorship, this argument that films were a form of social art became the standard M.P.P.D.A. defense of the industry against government intervention. When the National Board of Review was undermined by the passage of a New York state law in 1921 requiring the licensing of movies, the M.P.P.D.A. assumed leadership in advocating self-censorship.[19]

The public relations campaign of the M.P.P.D.A. increasingly included educational leaders who were supposed to help improve the image of the movie industry. But this relationship was not without problems for the movie industry. As will be shown in the next section, educators provided research that popularized the idea that movies had a detrimental effect on the health and morality of children and youth.

CLOSING THE GAP BETWEEN EDUCATORS AND THE MOVIES

When Will Hays first appeared before the National Education Association in July 1922, it was only six months after he had accepted the leadership of the M.P.P.D.A. and one month after the forming of its Public Relations Committee. At the time, the NEA was the largest and most important educational organization in the United States. Hays's pledge to accept the challenge "of the American mother" to provide worthy entertainment for American youth was made to an audience that had mixed feelings about the educational value of movies. On the one hand, many educators considered movies and movie houses a major competitor with schools for control of the minds of children. On the other hand, educators recognized the importance of using movies for instructional purposes.

As the relationship between the movie industry and the educational establishment evolved in the 1920s and 1930s, the two groups found ways to serve each others' needs. The movie industry welcomed the claim made by educators that schools could improve movies by educating future audiences, because it provided the industry with another argument against government censorship. The movie industry could claim that movies would improve as the tastes of audiences improved. Educators established movie appreciation courses in high schools, which benefited the movie industry by creating a ready-made audience for certain types of commercial movies. Furthermore, educators and the movie industry together developed classroom films. Thus, the movie industry used educators simultaneously for public relations purposes and to increase profits through the sale of classroom films. Educators benefited by receiving financial support from the movie industry, from the development by the movie industry of classroom films, and from the opportunity to justify the importance of the school in educating movie audiences. As we will see in Chapter 5, by the 1930s the values in movies and the values taught in schools became strikingly similar.

From the beginning, educators had had ambivalent feelings about movies. In 1914, Alfred Saunders, the manager of the Education Department of the early Colonial Picture Corporation, spoke to the NEA on "Motion Pictures as an Aid to Education." As one of the first representatives of the movie industry ever to speak to the NEA, Saunders was primarily concerned with selling films to public schools. After reviewing available movie projectors and films suitable for schools, he claimed that "every school that is equipped with a projecting machine may cover the cost of it by allowing the parents to attend exhibitions in the evening."[20]

Immediately after his presentation, the audience of educators began to debate the value of movies. They complained that movies were competing with the schools for control of children's minds. Peter Olesen, Superintendent of Schools from Cloquet, Minnesota, stated: "In less than twenty years, the motion picture business has secured a hold on the minds of people which is almost equal to that of the school and the daily press." Olesen warned that movies might actually possess a stronger hold on the mind of the child than did the schools:

> I believe that one reason why it is hard to interest some children in school today is that their minds have been filled and their imagination thrilled with too vivid motion pictures, and, when these children come to school, they are disappointed because the teacher cannot make the subject as interesting as a motion-picture show.[21]

Olesen, like other educators, argued that enlisting movies in the cause of education would solve the problem. This argument was presented at the 1914 NEA meeting by David Snedden, Commissioner of Education for Massachusetts and a pioneer in industrial education. Snedden argued that movies could have an important role in education because they presented material in a concrete fashion. Snedden argued that because of the "cheapening and vulgarizing of the motion picture, schools and other educational agencies have been loath to attach to it the importance which it deserves." But, he stressed, pressure from the education world on the movie industry could result in films that were of value for classroom instruction. Snedden's position was echoed by Nathanial Graham, Superintendent of Schools from South Omaha, Nebraska, who stated, "We all believe that encouragement by this body of educators will result in motion pictures being made available for every department of school work. Who can tell in how short a time motion pictures will be as great an accessory to education as is the printed text?"[22]

In the 1920s, educators were still debating the role of movies in education and society. Will Hays' appearance before the NEA in 1922 did little to ease educators' apprehensions about the effects of movies on children and concerns about the development of films for classroom instruction. A 1923 editorial in *The Elementary School Journal* complained that after Hays' speech little effort was made to involve educators directly in the movie industry. The writer griped that the only things the movie industry seemed to want of educators were to preview and publish a list of approved movies, and to help develop a market for classroom films. But, his argument continued, this was not enough. Noting that "the motion picture has come to be one of the most important sources of influence over the public mind," the writer argued that it "behooves everyone who is interested in the creation of sound attitudes among people at large and especially among pupils to study the problems which motion pictures have created."[23]

Despite this editorial, an NEA Committee to Cooperate with the Motion Picture Producers was formed. This committee received direct financial support from the M.P.P.D.A. as part of organization's general public relations campaign. The committee was chaired by one of the leading educational psychologists of the period, Charles Judd of the University of Chicago. Its membership included public school representatives from around the country. The M.P.P.D.A. financed a meeting in New York between the members of the committee and representatives of the movie producers. In addition, the M.P.P.D.A. provided $5,000 for the committee to investigate the use of films for classroom instruction.[24]

The report submitted by the committee to the NEA in 1923, one year after Hays had spoken to the membership of that organization, must have pleased the M.P.P.D.A. The report called for the discharge of the committee presenting the report and the creation of what would become the NEA Department of Visual Instruction, which according to the report should "be specifically instructed not to attempt to organize any plan of picture censorship."[25] The primary recommendation of the report was for the study of the use of movies for the purpose of classroom instruction. The M.P.P.D.A. was interested in having educators use old films for classroom instruction so that movie companies could make a profit from films too old for the general market. For this purpose, the M.P.P.D.A. sponsored committees of teachers to inspect the film vaults held by producers and select portions of these films that could be used in classrooms. Lists of these selections were given to movie producers so that they could put together classroom films from these old movies.

Despite Hays's speech and the M.P.P.D.A's financial support of work by the NEA, educators' general criticism of the effects of movies on children did not stop. The movie industry became increasingly concerned about this criticism in the 1920s as it tried to make its products attractive to middle class families. Colonel Jason S. Joy, M.P.P.D.A. Director of Public Relations, began his speech to the NEA annual meeting in 1927 by claiming, "The motion picture today is catering to the American family." As part of this effort, he stated, "the industry has been concerned for some time now in finding out exactly what the effect of pictures is—on behavior, as an educator, and as a force for good." Joy went on to cite a study conducted by the Psychology Department at Columbia University on the numbers of children attending movies and their frequency of attendance. For the purpose of the study, audiences were observed at twelve different theaters in New York City and children were surveyed in public schools. The study found that on average only 8 percent of movie audiences were under the age of 17 and that the children surveyed in schools attended movie houses on the average 1.15 times per week. Based on these figures, Joy claimed that movies had little effect on children. Furthermore, he argued that the movies children did see were of educational and moral value. He read to the gathered educators a list of the ten most popular movies selected by children, which included *Beau Geste, Ben Hur,* and *The Scarlet Letter.*[26]

After dismissing the claims of negative effects of movies on children, Joy outlined steps the movie industry was taking to make movies more attractive to educators and families. One step was the making of movies based on the "classics." However, as will be pointed out later, many of the "classics" were being shaped to meet the requirements of the movie code. Joy told the NEA, "This growing intimacy between the motion picture and the book has met with general although not universal approval. There have been those who feared that many people would 'take their reading out in looking'." But, he argued in reference to a report by the New Jersey Library Association, movies stimulated greater interest in reading the "classics" and historical novels. In addition, "classics" made into movies became more accessible to the general population. "Books on the shelves of libraries," he told the NEA, "make it possible for men to attain a certain amount of knowledge and information by hard work and application. But the moving picture, presented as an amusement, will in a few years make it impossible for any average man or woman to remain ignorant."[27]

In his speech, Colonel Joy also referred to cooperative work between the motion picture industry and American universities. This work was the precursor of the movie appreciation units that would appear in English courses in American high schools in the 1930s. Joy described the work of Will Hays and Nicholas Murray Butler, President of Columbia University, in planning a school of motion picture technology at Columbia. In addition, Joy announced that the Graduate School of Business Administration at Harvard University had just initiated a series of lectures on the industry to begin with lectures by Will Hays, and that Harvard planned to establish a film archive.[28]

Despite the M.P.P.D.A.'s public relations campaign, educators continued to complain about the detrimental effects of movies on children. Obviously, these complaints ran counter to the desire of movie producers to attract the American family to the movie theater. While educators were warning parents about the negative effects of movie attendance on their children, the movie industry was trying to convince parents of its educational value. Nonetheless, grumbling about movies continued. A major threat to the movie industry was an extensive series of research monographs called the Payne Studies.

The Payne Studies, according to the early historian of the M.P.P.D.A., Raymond Moley, were one of the major contributing factors to the final enforcement by the movie industry of a censorship code in the 1930s.[29] The research studies were organized in 1928 under the leadership of W. W. Charters, Director of the Bureau of Educational Research, Ohio State University. The idea for the research came from the Rev. William Short, a long-time critic of movies, who in 1927 organized the Motion Picture Research Council. In 1928 he brought together a group of educators, psychologists, and sociologists to discuss possible research studies on the effect of movies on children. Short soon received financial support from the Payne Fund for creation of the Committee on Educational Research and a series of research studies.[30]

Twelve studies were completed and published under the sponsorship of The Payne Fund. In addition, Charters himself published a final summary volume in 1933. The research was carried out by a formidable array of social scientists and educators, and published in a series of volumes by the Macmillan Company.[31] A popular summary of the studies was written under auspices of The Payne Fund by Henry James Forman and published in 1933 under the title, *Our Movie-Made Children*. The popularity of Forman's book resulted in seven reprintings between 1933 and 1935.[32]

Touching on parental fears, one of the Payne Studies concluded that movies had a detrimental effect on the health of children by disturbing sleep patterns. In cooperation with the Bureau of Juvenile Research in Columbus, Ohio, researchers wired the beds of children in a state institution to measure the amount of movement during sleep. The children were divided into different groups to measure the effect of movies and other conditions on restlessness during sleep. One set drank coffee at 8:30 p.m. Another group underwent sleep deprivation by being kept up until midnight and then awakened early in the morning. (This part of the experiment ended after complaints by matrons of the institution.) A third set of children was taken to the movies prior to going to bed.

The researchers found that movie attendance caused as much disturbance during sleep as drinking two cups of coffee at 8:30 p.m. The researchers wrote, "We can conclude...from our results that seeing some films does induce a disturbance of relaxed, recuperative sleep in children to a degree which, if indulged in with sufficient frequency, can be detrimental to normal health and growth."[33] The results of this study led Charters to warn, "Thus it appears that movies selected unwisely and indulged in intemperately will have a detrimental effect upon the health of children."[34]

Charters described the sleep studies as one link in a chain of negative effects of movies on children. Another of the studies found that children retained information from movies over long periods of time. A group of second and third graders remembered at the end of six weeks 90 percent of what they remembered from a movie on the day they saw it. Researchers also found that movies had a significant effect on the conduct and attitudes of children. One study compared the behavior of children who attended movies four to five times a week with those from similar economic and social backgrounds who went to movies twice a month. It was found that those who frequently attended movies, as compared with those who attended infrequently, had lower deportment grades in school, did more poorly on school subjects, and were rated lower in reputation by their teachers. A study of children living in congested areas of New York City arrived at a similar conclusion about the effects of movies on behavior. The researchers concluded from the statistics gathered in the study "that for this population there is a positive relationship between truancy and delinquency and frequent movie attendance."[35]

Another Payne Study focused on the effect of movies on the emotional responses of children. In this experiment, children were wired to galvanometers to measure their reactions to movies while they were seated in the balcony and rear seats of a movie theater in Columbus, Ohio. The galvanometers measured their responses to scenes depicting dangerous situations and containing sexual material. The study found that scenes of danger created the greatest reaction in nine-year-old children, and that the degree of reaction declined with age. Not surprisingly, teenagers had a greater reaction to sex scenes than did younger children. The researchers concluded that reactions to scenes of danger caused unnecessary fright in young children, and that teenagers' reactions to sex scenes were unhealthy.

Concern about the effects of movies was further heightened by research on movie attendance. As part of the Payne Studies, 55,000 children in 44 communities in Ohio were surveyed regarding movie attendance. It was found that children between the ages of 5 and 8 attended movies an average of 0.42 times a week, and that for 8-to-19-year-old children the attendance rate was 0.99 movies a week. The study determined that the average boy in this study between the ages of 8 and 19 attended 57 pictures a year and the average girl attended 46 movies during the same period of time. The specter of weekly movie attendance by youth heightened fears about the effects of movies.

In general, the Payne Studies presented a very negative portrait of the effects of movies on children. Movies, according to the Payne Studies, disturbed children's sleep, heightened their emotional feelings, influenced their social attitudes, caused daydreaming, taught lovemaking, and flooded their minds with ideas and facts that were retained over long periods of time. In addition, the studies linked movie attendance to poor grades, misbehavior in school, and juvenile delinquency.

Of particular importance for raising public anxieties about the effects of movies was the supposed link between movie attendance and delinquency. Henry Forman presented this argument in graphic detail in the concluding section of his popularized version of the Payne Studies. He wrote, "A number of adolescent and youthful criminals give circumstantial accounts of their path to, and arrival at, criminality, and, rightly or wrongly, but very positively, they blame the movies for their downfall." Forman reported that girl inmates in an institution for sex delinquents attributed "to the movies a leading place in stimulating cravings for an easy life, for luxury, for cabarets, road-houses and wild parties, for having men make love to them and, ultimately, for their particular delinquency." Citing one of the Payne Studies, Forman stated that in "a high-delinquency area and a region where most of the youth is of foreign-born parentage, the movie enters into innumerable patterns of their lives and constitutes, in effect, an institution of informal education, socially uncontrolled and wholly unsupervised." Forman's intention was to impress the reader with the evils of the movie house. Forman quotes the words of one Dr. Wesley Mitchell: "Motion pictures are one of the most powerful influences in the making of mind at the present time. They affect great masses of people during the impressionable years of childhood and youth."[36]

To counter the negative effects of movies, the Payne Studies recommended creating movie appreciation courses in public schools. It was assumed that the content of films was dependent on public demand and, therefore, improving public taste would directly influence the content of movies. One volume for the series, by Edgar Dale, Research Associate at the Bureau of Educational Research of Ohio State University, is entitled *How to Appreciate Motion Pictures: A Manual of Motion-Picture Criticism Prepared for High School Students.*[37]

Obviously, the movie industry supported this argument because it shifted the blame for the content of movies from the producers to the audience. Hiding behind the rhetoric of capitalism, movie producers argued that they were only responding to the market and were producing films to satisfy public demand, as defense against government censorship. The movie industry also supported movie appreciation courses because they promised to increase profits by requiring student attendance at movies. Movie appreciation courses improved the public image of the movie industry by presenting movies as educational.

The educational value of movies and the education of public taste became important public relations themes of the M.P.P.D.A. In 1931, Carl Milliken, Secretary of the M.P.P.D.A., addressed the annual meeting of the NEA on the suggestive topic, "How the Movies Will Enrich Life." Milliken told the gathered educators that weekly movie attendance by adults and children reflected the fact that "people have selected the motion pictures for their chief leisure-time activity, and you can do nothing to alter that fact even if you wished to do so." Milliken went on to argue that movies played an important role in controlling social discontent by easing the monotony of modern work. In describing industrial conditions, Milliken stated that "with monotony comes a tightening of nerves and a feeling which may be likened to charged water in a bottle. If there is no relief from the inner pressure the top flies off, and the result is impairment of the individual's health, or in the case of the group, social disorder."[38]

Milliken also contended that educators must accept the fact that movies were a more important influence on the public than other art forms. He claimed that for every one hundred people attending movies there was only one person who read a book and for every ten thousand people attending movies there was only one person going to a concert or an art museum. Given these conditions, Milliken told the school leaders, their responsibility was to educate students to accept only the best in movies. Milliken argued that movies provided lessons in geography, civics, ethics, geology, and literature. Despite the potential benefits of these educational opportunities, he stated that "until the theater-goer is trained to look for that which is best for him, the actual benefits are limited."[39]

He suggested two general ways teachers could use motion pictures. One was to direct school children to attend movies that contained material of educational value. This required teachers to develop classroom materials that would help students benefit from the educational content of films. The second way teachers could use motion pictures was in the classroom.

Milliken concluded his speech by placing the burden for the quality of movies on the tastes of movie-going audiences. He argued that improvements in movies depended on the education of future audiences: "The motion picture industry is interested in children, of course," he assured the educational professionals, "for it is interested in the character of audiences it will command tomorrow. Better audiences mean better pictures." To drive home his argument for shifting the responsibility for the content of movies from the producers to the market, he told the educators, "You must realize that however earnest the producers of motion pictures may be in their continuous efforts to raise the social and moral standards of motion picture entertainment, the most they can do is to set the minimum level of good taste. Above that [it] is the community itself which sets the fashion."[40]

Milliken's stress on the education of future audiences was already receiving attention in the world of education. In preparing the manual on motion picture criticism for the Payne Series, Edgar Dale worked with members of the National Council of Teachers of English and with William Lewin, Chairman of the Council's Committee on Photoplay Appreciation.[41] In addition, Dale received help from Paramount Studios and the M.P.P.D.A. In 1930 and 1931, Lewin had conducted studies on movie selection by high school students and educators. In an article for the National Council of Teachers of English in 1931, he reported his findings and suggested the establishment of a committee of educators to rate movies. Subsequently, the President of the National Council of Teachers of English asked Lewin to organize the Photoplay Appreciation Committee. Edgar Dale was made a member of the committee, and, in cooperation with the National Council and the Payne Fund, Dale's textbook, *How to Appreciate Motion Pictures: A Manual of Motion-Picture Criticism Prepared for High School Students,* was distributed to high schools throughout the country.[42]

Dale's volume for the Payne Studies opens with a chapter explaining to the high school reader how a movie appreciation course will provide standards for judging films and increase enjoyment by introducing students to techniques in film production. Except for Chapter 2 and the last two chapters of the book, the remaining nine chapters are devoted to film history and techniques. Chapter 2 is devoted to "Shopping for Your Movies," and warns the student, in words that were probably applauded by the M.P.P.D.A., "When you attend pictures of inferior value, you are voting for their continuance, because the only way they can be continued is through sufficient returns at the box-office."[43] The selection, he suggests to the high school reader, should be based not only on the entertainment value of films but also on "the social value, in other words, the effect that they are likely to have on persons who view them." Dale advised the high school student to select movies based on reviews in magazines. Dale cited as examples reviews from *Parents' Magazine,* which labeled films as suitable or not suitable for youth and children. In keeping with the idea that the content of films can be controlled by educating audiences, he concluded the chapter: "By shopping for your movies you will raise the whole level of motion pictures that are produced. Poor pictures will no longer be made, and there will be many more good ones."[44] Dale ended the volume on the same theme by telling the reader "you have the power to influence the future of motion pictures."[45]

The use of movie study guides became an important part of movie appreciation courses. In part, the study guides were supported by the movie industry because they were a form of advertising. While working with Edgar Dale, William Lewin organized a film study group at Central High School in Newark, New Jersey and wrote the book *Photoplay Appreciation in American High Schools* for the Committee on Photoplay Appreciation of the National Council of Teachers of English.[46] In 1934, the National Council published this manual by Lewin.[47] During the same time period, the supervisor of English for the school system pioneered the use of study guides for movies.

Lewin received support for his advocacy of movie appreciation courses from Walter Barnes, a professor at New York University and Chair of the Committee on Literature for the National Council of Teachers of English and later President of the Council. Barnes was a leading advocate of the idea that movies should be studied as a form of literature. In a paper delivered at the annual meeting of the National Council in 1931, Barnes argued that movies and radio programs were providing experiences for their audiences that were comparable to reading a book.[47] Since movies influenced the attitudes, conduct, and character of youth, he declared that "school authorities must widen the scope of their programs, and utilize, in all feasible ways, this new and potentially promising agency for education."[48] Lewin expressed the same sentiment: "So long as children attend theaters, schools must develop units of instruction in relation to attendance at theaters."[49]

The teaching of movie appreciation in high schools thus received strong support from the leadership of the National Council of Teachers of English as both a method for improving the quality of movies and in recognition of movies as a form of democratic literature. In his forward to Lewin's book, Barnes referred to movie houses as "people's theaters." Perhaps most important for movie makers, Barnes' forward rejected the use of censorship as a means of controlling movie content, in favor of educating both film makers and audiences. Barnes stated that the chief contribution schools could make to the quality of movies was "not, perhaps, through formal censorship (for that is a dubious and devious mode of control), but through systematic and constructive education."[50]

An important goal of the work of the National Council of Teachers of English was influencing movie selection by children and youth. The Photoplay Appreciation Committee chaired by Lewin gathered statistics on adolescent movie selection and attendance, and conducted a study comparing students receiving instruction in movie appreciation with those receiving no instruction. Not surprisingly, the study found that adolescents in the late 1920s and early 1930s primarily consulted their family and friends in the selection of movies. And, of course, this study also found that those attending the courses made better selections of movies, according to the criterion of the study, than did those who did not attend the course. The criterion used for determining what was a superior selection of a movie was based on comparison of student selections with teacher selections.

In addition, the study claimed that movie appreciation classes caused children and youth to select movies that had a positive effect on their conduct. As an example of the important influence of movies on conduct, the Committee quoted an eleventh-grade girl in Memphis: "After seeing *Sign of the Cross*, I went to church on a weeknight." In reference to the same movie, a twelfth-grade girl in Los Angeles wrote, "It made me glad I was a Christian; it made me stronger in my faith; it made me hold to my religion." Regarding the movie *Twenty Thousand Years in Sing Sing*, an eleventh-grade boy in Newark wrote, "It took away my tendency, more or less, from crime." And a boy in St. Cloud,

Minnesota, stated about the same film, "It influenced me to be careful of my actions, as it is difficult to escape the arm of the law."[51]

The movie industry was probably pleased that the National Council of Teachers of English was advocating attendance at particular movies as part of the general education of youth. Rather than viewing movie attendance in a negative light, it was being presented by the Council as an extension of the work of the school. In conclusions of the study, an eleventh-grade student was quoted: "Before this experiment [the movie appreciation course], I went to movies just to kill time; movies weren't even a favorite hobby of mine. I didn't realize that there could be both educational and enjoyable pictures.... I've learned to select the better pictures. I think now I'll go to more pictures and appreciate them more."[52]

The Photoplay Appreciation Committee concluded that movie appreciation courses combined with movie attendance had a positive effect on the character and education of students. In the words of the Committee, "Class instruction excels in developing appreciation of high ideals of character in screen portrayals, the greatest gain being in appreciation of honesty, with large gains registered also for bravery, devotion, and self-sacrifice.... Movie influence on instructed pupils...is generally in the direction of higher ideals."[53]

In a finding that also must have pleased the movie industry, the National Council of Teachers of English concluded that movie attendance increased the reading of those books on which screenplays were based. This conclusion provided justification for cooperation between the National Council of Teachers of English and the M.P.P.D.A. in the writing and distribution of more study guides to the public schools. In 1933, the Council established a central reviewing committee for films, which produced during that year study guides for the films *Emperor Jones, Little Women,* and *Alice in Wonderland.* In 1934, the work was transferred from the National Council of Teachers of English to the National Education Association's Division of Secondary Education. In 1934 and 1935, study guides were distributed to public schools for *Great Expectations, Treasure Island, Little Women, David Copperfield, Dog of Flanders,* and *Les Misérables.*[54]

The movie industry and, supposedly, public school teachers were ecstatic about the distribution of these guides. For the movie industry it meant increased attendance at particular movies, free publicity, and good public relations. By 1937, study guides and information about movies were being sent to teachers of English, history, geography, and the sciences. This information was to be used by teachers in directing students to see movies that illustrated material used in classroom instruction. It was estimated that by 1937 3 million students were receiving instruction in movie appreciation.[55]

The importance of study guides for profits for the motion picture industry was outlined in an article in the May 16, 1936, *Motion Picture Herald* on the marketing of *Romeo and Juliet.* The article reported that the M.P.P.D.A directed its marketing campaign at sixteen national social, community, and educational groups with an estimated membership of 36,211,395. Based on an average admission price of 25 cents, it was estimated that the potential gross from these groups was about $9 million. Contributing to the marketing campaign for *Romeo and Juliet*, the Department of Secondary Education of the National Education Association prepared a study guide which, according to the article, was expected to be used in every high school English class in the United States. In describing the relationship between the movie industry and the schools in the marketing of films, the article states, "Half a million copies of this study guide will be made available for use as text material in schools and to be taken home to be read by all the family. All of this has a definite relation to the box office potentialities." Adding to the impact of the study guide, exhibits on *Romeo and Juliet* were shown in schools, libraries, and museums in 50 cities in the United States. According to *The Motion Picture Herald*, these efforts made the film the number one box office success for September 1936, and one of the top ten box office successes in 1937 and 1938.[56]

The movie industry was also interested in increasing profits by using parts of old films to create movies especially for use in the classroom. In 1929, Will Hays organized a conference on character education which, as discussed in Chapter 2, was a popular topic in American education. The conference organized a Committee on Social Values in Motion Pictures which included, among its five members, two of the researchers for the Payne Studies: Mark May, director of the Institute of Human Relations at Yale University, and Frank Freeman of the University of Chicago. Membership also included a former president of the NEA, Florence Hale. The two other members were Miriam Waters, a penologist, and Howard Le Sourd of Boston University.

The first work of the committee was to select life situations from movies that could be used for character education. In 1934, the committee, working with Paramount Studios, produced eight films and accompanying manuals. Marketed under the series title "Secrets of Success," demand for the short films exceeded availability. The success of the series lead to another mutual endeavor, this time between the Progressive Education Association and the General Education Board of the Rockefeller Foundation.

In 1936, an Advisory Committee on the Use of Motion Pictures was created by the M.P.P.D.A. to review the educational value of old films that were no longer profitable in commercial theaters. This committee was headed by Mark May and included Will Hays, the presidents of five universities, the Executive Secretary of the NEA, and other leading educators. The work of these various committees, Raymond Moley wrote, "from the industry's point of view…gave promise of more than an answer to the question whether noncurrent material in its vaults could and would be used by teachers if it were made available."[57]

These developments in the relationship between the movie industry and educators were summed up by Will Hays when he appeared before the annual meeting of the NEA in 1939, seventeen years after his initial appearance before that organization. After reviewing the development of visual instruction in public schools, he focused on the projects that had developed between M.P.P.D.A. and the public schools. These included preparation of study guides for motion picture appreciation groups in high schools, excerpting material from feature films for character education and human relations films, and exploring the possibility of producing nontheatrical short subjects. Hays described how the industry opened its vaults to educators for the development of human relations and character films, and reported that the committee working on the project was now reviewing material for nontheatrical short subjects for use in public schools. Hays recognized that these activities were of commercial value to the movie industry but argued that it was the commercial development of the industry that had made it so important "as a conveyor of ideas." He referred to commercially developed movies as "a tremendous influence in conditioning the thoughts of men everywhere...the best available substitute for actual experience." Reflecting educators' arguments that students should be trained to gain moral and social lessons from movies, Hays added that motion picture appreciation courses are "courses in discrimination, in good taste, and not of the photoplay art alone or of the literature on which it is based, but discrimination in matters of conduct and custom, morals and ethics."[58]

Hays's speech reflected the mutually beneficial relationship that had developed between educators and the movie industry. On the one hand, the industry used educators for public relations purposes and to develop audiences for particular types of films. On the other hand, educators received direct financial support and aid in exploring the use of films in the classroom. All of this helped to narrow the gap between the movie industry and educators who were critical of the negative effects of movies on the morals and conduct of the public in general and on youth in particular. Of major importance in softening educators' criticism of movies was the adoption by the movie industry of a self-regulating censorship code. As will be examined in Chapter 5, this code brought the values conveyed by movies into closer agreement with those being disseminated by the public schools.

CHAPTER FOUR

CONTROLLING SEXUALITY: YOUTH CULTURE, THE NEW WOMAN, AND MOVIES IN THE 1920s

DURING THE 1920s, the public schools tried to put a brake on what some people were calling a revolution in sexual morality. Many Americans considered the forces behind this revolution to be the portrayal of love life in movies, the youth culture created by the social world of the modern high school, and the continuing struggle for female emancipation. Some educational leaders linked female emancipation to the collapse of the family and, consequently, to increased juvenile delinquency and poor school performance by children. Therefore, as pointed out later in this chapter, an important aspect of education programs in public schools was control of female sexuality. The tension between the moral objectives of public schools and the content of movies would reach some resolution in the early 1930s when the movie industry adopted a self-regulatory code. But during the 1920s there was a clear conflict between the world presented to the public by movies and the values disseminated by the schools.

In addition, there was a tension in public schools between the social world being fostered in the modern high school and the attempt by educators to control adolescent sexuality. Educators expressed alarm about the revolution in sexual morals, particularly among women. In part, the sexual revolution was linked to expanding enrollments in colleges and high schools, which created concentrated populations of youth and opportunities for the relatively new practice of dating in pairs. In their history of sexuality in America, John D'Emilio and Estelle Freedman write about the 1920s, "Sexual innovation played a key role in this new world of youth. Particularly in coeducational institutions, heterosocial mixing became the norm. Young men and women mixed casually in classes, extracurricular activities, and social spaces, with a great deal of freedom from adult supervision."[1] By the 1920s, as D'Emilio and Freedman indicate, high school was a mass institution attended by almost three-quarters of American youth. Within this new social world of the high school of the 1920s, dating in pairs replaced the nineteenth-century practice of informal socializing in groups. The high school date provided greater opportunity for sexual freedom

67

than had previous forms of socializing among young men and women.

It would be difficult to determine the exact contribution of movies, of the struggle for female emancipation, and of the social world of the high school to a loosening of sexual morality in the 1920s. But certainly there is evidence that sexual standards did change during this period. A 1939 survey of college-educated women reported that in the survey only 26 percent of the respondents born between 1890 and 1900 had had premarital sex as compared to 69 percent of those born after 1913. Another study that suggested increased sexual activity among unmarried women found a steady rise in the number of pregnant brides after 1900.[2]

Educators and many social commentators of the 1920s were concerned about increased sexual aggressiveness and pursuit of pleasure among American women. The Kinsey Study of the early 1950s showed a steady increase in the number of women achieving orgasm in marriage beginning with the cohort born in the very first part of the twentieth century. Kinsey found that more than a third of the women born before 1900 remained clothed during sex, in contrast to 8 percent of those born during the 1920s.[3] These changes in sexual morality might not have been just a product of the 1920s, since there is some evidence of changes prior to World War I.[4]

In any case, many people in the 1920s linked movies to changes in adolescent morality. There is some evidence for this assertion. For example, Herbert Blumer, associate professor of sociology at the University of Chicago, conducted a Payne Study on the relationship between changes in sexual behavior and movies. This study is important from two standpoints. First, the study seems to demonstrate the important role of movies in the sexual revolution of the twentieth century. Second, the study added significantly to fears that movies were having a detrimental effect on the population.

Blumer asked 1,800 high school and college students, office employees, and factory workers to keep journals on the effect of movies on their lives. One of the major conclusions Blumer reached after reading the journals was that movies played an important role in teaching lovemaking. Blumer wrote, "They [the journals] force upon one the realization that motion pictures provide, as many have termed it, 'liberal education in the art of loving'."[5] Typical of the journal entries was a male college sophomore who recounted, "She would make me go with her to see [a movie]...and then when we returned home she made me make love to her as she had seen the other two on the screen." Another college male wrote, "The technique of making love to a girl received considerable of my attention, and it was directly through the movies that I learned to kiss a girl on her ears, neck, and cheeks, as well as on the mouth." A statement in the journal of a female high school sophomore was typical of those found in other journals by girls of her age: "I have learned quite a bit about love-making from the movies."[6]

Blumer concluded that in addition to teaching teenagers about lovemaking, movies were taking over the fantasy world of youth. He claimed that 66 percent of 458 journals written by high school students provided evidence that movies were linked to daydreaming. Part of the criticism of movies during the period was that they were inciting the lustful propensities of youth.

Another Payne Study concluded that aggressive female sexual behavior portrayed in movies did not conform to the public values of the 1920s. In order to determine values in relation to the content of movies, Charles Peters, Professor of Education at Pennsylvania State College, organized fourteen categories representing distinct types from the general population.[7] The social categories ranged from middle-aged college professors to Western Pennsylvania miners and their wives and children. The members of each social category rated movie scenes according to whether or not they thought the content was above or below standards of public morality and political attitudes. In other words, this research method used publicly expressed standards of morality and politics to judge the content of movies.

The members of the fourteen social categories were asked to judge movie scenes according to that portrayal of (1) democratic attitudes and practices, (2) the treatment of children by parents; (3) kissing and caressing, and (4) aggressiveness of a girl in lovemaking. The movie presentations of only one of these was rated by all of the different social categories as being below the moral standards of American society. "Treatment of children by parents" and "democratic attitudes and practices" in movies were rated by all categories as above the average standards of society. "Kissing and caressing" movie scenes were found to parallel general moral standards. Only the fourth movie portrayal, "aggressiveness of a girl in lovemaking," was rated as below general moral standards.

A combination of the publicized sex life of movie stars and the portrayal of passion on the screen contributed to the sexual education of youth during the 1920s. With the advent of movies came the modern phenomenon of movie stars whose lives were followed in close detail by magazines and newspapers. During the 1920s, movie stars began to comment in public on their love life and divorces. As film historian Robert Sklar writes about the 1920s, "There is no way to show a cause-and-effect relation between Hollywood's pleasure principles and the gradual loosening of sexual restraints.... But Hollywood's sexual behavior was the most publicized frontier of a new morality."[8]

The world of passion and sensuality depicted in films of the 1920s would later be curbed by the movie code of the 1930s. Some films of the pre-code period provided audiences with glimpses of nude female bodies. For example, after 1918, director Cecil B. DeMille began to make films that showed risqué extramarital tales. In one of his films, *Male and Female* (1919), a film criticized for its immorality, Gloria Swanson briefly reveals her breasts as she steps out of a bathtub. DeMille produced a whole series of films for the 1920s that dealt with issues of sexual morality and provided movie audiences with a world of sensuality. Europeans were very often used in movies to portray sexual desire, European women were frequently used to depict aggressive female characters.[9]

Two movie stars who probably haunted the daydreams of adolescent males and females in the 1920s were Rudolph Valentino and Greta Garbo. It is certainly conceivable that some of the men and women in Blumer's study who were learning lovemaking from movies were learning it from films such as Rudolph Valentino's *The Sheik* (1921) and Greta Garbo's *The Temptress* (1926). Valentino brought a new image of masculinity to American moviegoers-that of a man devoted to heightening the sensual relation of women. Greta Garbo, a female Valentino, showed American audiences the passionate side of female nature. Valentino taught men how to be sensual and passionate, and Garbo taught the same lessons to American women.[10]

Along with the movies, the women's suffrage movement contributed to fears among some Americans that female aggressiveness would undermine the American family. In 1920, resistance to the ratification of the Nineteenth Amendment, which gave the vote to women, was primarily from those fearing that women would step outside their traditional domestic roles. In *At Odds: Women and the Family in America from the Revolution to the Present,* Carl Degler concludes, "The reason why women, alone of all social groups, organized against their own political emancipation is that many women perceived in the suffrage a threat to the family, a threat so severe that the vote did not seem worth the possible cost."[11] Even after ratification of the Nineteenth Amendment, women did not rush to exercise their right to vote. It was not until 1956 that the proportion of women voters equaled that of men.[12]

In the popular press of the 1920s and the complaints of conservative religious leaders, female political emancipation was often linked to decline in sexual morality and from this to the collapse of the family. For instance, fear of the effect of female sexuality on society was reflected in a 1922 national survey on youth conducted by *The Literary Digest.* The magazine concluded from the survey that the overriding concern about the younger generation was the decline of sexual morality. The survey questioned high school principals, college presidents and deans, the editors of college newspapers, and the editors of religious weeklies across the country. The editor of the conservative religious journal, *Moody Bible Institute Monthly,* responded to the survey with the declaration that in both manners and morals society "is undergoing not a revolution, but a devolution. That is to say, I am not so impressed by its suddenness or totalness as by its steady, uninterrupted degeneration."[13] From a college newspaper editor at the University of Pennsylvania came the opinion that "the modern dance has done much to break down standards of morals." Dealing directly with the issue of female sexuality, the editor complained, "To the girl of to-day, petting parties, cigarette-smoking, and in many cases drinking, are accepted as ordinary parts of existence.... She dresses in the lightest and most flimsy of fabrics. Her dancing is often of the most passionate nature."[14]

Female political emancipation was often tied to other changes in the world of the 1920s as well. As noted in *The Literary Digest* 1922 survey on youth, fears of the effect of modernity on youth centered on the new technological and social changes, particularly the growing economic independence of women. Some citizens feared the independence provided women by the automobile. Others focused on the economic emancipation of women and the resulting changes in the family structure.

One criticism was of the image of female sexual aggressiveness projected on the movie screens. According to nineteenth-century values, women were to be the vessels of virtue who checked the passions of men. Loose sexual morality among women meant, in the minds of many in the 1920s, the release of passions among men which, in turn, would cause the decay of civilization.

Many writers placed their discussion of these changes under the category of the "youth problem." Some saw the cause of the youth problem in the changes brought on by modern living. Typical of these feelings were those of the headmaster of the Lawrenceville School, who in 1926 lamented the maelstrom his students would be entering. He wrote that, when he was eighteen, life was less difficult because there was no "Prohibition," "ubiquitous automobile," "cheap theater," "absence of parental control," or "emancipation of womanhood."[15]

Fears of sexual hedonism were evident in articles written by two "representatives" of the younger generation on the question, "Has Youth Deteriorated?", published in 1926 by *Forum*. The affirmative answer to this question alluded to unrepressed sexuality causing chaotic and uncivilized disorder. Young people today, one of the youth representatives stated, "rush in an impetuous, juvenile stampede, not knowing what lies ahead. They have hurled aside all conventions; accepted standards are 'nil.'... 'Liberate the Libido' has become, through them, our national motto."[16] The other article stressed the idealistic aspects of youth. This author of this article claimed, "Beauty and idealism, the two eternal heritages of Youth, are still alive. It is a generation which is constituting the leaven in the rapid development of a new and saner morality."[17]

Both Forum articles stressed that the central concern about youth was sexual standards. As one of the young writers stated,

> This tremendous interest in the younger generation is nothing more nor less than a preoccupation with the nature of that generation's sex life. What people really want to know about us, if they are honest enough to admit it, is whether or not we are perverted, whether we are loose, whether we are what they call immoral; and their curiosity has never been completely satisfied.[18]

To counteract the supposed effects of movies, female emancipation, and automobiles on the sexual morality of youth, educators argued that character education could channel the sexual energies of youth into socially useful pursuits. The argument that sexual energies could be channeled, as discussed in the next section, provided educators with another justification for school athletics, extracurricular activities, school clubs, and youth organizations. Of course this justification would turn out to be self-defeating if, in fact, the social world of the high school itself was a contributor to the revolution in sexual morality. In this particular context, it can be argued that the organization of the modern high school was designed to control and channel adolescent sexuality, but in practice it provided opportunities for the expression of a new sexual freedom.

SEX AND ADOLESCENCE

In their thinking about the morality and sexuality of youth, educators were strongly influenced by the pioneer work on adolescent psychology of G. Stanley Hall. Hall was a leader of the child study movement in the 1890s. His two-volume work on adolescent psychology was published in 1904. In the introduction to this classic work, Hall stated, "The whole future of life depends on how the new powers [in emergent adolescent sexuality] now given suddenly and in profusion are husbanded."[19] Hall's psychological theory of adolescence was premised on the belief that sexual drives could lead a person either to do good or evil. Consequently, according to Hall, the future of society depended on proper control of sexuality. If left unbridled, sexual drives would lead civilization down the path of immorality, which would mean, from Hall's perspective, the decline of modern civilization. On the other hand, Hall argued, sexual drives could be channeled into activities that would benefit society.

Hall proposed his theory of adolescent development during the period of the social purity movement of the latter half of the nineteenth century. This movement was composed of a variety of organizations that sought to curb male sexuality. According to Carl Degler, a major impetus for this movement was the desire among women to limit childbirth. The social purity movement attempted to control male sexuality outside of marriage by eliminating prostitution, and to limit it within marriage as well. What frightened social purists in the 1920s was the increase in premarital and extramarital sexual activities. These changes threatened the basic aims of the social purity movement.[20]

Hall shared with the social purity movement a belief in the cultural determination of sexuality, in other words, that the function that sexual drives play in the life of an individual is determined by cultural conditions. Sexual drives could function purely for purposes of reproduction or they could be channeled into other activities such as forms of social service. Neither Hall nor the social purists denied the strength of sexual passion. In fact, throughout the nineteenth century there was a general recognition of the power of sexual drives, particularly among women. It was often believed that female sexual drives were stronger than those of males and that male passion was more easily satisfied than female passion. Also, it was a widely held belief that female orgasm was necessary for conception.[21] Contradicting this image was indeed a survey of one thousand women who reached marriageable age before World War I, of which 75 percent were born before 1890. Seventy-four percent reported using some form of birth control and that reasons other than conception justified sexual activity. Forty percent reported having sexual intercourse more than twice a week and 80 percent reported sexual intercourse at least once a week.[22]

In trying to control and direct sexual passions, the social purity movement tried to create an image for the public that sexual passion was not a major element in most people's lives. In part, it was hoped that this image could be sustained through the censorship of sexual scenes in movies, radio, and literature, and by the highly moral values contained in sex education courses in public schools and the lack of discussion of sexuality in other parts of the school curriculum. Certainly, in the public school curriculum historical figures were never portrayed as having an active sex life. The movie code of the 1930s, as Chapter 5 will demonstrate, removed any hint of sexuality from marriage even to the point of having married couples sleep in separate beds!

Hall's psychological theories and the work of other educators in the early part of the twentieth century were designed to control sexuality and create a belief that it was good to channel sexual desire into nonsexual social activities. To explain the social role of sexual desires, Hall used the theory of *recapitulation*. According to this theory, each stage of human development is matched to a stage in the evolution of society. The stage of individual development between the ages of 4 and 8, corresponds to the cultural epoch when hunting and fishing were the main activities of society. From 8 to 12, the child recapitulates the humdrum life of savagery. During puberty, the flood of sexual passions forms the social person. In describing this stage of human development, Hall states, "The social instincts undergo sudden unfoldment and the new life of love awakens."[23]

Within the context of Hall's theories, the control of adolescent sexuality was essential for the improvement of society. In fact, he argued that social institutions should be evaluated according to how they utilized adolescent drives. Hall believed that the proper training of youth was the panacea for most social problems. The "womb, cradle, nursery, home, family, relatives, school, church, and state," Hall wrote, "are only a series of larger cradles or placenta, as the soul...builds itself larger missions, the only test and virtue of which is their service in bringing the youth to fuller maturity."[24]

Hall recommended that social organizations direct adolescent sexual drives toward social ideals. This argument contained a conception of youth that made the pursuit of ideals a function of romantic impulses. In other words, Hall argued, the sexual drives of youth could be directed toward the ideals of charity, social service, and social duty. This could be accomplished by placing youth in social situations that would allow for the attachment of romantic impulses to social ideals. These social institutions could range from boys clubs to the high school. Social organizations were to utilize the natural instincts of youth and "so direct intelligence and will as to secure the largest measure of social service, advance altruism, and reduce selfishness, and thus advance the higher cosmic order."[25]

Therefore, educators could use Hall's arguments to justify expanding the social role of the school as a means of guarding adolescent sexuality against the temptations of modernity and as a means of attaching it to social ideals. The argument could also be used to differentiate types of character education according to age. For example, the 1911 report of the NEA Committee on a System of Teaching Morals in the Public Schools proposed teaching morals to lower grades through routine practice, while high school grades were to use cooperative social activities, student government, and a curriculum that dealt with the relationship between the individual and society. In justifying these different methods, the report defines adolescence in language similar to that used by Hall. The report states that adolescence is "the time of life when passion is born which must be restrained and guided aright or it consumes soul and body. It is the time when social interests are dominant and when social ideals are formed."[26]

Other educators echoed Hall's arguments in their discussions of adolescent education. In *The High-School Age,* Irving King, Professor of Education and social education advocate at the University of Iowa, argued in 1914 that a high school education must provide the adolescent with opportunity for social service, because at the age of 16 "youth emerges from the somewhat animal-like crassness of the pubertal years and begins to think of his social relationships, his duties and the rights and wrongs of acts."[27] Reflecting a belief that education could lead youth to accept social ideals, he continues, "Every youth is…an incipient reformer, a missionary, impatient with what seem to him the pettiness and the obtuseness of the adult world about him." The same sentiment is echoed by Michael V. O'Shea, Professor of Education at the University of Wisconsin, in *Trend of the Teens,* published in 1920. According to O'Shea , the "reformer…realizes that if he would get his cause adopted he must appeal to youth.…Youth longs for a new order of things."[28]

Attitudes about the sexuality of youth played two major roles in the character education movement. First, sex education was considered part of character education. An important theme in sex education was maintaining what was considered the traditional role of women, in other words, curbing female sexuality. Second, prevalent ideas about adolescent sexuality were used to justify character education methods in high schools.

Concern about curbing female sexuality was directly related to arguments regarding the protection of the family unit. A persistent claim in the 1920s and early 1930s was that an increasing divorce rate was causing increased juvenile delinquency. A logical conclusion of this argument was that the emancipation of women was causing instability in marital relationships, which, in turn, was increasing the number of juvenile delinquents who might later become hardened criminals.

Typical of educators' responses to the increasing divorce rate was William Bagley's address to the annual meeting of the Department of Superintendence of the NEA in 1929. Addressing superintendents of local public schools, Bagley cited statistics that divorces had doubled in the last generation and that one marriage out of six would end in divorce. He claimed that while he had no prejudice against divorce, he did "know that broken homes are cruel wrongs to children, and every pertinent investigation shows that from broken homes an entirely disproportionate number of delinquents, criminals, prostitutes, and other social misfits are recruited."[29]

At the same meeting, John Tigert, President of the University of Florida and former U.S Commissioner of Education, argued that the increase in crime could be directly related to the "disappearance of the American home with its evenings of fireside dogma and parental control."[30] Other educators expressed similar sentiments. Writing in a 1930 issue of the *Journal of Education,* educator Frank Eversull worried that the "emancipation of women is upon us. The extension of leisure time further complicates our problem." "How," he asked, "can our youth meet this new world?" He argued that one must answer this question or be "lost in the oblivion of crime and its attending evils of broken homes, divorces, companionate marriages and the host of other outrages which daily adorn the columns of the metropolitan newspapers."[31]

A similar connection between crime and broken homes was made in the 1926 report of the NEA's Committee on Character Education. The Committee noted that there did not exist any scientifically determined causes for juvenile delinquency and the actions of adult criminals. But while recognizing the lack of scientific agreement on the causes of crime, the Committee formulated what it called "a pluralistic theory of causation." This theory was the Committee's synthesis of existing arguments regarding the causes of crime. In their formulation, the causes of delinquency were divided into "Factors which enfeeble social control" and "Factors which enfeeble self-control." They further divided each of these categories into "chronic" and "acute." Under chronic factors hindering social control, the Committee listed defects in the political, economic, and social organization of society; problems in urbanization and the physical environment; and, in the words of the report, "changing mores and group conflict, e.g., with regard to sex; use of alcohol, tobacco, etc." Under acute factors hindering social control, they listed family disorganization and "unwholesome leisure activities" along with neighborhood disorganization and lack of educational activities. And under hindrances to self-control, the Committee listed, "personal disorganization from excesses, e.g. sex; use of alcohol, narcotics, etc."[32]

An interesting fact about discussions of juvenile delinquency in the 1920s is that statistics presented during that period showed an actual decline in rates of delinquency. This decline was reported by the Children's Bureau of the United States Department of Labor to, among others, the annual meeting of the NEA in 1927. Speaking to the Department of Secondary School Principals of the NEA in 1927, Walter May, Deputy Commissioner of Education of New Hampshire, reported the Bureau's study of delinquency rates in fourteen cities between 1880 and 1923. The study found that in nearly all the cities the delinquency rate was lower in 1924 or 1925 than in 1915. In addition, the admission rate to institutions handling delinquents below the age of 18 had declined from 171.7 per 100,000 in 1910 to 161 per 100,000 in 1923. The admissions to prisons of persons between 18 and 20 had also declined from 12.1 percent in 1890 to 9.4 percent in 1923. Despite this apparent decline in juvenile delinquency, educators persisted in warning that female emancipation, broken homes, increased leisure time, the automobile and movies, were causing increased crime among young people. But even after presenting the statistical facts on the decline of juvenile delinquency, May told the gathered secondary school principals, "We know also that while there may be no proportionate increase in youthful delinquency, the actual number of youthful delinquents is all too large and challenges the three institutions...the school, the church, and the home."[33]

So, despite statistics that could have been used to support a different argument, educators continued to propose limitations on and control of adolescent behavior as a solution to delinquency. Of major importance to these educators was the control of adolescent sexuality, particularly female sexuality, as a means of establishing social ideals, protecting the traditional family structure, and reducing crime.

SEX EDUCATION

The 1926 report of the Committee on Character Education of the NEA recommended sex education as a means of combatting the decline of the family and regulating sexual impulses for the good of society. The report states that a purpose of human life is, "The creation of one's own home and family, involving first the choice and winning of, or being won by, one's mate." The Committee report went on to argue that sex education in schools could play a role in preparation of youth for this life purpose. "The recent activities," the report states, "in sexual and social hygiene are in the nature of forerunners to this work."[34]

The type of sex education advocated by the NEA was modeled on the work of a member of the NEA's Character Education Committee, Thomas Galloway. Galloway was Associate Director of the American Social Hygiene Association Department of Educational Measures, and the author of its official training manual, *Sex and Social Health: A Manual for the Study of Social Hygiene*. Galloway was also author of a number of other books, including *The Sex Factor in Human Life* and *Biology of Sex*.

The American Social Hygiene Association was organized in 1905 by a New York physician, Prince Morrow, for the purpose of combatting the spread of venereal diseases. Prior to World War I, the Association enlisted the aid of superintendents of schools and teachers organizations in an educational campaign against such disease. In 1912, the NEA endorsed sex education. After World War I, the Social Hygene Association focused its educational campaigns on trying to limit sexual activity to marriage. This limitation, the Association believed, was necessary for the protection of the family and the stability of society.[35]

Galloway's preface to the official training manual, *Sex and Social Health,* gives as its purposes providing a text to guide community discussion; a textbook for parent-teacher groups and for teacher training programs; and a reference book.[36] The premise of the manual is that "reproductive processes and the associated sexual impulses are not individual but social privileges and phenomena."[37] The social obligation of the individual, according to the manual, is to use one's sexual drives for the benefit of society. This includes selective breeding: "Doubtless, if human mating and reproduction were controlled as in the domestic animals, we could by generations of selective breeding secure pure races of men well endowed with any desired quality of body, or capacity, or disposition now found among us."[38] The Association, in advocating eugenics, admitted, however, that it could never be achieved. But even if control of human breeding was not possible, the manual argues, it is possible to educate the individual to make a proper selection of a mate. Within this context, sex education would aid in the improvement of the race. Furthermore, the manual advocated that sexual intercourse be confined to marriage.

The purpose of both sex and marriage, in the framework of this argument, is the production of children for society. In the words of the manual, sex control is necessary for "proper home functioning, which includes the comfort and happiness of all, maximum development of the mates, proper child production, and effective personal and social education of children."[39] Also, according to the manual, the reason sexual intercourse outside of the bounds of marriage should be avoided is because of its potential threat to the stability of the family. The manual states that physical "intercourse …without the social sanction of formal marriage…wholly ignores the interest of society in all questions of sex and reproduction."[40]

For all these reasons, the manual states, sexual abstinence, except among married couples, is necessary for the good of society. In italic letters, the manual informs the reader, *"If abstinence is desirable or necessary, it is primarily because of the effects of sex behavior on the home, on the emotional qualities in the individual upon which the success of the home is based, and on the larger society which depends on the home and on personal character."*[41] The manual made a similar argument when it warned that sexual intercourse outside the institution of marriage would not only weaken the family structure, but cause diseased and defective individuals, prostitution, and the shame of an illegitimate pregnancy.

Premised on the idea that sexual intercourse is a social privilege, the goal of sex education, as stated in this American Social Hygiene Association manual, is to educate people so that they will have sexual intercourse only within the confines of marriage. Interestingly, the manual states that the goal of teaching facts of venereal diseases is "that they make an appeal to fear."[42] Thus, the clearly articulated goal of the manual was to establish sex education programs that would attempt to stem the tide of the growing sexual revolution.

Paralleling the psychological theories of G. Stanley Hall, the manual argues that sexual energies should not be repressed but should be channeled into socially constructive activities. In making this argument, the manual makes a traditional distinction between male and female sexual drives, portraying the male as the pursuer and the female as the pursued.

In fact, the manual states that feminists are wrong in attacking these distinctions as social. "Defense and chivalry in males," the manual claims, "are probably correlated with this tendency of pursuit, biologically." And, in reference to feminists who attacked this idea, the manual continues in the next sentence, "It is certainly not a mere matter of conventional patronizing growing out of a feeling of superiority, as resented by the feminists."[43]

In the same vein, the manual contends that unused female sexual energies are expressed differently than those of males. This particular argument is based on the idea, given in the manual, that humans have more sexual energy than they can ever possibly use. Consequently, this sexual energy is drained off into other activities. "In women," the manual states, "apparently more of the sexual interest expresses itself in these less physical and more spiritual ways. This is probably connected with her biological specialization of reproduction. It is here chiefly that women differ from and surpass men."[44] The "biological specialization of reproduction," according to the manual, results in feminine characteristics that play an important social function. These include, as stated in a section on building the "Right Feminine Qualities and Attitudes in the Girl," "an appreciation of male restraint and chivalry without any taint of losing personal independence by becoming parasitic upon strength; a sense of power over men by virtue of her attractiveness, with an attitude of using this power for social rather than selfish ends." And, to counter the movie-screen image of aggressive female love-making, the manual argues that proper feminine qualities include "purity as a social obligation, a restraining rather than an inciting attitude toward the male, and a sense of obligation for conserving and 'mothering' life."[45]

The manual gives a scientific tone to its attack on aggressive female sexuality by citing both biological and social reasons for sexual differences between males and females. For instance, the manual gives biological reasons for wives playing a maternal role in relationship to their husbands. The manual states, "Very often the attitude of the wife to the husband is much more that of mothering than of mating. This connection is shown on the physical plane by the mingling in the female of the influences of the sexual and the reproductive internal secretions." In general, the manual argues, male aggressiveness is related to localized sexual energy in the "generative organs," while female sexuality is less localized and less intense. The combination of biological factors and social repression results, according to the manual, in women being more "capable of control [of sexual drives], of suppression, and of refinement into more intellectual and aesthetic forms than...most men."[46]

As in the theories of G. Stanley Hall, the manual uses the concept of sexual energy and surplus sexual energy to justify supposed differences in aggressiveness between females and males, and to suggest means of controlling sexual impulses. The image created by the manual is of human sexual energy permeating all social activities. Sexual energy is to be directed toward socially constructive activities. The manual rejects the idea of attempting to repress sexual energy except in emergency situations. Repression, it argues, results in the breaking down of character and the molding of submissive and obedient children. Its repression, as opposed to its expression in socially useful and virtuous acts, is impossible and only results in weakening human character and detracting from the quality of human life.

This attitude toward sexual energy is reflected in a poster issued in 1922 by the American Social Hygiene Association. The poster is titled "The Sex Impulse and Achievement" and pictures a group of young men running hurdles.[47] Under the picture is the statement:

> The sex instinct in a boy or man makes
> him want to act, dare, possess, strive.
>
> When controlled and directed, it gives
>
> ENERGY, ENDURANCE,
> FITNESS.

Using the concept of redirected sexual energy, the manual provides an interesting argument for the sexual underpinnings of democracy. It asserts that sexual drives contribute to the development of "social and unselfish motives" that make possible a cooperative society. Using a social definition of democra-

cy, the manual contends that this cooperative spirit, growing out of sexual energy directed toward the good of society, is the basis for a modern democracy:
"Clearly this sense of the worth of social sacrifice and democracy, which is so
largely the gift of the sex and reproductive processes, can in turn be applied
most effectively to the guidance of sex impulses themselves."[48]

With regard to adolescent sexual energy, the manual calls for draining
the energy away from sexual thoughts and activities to "constructive" interests:
"If young people are given many wholesome, attractive enterprises which
strongly appeal to them personally during the whole of childhood and adolescence, there is much less likelihood that they will be drawn into sexual or other
errors and excesses."[49]

Thus, it is clear that the sex education proposals of G. Stanley Hall, of
the Social Hygiene Association, and of many educators focused on the idea of
channeling sexual energy into socially approved activities. Following in the tradition of Hall, the power of sexual impulses was not denied—rather, control of
these impulses was advocated as a means of shaping personality. Control was to
be taught through sex education, which was considered a means of curbing the
sexual revolution and protecting the traditional family. A key element in the
process was to be the limiting of aggressive female sexual behavior.

CONCLUSION

To the social purity movement, movies, youth culture, and female emancipation threatened the very foundations of civilization. In particular, movies
and movie stars seemed to be breeding a new climate of sensuality and lust. For
many educators and religious leaders, control of adolescent sexuality unleashed
by these forces was essential for the progress of society.

Some educators believed sex education and the social world of the modern high school would tame sexual drives. Athletics, school spirit, clubs, student
government, and other extra-curricular activities were to channel sexual energy
into social service. Ironically, these social activities promoted the very youth
culture that seemed to be causing the sexual revolution, but no one seemed to
recognize this at the time.

The psychological energy for the "live wires" and "go-getters" was to
come from redirected sexual energies. It was hoped that the social whirl of the
high school would prepare youth for the organized life of the modern corporation. Channeling sexual energy into high school activities would result, some
believed, in the eventual channeling of sexual drives into the social life of the
modern corporate and bureaucratic structure.

In the 1930s, the movies joined the schools in the dissemination of a
similar set of sexual values. As the next chapter will show, the Legion of
Decency, an organization created in the 1930s by the Catholic Church, forced

Hollywood producers to make films that conformed to the Church's moral and social standards.

Of course, the sexual values of all U.S. citizens were not represented by the middle class reformers and religious organizations leading the social purity movement. Since the sexual revolution continued on through the twentieth century, one could conclude that the social purity movement might have represented the values of only a minority of the population. These differences in sexual mores created a tension between the private lives of many citizens and the sexual values disseminated by public schools and movies of the 1930s and 1940s.

CHAPTER FIVE

MOVIES AS A FORM OF PUBLIC EDUCATION: THE FILM PRODUCTION CODE OF 1930

"THAT EDUCATORS AND motion picture producers have certain specialized and mutual interests in the motion picture as a purveyor of ideas and motivator of activities even the layman has come to realize," Will Hays told the delegates at the 1939 meeting of the National Education Association. As Hays indicated, an enduring truce had been reached with educators when the film industry adopted in the 1930s a self-regulating censorship code. In Hays's words, the censorship code required that in films, "crime, wrongdoing, evil, or sin shall not be made attractive; that correct standards of life shall be presented; that law, natural or human, shall not be ridiculed, or sympathy created for its violation."[1] It was the standards of this code, Hays maintained, that made it possible to bring together the world of the movies and the schools as purveyors of ideas.

The adoption and enforcement of the movie code at the point of production resolved the debate discussed in Chapter 1 over government censorship versus self-censorship by the industry. While the movie industry tried to avoid all forms of censorship, intense economic pressures placed on the movie industry by religious organizations—particularly the Catholic Church, educators, and other concerned groups—resulted in the enforcement of the production code Hays proudly referred to in his 1939 speech to the NEA. Like other proposals for self-censorship, the production code was designed to shape movies so that they taught audiences approved moral, political, and social values.

As a Presbyterian elder, Hays was not opposed to religious morality influencing the content of motion pictures. The main stumbling block to the enforcement of self-censorship in the 1920s was the resistance of members of the Motion Picture Producers and Distributors Association. Although Hays was hired to improve the public image of the industry, movie producers were wary of direct interference in movie production. It was not until 1933, with publication of the Payne Studies and organization of the Legion of Decency by the Catholic Church, that movie producers agreed to the strict enforcement of the production code.

Hays's first efforts at censorship occurred after a storm of protest by religious groups in 1923 against a movie version of the best-selling novel by Homer Croy, *West of the Water Tower,* which dealt with illegitimacy and a dissolute clergyman. While religious groups objected to the portrayal of the clergyman, the National Congress of Parents and Teachers feared that a movie based on the novel would increase sales of the book. Despite these objections, the movie was produced and released. As a result of continued protests, however, Hays was able to convince the members of the M.P.P.D.A. to require his office to review all books and plays that might interest movie producers.[2] In 1927, Hays expanded the movie self-censorship by adopting a list of "Don'ts and Be Carefuls." In 1930, this list was replaced by a more extensive "Code to Govern the Making of Talking, Synchronized and Silent Pictures." The enforcement of the 1930 code was made complete by a 1934 agreement among members of the M.P.P.D.A. that no movies would be released that were not approved by a new Production Code Administration.

The actual writing and enforcement of the code was dominated by representatives of the Catholic Church. This was a reflection of the militancy of the Catholic Church regarding the content of movies, and its ability to ban movies to its parishioners and to hinder export to predominantly Catholic countries.

The authors of the code were Martin Quigley, a Catholic publisher of *The Motion Picture Herald,* and Daniel Lord, S.J., a Catholic priest, and also a Professor of Dramatics at the University of St. Louis. In 1936, the code received the official blessing of the whole Catholic Church when it was endorsed by the Pope.[3] The efforts of the Catholic Church received strong support from other religious organizations, including the Federal Council of Churches of Christ in America and the Central Conference of Jewish Rabbis.[4] It was the protests of these religious groups, as explained later in this chapter, that resulted in the complete enforcement of the code by the M.P.P.D.A. in 1934.

The 1930 code was premised on the idea that entertainment should provide audiences with moral, social, and political lessons. The code was designed to shape the content of movie scripts and filming techniques, and, at the same time, eliminate objectionable scenes and dialogue. In *Decency in Motion Pictures,* Quigley argues that the motion picture should be a form of entertainment that establishes ideals for its audiences. He rejects the argument that art should be free to follow its own development, arguing instead that, particularly for youth, art should provide guiding ideals for living in the world. Quigley rejects government censorship of movies because such censorship turned decisions about morality over to the democratic process. Since morality, at least from Quigley's Catholic point of view, is determined by God, it should not be influenced by the whims of democratic decision making. Therefore, Quigley maintained, self-regulation of the production of movies was preferable to government censorship.[5]

The code written by Quigley and Lord, and approved by the M.P.P.D.A., contains a social analysis of art. The code argues that traditional forms of art appeal in different ways to different social classes and groups of people. In the words of the code, "Music has its grades for different classes; so has literature and drama." But movies appeal "at once to every class—immature, developed, undeveloped, law abiding, criminal." In addition, the mobility and ease of distribution of movies makes it possible to reach "places unpenetrated by other forms of art." Therefore, the code states, "it is difficult to produce films intended for only certain classes of people."[6]

The argument that movies, unlike traditional art forms, could not be restricted to certain classes of people was a major reason given by the code for the necessity of censorship. As the code states, "The exhibitor's theatres are built for the masses, for the cultivated and the rude, the mature and the immature, the self-respecting and the criminal. Films, unlike books and music, can with difficulty be confined to certain selected groups." The code argues that books depend on words and the imagination of the reader, while movies depend on the vividness of presentation of visual and sound effects. The code states that, unlike plays, films need censorship "because of the larger audiences of the film, and its consequential mixed character. Psychologically, the larger the audience, the lower the moral mass resistance to suggestion." Consequently, according to the code, movies cannot be given as wide a latitude in content as books and plays.

The code also stresses the important social role of entertainment and art. As an example, baseball and golf are described as being morally uplifting sports, whereas cockfights and bullfighting are said by the code to be degrading. In the words of the code, "correct entertainment raises the whole standard of the nation. Wrong entertainment lowers the whole living conditions and moral ideas of a race."

After presenting its justification for self-censorship of the industry, the code states the guiding principles for the production of movies. These principles shaped the content of movies from the 1930s to the 1960s. The guidelines of the code can be divided into the categories of (a) religious; (b) moral; (c) offensive to certain individuals; (d) criminal; and (e) political. The guidelines for religious content in movies deal with situations that might be offensive to organized religious groups. The guidelines for morality are concerned with the portrayal of good and evil, and specific sexual situations. The standards for content "offensive to certain individuals" refers to movie scenes that might spark racial tensions or might be found objectionable by some people or organized groups because of their personal tastes or beliefs. Guidelines for eliminating movie scenes depicting crimes against the law reflect the feelings expressed by educators and religious leaders that movies were teaching people how to be criminals and making criminal actions acceptable. The political restrictions of the code deal with attitudes toward the law, the justice system, the U.S. political system, and foreign countries.

In writing the 1930 code, Quigley and Lord followed the general restrictions of the 1927 list of "Don'ts and Be Carefuls." The major complaint of religious groups about the 1927 list was its lack of detail and enforcement. We can compare the 1927 list to the 1930 code, dividing it also into the categories of (a) religious; (b) moral; (c) offensive to certain individuals; (d) criminal; and (e) political. In addition, the 1927 list has been separated into what "shall not appear in movies," and what required "special care."[7]

Don'ts and Be Carefuls (1927)

Shall Not Appear in Movies

A. Religious
1. Pointed profanity...this includes the words "God," "Lord," "Jesus," "Christ"...;
2. Ridicule of the clergy.

B. Moral
1. Children's sex organs;
2. Any licentious or suggestive nudity...;
3. Any inference of sex perversion;
4. White Slavery;
5. Sex hygiene and venereal diseases.

C. Offensive to Certain Individuals
1. Miscegenation (sex relations between the white and black races);
2. Scenes of actual childbirth....

D. Crimes Against the Law
1. The illegal traffic in drugs.

E. Political
1. Willful offense to any nation, race or creed.

Special Care

A. Moral
1. The sale of women, or a woman selling her virtue;
2. First-night scenes;
3. Man and woman in bed together;
4. Deliberate seduction of girls;
5. The institution of marriage;
6. Excessive or lustful kissing....

B. Offensive to Certain Individuals
1. Brutality and possible gruesomeness;

    2. Actual hangings or electrocutions as legal punishment for crime;

    3. Apparent cruelty to children and animals;

    4. Branding of people and animals;

    5. Surgical operations.

C. Crimes Against the Law

    1. Sympathy for criminals;

    2. The use of firearms;

    3. Theft, robbery, safecracking, and dynamiting of trains, mines, buildings, etc. (having in mind the effect which a too-detailed description of these may have upon the moron);

    4. Technique of committing murder by whatever method;

    5. Methods of smuggling;

    6. Rape or attempted rape.

D. Political

    1. The use of the flag;

    2. International relations (avoiding picturizing [sic] in an unfavorable light another country's religion, history, institutions, prominent people, and citizenry);

    3. Attitude toward public characters and institutions;

    4. Sedition;

    5. Titles or scenes having to do with the law enforcement or law-enforcing officers.

The 1927 code reflects many of the complaints about movies. The prohibition of negative statements about the clergy and of religious oriented profanity were in response to criticism from religious groups. Moral prohibitions were those advocated by the social purity movement. Banning movie portrayal of miscegenation reflected worries about local government censors, particularly those in the South. Fears that movies would stimulate criminal actions prompted prohibition of scenes of illegal drugs. Warnings about scenes involving crimes against the law are a major part of the Special Care section of the 1927 code as reflected in cautions about movie scenes depicting theft, robbery, safe-cracking, and the dynamiting of trains affecting "morons" in audiences. The code reflects a concern with maintaining a positive image of government by cautions regarding scenes with public characters and institutions, sedition, and the flag. And, of course, concerns about foreign censors and domestic race riots led to prohibitions against offending any nation, race, or creed.

The 1930 code was far more extensive, explanatory, and detailed. It gives as its first general principle, "No picture shall be produced which will lower the moral standards of those who see it. Hence the sympathy of the audience shall never be thrown to the side of crime, wrong-doing, evil or sin." This

First general principle envisions a moral world where good always triumphs over evil and good people are always justly rewarded. It is a movie-made world where cowboys in white hats always beat the bandits in black hats. The code states that movies must avoid scenes where "evil is made to appear attractive or alluring and good is made to appear unattractive." Distinguishing between sympathy for a crime or sin as opposed to sympathy for the plight of a sinner, the code warns against the sympathy of the audience being directed toward behavior that would generally be considered a crime or sin.

Supporting the creation of a moral universe in movies where triumphal good always holds sway over evil, the second general principle of the 1930 code states, "Correct standards of life, subject only to the requirements of drama and entertainment, shall be presented." The code doesn't give a specific definition of "correct standards of life," only stating that the plots and characters in movies should develop the "right ideals and moral standards." This is to be accomplished by movies' giving audiences a model for moral living. In the words of the code, "If motion pictures consistently hold up for admiration high types of characters and present stories that will affect lives for the better, they can become the most powerful natural force for the improvement of mankind."

The third general principle of the 1930 code protects the image of laws and governments. It states, "Law, natural or human, shall not be ridiculed, nor shall sympathy be created for its violation." Natural laws are defined by the code as the principles of justice dictated by a person's conscience. With regard to human law, the code specifies that audience support should always be developed for government laws, and warns against movies that are sympathetic to the commission of crime and do not favor the law. In addition, according to the code, "The courts of the land should not be presented as unjust." While individual court officials might be portrayed in movies as unjust, the code warns that "the court system of the country must not suffer as a result of this presentation."

Following the three general principles in the 1930 movie code is a list of particular applications which are only slightly different than the list in the 1927 "Don'ts and Be Carefuls." The main differences are the addition of warnings about the portrayal of the "use of liquor in American life," "undressing scenes," "indecent exposure," "dancing costumes," and "obscenity in word." And, in addition to all the other warnings of the 1927 movie code, the 1930 movie code states, "The treatment of bedrooms must be governed by good taste and delicacy."

As elaborated later in this chapter, the content of movie scripts and methods of filming were changed to meet the requirements of the 1930 code. When applied from the inception of a movie's production, the 1930 code created for an unsuspecting audience a particular moral and political vision of the world. This movie-made world was designed to avoid any threat to established social and political systems.

While educators and religious groups were initially pleased with the 1930 code, they were not pleased with the method proposed for its enforcement. A Production Code Administration was established as part of the M.P.P.D.A which had the responsibility for reviewing scripts and films, to recommend changes based on the requirements of the code. Originally, the procedure for enforcement of the code allowed a movie producer to appeal any proposed changes to a panel of three other producers. An article in *The Literary Digest,* a magazine that supported a national boycott of movies to demand enforcement of the code, argued that, under this method of applying the code, "mutual backscratching and eye-winking were inevitable…. So, in practice, the producer usually won out in his dispute with the code administration."[8]

In 1933, the Legion of Decency was organized at a meeting of the National Catholic Welfare Conference to force the movie industry into applying seriously the requirements of the code. In language that left little doubt about the Conference's attitude toward Hollywood, the administrative committee in its recommendation for the creation of the Legion of Decency stated, "The pest hole that infects the entire country with its obscene and lascivious moving pictures must be cleansed and disinfected: The multitudinous agencies that are employed in disseminating pornographic literature must be suppressed."[9] The strategy of the Legion of Decency was to apply economic pressure on Hollywood by calling on the public to boycott "objectionable" movies. Father Lord, as one of the codes's authors had provided a model for the Legion of Decency, organizing the Sodality of the Blessed Virgin in Chicago. He claimed that its boycott of one picture cost the industry $125,000, and that a major movie industry official had tried to appease the Sodality but, in Lord's words, "They gave that picture such a beating that the industry has never forgotten."[10]

The Legion of Decency, with the support of the Catholic hierarchy, asked Catholics in local churches to sign a pledge that they would "remain away from all motion pictures except those which do not offend decency and Christian morals." The pledge opened with a call for unity in protesting the supposed threat to youth, country, home life, and religion, and it included a promise to also boycott objectionable magazines and books. The signer of the pledge promised to condemn movies that were promoting a "sex mania in our land" and to "do all that I can to arouse public opinion against the portrayal of vice as a normal condition of affairs, and against depicting criminals of any class as heroes and heroines, presenting their filthy philosophy of life as something acceptable to men and women."[11]

By June 1934, the Catholic Church claimed that 20 million people had signed the pledge. In addition, the pledge was endorsed by the Federal Council of Churches of Christ in America and the Central Conference of Jewish Rabbis. Besides economic pressure at the box office, another tactic used by the group responsible for distributing the Legion of Decency's pledge, the administrative committee of the National Catholic Welfare Conference, was to send question-naires to priests in all parishes in the United States asking for the names of local theaters and the names of banks holding mortgages against theater properties. Crusades against objectionable movies led by priests in cities throughout the United States added to these pressures. Reflecting the attitude of religious lead-ers involved in these local campaigns, the Rev. James Cassidy of Fall River, Massachusetts, declared, "If these [motion-picture theaters] doors of degrada-tion are to be shut, then hear ye well and heed! They must be shut from the out-side; they will never be locked from the inside while the nickels and dimes and the quarters and the halves continue to roll in from the outside."[12]

In response to public reaction to *Our Movie-Made Children,* the popular version of the Payne Studies published in 1933, the mounting protests of the Legion of Decency, and renewed calls for federal legislation to censor movies, Will Hays decided to take steps to ensure the enforcement of the movie code. In June 1934, he dispatched Martin Quigley and Joseph Breen to a meeting in Cincinnati of the Catholic Bishops Committee. Joseph Breen had been hired by the M.P.P.D.A. in 1933 to enforce the code. Before assuming that, he had han-dled public relations for the M.P.P.D.A. Breen had a history of strong relation-ships with members of the Catholic Church. In 1926, he was hired by one of the later leaders of the Legion of Decency, Cardinal Mundelein, to handle press relations at the Eucharistic Congress in Chicago.[13] *The Literary Digest* reported that he promised at the June 1934 meeting of the Bishops Committee to "rid Hollywood of its dirt." The magazine described Breen as a good Catholic father of six children.[14]

When Quigley and Breen promised that the industry would take steps to enforce the code, the bishops agreed to relax the pressures from the Legion of Decency. Quigley and Breen reported to Hays the discussion with the bishops and, as a result of that discussion, the Production Code Administration was established on July 1, 1934 with Joseph Breen as its leader. The Production Code Administration changed the appeal process from one that used other pro-ducers to one that relied on decisions by the directors of the M.P.P.D.A. The decisions of the directors was considered final. It was agreed among the mem-bership of the M.P.P.D.A., which included all the major film studios, that no films would be released that did not have the approval and seal of the Produc-tion Code Administration. If a picture were released by a studio without a seal of approval, the studio would be fined $25,000. Under this system, Breen became a real dictator of morality, and the content and filming of movies were shaped according to the canons of the movie code.[15]

The Production Code Administration focused its work on the shaping of movies so that they conveyed the moral and political themes of the movie code. Producers submitted screenplays and movies to Breen's office, which then issued lists of "corrections." In retrospect, much of what was censored by

Breen's office seems unimportant, but understandable in the context of the Production Code Administration's goals of protecting the industry from criticism and protecting the morality of the nation. For instance, Breen wrote to Jack Warner, president of Warner Brothers Studios, criticizing lines and parts of the plot of the famous film *Casablanca* starring Humphrey Bogart and Ingrid Bergman because they suggested loose sexual mores and a lack of seriousness about marriage bonds. As part of his criticism of the plot, Breen states, "The following lines seem unacceptably suggestive: 'It used to take a villa in Cannes...and a string of pearls [in reference to seduction]. Now all I ask is an exit visa;' and 'How extravagant you are throwing away women like that. Some day they may be rationed'." A major concern was the suggestion in the plot that Ilsa (Ingrid Bergman), a married woman, had carried on a love affair with Rick (Humphrey Bogart) in Paris. In his letter to Warner, Breen says "a suggestion of a sexual affair [between Ilsa and Rick]...would be unacceptable if it came through in the finished picture. We believe this could possibly be corrected by replacing the fade-out...with a dissolve, and shooting the succeeding scene without any sign of a bed."[16]

The 1930 movie code's distinction between movies and books is highlighted by the censorship of novels adapted for the screen. The introduction to the code called for the censorship of movies, but not books, because books only appealed to only certain groups in society, whereas everyone attended movies. Thus what was acceptable in book form was not acceptable in movies. Of course, this meant that the study guides and exhibits for the great classics brought to the screen, the product of cooperative effort between the movie industry and educators, had to meet the requirements of the Production Code Administration. As moral guardian of the "art of the multitudes," Breen's office was not going to allow the portrayal on the screen of material from novels that might threaten sexual morality, the family, and marriage.

For instance, Leo Tolstoy's great novel, *Anna Karenina,* on an adulterous relationship became a major problem for the Production Code Administration. After much discussion, M-G-M agreed with the Breen office to change the plot of the novel in its movie production so that the "'matrimonial bond' would be 'positively defended'." Breen's office wanted Anna to frequently affirm "the sanctity and inviolability of marriage as a sacrament and as a civil contract." Other characters in the novel were given prominence in the movie as a means of highlighting the value of marriage, for example, a newly married, happy young couple and another couple reluctant to divorce. Karenina was never to be portrayed in the movie as being happy with her lover. The censorship office and the producers agreed to eliminate any mention of the illegitimate child Karenina bears her lover in the novel.

After freely changing the novel's plot, Breen's office demanded changes and deletions in individual lines in the movie script. For example, Breen asked for deletion of the speech by Anna Karenina; "Am I ashamed of anything I've done? Wouldn't I do the same again tomorrow? Who cares what people say so long as I love you and you—change." Breen also wanted changes in the way the movie was filmed so that adulterous sex was not accentuated. His office recommended that scenes should not be played in Anna's bedroom but should be filmed in the living room or boudoir.[17]

The censorship of plots, lines, and settings by the Breen office would, according to the movie code, create morally uplifting films that showed good always triumphing over evil. In addition, Breen's office looked carefully for any scenes that might portray the law or the legal system in a negative light. For instance, Breen wrote to Warner of Warner Brothers regarding the film, *The Maltese Falcon,* "Spade's speech about the district attorney should be rewritten to get away from characterizing most district attorneys as men who will do anything to further their careers. This is important."[18]

The movie code not only extended such protection to courts, district attorneys, and the entire legal system, it also guarded lawyers from approbrium. The Production Code Administration suggested that if a movie presented "the wrong kind of lawyer," then the producer should balance the picture with the "right kind of lawyer." A statement from the Production Code Administration states, "We, never, in our experience, have approved a picture wherein it was indicated, in the final summation, that unethical or dishonest lawyers are sympathetic characters, or that there is any approval, in the end of the story, of these unethical practices...."[19]

As for political matters, in general, both movie producers and censors tried to avoid any criticism of government or any direct ideological statements about politics or economics. By avoiding political statements and criticism of government, movies were, of course, supporting the status quo. One major, and consequently, controversial exception, was Charlie Chaplin's 1938 attack on fascism in the film *The Great Dictator.* The movie was quickly banned by the Chicago police, who feared that it would offend Chicago's German population.[20] Raymond Moley, sympathetic historian and supporter of the Hays office, criticized Chaplin's film because, "Nothing hurts a picture's chance of success more than the whisper that it contains 'propaganda'." He argued that the film failed at the box office because of the mixing of art with politics.[21]

After the movie code went into effect, members of the M.P.P.D.A. avoided films with controversial political themes. It was reported in the 1930s that even if a film script passed the movie code, its production and distribution could be hindered for political reasons. An article in a 1938 issue of *The Nation* by Winchell Taylor complains about behind the scenes censorship by Will Hays. Writing about the problems faced in the distribution of *Blockade,* an anti-fascist film about the Spanish Civil War, Taylor claims,

If it happens that Will Hays doesn't like a movie but can't find that it violates the motion-picture production code for which he is the watchdog, he can pick up the telephone, call up, let's say, Louis Mayer, and say he thinks such and such a film will have a bad effect on business.... Mr. Mayer then calls Schenck of Loew's, Kent of Fox, and Freeman of Paramount, and presto! three of the most powerful theater chains refuse to run the film.

In the case of *Blockade*, Taylor reports, the Fox West Coast theater chain refused to run it as a regular first feature despite its early financial success at the box office. The reason, he argues, was the presence of Catholic pickets at its first showings, and objections raised by the Knights of Columbus because the Catholic Church considered the movie "war propaganda" against the fascist leader Generalissimo Franco.[22]

The tendency in the 1930s was to brand as anti-American propaganda any film that appeared to be anti-fascist, pro-Communist, or critical of American society and government. On the other hand, however, Hollywood was willing to make films for the explicit purpose of spreading pro-American propaganda. Actor Douglas Fairbanks, Jr., explained the position of the movie industry on this issue in an address to the 1939 convention of the NEA.

Fairbanks told the educators that propaganda could be "a force for good as well as for evil," and referred to teaching about American government in public schools as good propaganda. "When you, in the exercise of your profession," he said to the convention, "teach that we live under the best possible form of government, that is propaganda." Fairbanks drew a parallel between the role of the public schools and that of the movie industry in educating the public by describing how the movie industry was beginning to make movies that were explicitly for propaganda purposes. He told the school people, "some of the best pictures in recent months and some of the most entertaining as well have been based on historic incidents which in themselves serve to emphasize the merit of democracy." As an example, the actor described how a statement made by Andrew Jackson to Sam Houston in the film, *Man of Conquest* consistently caused audiences to applaud. In the movie, Jackson tells Houston, "Don't ever forget that this is still the only country where a man can give the President a good cussing out and the only thing the President can do is to cuss right back or go fishing."[23]

In his study of American political movies, film historian Terry Christensen argues that Hollywood movies rarely present problems with the American political system. "This reduces politics," he writes, "to a need for occasional individual action to regulate an essentially good, smoothly functioning process by pointing out flaws in the form of bad individuals and sometimes bad organizations like gangs, machines, and corporations."[24] He found that most political movies present politics and politicians as corrupt, and that corruption is overcome by the work of an individual or the triumph of the political system as a whole. Christensen gives as an example one of the most popular films of all time, *Mr. Smith Goes to Washington* (1939). The movie is about a naive individual, Smith, who, because of a political feud, is selected over regular politicians to fill the post of a dead U.S. senator. Once in Washington, Mr. Smith decides to sponsor a bill for a boy's ranch in his home state, only to be confronted by the fact that the proposed land is part of a corrupt water project being sponsored by the state's other senator. The conflict is resolved with the suicide of the corrupt senator and the triumph of Mr. Smith. Christensen writes that the director's message "is limited and simplistic: there is a problem because something isn't working properly, but the problem is minor, caused not by faults in the system or its institutions, but by bad men; good men, supported by the people, can fix things up."[25]

While individual triumph over evil was often portrayed, scenes of collective action were avoided. The Production Code Administration warned against mob scenes that might cause political and social unrest. Movie producers learned the consequences of not heeding that warning when scenes of looting in the film, *The Good Earth,* were cut by censors in England, Hungary, and Quebec.[26]

In addition, movie producers resisted the formation of unions within their own industry, and were generally anti-union. Consequently, films rarely dealt with labor relations or class conflict. The political conservatism of producers was reflected in their campaign against Upton Sinclair's run for Governor of California in 1934 on the ticket of the Democratic Party. The movie studios filmed anti-Sinclair trailers that looked like newsreels and distributed them throughout the state.[27]

The conservatism of movie producers and the Production Code Administration was also reflected in changes made in the plot of John Steinbeck's *Grapes of Wrath* when the novel was adapted to the "art of the multitudes." Steinbeck's novel is a radical depiction of the plight of Oklahoma farmers during the Depression as they migrate to California in search of jobs. The novel is an indictment of the economic system that allows the creation and continuation of poverty and it is a call for action. The movie changes Steinbeck's message by eliminating criticism of the economic system, and by placing faith in individuals to adjust and survive economic problems. This change is exemplified by the difference in the endings of the book and movie. Near the end of the book, the family first enters a migrant camp that is operated by the government and then moves on to a camp operated by the growers. In the growers' camp, one of the main characters becomes actively involved in union organizing. Steinbeck believed that one answer to migrant problems was unionization. The book ends with the union being broken and a woman breast-feeding a starving man. The film reverses the order of camps visited, to show the family moving from the growers' camp to the government camp. On their arrival at the government camp, the film shows a cleanly dressed attendant welcoming the family and explaining that it is a government operated cooperative. The government camp represents the New Deal programs of the Roosevelt administration. Rather than ending in despair, the movie ends in the government camp with a speech that implies all will be well.[28]

The Production Code Administration censorship of film scripts dealing with foreign countries resulted in movies that presented an unrealistic view of such countries. The movie industry was concerned about scenes that might offend foreign censors and cause the banning of films. For instance, in 1922 the M.P.P.D.A. adopted a resolution "that the occasional and thoughtless practice of representing Mexican characters in American motion picture productions as dictators, bandits and in other offensive manner[s]...interfere[s] with the establishing and strengthening of cordial relations, commercial and otherwise."[29] This concern was affirmed in the 1927 and 1930 codes' prescription for the respectful treatment of other countries and their peoples.

An example of the censorship of scripts dealing with foreign countries is the correspondence regarding the movie, *The Treasure of the Sierra Madre*. In reference to the original film script, Breen wrote Warner in 1942 that it was unacceptable because of "the sordid locales, such as the Mexican saloon and gambling joints, the Mexican flophouses; the extremely derogatory presentation of Mexican nationals...the barefoot Mexicans...and the derogatory statements about Mexico, its people, and its institutions made by the American characters."[30]

Concern with offending foreign countries extended to small details. Addison Durland, the Production Code Administration's expert on Latin America, wrote Warner regarding a film set in Brazil, *Now Voyager,* "In our opinion the ramshackle car in which your characters make the trip [to Rio] should be eliminated. Rio is justly proud of its modern system of transportation; we would expect to see a modern taxicab."[31]

In summary, fears of government censorship, a desire to maintain good public relations and attract families to movies, complaints by educators about the effect of movies on children and youth, and pressures from religious organizations forced the movie industry to adopt a censorship code that shaped the moral, social, and political content of movies. After 1934, movie audiences were presented with an image of a moral world in which good always won out over evil, collective action resulted not in social progress but in mob violence, and social problems were not systemic but were usually resolved by individual action. Audiences saw a world where government was benign and the good citizen did not try to change basic political processes but reformed government by getting rid of corrupt politicians. In addition, at least until the propaganda films of World War II, movies presented an uncritical and superficial view of the nations of the world.

MOVIES AS IDEOLOGICAL MANAGEMENT

One justification that was used for enforcement of the motion picture code was that it protected the moral and political values of the majority of the population. It could be argued that such a justification fits a theory of democracy based on the idea that a majority has the right to control the content of mass media, and that this control is necessary for the preservation of social order and democratic values.

A problem with this argument, however, is that in all likelihood the movie code did not reflect the moral and political values of many members of the population. In other words, censorship according to the standards of the movie code might not have been a demand of something called "the public" or "the people" but of a small but loud and active group we can call the "guardians of morality." These guardians of morality represented the value system initially pushed forward by the social purity movement discussed in Chapter 3. Their ability to impose their values on the content of movies, regardless of the will of the general public, was a result of the economics of the film industry and of the ability of organized interest groups to influence government and business.

To appease these moral guardians and to avoid government interference through censorship and anti-trust action, the movie industry mounted a public relations campaign that resulted in the acceptance of the moral standards of the social purity movement and of political values that would not offend government officials or cause social unrest. The critics of movies, while not necessarily representing the general public, were able to achieve victory because of their public demonstrations and economic threats. Stated more simply, the movie industry felt called upon to appease the most vocal and powerful. The result of this appeasement, as Will Hays suggested to the NEA, was to have American movies join with schools in the 1930s as ideological managers of American society.

CHAPTER SIX

EDUCATORS VERSUS COMMERCIAL RADIO: THE TRIUMPH OF CONSUMER CULTURE IN THE 1930s

"BRITISH VS. AMERICAN Radio Slant, Debate Theme in 40,000 Schools" headlined a front-page story in 1933 in *Variety,* the theatrical trade journal. The pro-industry weekly reported that, in radio circles, the selection of this theme for national high school debates was thought to be part of an "anti-radio" propaganda campaign being waged by educators, religious groups, and nonprofit organizations against the American system of broadcasting. *Variety* liked to use the term "anti-radio" when referring to these opponents of commercial radio who wanted the federal government to license more educational and nonprofit radio stations. "Anti-radio" groups worried that profits from advertising were increasingly determining the content of radio programming and that, consequently, commercial radio was destroying American national culture. In the end, the victory of commercial broadcasting helped to create a national consumer culture by surrounding entertainment with increasingly sophisticated advertisements.

The central issue in the high school debates was whether radio should be privately owned and financially supported by advertising, or like the British system, operated by the government and supported by some form of taxation. The major radio networks feared that with an estimated attendance of one hundred persons at each debate, as many as 4 million people might hear the question being discussed. "Many, perhaps most," *Variety* lamented, "of these people have been unaware of the existence of the question."[1]

As they had with movies, many educators thought commercial radio was threatening the central role of the school in shaping the public mind. In the debate over the organization and control of radio in the 1920s and early 1930s, a major issue was the role of radio in influencing the development of a national culture. The common school system was established in the early nineteenth century to educate youth in a common set of political, social, and moral values. In the minds of many educators, the common education received by Americans in public schools was a central factor in maintaining a national culture. Radio threatened this function of the school by penetrating the home and all regions of the country. Because of the potential of radio to create common national values, educators argued that they were the ones who should be in control of radio programming and they criticized the idea that the content of radio programming should be determined by advertising.

The radio industry responded with the argument that commercial programming fostered a democratic culture. This response assumed that listeners voted for the type of culture they wanted by turning the radio knob to their favorite programs. Operated as a business, industry leaders argued, commercial radio responded to the choices made by listeners. What educators wanted, they argued, was to impose a culture on the population. On the other hand, private broadcasters argued, commercial radio reflected listener's choices and, consequently, it was fostering the development of a truly democratic culture.

The debate between educators and commercial radio interests reached a peak in the early 1930s. By the 1930s, commercial radio networks dominated the airwaves. But they operated under a constant fear that government action might take away their newly established dominion. They were particularly concerned about educators who, in addition to their concern about the influence of radio on national culture, were fighting mad about their recent loss of radio licenses as a result of government favoritism toward commercial radio and of actions taken under the Radio Act of 1927, which created the Federal Radio Commission (FRC). Meeting in 1928, the FRC adopted a new allocation plan for the distribution of licenses as a means of eliminating interference in broadcasting. Under this plan, radio stations with the greatest financial resources, the most expensive equipment, and the most varied programming were favored in the issuance of licenses. Therefore, commercial broadcasters were favored over educational broadcasters.[2] Writing in the mid-1930s for the National Advisory Council on Radio in Education, a pro-educational broadcasting group, a Professor of Education at Adelphi College, S. E. Frost, determined that, between 1921 and 1936, 202 licenses had been granted by the government to educational organizations. As of January 1, 1937, however, there were only 38 licenses still held by educational institutions. The loss of many of these licenses was due to inactivity and financial failure, as well as to government favoritism toward the large networks.[3]

The triumph of the large commercial networks—what is referred to as the American broadcasting system-over nonprofit radio took place during the 1920s. During the early development of radio as a form of entertainment, paid advertising did not play a dominant role. Westinghouse Electric Company initiated American radio programming in 1920, when it began broadcasting over KDKA in Pittsburgh, as a method of enticing the public to purchase radio sets. These early programs were not sponsored by commercial advertisers. During the same period, educational and religious groups obtained licenses and they also did not rely on advertisers. The first commercial sponsorship of radio programming occurred on August 28, 1922, when WEAF in New York City aired paid commercials for a tenant-owned apartment building. By the mid-1930s the radio broadcast system was characterized by private ownership and commercial sponsorship. It was dominated by two networks.[4]

The basic structure of the American broadcasting system emerged between 1926 and 1934. The first major network, the National Broadcasting Corporation (NBC), was organized in 1926 under the combined ownership of the Radio Corporation of America, General Electric, and the Westinghouse Corporation. American Telephone and Telegraph had originally planned to participate in the ownership of NBC, but backed out when an agreement was signed with NBC to continue its use of American Telephone and Telegraph's telephone wires as their broadcast network. Until 1943, NBC operated a Red network and a Blue network. Forced by the government, NBC sold the Blue network, which became the American Broadcasting Company (ABC). The Columbia Broadcasting System (CBS) was formed in 1928 under the leadership of William Paley, with Paramount-Publix, the movie giant, holding a 49 percent partnership. Providing some competition with these broadcasting giants, the Mutual Broadcasting System was formed in 1934.[5]

Dependent on government licensing, commercial networks worried about offending politicians. Networks also didn't want to alienate advertisers and the public. For example, "blood-and-gore" types of children's programs were created to attract more juvenile listeners. But parents' organizations complained that radio was causing emotional disturbance in children and teaching them crime. Commercial broadcasters wanted to generate as much revenue as possible through increased advertising, but they feared that too much advertising and the wrong type of advertising would turn the public against commercial radio. As shown in Chapter 7, the networks ultimately created self-censorship codes. These codes affected the content of children's programs. Like the movie codes, broadcast codes were designed to present children with radio programs that taught particular moral and social lessons.

EDUCATORS AND THE AMERICAN BROADCASTING SYSTEM

In January 1934, five months after the theme of the American versus the British broadcasting system was selected as a topic for national high school debates, *Variety* again expressed concern that the debates were supporting legislative attempts to undermine commercial radio. In this article, *Variety* outlined the different sides of the debate. Central to the defense of the American system was its sensitivity to public tastes and opinions. Because sponsors of American broadcasting wanted large audiences to hear their advertisements, it was argued, programs were written to meet public demand. On the other hand, since British radio depended on direct government support, public tastes were neglected. Furthermore, government control of radio resulted in censorship. In the high school debates, opponents of the British system frequently cited the case of Mahatma Gandhi being barred from British radio. They also argued that the method of financing British radio, a tax on radio sets, was a nuisance.[6]

On the other side of the debate, supporters of the British system attacked government regulation of American broadcasting as a contrivance to protect monopolistic control by the major networks. In addition, high school debaters argued that radio advertising cost the consumer $1.50 per year. They also contended that the American broadcasting system made it difficult for educational institutions to compete for air time and that the intelligent minority of the population had no voice in radio programming. Furthermore, they claimed, commercial radio was destroying the newspaper industry and serving as a propaganda agent for utility companies.

Commercial networks were nervous about the national high school debate theme because a vocal coalition of educators, religious organizations, and other interested groups were demanding that 25 percent of all broadcasting licenses be given to nonprofit institutions. Leading this movement was the National Committee on Education by Radio. Formed in 1930, the Committee was funded by the Payne Foundation and had representatives from eleven major national educational organizations, including the National Education Association, the National Catholic Education Association, the American Council on Education, the National Association of State Universities, and the National Council of State Superintendents of Education.[7]

Like the advocates of self-censorship of movies who wanted entertainment to be a vehicle for moral and civic values, the members of the National Committee on Education by Radio were primarily concerned about radio programming's serving as an instrument for building a national culture. Critics frequently pointed out that radio's influence on the public was similar to the socially and morally negative influence of movies. When the Committee met in May 1934, in the midst of efforts to get Congress to grant 25 percent of broadcast licenses to nonprofit stations, the Committee selected as its topic, "The Use of Radio as a Cultural Agency in a Democracy."

The general tenor of the conference was reflected in the question posed for the first morning session of the conference: "A National Culture—By-Product or Objective of National Planning?" The topic was first discussed by Jerome Davis, a member of the Executive Committee of the American Sociological Society and a faculty member at the Yale Divinity School. After reviewing the rise of commercial radio and the decline of educational radio, Davis argued that radio in the 1930s was distributing negative cultural values through advertising:

"Children are told that when they drink Cocomalt they are cooperating with Buck Rogers and heroine Wilma.... I am not questioning the quality of Cocomalt, but the outrageous ethics and educational effects of this advertising on the child mind." Davis argued before the gathered educators that on the other hand, if it were possible to plan programs "for the younger generation on an educational instead of a profit basis, the dramatic adventures of historical figures in American life—those who have really contributed something to the welfare of the nation and the world—could be told." Davis lashed out against profit-driven programming, and the quality of music and programs on commercial radio, and he concluded with a demand that commercial radio be required to devote at least 20 percent of its programming to educational programs.[8]

Joy Elmer Morgan, editor of the *Journal of the National Education Association* and chair of the National Committee on Education by Radio, echoed Davis's sentiments by warning the same audience, "You will discover that the advertising agency is taking the place of the mother, the father, the teacher, the pastor, the priest, in determining the attitudes of children."[9] Based on a pursuit of profits, these two media, she argued, were spreading a form of entertainment that was the negation of culture and positive values: "America today is operating on a momentum which was acquired in the days before radio. It is operating on a momentum which the people acquired before the motion picture began teaching crime and gambling and the cheap and flippant attitude toward the verities of life." Morgan worried about the effect on the United States when the generation being raised in the age of commercial media reached adulthood. "No one knows what will happen," she told her sympathetic audience, "when this country comes into the hands of those who have been exposed to the propaganda of the money changers and to the debasing material which they have broadcast into the lives of the people."[10]

In answering the NEA session's question, "Is culture a by-product or an objective of national planning?", Morgan listed three requirements for the building of a culture: freedom of speech, the idea of progress, and planning. Freedom of speech, she argued, provided the opportunity for the creation of new ideas in science and in social and political thought. Without advances in these areas, culture remained static. She related the idea of progress to the development of the public school system in the United States, stating that it was Horace Mann's belief in the possibility of progress through the improvability of humans that led to his crusade for common schools. And it was the common school of the 1890s, Morgan claimed, that made possible the rapid advances in American civilization in the 1890s and early 1900s.[11] Finally, Morgan related the concept of planning to the development of the public school. From her perspective, planning, accompanied by freedom of thought and a belief in progress, made possible the advance of civilization. "The common school," she stated, "is an example of far-sighted planning. It does not expect to make a profit today or at the end of the month or even at the end of the year."[12] The common school exists to serve society and therefore its use can be planned.

Therefore, according to Morgan's concept of the development of culture, public schools advance culture while movies and radio destroy culture. While failing to mention the lack of freedom of thought in public schools, she argued that radio and movies hindered the advancement of civilization because profits took precedence over freedom of thought, the idea of progress, and socially meaningful planning. Her answer for making radio an important contributor to the advancement of culture was elimination of private ownership of broadcasting, determination of program content according to listener's particular interests, and promotion of the cultural uses of radio over commercial uses.

In addition, she argued, the child needed to be protected against commercial exploitation. She told fellow educators, "We should look upon the effort to go over the heads of parents, the church, and the school, to the child mind with something of the horror that we would look at the poisoning of a spring or well."[13] Finally, she argued, freedom of speech on radio needed to be protected from commercial and political interests.

There was strong agreement among discussants about Morgan's speech. James Rorty, representing the censorship committee of the American Civil Liberties Union, agreed with Morgan's statements about advertising and culture and added that educators should claim 100 percent interest in radio broadcasting because the "use of this major social instrument [radio], unless the whole concept of culture is to be made ridiculous, is a function of education and cultural leadership."[14] In response to the speech, James Cooke of the Presser Foundation expressed concern about to America's national culture after hearing a group of boys in the Middle West singing, "My country 'tis of thee, sweet land of Dillinger, of thee I sing." The reference to a gangster in a patriotic song confirmed his belief that radio and movies were undermining American ideals. He told the audience that the children's rendition of the song "simply meant that a brigand has become the most publicized person of our times thru [sic] the press, through the movies, and thru [sic] the radio, and it merely indicates what great power is given to the radio in this connection."[15]

The last session of the second day was devoted to a discussion of the "Report of the Committee on Fundamental Principles Which Should Underlie American Radio Policy." The report contains a summary of the opinions held by representatives from the major educational organizations attending the conference regarding national radio policy. The report, like discussions of self-censorship in the movie industry, stresses the importance of using radio as a means of social control. In fact, it emphasizes the importance of exercising conscious control for this purpose. The report opens, "Radio broadcasting—this great, new agency—should be so guided and controlled as to insure to this nation the greatest possible social values. And, the report continues, "The social welfare of the nation should be the conscious, decisive, primary objective, not merely a possible by-product incidental to the greatest net returns to advertisers and broadcasters."[16]

To achieve this conscious control over the social values promoted by radio, the report recommends that listener needs and desires take precedence over commercial interests; that minority groups gain access to radio; that the "impressionable, defenseless minds of children and youth...be protected against insidious, degenerative influences"; and that controversial issues and America's best culture be broadcast over radio. And, with regard to the issue of ownership, the report makes a general statement that, "The government should cease incurring expense for the protection of channels for the benefit of private monopoly without insuring commendable programs satisfactory to citizen listeners."[17]

Broadcasters countered the criticism from educators by launching a campaign to prove that commercial radio brought educational programs to the American home. "Strategy of commercial broadcasters," *Variety* summarized in May 1934, "will be to demonstrate as completely as possible that adequate opportunity is afforded under present setup for non-profit programs." Like the movie industry, broadcasters took their campaign directly to the educators. "The first shot in the defensive campaign was fired several weeks ago," *Variety* reported, "when Merlin H. Aylesworth, president of NBC, told the National Education Association convention that 'education gets a 50-50 break over our networks'."[18]

In a speech before the NEA 1934 annual meeting, "Radio As a Means of Public Enlightenment," Aylesworth told the delegates that radio had joined with the church, the home, and the school as a source of public enlightenment. The American broadcasting system, he maintained, provided the greatest variety of programming of any system in the world. He claimed that 20 percent of programs broadcast on commercial radio was educational, while 30 percent was of "educational value." These figures were used to claim that a total of 50 percent of network radio was devoted to educational programming. In giving examples of educational programs, he referred only to NBC's Music Appreciation Hour, which he said was heard weekly in fifty thousand schools by six million children. Educators in the audience must have wondered what programs constituted the remainder of the 50 percent of educational programming.[19]

Aylesworth also answered charges that the two major networks were showing favoritism toward the Roosevelt Administration and Democratic Party as a method of protecting their monopoly over radio. Aylesworth countered that representatives of the federal government were allowed to explain administration policies over the radio and opponents were allowed to voice their opinions. And, in what became one of the standard defenses used by networks for freedom of debate on radio, Aylesworth stated, "The only qualification a man needs to speak on an NBC network is that he be a responsible citizen, representing a responsible group of citizens, with something important to say."[20]

Organized labor was one group that claimed its opinions were being excluded from commercial radio. Whether or not representatives from labor and labor organizations were included in Aylesworth's definition of "responsible citizen" and "responsible group" is open to speculation. But from the standpoint of the American Federation of Labor, commercial radio was not working in the interests of the laboring person. In 1926, the Chicago Federation of Labor established station WCFL as the only station in the United States operated by organized labor. In 1934, the American Federation of Labor joined with educators and religious organizations in the attempt to gain 25 percent of licenses for nonprofit broadcasting. The goal of the American Federation of Labor was to establish eleven more radio stations to counter what it believed was the conservative economic philosophy disseminated by the major networks.[21]

In early October 1934, advocates of nonprofit radio took their arguments directly to the Federal Communications Commission (FCC). *Variety* claimed that Joy Morgan, now president of the NEA, and the leaders of the National Committee for Education by Radio were "stage-managing the show for proponents of educational broadcasting."[22] Apparently, advocates of nonprofit radio tried to avoid a direct confrontation with the networks by affirming their belief in the American broadcasting system while asking for a separate network for nonprofit educational radio broadcasting that would hold 25 percent of the broadcasting licenses.[23]

The National Association of Broadcasters (NAB) organized network opposition to the proposal for granting 25 percent of radio licenses to nonprofit stations. The NAB was originally organized in 1923 to deal with the issue of payments for music used on radio. Over the years it had evolved into a trade association dealing with all issues involving the industry's relationship to government, advertising, and broadcasting standards. In testimony before the FCC in 1934, the NAB estimated that requiring 25 percent of radio licenses for nonprofit stations would result in the loss of 100 commercial radio stations. They argued that networks were willing to cooperate with educational and religious groups, and they denied allegations that networks gave only the most useless and unprofitable daytime hours for educational and religious programming. The NAB and the networks claimed that the public did not want educational radio because it was generally uninteresting and boring. The Vice-president of CBS, Henry Bellows, told the FCC that most colleges wanted free time only to broadcast football games and "dry" talks.[24] NBC submitted a statement by Henry L. Mencken that "educational programs are puerile and dull and ...there is no evidence that the calibre of their broadcasts would be any better 'if they had all day'."[25]

The most articulate defense of the broadcasting industry was presented to the FCC by CBS President William Paley. Like Aylesworth's speech before the NEA, the title of Paley's address, "Radio As a Cultural Force," suggested rebuttal of the arguments expressed at the May meeting of the National Committee on Education By Radio. Paley justified the American broadcasting system in the context of a market economy. Since radio is operated as a business, he argued, broadcasters must provide programs that attract listeners. Therefore, the first problem for the networks is to win an audience and then hold that audience. In addition, his argument continued, radio, unlike newspapers, cannot be geared for a special audience. It must have universal appeal. To achieve these goals, Paley maintained, radio programs had to appeal to the emotions and self-interest of listeners, as well as to their intellect.

Paley dealt with a issue in ideological management: Should a group such as educational and religious leaders determine what is the best programming for listeners, or should that be determined by the selections of individual listeners? The arguments presented by the members of the Committee on Education by Radio suggested that a group of intellectual and moral leaders should decide what is best for the public and that radio should be turned into a form of public education. Paley, on the other hand, justified the American broadcasting system by claiming that it was democratic because it was based on listener selection. Paley stated, "We cannot assuredly, calmly broadcast programs we think people ought to listen to, if they know what is good for them, and then go on happily unconcerned as to whether they listen or not."[26]

Paley also attacked the format of educational radio as undemocratic because, in his opinion, it had underlying aristocratic assumptions. Quoting from an article he wrote for the *Annals of the American Academy of Political and Social Sciences,* he argued that the public school system in the United States had created independent and critical thinkers. This form of democratic education, he stated, prepared citizens for direct application of the humanities and arts, as opposed to the aristocratic concept of education, which emphasized learning for learning's sake. In his words, "Experience has taught us that one of the quickest ways to bore the American audience is to deal with art for art's sake, or to deify culture and education because they are worthy gods."[27]

In the context of the preceding argument, Paley justified the content of commercial radio by claiming that it was a part of democratic culture. He claimed that scholars who thought the goal of education should be learning for learning's sake would be shocked that "we even went so far as to classify a broadcast of the World's Fair opening as an educational program."[28] In other words, according to Paley, radio made possible the direct experience of events by the masses of people, which he claimed was a form of democratic learning. Incidentally, this broad definition of democratic education is probably what allowed NBC to claim that 50 percent of its programs were educational and Paley to claim in his statement to the FCC that CBS devoted 2,207 hours to educational programming during the first nine months of 1934. It also allowed NBC to claim that "Amos 'n' Andy" was educational and to have the actors perform a comedy routine before the Commission as an example.[29] Paley specifically named in his statement to the FCC CBS's "American School of the Air" and "Church of the Air" as educational radio programs. Paley went on to argue that for "radio's democratic audience" history should not be presented as dry facts but as a living experience and that science should not be discussed as abstract theory but "as an answer to the daily needs of man in his struggle with his environment."[30]

Paley and members of the National Committee on Education by Radio agreed that radio played an important role as an educational force in the development of a national culture. Where they differed was over the control and form of this new means of mass education. Obviously, both groups wanted control over radio programming and each provided arguments to justify control "being" in their hands. Educators on the National Committee on Education by Radio believed that intellectual leaders like themselves should determine what was "good" or "best" for the education of the general public. On the other hand, leaders in the radio industry justified their control by claiming that if education over radio were to be effective it had to be packaged as entertainment that appealed to the masses. In addition, the radio industry argued that the only assurance that entertainment radio would continue was that broadcasting remain a business dependent on pleasing audiences. Of course, one issue not stressed by the radio industry was that programming also had to appeal to the sponsor.

Therefore, at least from the standpoint of the President of CBS, William Paley, the development of a national culture by radio was to be a product of entertainment surrounded by the slogans of advertising. Of course, Paley did argue that radio should be thought of only as supplemental to formal schooling. In his words, radio "cannot take the place of the classroom and the lecture platform."

Paley handled the issue of censorship by invoking the economic power of the marketplace. Quite simply, he claimed that censorship was bad for business. He denied that CBS exercised an editorial "blue pencil" and cited the example of a "businessman" opponent of the Roosevelt Administration who was granted broadcast time. Paley reported that the businessman had exclaimed, "I thought you fellows broadcast only Administration talks." It would be shortsighted editorial policy, Paley argued, to exclude anti-Administration views, because "intelligent controversy is one of the quickest roads to audience interest."[31]

In summary, Paley's defense of the radio industry against attacks by educators was based on the idea that individual choice (which in this case meant turning the dial on a radio) should determine culture-not educators and intellectual leaders. "It is worth repeating here," Paley concluded his presentation to the FCC, "we conceive of education by radio not in the narrow classical sense, but in the broadest humanitarian meaning. Nor, in our democratic society, is culture merely a matter of learning the difference between Bach and Beethoven...but it is equally a knowledge of how to rear a family in health and happiness—or to spend leisure wisely and well."[32]

Of course, as noted earlier, industry leaders failed to mention that the content of programming was not just a matter of listener choice. In fact, commercial radio frequently exercised its own blue pencil to censor certain program material, including song lyrics. This censorship was not in response to popular demand, but rather a result of network fear of protest from advertisers and from the religiously conservative. In addition, broadcasters feared offending political leaders because of the industry's dependence on government licensing. In reality, democratic choice as the determining factor in radio programming was seriously compromised by the economic and political needs of the broadcast industry.

Siding with the radio industry, the FCC reported to Congress that commercial radio was providing adequate educational programming. What was needed, the Commission argued, was cooperation between broadcasters and the educational community. For this purpose they created the Federal Radio Education Committee, which became another platform for the debate over the role of education in the American broadcasting system.

Obviously, the creation of the Federal Radio Education Committee as an alternative to the 25-percent-allotment plan was favored by the broadcasting industry but not by the members of the Committee for Education by Radio. The goal of the Federal Radio Education Committee was to establish cooperation between educators and the commercial broadcasters, and to support studies on the educational use of radio. These activities posed no threat to the broadcasting industry and, in fact, provided a means for commercial broadcasters to claim that they were serving the public interest. Educators did gain federal assistance in the development of education by radio, but they lost it in their attempt to create an educational network.

The Federal Radio Education Committee was formally organized during late 1935 and early 1936 under the chairmanship of the U.S. Commissioner of Education, John Studebaker. Reflecting the industry's support of the Committee, funding was provided by the National Association of Broadcasters and the industry-sponsored National Advisory Council on Radio. Additional funding was received from the Carnegie Corporation and the U.S. Office of Education. After five programs were created, Studebaker claimed they had been successful in creating educational programs that could compete on radio with commercial programming. The programs included "The World Is Yours," done in cooperation with the Smithsonian Institution and broadcast over NBC; "Answer Me This," containing questions and answers that were to educate the listener; "Have You Heard," a natural science program; and a CBS safety program titled "Safety Musketeers."[33]

In addition, the Office of Education encouraged college and high school courses in radio production. The formation of the Federal Radio Education Committee did seem to mute the protests of educators against commercial radio. A whole slate of defenders of the American broadcasting system, including the

Chair of the FCC, the President of RCA, and the federal Commissioner of Education, spoke at the Committee's first national conference in Washington, D.C., in December 1936.[34]

At the first session of the conference, Anning S. Prall, Chairman of the FCC, argued that educational goals should be combined with the basic structure of the American broadcasting system by developing radio as a form of democratic propaganda.[35] After noting the sinister connotation of the word "propaganda," Prall told his audience, "Yet propaganda, radio's greatest function in Germany and Russia, can spread the ideas and ideals of America, can 'sell' America to Americans, and thus forge a weapon of national unity that no other agency can create. Why cannot propaganda be used for good as well as for evil ends?" Answering his own question, Prall argued that educators would be the best people to assure that propaganda on radio could be for "good" ends.[36]

Prall concluded that radio was a form of public education and that it should remain in the hands of commercial broadcasters. To develop the educational or propaganda side of radio required cooperation between educators and commercial radio networks. However, Prall did not seem to see any conflict between profit motives in advertising and the development of a national culture. Prall ended his statement on propaganda with a call to educators to use their skills for radio. "Who are so well equipped, " he asked rhetorically, "as those engaged in the education of our youth to guarantee an unselfish, idealistic, and patriotic extension, through radio, of the ideals of citizenship, which they are now engaged in presenting in the narrower field of their individual classrooms?"[37]

Following Prall's remarks, Studebaker, U.S. Commissioner of Education, also raised the problem of public education through a privately owned industry. Studebaker asked, "How can public enterprise use a utility which is privately controlled?" In answer to his own question, Studebaker pointed out the attempts to protect public education from outside influences through separate financing by taxes and through rules governing the relationship between school administrators and salespeople. But in the case of radio, he stated, educators must deal with the world of business. In fact, to effectively use radio for educational purposes, educators needed to learn the techniques of the world of privately owned entertainment. In language similar to that used in the discussion of ideological management, Studebaker told the delegates to the conference, "Education through radio will become a vital and permanent factor in the dissemination of knowledge and the development of social insight when we do the job of educating over the air as effectively for our purposes as the commercial broadcasters do their job of entertaining."[38]

In 1937, the second Educational Broadcasting Conferences opened in Chicago with a defense of the radio industry by the head of CBS, William Paley, and a weak plea by the chair of the Committee for Education by Radio for state radio planning.[39] The movement for more educational radio stations lost steam; educators seemed resigned to accepting only a few low-power stations at educational institutions.

THE TRIUMPH OF CONSUMER CULTURE

If one accepts the argument made in the 1930s that the struggle between private interests and educators for control of radio was in fact a struggle over who should determine national culture, then the victory of private interests meant that advertising would have a major influence on national culture. With each radio program wrapped in the slogans of its sponsors, listeners were steadily bombarded by pleas to buy products. With increasing sophistication in marketing, advertising became a form of entertainment that competed with programming material for the attention of listeners. Advertising jingles and slogans became a part of the American way of life.

The "American system of broadcasting" was eventually extended to television. Together, radio and television acted as a powerful influence on the direction of American culture. From the standpoint of educators and religious groups in the 1930s, the influence of broadcasting on national culture should have remained in the hands of government. Broadcasting, they felt, should be treated in the same manner as public schools. The control of dissemination of knowledge, they argued, should remain in the hands of elected public officials and their expert empoyees.

Commercial broadcasters claimed that their influence on national culture was democratic, because listeners could exert control by selecting programs. This consumer model of democracy, where choice determines product, was never a reality, of course. There are only a limited number of networks available for consumer choice and, as pointed out in more detail in later chapters, sponsors exert a great deal of influence over the content of programming. In addition, the next chapter will show that broadcasters adopted standards that effectively censored program material.

Therefore, broadcasters' claims that consumer choice created a democratic culture were false. Commercial broadcasting made the selling of products into a form of entertainment. Penetrating rural and urban homes across the nation, broadcasting made commercial products identifiable to all listeners. Public school leaders had once dreamt of creating a national culture through public schooling, but radio and television might have proved more influential. Broadcasting helped create a shared national culture by establishing a common knowledge of consumer items and a shared experience of sponsored radio and television entertainment.

CHAPTER SEVEN

CRIME AND GORE IN CHILDREN'S RADIO

IN DECEMBER 1934, Thomas Rishworth, the director of radio station KSTP in St. Paul, Minnesota, made the mistake of challenging the local Parent-Teachers Association (PTA) to stop their "glib" criticism of children's radio programs and offer constructive advice. He was tired of hearing the Minnesota PTA complain that radio broadcasts were disturbing children with tales of blood and gore, causing them to toss and turn in their sleep, and making them miss meals when their favorite programs were on the air.[1]

One week later representatives of the PTA, Boy Scouts, and other community organizations met with Rishworth to discuss the problems of children's radio. Besides the complaints already mentioned, John Donahue, a probation officer in St. Paul, stood up at the meeting and warned that radio programs like "Jack Armstrong" were causing law-breaking tendencies among the communities' children, in part, he argued, by the portrayal of likeable villains.[2]

Contrary to Rishworth's original intentions, the meeting ended with a call for boycotts of advertisers and strict censorship of radio listening by parents. Even the trade newspaper, *Variety,* was caught by surprise. Its original article on the story gave the impression that Rishworth would easily handle the critics of children's radio. After the critics announced a boycott of advertisers, *Variety,* in an article titled "Air Reformers After Coin," claimed that the real goal of critics in St. Paul was to make money in the radio business by trying to peddle their own scripts to commercial sponsors.[3]

The interaction between Rishworth and the local PTA exemplified the protests against children's radio that began shortly after the broadcast over NBC on April 6, 1931, of the first children's radio serial, "Little Orphan Annie." Serialized adult mystery drama began in 1929 with the broadcast of "True Detective Mysteries." The most popular of the mysteries, "The Shadow," appeared in the same year as "Little Orphan Annie." Children in the 1930s probably listened to both the mystery programs and late afternoon children's programming. CBS began broadcasting "Buck Rogers in the Twenty-fifth Century" in 1932, and in 1933, the "Lone Ranger" and "Jack Armstrong, the All-American Boy" made their debuts. By 1938, the most popular children's serials included these programs and, "Dick Tracy," "Don Winslow of the Navy," "Terry and the Pirates," and "Tom Mix."[4]

"Buck Rogers in the Twenty-fifth Century" and "Tom Mix" could be placed at opposite ends of a scale measuring parental fears about children's radio. According to historian Raymond Stedman, "The agitated fantasy of "Buck Rogers" must have been at the heart of many of those articles expressing worry about radio's effect on young minds."[5] In the daily fantasy series, Buck Rogers battled fleets of spaceships, missiles, death rays, and other futuristic weapons to save the universe from destruction.

At the other end of the scale, "Tom Mix" provoked little apprehension in parents. In fact, "Tom Mix" was a model for the type of children's programs championed by the 1935 CBS radio code. In what became the classic cowboy drama of radio and movies of the 1930s, the good cowboy Tom Mix always won out against the evil of the bad cowboy. The epigram of "Tom Mix" was, "Lawbreakers always lose. Straight shooters always win. It pays to shoot straight!" The sponsor, Ralston Cereals, tried to win parental support of the program by placing promotional advertising in *Parents Magazine*.[6]

But even programs emphasizing the pursuit of evil contained elements that were thought to be disturbing to children. In the first episode of the "Lone Ranger," the hero is restored to health by what would later be his faithful Indian companion after being shot in an ambush that left his five companions dead. "The Shadow" opened with the chilling question: "Who knows what evil lurks in the hearts of men? The Shadow knows."[7]

National magazines complained about these scary statements and forms of violence. A 1933 editorial in *Parents Magazine,* written in response to the many complaints received in their offices about children's programs, was accompanied by a cartoon depicting a frightened young girl sitting on the floor next to a radio spewing forth the words, "Scram! Don't Shoot! Kidnapped! They're Going To Kill Me! Help! Murder! Bang! Bang! Kill Him! Police!" The editorial explained that the majority of complaints it received were about the high pitch of fear and emotional excitement radio caused in young children. The editor urged parents to write sponsors protesting the quality of children's program.[8]

The editorial in *Parents Magazine* mirrored the criticisms that eventually caused the broadcasting industry to adopt self-regulating codes. In many ways, the radio codes were like the one enforced by the movie industry. Under the code, children's programs were to teach moral lessons through the adventures of heroes. The last section of this chapter will demonstrate that, after the adoption of the radio code, the standard format for children's radio became superheroes warring against the representatives of evil. Like the movies, good was always to triumph over evil.

THE CAMPAIGN TO CLEAN UP CHILDREN'S RADIO

Parental complaints about children's radio were primarily voiced through PTAs and women's clubs. For example, in February 1933, the Central Council of the PTA of Rochester, New York, issued a public statement that, according to *Variety,* declared "the crime ideas [in radio programs] harmful to the moral fibre of children and the bloodcurdling situations tend to excite youngsters in a manner to interfere with their sleep." The PTA sent protests to local stations with hints of a boycott of advertisers.[9] A few months later the California State PTA issued a list of "bad" radio programs and called for unofficial censorship of programs broadcast between 5 p.m. and 8 p.m.—the prime hours for children to listen to radio. The California PTA expressed concern about "all programs emphasizing killing, robbing, impossible or dangerous situations."[10]

The actions of PTA groups affected network broadcasting. In February 1933, NBC announced that, in response to mounting complaints that children were trying to mimic the action of criminals appearing on radio programs, it would begin to "blue pencil" radio scripts with criminal themes.[11] Advertisers began to show concern: *Variety* announced that August, "Commercials are yielding to the agitation of PTA associations." The advertising agency for Jello led the way by shifting from sponsorship of horror programs to a radio version of *The Wizard of Oz.* Members of other advertising agencies expressed surprise that protests had not started sooner because horror was overdone on radio.[12]

The National Council of Women, representing twenty-eight national women's organizations, took an active role in criticizing children's radio. The head of the Council's Women's National Radio Committee, Mrs. Harold V. Milligan, indicated that the organization's concern about children's radio was sparked by a study conducted by the Woman's Club in the wealthy Westchester County, New York, community of Scarsdale.[13] Protests erupted in Scarsdale in 1933 when Mrs. George Ernest, head of a committee of Scarsdale women, organized a meeting on children's radio at Teachers College, Columbia University. The group rated forty children's programs and found only five suitable, according to their judgement. The rest were condemned because they "keep the children in emotional suspense and excite them so they can't sleep." The committee issued a statement objecting to mystery thrillers because "children don't just hear it and forget it, but they carry the story in their mind from day to day, or week to week."[14] To provide an alternative to existing children's programs, the Scarsdale Woman's Club wrote an unsuccessful radio serial titled "Westchester Cowboys."[15]

Mrs. Milligan, of the Women's National Radio Committee, laced her attack against children's radio with strong feminist language. In a 1935 letter to *Variety,* she described the Committee as the first coordinated effort by women to register their complaints against radio, which, in her words, is "man-made" and "man-regulated."[16] The following year at a national radio conference she declared, "Women vote, and they have influence on public opinion, yet big business does very little to indicate its willingness to earn the respect of millions of women who are serious about the one problem—children's programs on the radio."[17]

The Women's National Radio Committee was also worried about the effects of advertising. To capture the child's attention, she argued, advertisers made programs highly stimulating; advertisers were also exploiting children as consumers. Urging parents to counter the work of advertisers, she reported, "Some parents have met the 'box-top' problem by suggesting that if the child wants the prize offered for sending in a certain number of box tops, he pay for the package out of his own allowance."[18]

The Women's National Radio Committee established a system of awards to promote what they thought was good children's radio. Sometimes the rewards went to programs that could not find commercial sponsorship. Thus one award went to the CBS historical program "Wilderness Road" which failed to remain on the air because of lack of sponsorship. Some member organizations of the National Council of Women actually sponsored radio programs. For instance, the American Legion Auxiliary, one of the member organizations, sponsored a radio dramatization of James Truslow Adams' *The Epic of America* and offered prizes for the best children's essay on "What the 'Epic of America' Has Taught Me About the Future of America."[19]

Modeling themselves after the movie industry, the radio networks reacted with a public relations campaign. That the radio industry was borrowing methods from Will Hays's Motion Picture Producers and Distributors Association was boldly stated in a headline in *Variety,* "Radio Wants Clubwoman Good Will: Offer Transmitters to Gals with Messages—Will Hays Started It." The CBS Chicago affiliate, WBBM, offered free air time to local women's clubs, the DAR, and PTAs.[20]

In 1935, the FCC responded to complaints abut children's radio programming from PTAs and women's clubs. On April 3, 1935, *Variety* announced, "Deluged with bleats from educators and parents, [FCC Chairman] Commish is agreed that if broadcasters do not move on their own to cook up more satisfactory entertainment for children, the government must apply the whip." The FCC admitted that under its "anti-censorship" clause it could not directly control the content of children's radio, but it could threaten stations with the possibility of taking away their licenses by stringently applying the public service requirement and by rigidly enforcing technical rules. The FCC was receiving pressure also from the White House and Congress to do something about "Goose-Pimple Kid Shows." In the words of *Variety,* "Kids' programs of blood-and-thunder type appear doomed under new drive."[21]

By May of 1935, the FCC radio cleanup was in full swing. Its efforts at improving radio programming extended beyond just children's radio. Admitting that it could not directly censor radio, the FCC let radio stations know that it was concerned about the following types of programming and advertising:

1. lotteries
2. fortune tellers
3. racing tips
4. blood and thunder kids' programs
5. birth control compounds
6. fat-removing compounds.[22]

In June of 1935, the FCC instructed its field personnel to report radio broadcasts that seemed to violate these restrictions. Besides objectionable advertising and religious and medical programs, *Variety* claimed that the FCC included in its list "attacks on government officials or governmental departments."[23]

The editors of *Variety* reacted to public and government pressures on the broadcasting industry with an editorial entitled, "Radio Should Fight Back."[24] A letter printed on the page opposite the editorial quoted the Superintendent of New York City public schools declaring at a meeting of the American Council of Education that improving home conditions for children was made difficult by the domination of radio programming during the family hour between 5 p.m. and 8 p.m. The Superintendent had asked the gathered educators, in reference to radio, how the home could be improved "when anti-social, immoral and other destructive conditions present insurmountable obstacles?" The letter in *Variety* pointed out the PTA's adoption of a resolution for changing radio programming.[25] *Variety*'s editorial response to the letter called critics of radio broadcasting "the enemies." The editorial stated, "Whether they admit it or not, censorship of radio is what the enemies of the industry want. Radio has censorship already—more than enough.... There are plenty of things wrong with radio, but censorship is not the remedy."[26]

THE RADIO CODE

The broadcasting industry's response to public and government pressure paralleled that of the movie industry. The networks proclaimed the institution of self-censorship codes and the Philco Corporation announced in early June 1935 the establishment of a Radio Institute of the Audible Arts, modeled on the Hays organization in the movie industry. The stated purpose of the Institute was to hold off government censorship of radio by recommending programs and acting as a clearinghouse for information. The Institute compiled a mailing list of five thousand women's clubs, PTAs, and other interested groups.[27]

The most widely publicized response was the CBS announcement in May 1935 of a self-censorship code designed to clean up broadcasting.[28] This was not a surprise move on the part of CBS. In his annual report to its board members in 1933, CBS President Paley had argued against government censorship of network programming and advocated voluntary censorship.[29] Even before 1935, CBS had adopted a number of standards to guide programming. In 1928 and 1929 CBS issued guidelines for dealing with controversial public issues, and in 1931 it banned attacks on religious groups. Some standards regarding advertising were established in the early 1930s.[30]

NBC reacted to the CBS 1935 code by claiming that it had adopted a similar code in 1934.[31] But NBC did not pull together its broadcasting standards into a single booklet for public distribution until 1939. Prior to 1939, NBC claimed that its broadcast standards were stated in personal letters to advertisers.[32]

CBS President Paley informed the public of the code in a broadcast over the Columbia network on May 14, 1935. Paley began by reminding his listeners how radio permeated the lives of most Americans. "You hear the voices of Columbia," Paley said, "for many hours each day. These voices are familiar in your home, perhaps in your workshop, and even in your automobile and the restaurants and theaters you visit." In words suggesting that radio had caused changes in social relationships, Paley continued, "These voices are frequently more familiar comrades than some of your closest personal friends." After painting a picture of the intimate and personal relationship between the listener and the broadcaster, Paley went on to describe the general outlines of the new broadcasting code.[33]

The files at the CBS Reference Library in New York City indicate that the self-censorship code was issued as part of a well-orchestrated public relations campaign. The code was immediately distributed to important public leaders, and their responses were carefully collected and used in public relations announcements. The code was distributed with an announcement that CBS was employing Prof. Arthur Jersild of Columbia University Teachers College, as a consulting psychologist for children's programming.

Appropriately, Prof. Jersild's major area of research was children's fears. Unlike others, Jersild did not attack radio and movies for causing children's fears nor was he a strong advocate of censorship. This was probably why CBS executives selected him as a consultant. Jersild believed that it was hard to blame radio and movies for children's fears because previous generations experienced similar fears. On the other hand, his data did indicate that movies and radio thrillers were a source of many children's fears. But he was hesitant about censoring children's programs to remove fear-provoking material. In a book he coauthored with another child psychologist, Frances Holmes, Jersild wrote, "The use of fear-inspiring materials in books, radio programs, and moving pictures designed for children might, no doubt, be controlled to some degree by rigid censorship." But, he continued, this type of censorship might protect some individuals at the expense of others. Therefore, he argued, parents of susceptible children should exercise control over their movie going and radio listening. Obviously, this approach to control of children's radio was more palatable to radio executives than outright government censorship.[34]

Two months after issuing of the code, CBS announced the creation of an Advisory Committee on Children's Programs. Reflecting the astute public relations strategy of the network, one of the four members of the advisory was Mrs. Harold Milligan, member of the Executive Board of the National Council of Women and Chair of the Women's National Radio Committee. The other three members of the Advisory Committee were, Mrs. William Barclay Parsons, President of the Parents League; Newel W. Edson, National Chairman of the Social Hygiene Committee of the National Congress of Parents and Teachers; and Mrs. Henry Breckinridge, Chairman of the Municipal Arts Committee.[35]

In its official announcement, CBS described the formation of the Advisory Committee as the final step in creating the administrative machinery to control the content of advertising, to limit the length of advertising announcements, and to bring "children's programs up to a level generally approved by parents and authorities on child health and child psychology." In addition, CBS announced that the Child Study Association would work with this newly formed Advisory Committee.[36]

CBS's policies were directed at the two major complaints about American broadcasting—advertising and children's radio. Of central importance for the future of children's radio programs was the code's emphasis on providing children with moral and social heroes. The code recognized the importance of hero worship in a child's life. "Superman," "The Lone Ranger," and "Tom Mix" exemplified the heroic model recommended in the CBS code. Like the movie code, the CBS code also emphasized the importance of not teaching children anti-social behavior by presenting crime and criminals in a positive light. In addition, the code tried to answer complaints from women's clubs about the quality of advertising on children's programs.

The opening statement of the 1935 CBS code directly links the necessity of self-censorship with corporate profits: "It is incumbent upon the broadcaster constantly to examine general policy so as to assure steady progress in building and holding radio's audience. Such watchfulness serves the interests of the audience, of the advertiser, and of the broadcasting companies alike."[37] Without mentioning the complaints of public groups and government officials, the code refers to the current concern of the broadcasting industry with children's programs and "unpleasant discussions of bodily functions, bodily symptoms, other matters which similarly infringe on good taste."[38] This last item referred to advertising such items as laxatives.

The section on children's programs begins with a discussion of differing opinions among parents and authorities regarding which programs are suitable for children, and the attempt by commercial sponsors to provide appropriate programs. But even with these considerations, the code argues, it is necessary to eliminate instances of poor judgment. The code disclaims any attempt by CBS to be "arbiter of what is proper for children to hear...." But the code states that CBS "does have an editorial responsibility to the community, in the interpretation of public wish and sentiment, which cannot be waived."[39] Using this justification, the code provides the following forbidden themes and dramatic treatments for children's programs:

1. The exalting, as modern heroes, of gangsters, criminals and racketeers will not be allowed.
2. Disrespect for either parental or other proper authority must not be glorified or encouraged.
3. Cruelty, greed, and selfishness must not be presented as worthy motivations.
4. Programs that arouse harmful nervous reactions in the child must not be presented.
5. Conceit, smugness, or an unwarranted sense of superiority over others less fortunate may not be presented.
6. Recklessness and abandon must not be falsely identified with a healthy spirit of adventure.
7. Unfair exploitation of others for personal gain must not be made praiseworthy.
8. Dishonesty and deceit are not to be made appealing or attractive to the child.[40]

After stating these prohibitions, the code presents an argument for using hero worship as a central feature of children's programming. The code argues that, for children of elementary school age, programs should provide entertainment of a moral nature. The code notes that children's literature continues to provide "heroes worthy of the child's ready impulse to hero worship, and of his imitative urge to pattern himself after the hero model." Literature of this sort, the code claims, "succeeds in inspiring the child to socially useful and laudable ideals such as generosity, industry, kindness and respect for authority.... It serves, in effect, as a useful adjunct to that education which the growing and impressionable child is absorbing during every moment of its waking day."[41] The section on children's programming concludes with an announcement of the appointment of an Advisory Committee and a psychologist to help achieve broadcast standards. The remainder of the code is devoted to prohibiting the advertisement of depilatories, deodorants, and laxatives, and guidelines for limiting the percentage of programming devoted to advertising.

Within days of its distribution, CBS collected and distributed responses to its new code. On May 15, 1935, a day after Paley's broadcast, CBS issued a press release of others' praise for the new policies. From a political standpoint the most important congratulations came from FCC Chair Anning Prall, who wrote, "Such an example of wise leadership can hardly fail to exert a profound influence on American broadcasting generally...[and] can only...enhance radio's unique influence in our modern ways of living and thinking...."[42] The Women's National Radio Committee wrote, "Delighted to hear about Columbia's new policy regarding advertising and children's programs. Its adoption will mean the beginning of a new era in broadcasting as you have set a standard as high as any outside agency could desire."[43] The President of NEA responded to the code, "Educators and parents are strongly in sympathy with your objectives in the production of more wholesome broadcasts."[44]

Like the CBS code, the NBC code, released in 1939, linked self-censorship to protection of markets. The code argued that enforcing self-censorship would avoid the broadcasting of anything that "might in any way divert part of an audience from one network or station to another." the NBC code banned advertisements dealing with speculative finances, personal hygiene, weight-reducing agents, fortune tellers, professions, cemeteries, alcoholic beverages, and firearms.[45]

Children's programs were to stress law and order, adult authority, good morals, and clean living. Like the CBS code, heroes were to play a role in shaping children's morality. The NBC code states, "The hero or heroine and other sympathetic characters must be portrayed as intelligent and morally courageous...and disrespect for law must be avoided as traits in any character that may be presented in the light of a hero to the child listener."[46] In addition, the code states that programs should emphasize mutual respect, fair play, and honorable behavior. Adventure stories were singled out for special attention because of their potential to emotionally upset children. Prohibited from adventure programs were kidnapping, torture, extreme violence, horror, superstition, and "morbid suspense."

Children's programs were also covered by eleven "Basic Program Standards" that were to be applied to all NBC programs. Three of these standards dealt with presentations that might offend religious groups, such as irreverent references to God, material offensive to particular religious views, and sacrilege. Included in the standard on material offensive to religious groups was a ban on statements against racial groups. The standards also discouraged murder and suicide in programs, and prohibited descriptions of insobriety and "antisocial" practices. One standard reserved the use of "FLASH" for genuine special news programs, and another warned against false statements. Except in factual news statements, there were to be no references to people featured in criminal and sensational news stories. Reflecting broadcasting's concern over offending important people and other countries, one standard reads, "Figures of national prominence as well as the peoples of all nations shall be presented with fairness and consideration."[47]

RADIO AND COMIC BOOK HEROES

By the end of the 1930s, children attending movies and listening to the radio were receiving similar messages about the triumph of good over evil. In the case of radio, moral messages were being conveyed through the adventures of superheroes. Many of these superheroes could also be found in comic books, which first made their appearance in 1929 when George Delacorte decided to take the comics from newspapers and present them in a tabloid-size book. This first comic book, *The Funnies,* had little success and was discontinued after thirteen issues. Several years later, however, M. C. Gaines successfully marketed reprinted newspaper comics. In 1935, Delacorte and Gaines teamed up to produce *Popular Comics,* which contained comic strips that were also popular radio programs, such as "Dick Tracy" and "Terry and the Pirates." Therefore the production of comic books paralleled the development of children's radio. But unlike the radio industry, the comic book industry did not adopt a code until the 1950s.[48]

The moral and political message of children's radio in the second half of the 1930s emphasized the ultimate triumph of good, the importance of obedience to the law, and patriotism. For instance, the adventures of Superman on radio and in comic books were an important vehicle for these messages. Making his appearance in the June 1938 issue of *Action Comics,* Superman was quickly adapted to radio. Children grew accustomed to hearing over the airwaves the famous lines spoken by the hero as he changed from Clark Kent to Superman to fight for justice:

> This looks like a job for (voice drop)
> Superman!
>> Now off with these clothes!
>> Up, up and awa-a-a-ay!
>> (swoosh).[49]

Supermen of America Clubs sprang up around the country, whose members pledged to "do everything possible to increase his or her STRENGTH and COURAGE, to aid the cause of JUSTICE...."[50]

A striking feature of the history of Superman comics are the changes in Superman's character. In 1938, Superman was portrayed as a humanitarian fighting against unjust social conditions. In one 1938 episode, Superman forces a mine owner to improve safety conditions by causing a cave-in that traps a group of the owner's affluent friends. In a 1939 episode, Superman is at odds with the law when he rescues a juvenile delinquent from a police paddy wagon. He then destroys the slum buildings that supposedly caused the delinquency. When the publishers discovered that many of the episodes pitied Superman against an unjust legal system, they forced the creator, according to historian Thomas Andrae, to "make Superman operate within the law and to confine his activities to fighting criminals." By 1942, Andrae states, "His struggle against evil becomes confined to the defense of private property and the extermination of criminals; it is no longer a struggle against social injustice, an attempt to aid the helpless and oppressed."[51]

The popular "Don Winslow of the Navy" carried a patriotic message in its programs and through the creed adopted by children joining its club, the Squadron of Peace. The Don Winslow Creed begins, "I consecrate my life to Peace and the protecting of all my Countrymen wherever they may be." Reflecting the moral education goals of children's radio, the Creed, in reference to the fictitious enemy, Scorpia, states, "My battle against Scorpia represents the battle between Good and Evil." The Creed ends with the command, "Love your country, its flag and all the things for which it stands. Follow the advice of your parents and superiors and help someone every day."[52]

Like "Don Winslow of the Navy," "Terry and the Pirates" took its listeners on adventures in Asia to battle with the forces of evil. During the 1940s, this program took on a definite patriotic ring as the "enemies" were in fact America's foes in World War II. For instance, a typical episode of "Terry and the Pirates" opened with the announcer describing, "Somewhere in Calcutta is a master spy, a Nazi enemy agent. That German operator is the evil genius who is helping the Japs in nearby Burma to improve their deadly robot bombs."[53]

In the 1940s, the heroes of radio and comic books would be joined by a whole brigade of defenders of justice and good against the forces of crime and evil. Batman and Robin, Captain America, Captain Marvel, The Spider, and Spy Smasher were only a few of the characters waging a relentless battle for good. After World War II, many of these heroes formed the Justice League of America to launch a coordinated effort to end crime in the United States.

As the radio and comic book heroes and the movies of the 1930s taught children moral and political lessons that were very much like the character education programs in schools in the 1920s, educators reshaped educational programs to meet the problems posed by the Depression and the rise of fascist governments in Germany and Italy. As I will discuss in the next chapter, these changes would bring down the wrath of the "patriotic" organizations, particularly, the American Legion, the DAR, and the Sons of the American Revolution. The efforts of these groups before, during, and after World War II made the message of the schools closer to the moral examples set by the radio and comic book heroes.

CHAPTER EIGHT

PROGRESSIVISM AND SUBVERSION IN THE 1930s

IN THE 1930s, there were serious conflicts between patriotic and progressive groups over educational policy and classroom practices. Progressive policies found greater acceptance in the schools because of the doubts about capitalism raised by the Depression and the development of fascism. But these progressive policies were often modified by continued pressure from conservative educators, the American Legion, and some politicians who wanted schools to continue fighting subversion in American society.

In contrast to the passive character traits and desire in the 1920s to produce "go-getters" and "live wires," public schools by the end of the 1930s were concerned with preparing students for a world divided between totalitarianism and democracy. This vision of the world contained important variations on the anti-Communist themes of the 1920s. In the 1920s, the primary concern was convincing students of the evils of Communism by comparing economic systems. But in the 1930s the emphasis in these arguments shifted from economic to political concerns. Fascism, Nazism, and Communism tended to be lumped together under the label of "totalitarianism," while opposing political systems fell into the category of "democracy."

Beginning early in the 1930s, educators began to worry about the role of propaganda on citizens. "The present age might well be called the age of propaganda," wrote the Commission on Character Education for the 1932 yearbook, *Character Education,* of the Department of Superintendence of the NEA. "With the development of the press, the cinema, and the radio, instruments have been forged through which ideas, attitudes, and philosophies may be quickly impressed upon vast populations," continued the Commission. "And in every society there are powerful minority groups struggling for the control of these instruments and bent on conserving or grasping special privileges of all kinds."[1]

By the late 1930s, schools combined concerns with propaganda with preparing students to resist the temptations of totalitarianism. A cartoon in the study guide for a 12th grade unit on "Democracy and Its Competitors" at Theodore Roosevelt High School in Des Moines, Iowa, in the late 1930s shows a perplexed man sitting in his robe and slippers reading a newspaper. Swirling around his head are the words "Communism," "Nazism," "Fascism," "Totalitarianism," "Anti-Semitism," and "Reciprocal Trade Agreements." The caption under the cartoon declares, "What this country needs is a good 5-cent dictionary." The study guide warns that many Americans are as confused as the man in the cartoon with the "isms" and political labels of the 1930s. The school's list of "isms" and political labels includes, "Communism, sovietism, socialism, national socialism, nazism, Bolshevism, fascism, nationalism, Americanism, red, radical, conservative, reactionary, and liberal." In units with titles such as, "Democracy and autocracy compared," the study guide lumped together the United States, France, and England in the democratic camp, and Germany, Italy, and the USSR in the autocratic camp.[2]

Reflecting these concerns with world politics, the NEA and the American Association of School Administrators organized in 1935 the Educational Policies Commission for the purpose of improving education for "democratic citizenship." An important legacy of the work of the Educational Policies Commission conducted in ninety high schools in twenty-seven states between September 1939 and January 1940 is a survey of actual instruction in citizenship. This survey, *Learning the Ways of Democracy: A Case Book in Civic Education,* provides snapshots of the actual ideas and values that a large sample of American high schools were trying to disseminate to their students just at the outbreak of World War II.

The survey found high schools emphasizing the study of public opinion so that students could protect themselves against the propaganda of totalitarian governments. For instance, a ninth grade unit on public opinion in the Cleveland public schools focused on issues of free speech and the censorship of newspapers, radio, and movies. Students studied "The Struggle for Personal and Political Liberty." The major objective of the unit was,

> To appreciate the time and the individual sacrifices required to establish the personal and political liberties enjoyed in America today; to sense the dangers now threatening to destroy these liberties; and to strengthen the spirit of resistance to such destructive forces.[3]

In the twelfth grade, Cleveland students were again exposed to the issue of public opinion with a unit on "Civil Rights—Significance and Repression." In this unit, students studied the development of civil liberties from the Magna Charta to the Constitution; the Bill of Rights; the repression of civil rights including the activities of the Ku Klux Klan, and the effects of repressive legislation; and the comparison of civil liberties under democracy, communism, socialism, and fascism. The final part of the unit related civil liberty to public opinion.[4]

The examination of free speech and propaganda raised questions about the "Red Scare" of the 1920s. Twelfth grade classes in Rochester, New York, focused on the problem: "What serious questions exist in American democracy today concerning public opinion?" The students were specifically told to discuss, "What is a 'red scare'? Look up the Lusk Laws 1921 in New York State."[5]

A theme in these courses of study was that propaganda was not a problem in a democratic society because of the freedom to debate different opinions. In such debate, individuals test the validity of their beliefs. For instance, a study guide for the eighth grade in Schenectady, New York, stressed the importance of using actual concrete information in forming opinions according to the guide, "in a democracy where free speech and free press are so highly prized, this is very important." The guide called for a study of newspapers, magazines, books, radio, and motion pictures as agencies "which aid in opinion expression and formation."[6]

Study guides included sections dealing with threats to freedom of speech. The high school study guide for Rochester, New York, contained a unit that opened with the question, "What serious problems exist in American democracy today concerning public opinion?" The guide lists the following topics:

1. current threats to civil and political liberty;
2. academic freedom and discussion of public problems in the classroom;
3. extension of procedures of scientific thought to public and personal problems.[7]

The Commission was pleased at the willingness it found to discuss controversial issues. The members of the Commission wrote, "Freedom of discussion of controversial subjects is more than a right.... If citizens do not have this right, they are unable to make intelligent decisions, and control passes into the hands of those individuals who are adroit enough to attain positions of power and influence."[8]

The Commission's examples of controversial discussions were mainly around the issue of propaganda. In a Modern Problems class in South High School, Omaha, Nebraska, students discussed a mimeographed sheet distributed in the community entitled, "Finns Hailed Soviet Aid." At the time, newspapers were presenting the same news that the handbill addressed as an attack by the Soviets on Finland. As transcribed by the staff of the Commission, students in the Omaha classroom argued that free speech was necessary to combat the type of propaganda represented by the mimeographed sheet, while the right to distribute the mimeographed sheet was necessary for the maintenance of democracy. According to the Commission, the important lesson for the students in the discussion was that the free press was the antidote for the type of propaganda in the mimeographed sheet. In response to the teacher's question, "Do you think that the city should pass an ordinance forbidding the distribution of handbills like this one?", the concluding, and typical, response recorded by the Commission staff was, "Suppression would do more harm to democracy than anything. It would make our newspapers like the Russian newspapers."[9]

Most of the distinctions made with regard to propaganda hinged on arguments for a free press. But by 1941, radio had replaced newspapers as the major source of news for most citizens in the United States.[10] And, of course, radio could hardly be considered free, with government licensing and regulation, interference from politicians, pressures from advertisers, and the networks' own censorship codes. From the 1930s into the 1950s, most movies watched by Americans also went through the hands of industry censors. Indeed, as pointed out throughout this volume, free speech did not exist in public schools, either. There were many different forms of censorship in the United States. Therefore, the real differences between the United States and totalitarian governments was the lack of a single agency and a unified policy controlling propaganda and the distribution of information.

What schools were accomplishing by the late 1930s was the creation of an image of a world divided between democratic and totalitarian forces. Skipping over meaningful political differences between governments lumped under each category, this image matched the world being portrayed on children's radio and in movies. It was a world divided between the forces of good and the forces of evil.

GOOD AND EVIL IN AMERICAN SCHOOLS

The Depression caused a split between the U.S. business community and the educational establishment, represented by the National Education Association. Faced with economic hard times, the business community sought reductions in school spending. In reaction to these cuts, the NEA strengthened its relations with the American Legion.

The American Legion sided with public schools in resisting cuts in school funding. In 1933, J. W. Crabtree, Secretary of the NEA, asked the American Legion to help fight against proposed cuts in educational spending. Representing the NEA, Crabtree stated at the annual convention of the Legion, "Forces in this nation [are] working to cut the cost of public education regardless of damage to childhood." The American Legion responded with a resolution demanding that "education be given its proper consideration by legislative bodies and…not be made to bear a major part of the sacrifices for economy." At the NEA convention the following year, the National Director of the Americanism Commission of the American Legion declared, "The educators of America are combining forces with the American Legion in a great battle to defeat any plan which seeks to curtail the activities of our schools."[11]

It was primarily the business community that demanded cutbacks in funding and school programs. As the Depression worsened school leaders became more critical of business leaders who were campaigning cut school taxes.[12] For instance, when the Depression hit Detroit, school revenue plummeted from $17,885,000 in 1930/1931 to $12,875,000 in 1932/1933. Furthermore, the student population increased, and debts continued from the school-building boom of the 1920s. Faced with these conditions, members of the business and financial community called for reductions in teachers' salaries and educational programs. The school board accepted the idea of salary reductions but resisted cutbacks in educational programs. While the fight over money strained the relationship between the schools and the business community, they did work together on some issues, such as resisting demands by Communist groups to hold weekend rallies in the schools.[13]

In 1938, as part of a public relations campaign to fight cutbacks, the NEA and the American Legion formed a joint committee "to confer and cooperate...so that we shall have 'better Americans thru better schools'." At the preliminary meeting, the American Legion pledged its support for federal aid to public schools.[14] In their mutual pledge of support, the two organizations agreed that federal aid should not mean federal control of public schools.[15]

Legion posts tried to protect local school budgets. Paul Griffith, as Chairman of its National Americanism Commission, outlined the Legion's strategy in a 1934 article in *American Legion Monthly*. Crabtree wrote,

> Some posts, faced with a school emergency have rallied the voters to the polls or to town meetings [and] have succeeded in getting through extra appropriations to keep schools open or to reopen closed schools. Others have organized money-raising projects and turned the funds over to school authorities. In the State of Alabama, Legionnaire petitions were responsible for a special session of the Legislature which appropriated funds to keep schools open. In Kentucky and in Wisconsin, to mention two States particularly, Legionaries have done valiant work for the schools....[16]

Griffith declared that adequate funding of public schools was essential in the fight against Communism and fascism.[17]

In 1934, Edward Hayes, National Commander of the American Legion, told the delegates to the NEA convention, "I pledge to you the tireless and loyal support of our 11,003 posts of the American Legion, in making of our schools the guardians of good citizenship...." The Secretary of the NEA, Crabtree, responded to this pledge with a declaration of pride in "cementing the relationship" between the two organizations and in the fact that "the members of the Legion, if need be, will fight as hard to save the schools as they did to save a world."[18] In 1935, the Legion voted to continue to work cooperatively with the NEA and the Parent-Teachers Association in supporting federal aid to education.[19]

While defending school budgets, the Legion continued its commitment to eliminate subversion in schools, which in the 1930s meant both fascism and

Communism. At their annual convention in 1935, the American Legion passed a resolution against "the advocacy in America of Nazism, Fascism, Communism, or any other isms that are contrary to the fundamental principles of democracy, as established under the Constitution of the United States." Local branches of the Legion's Americanism Commission were ordered to give close attention to possible "subversive" activities in their local communities.[20]

In 1934, the Legion thanked the NEA for its fight against subversion and stated that all Legion posts were assisting "local school officials in preventing such teaching."[21] Over the years, the joint NEA–American Legion committee expanded its interests to issues of subversion in the schools.[22]

This expanded activity included an interesting plan to influence citizenship training in schools. Beginning in 1941, the joint committee of the NEA and American Legion compiled a list of public school teachers who were also members of the American Legion. The report of the committee in 1941 states, "Fortunately, 12,000 Legionnaire-schoolmasters have the combination of experience and training essential to the promotion of understanding and goodwill in both patriotic and professional organizations." The committee tried to enlist these "fellow-workers" in a campaign to achieve the "common educational objectives" of financial support for the schools and "citizenship for the American way of life."[23]

By 1943, the major occupation of the joint committee was compiling a list of people holding joint membership in the NEA and American Legion, and the creation of local Legionnaire Schoolmasters Clubs. Of course, 1943 was the middle of World War II and the American Legion was planning for the expansion of its ranks by the recruitment of veterans at the end of the conflict.[24] In 1944, nine out of the eleven items on the program of the joint committee were related to recruiting for Legionnaire Schoolmaster Clubs and working for common educational objectives. The other two items urged local school boards and tax associations to provide adequate funding for public schools, and called for federal aid to education.[25] When World War II ended, development of Legionnaire Schoolmaster Clubs remained a major item of the program of the joint committee.[26]

During the 1930s, the Legion continued to advocate the firing of "disloyal" teachers. One of its objectives was to require loyalty oaths of all teachers. The Legion considered even any opposition to loyalty oaths as the work of "subversive" elements in American society. In 1935, the Americanism Commission reported that eight states had passed legislation requiring loyalty oaths of teachers. Other reports indicated that by 1935, twenty states required teachers' loyalty oaths.[27] Besides the actions of state governments to impose loyalty oaths on teachers, Congress in 1935 passed an appropriation bill containing a rider forbidding the payment of salary to any teacher spreading the doctrines of Communism. The rider kicked off a storm of protest lasting until 1937, when President Roosevelt got the act repealed.[28]

In 1934, the American Legion detected another source of subversion in American education. Speaking for the American Legion, Russell Cook, Director of the National Americanism Commission, warned delegates to the 1934 NEA convention, "In the last few years there has grown up a movement in which too many of our teachers are creating ideas in the schoolroom for what is called a new social order." Referring to social reconstructionists, Cook told the convention, "The American Legion is opposed to that movement. We say that it is not the mission of the teacher to lead the child into believing we should have a new social order...."[29]

The social reconstructionism movement is most often identified with a speech given by George Counts, a professor at Columbia University Teachers College, at the 1932 annual meeting of the Progressive Education Society. The speech was originally called, "Dare Progressive Education Be Progressive?" and it was distributed in pamphlet form with the controversial title of "Dare the Schools Build a New Social Order?" In the speech, Counts attacked capitalism as being "cruel and inhuman" and "wasteful and inefficient." He argued that the development of modern urban-industrial society made obsolete concepts of competition and rugged individualism. A new economic system, he argued, would free people from poverty.[30]

Counts proposed that teachers should assume leadership in the reconstruction of society. In Count's vision, teachers would lead children down the path of social reconstruction by openly admitting that all teaching was indoctrination. Once this was out in the open, the teacher could rationally select which principles would be indoctrinated into the child. Count's hope was that teachers would indoctrinate students in a progressive economic philosophy. Counts stated, "If democracy is to survive, it must seek a new economic foundation.... Natural resources and all important forms of capital will have to be collectively owned."[31]

Social reconstructionists were a small but vocal group in the 1930s. At the 1932 convention of the NEA, the Committee on Social-Economic Goals for America issued a report in which direct reference was made to the importance of Counts' questions "Dare the School Build a New Social Order?" The report, which urged the NEA to assume leadership in constructing the new social order, states, "The NEA is saying, and I hope saying more or less militantly, that a social order can be built in which a social collapse such as the present one will be impossible."[32] The committee's resolution was accepted without major debate by the convention. Although the NEA never took on militant and radical leadership during the 1930s, the very act of approving the report indicated growing militancy among some educators and the association's tension with the business community.

Most of the educators associated with social reconstructionism were on the faculty of Columbia University Teachers College. The group came to be identified as "frontier" thinkers. In 1933, they began a journal called *The Social Frontier,* which was later renamed *Frontiers of Democracy.* The major leaders of the movement, George Counts, William H. Kilpatrick, John Childs, and Harold Rugg, were a favorite target of patriotic organizations both before and after World War II. In the minds of members of patriotic organizations, the existence of these educators seemed to validate the notion of subversion in the schools.

Many leaders of patriotic societies considered social reconstructionism to be the worst form of progressive education. As indicated in the next section on conservative attacks on textbooks, Augustin Rudd, who campaigned to get Harold Rugg's textbooks off the market, blamed the supposed deterioration of public schools and their infiltration by subversives on what he called "hard" as opposed to "soft" progressivism. In 1940, Rudd was made chairperson of the newly organized Guardians of American Education. The specific goal of this organization was to combat social reconstructionist thought in education. The first publication of the organization stated as a goal the defeat of "left-wing...educational leadership...[which is trying to replace] our American way of life...[with] a 'new social order' based on the principles of collectivism and socialism." The publication also asked, "How long shall we continue to permit our public schools to be used as a breeding ground for alien ideologies?"[33] As Chairman of the Guardians of American Education and the Educational Committee of the New York Chapter of the Sons of the American Revolution, and member of the American Legion, Rudd's criticism of social reconstructionism continued into the late 1950s. In 1957, he published *Bending the Twig: The Revolution in Education and Its Effect on Our Children.* The original progressivism of John Dewey, Rudd argued, was primarily concerned with classroom methods and was dominated by a visionary idealism about the development of human beings. This form of progressivism Rudd labeled "soft progressivism." In the 1930s. he argued, soft progressivism was replaced by a hard form emphasizing political objectives. Rudd states, regarding hard progressivism, "Encouraged by the depression and the social and political climate of the times, this cult became more militant as its power increased. Thus it was that the educational reform movement growing out of Dewey's leadership gave birth to a political and social reform movement of even greater significance."[34]

Rudd identified George Counts and Harold Rugg as the ring leaders of hard progressivism. In Rudd's words, "Dr. George Counts...was a militant 'hard' Progressivist who demanded that teachers reach for power," and Harold Rugg was "a leading Frontier Thinker,...an ardent crusader and an expert in the techniques of indoctrination in the classrooms of the nation. Incidentally, he was an extremely successful seller of textbooks."[35] For Rudd, Columbia University's Teachers College was "the fountainhead of the movement, and the executives and authors featured in the magazine were drawn largely from the 'ivory towers' on Morningside Heights."[36]

Particularly distressing to Rudd were statements in the journal *The Social Frontier* calling for economic planning and the presenting society as a collective organization. To substantiate his argument, Rudd quoted from the lead editorial of the first issue of the journal: "For the American people the age of individualism in economy is closing and the age of collectivism is opening. Here is the central and dominating reality in the present epoch...." To Rudd and other members of patriotic organizations these words represented part of a subversive plot to undermine American capitalism. Rudd found particularly upsetting a statement in the April 1935 issue of the journal: "The end of free enterprise as a principle of economic and social organization adequate to this country is at hand."[37]

During the late 1930s and early 1940s, the attack on social reconstructionism centered on Harold Rugg's textbook series. For patriotic groups, these books represented the inroads social reconstructionism had made into the nation's public schools. For these groups, the Rugg books were proof that subversives were controlling schools and indoctrinating children.

GOOD AND EVIL IN AMERICAN TEXTBOOKS

"I am here, not thinking that I was going to be at all, but I am and I want to say just a few words," a huge middle-aged woman in the early 1940s shrieked at a public hearing about Harold Rugg's social studies textbook series. "Righteousness, good government, good homes and God—most of all, Christ—is on trial today," she continued. Even though she had not read any of the Rugg books, she knew they were bad. "You can't take the youth of our land and give them this awful stuff and have them come out safe and sound for God and Righteousness." At another meeting, according to Rugg, a youth of twenty leapt into the air waving his arms and shouting, "If you let these books go in and if what I've heard is true, it'll damn the souls of the men, women and children [in] our state."[38]

During the Depression, the controversy over the Rugg books highlighted the divisions within the educational community, and between educators and groups outside the educational establishment. At the peak of their popularity in 1938, 289,000 copies of Rugg's texts were sold.[39] Rugg estimated that during the 1930s, the books were used in over five thousand schools by several million school children.[40] The story of their demise provides insight into the role of patriotic organizations in influencing the content of instruction in public schools. After the criticisms of the series began, annual sales plummeted to 21,000 copies.[41]

The Rugg texts began as a series of pamphlets written during the 1920s as part of an effort to develop an integrated approach to the teaching of history, economics, and sociology to junior high school students. In 1920, Rugg published his own "Social-Science" pamphlets to be used on a trial basis at the Lincoln School of Teachers College, Columbia University. Between 1927 and 1931, Rugg pulled together the pamphlets into six six-hundred-page books for senior and junior high school students. Published by Ginn and Company during the years 1933–1936, the series was expanded to include grades 3 through 6.[42]

The series' premise was that children should be educated to assume intelligent control of their institutions and environment. The books did not advocate Communism or socialism, but they did argue that intelligence should be applied to planning the economy and operating public institutions. The series presented a history of the United States that depicted its transformation from an individualistic agrarian society to a collective industrial society. Rugg's message was that modern urban and industrial society required cooperative planning. In the modern world, corporations, factories, public institutions, and urban living all depended on cooperative behavior. In addition, the complexity of modern life required cooperative planning to achieve economic and social goals.

An example of Rugg's message can be found in his ninth-grade textbook text entitled *Citizenship and Civic Affairs*. The last chapter of the book, "The American Spirit," reviews America's transition from a simple agrarian to a complex urban-industrial society. Rugg argued that the transition required "more and more emphasis on 'social cooperation'." Modern problems, he wrote, now extend into all families and touch all people. "There is a word to describe these problems that touch the public as a whole," Rugg states in his textbook. "They are called 'social' problems. So we can say, too, that in trying to solve them by the joint efforts of all, 'social' co-operation was being used." Following this is a section entitled "So the Americans came to say 'We' more and 'I' somewhat less," which describes how America's many social problems can only be solved by communities' taking action as a whole. The section ends with a statement showing the balance in modern society between individualism and cooperation: "In many ways the individual man and woman were left free to work out their own lives, but in certain others they had to do as the community, the state, and the nation as a whole decided. Thus increasingly the Americans came to say 'We' more and 'I' somewhat less."[43]

It was exactly this emphasis on cooperative social and economic planning the caused the wrath of patriotic organizations and individuals. The first major attacks against the Rugg textbooks came from the Hearst newspapers and B.C. Forbes, financial writer and founder of *Forbes Magazine*. Forbes conducted his campaign at both the national and local level. As a member of the school board of Englewood, New Jersey, Forbes tried unsuccessfully to have the books removed from the community's schools. At the national level, Forbes wrote critical articles for *Forbes Magazine* and for the Hearst newspapers. His opening salvo in *Forbes Magazine* came in an August 1939 article that called Rugg's books, "viciously un-American.... [Rugg] distorts facts to convince the oncoming generation that America's private-enterprise system is wholly inferior and nefarious." In words that must have made the textbook industry shudder, Forbes wrote, "I plan to insist that this anti-American educator's textbooks be cast out.... I would not want my own children contaminated by conversion to Communism."[44] In his column for the Hearst newspaper chain in 1940, Forbes asked the question every week: "Are too many educators poisoning the minds of the young generation with prejudiced, distorted, unfair teachings regarding the American system of economy and dazzling them with overly-rosy [sic] pictures of conditions in totalitarian countries?"[45]

The Advertising Federation of America joined the battle in early 1940 with a pamphlet entitled, "Facts You Should Know About Anti-Advertising Propaganda in School Textbooks." The pamphlet was specifically directed at the Rugg books that contained lessons about why consumers should look out for false advertising claims. As an example of what the Federation believed was an attempt to turn students against advertising, the pamphlet cited the opening section of a chapter on advertising in one of Rugg's books which begins,

Two men were discussing the merits of a nationally advertised brand of oil.
"I know it must be good," said one. "A million dollars' worth of it is sold each year. You see advertisements of that oil everywhere."
The other shook his head. "I don't care how much of it is sold," he said. "I left a drop of it on a copper plate overnight and the drop turned green. It is corrosive and I don't dare to use it on my machine."

The pamphlet issued by the Advertising Federation objected to this anecdote because it was hypothetical and bred distrust of widely advertised products among students.[46]

In April 1940, the President of the Advertising Federation issued a letter to large advertisers that opened: "Advertised products are untrustworthy! That is the lesson taught to the children in 4,200 school systems by a social science textbook of Professor Harold Rugg of Teachers College, Columbia University."[47]

The American Legion quickly joined the battle in September 1940 with an article, later distributed as a pamphlet, in the *American Legion Magazine* by O.K. Armstrong entitled, "Treason in the Textbooks." The cartoon for the article depicts Rugg as a devil putting colored glasses over children's eyes. The caption on the picture states, "The 'Frontier Thinkers' are trying to sell our youth the idea that the American way of life has failed." The Legion article and pamphlet also listed several other books and *Scholastic Magazine* as being subversive.[48]

As already pointed out, Rudd placed Harold Rugg and his textbook series at the center of an attempt to overthrow American institutions. Rudd wrote, "He [Rugg] was one of the principal architects of the ideological structure known as the 'new social order'." From his faculty position at Columbia University Teachers College, Rudd stated, "His propaganda and doctrines were spread throughout the United States. He also exercised a strong influence...through his Teachers Guides, which interpreted his economic, political and social philosophies to thousands of classroom teachers using his social science courses."[49]

The combined attack of the Hearst newspapers, *Forbes Magazine,* the Advertising Federation, and patriotic organizations resulted in dramatic actions by local school boards. In September 1940, *Time Magazine* reported that the members of the Binghamton, New York, school board had called for public burning of Rugg's textbooks. In the words of the *Time* article, "But last fortnight Rugg book burnings began to blaze afresh in the small-town, American Legion belt. In rapid succession the school boards of Mountain Lakes and Wayne Township, N.J., banished Rugg texts that had been used by their pupils nearly ten years. Explained Wayne Township's Board Member Ronald Gall: "In my opinion, the books are un-American but not anti-American...."[50]

Particularly dramatic were the events in Bradner, Ohio where the community divided over the issue of "teaching Communism" in the schools. According to a Cleveland newspaper account of the events, "The rural Red hunt...has resulted in: explosion of a dynamite charge and the burning of a fiery cross in front of the home of...[the] school board president." The explosions and cross burning were accompanied by the spectacle of school board members shoving books into the school furnace.[51]

Rugg's publishers, Ginn and Company, did not take lightly this attack against a highly profitable series of books. They financed Rugg to travel to communities where the series was under attack. But, as Rugg reported, most of these visits proved unsuccessful. From his perspective, communities were whipped up to such a level of hysteria that little could be done to stop school systems from rejecting the books. When Rugg appeared in Philadelphia at a public hearing, a participant pointing his finger at Rugg exclaimed, "There sits the ringmaster of the fifth columnists in America financed by the Russian government. I want you people to look at him."[52]

According to Rugg's description, a typical pattern at the public hearings he attended around the country was for a representative of a patriotic organization, usually the American Legion or Daughters of the American Revolution, to charge that Rugg's books were poisoning children's minds with pro-Communist propaganda. Typically at these hearings, someone would wave a copy of Elizabeth Dilling's *The Red Network* as proof of Rugg's Communist leanings. Dilling's book contained nine lines referring to a five-page speech Rugg gave in 1933 on world youth movements in which he made a favorable reference to the Communist Youth Association. After responding to this charge, Rugg claimed, he would then be charged with writing for the Communist newspaper, *The*

Daily Worker. Rugg responded, "I have never written one line for *The Daily Worker* in my life or authorized anyone else to do so in my name."[53]

A frustrating part of the public meetings for Rugg was the open admission by many of his critics that they had never read any of his books. Person after person at these hearings, Rugg wrote, would begin their statements with the phrase: "I haven't read the books, but..." The phrase would be followed with comments such as, "He's from Columbia, and that's enough"; "I have heard of the author, and no good about him"; and "my brother says the schools and colleges are filled with Communists."[54]

The demise of the Rugg books sent a warning to textbook publishers that right-wing organizations would respond vehemently to the publication of any public school textbook critical of the United States or suggesting the importance of collective planning. But many students, particularly those of junior high school age in the 1930s, did encounter one of the few sets of textbooks in the history of American schools to present a critical view of American institutions and to suggest alternatives to the free enterprise system. Unlike textbooks of the 1920s and postwar years, the Rugg books were specifically designed to educate critical and active citizens. After the experience of Ginn and Company, other publishers were wary of textbooks that might bring down the wrath of the political right. This lesson was reinforced during the Red Scare after World War II.[55]

CONCLUSION

As America entered World War II, movies, radio, textbooks, and the public schools were presenting a similar image of a morally and politically divided world. The purging of the Rugg textbooks represented the triumph of patriotic over progressive forces in the control of knowledge disseminated to the American people. The movies showed a world divided between the forces of good and of evil, with good always triumphing in the end. In movies, government was presented as benign and without criticism. From radio, children were receiving an image of a world protected by superheroes who always triumphed over injustice and immorality. At school, children were learning that the world was divided between democracy and totalitarianism, and, of course, democracy was good and totalitarianism was evil.

Obviously, these images justified America's entry into World War II and prepared the population to believe in the ultimate triumph of the forces of democracy over those of totalitarianism. These images also set the stage for Americans to carry the fight against totalitarianism into the post-World War II era. The Cold War against the Soviet Union was justified as a war against the forces of evil, immorality, and injustice by the images created by movies, radio, and the public schools.

These simplistic images allowed people to live with contradictions. In a neatly divided world, one did not worry that some nations in the democratic camp might be oppressive and disregard the political and economic rights of their citizens. According to these images, if governments were on the side of the United States in the Cold War, then they had to be good. And, of course, the reverse was true. All countries associated with the Soviet Union were evil, unjust, and immoral. And, of course, these images covered most aspects of a society. Everything about the enemy was evil and sinister.

In this particular world of images, the United States was the super hero fighting a war for good and justice. The United States was the cowboy in the white hat on the movie screen, the Superman and Captain Marvel on radio and in comics, and the leader of the forces of democracy portrayed in public schools.

These images of the world were not accidental. They were the product of a combination of economic and political influences. The movie and broadcasting industries imposed censorship to protect their economic control of the market and, in the case of radio, to avoid offending advertisers. In addition, both industries felt pressure from a variety of interest groups. The public schools and the textbook industry also felt pressure from outside groups. The climate created by the Depression did allow ideas to creep into the schools that might raise questions about American institutions and government, but these were quickly snuffed out by the reaction of the political right. In addition, schools had their own economic needs and were controlled by legislation. All of these forces came together by the beginning of World War II to create a situation where the schools, radio, and movies were disseminating similar messages to the American population.

CHAPTER NINE

A WORLD DIVIDED

ELMER DAVIS, DIRECTOR of the Office of War Information (OWI), wrote in 1943, "The easiest way to inject a propaganda idea into most people's minds is to let it go in through the medium of an entertainment picture when they do not realize that they are being propagandized."[1] In the same year, a *Collier's* article defended the idea of Hollywood actors and other motion picture personnel being exempted from military service. "The movies," the article states, "are one of our lines of defense. It is as stupid to throw away a Mickey Rooney or a Henry Fonda as it would be to draft an airplane designer to make him a grease monkey."[2]

Also in 1943, Price Gilbert, a former advertising manager for Coca-Cola, created as a joke, after the OWI was taken over by representatives of the advertising world, a poster of a Coca-Cola bottle wrapped in an American flag. Below this symbol of Americanism was inscribed, "Step right up and get your four delicious freedoms. It's a refreshing war."[3]

During World War II, most combatants believed the war required management of ideas as well as armies. Not wanting to take second place to radio and movies in this aspect of the war effort, John Studebaker, U. S. Commissioner of Education, reported to the 1943 annual meeting of the NEA that since 1940 public schools and colleges had trained over six million workers for war industries and provided a clear notion of the war's goals through education "in the thousands of schoolrooms serving the millions all over this land—in the daily 'Pledge of Allegiance' to the flag, in history classes, in reading and literature classes, in student councils, and on the playgrounds and athletic fields of a quarter of a million schools."[4]

There was acceptance by members of the OWI that ideological management involved not only the dissemination of information, but also the planting of messages in movie and radio entertainment. Similar to the industry control over the content of radio and movies in the 1930s, the federal government treated entertainment as a form of public education. At least in the minds of the OWI, this could be conducted in a subtle manner. Movie scenes of crowds with men and women in uniforms, teenagers aiding in war activity, and displays of war posters could be used to depict a nation united around the war effort. But concerned about

137

entertainment and profits, Hollywood did not limit itself just to subtle forms of propaganda but openly engaged in a campaign to build hatred of the enemy.

Developments in the 1930s also served as a prelude to the events of the 1940s. The moral struggle between good and evil portrayed on the movie screens of the 1930s was easily translated into a war message. World War II could be portrayed as a battle between the forces of darkness and light. The superheroes of the radio serials could now don uniforms to fight the Axis powers. And public schools could define democracy in the context of a world struggle between democratic and totalitarian forces.

Of course, resistance developed to this campaign of ideological management. Members of the OWI and some journalists complained about the simplistic war messages being transmitted to the public by movies and radio. Some members of the OWI argued that the United States should be engaged in a campaign of truth and not propaganda. Of course, any management of information makes it difficult to maintain a sharp distinction between the two. And, of course, social reconstructionists such as, Harold Rugg, continued to campaign for progressive ideas in the classroom.

During World War II there were important developments in the flow of ideas in American society. Of great importance was the development of radio as the major source of news for the American public. The various economic and political forces affecting radio influenced the content and form of news received by the public. The war also sharpened the image of good and evil struggling for world domination. This image easily carried over into the postwar period when Communism became again the sole symbol of world evil for most Americans. The war also reaffirmed and strengthened the relationship between business and the public schools. From World War II to the end of the 1990s, the curriculum and content of instruction in schools would be strongly influenced by the needs of business.

World War II profoundly impacted the images of women and African-Americans disseminated to the public. Suddenly, married women and African-Americans were needed in the labor market. There was an attempt to reverse the belief that working mothers would cause the downfall of morality and civilization. Against a background of racial tensions, there were attempts to alter images of African-Americans.

This chapter will discuss the continued dissemination of images of a world divided between the forces of good and evil. It concludes by considering the impact of war mobilization, working mothers, and African-Americans on ideas disseminated to the public.

OBJECTIVE NEWS AND PROPAGANDA

Radio and public schools faced similar problems in discussing civic affairs and world events. Both institutions feared stirring the pot of controversy.

Broadcasters worried about complaints from government officials and advertisers, while school officials felt pressure from local American Legion posts and other community groups. Certainly, the story of Harold Rugg's textbooks, discussed in the previous chapter, sent a chill through the publishing industry. For broadcasters, textbook publishers, and school people, controversy meant headaches, loss of financial support, and possible loss of jobs.

But how could one present the news of the day without offending some group in society? This question became extremely important in the 1940s when, according to radio historian David Culbert, radio replaced newspapers as the major source of news in the United States.[5] It is very difficult to present news free from some form of political bias. First, there is the decision about what to report. Given a limited amount of time for a news broadcast there has to be some form of selection. Consider economic news: One person may give first consideration to news of strikes and welfare conditions, while another may select reports on stock market activities and business investments. In addition to topic selection, there is the problem of content and interpretation. Obviously, a conservative is going to have a different idea about the important, newsworthy circumstances surrounding a war or a strike than a radical. In other words, it is very difficult, if not impossible, to abstract news from a political context.

To overcome this problem, news broadcasters in the 1940s tried to project an image that they were presenting news in an objective and politically neutral manner. While it was impossible for radio broadcasters to achieve political neutrality and objectivity, they attempted to convince listeners that the news they were hearing was free of bias.

The creation of the myth of objective and neutral news encountered resistance. In 1942, pioneer radio news broadcaster H.V. Kaltenborn organized the Association of Radio News Analysts for the purpose of protecting the right of radio news commentators to express their opinions regarding controversial material. At issue was the right of owners of the broadcast industry to censor news. It was on this issue that the Association and the industry parted company. Paul White, director of news broadcasting for CBS, stated in rejecting the organizations' position: "Just as I believe that no news reporter should go on the air until his script has gone over the copy desk to be checked for errors of fact, grammar, and news judgment, so do I feel that no news analyst should broadcast without editorial supervision of his script."[6]

White claimed he was exercising censorship for the purpose of making news objective and neutral. He stated that the function of the news analyst was "to marshal the facts on any specific subject and out of his common or special knowledge to present those facts so as to inform his listeners rather than to persuade them." White argued, "Ideally, in the case of controversial issues, the audience should be *left with no impression* [emphasis supplied] as to which side the analyst himself actually favors."[7]

On the other hand, the right of sponsors and owners to determine news broadcasters' political statements was objected to by government officials. The New Deal Chairman of the Federal Communications Commission (FCC), James Fly, complained in 1943, " I heard a so-called news program last night. Through the months it has been tending more and more to get away from the news of the day to the philosophies of the particular sponsor." Fly believed the problem went beyond explicit statements by the news broadcaster. He stated, "Things like that [giving the sponsor's philosophy] are done in a somewhat subtle if not over-subtle manner. Only by careful listening do you discover that he is not giving you news or comment on the world news, but is peddling ideas to you from company headquarters."[8]

The code of the trade association of the radio industry, the National Association of Broadcasters (NAB), attempted to appease liberals', such as Fly, fears of subtle indoctrination by advocating neutrality in news broadcasts:

> News shall not be selected for the purpose of furthering or hindering either side of any controversial public issue nor shall it be colored by the opinions or desires of the station or the network management, the editor or others engaged in its preparation, or the person actually delivering it over the air, or, in the case of sponsored news broadcasts, the advertiser.... News commentators as well as other newscasters shall be governed by those provisions.[9]

Justifying their actions by referring to the NAB code, news directors in the 1940s freely censored news items. In 1943, *Newsweek* listed a whole series of incidents of censorship by news directors at NBC, ranging from comments on actions by U.S. Senators to the refusal of American seaman to unload cargo. When famed news commentator Walter Winchell had material regarding a member of the House of Representatives and the press chief for the Democratic party censored by NBC, he commented, "My fangs have been removed and my typewriter fingers rapped with the butt of a gun."[10]

The FCC also pressured news broadcasters to appear "objective." The demands for objectivity were a product of President Roosevelt's objections to news broadcasts attacking his administration. Throughout the 1930s, radio broadcasts were the center of political controversy. Particularly galling to Roosevelt was radio commentator Boake Carter's open advocacy of an isolationist foreign policy.[11] In the 1936 presidential campaign, Roosevelt was also disturbed when 95 percent of American newspapers, many of which owned radio stations, opposed his election. In order to sever the ties between newspapers and radio stations and to control criticism of his foreign policy, Roosevelt in 1939 appointed Fly as Chairman of the FCC. One commentator referred to Fly as the "cockiest Fourth New Deal wight who ever figuratively and gleefully cut a Tory's throat or scuttled an economic royalist's ship."[12]

In 1941, under Fly's leadership, the FCC issued the Mayflower Doctrine requiring objectivity in radio newscasts. The doctrine resulted from a case involving the application by the Mayflower Broadcasting Company to operate over a frequency used by one of two stations owned by John Sheppard III, his Yankee Network. Sheppard was sponsoring the broadcasts of the right-wing news commentator, Father Coughlin, who consistently attacked Roosevelt as "Franklin Doublecrossing Roosevelt." While denying the license to Mayflower Broadcasting, the FCC criticized Sheppard's activities as a "serious misconception of...duties and functions under the law."[13]

In its decision in Sheppard's favor, the FCC nevertheless criticized the Yankee Network for broadcasting editorial support for political candidates and the presentation of a political point of view. The decision states, "No pretense was made at objective, impartial reporting. It is clear—indeed the station seems to have taken pride in the fact—that the purpose of these editorials was to win public support for some person or view favored by those in control of the station." Without any discussion of the difficulty, if not impossibility, of objective news reporting, the decision declares, "Radio can serve as an instrument of democracy only when devoted to the communication of information and the exchange of ideas fairly and objectively presented."[14]

There is some evidence that radio might have been effective in conveying an image of neutrality and fairness. During the war, Paul Lazarsfeld conducted a survey of public attitudes regarding radio. His survey found that in picking the fairest medium for the presentation of news the public gave radio a high vote of confidence (81%) as compared to magazines (45%) and newspapers (39%). In comparing radio to other American institutions regarding the quality of performance, he found the public putting radio at the top of the list, followed in order by churches, newspapers, schools, and local government.[15]

The Office of War Information (OWI) also tried to project an image of neutrality. The initial claim of neutrality and objectivity was made by poet Archibald MacLeish, who was appointed in 1941 by President Roosevelt to head the Office of Facts and Figures in the Office of Civilian Defense. In 1942, MacLeish was made co-director of the newly created OWI.[16]

Archibald MacLeish encountered the same difficulty in distinguishing the management of information in a democratic society from propaganda in a totalitarian society as broadcasters had in claiming to be objective and neutral as opposed to biased and political. His ideas mirrored the instruction the public schools' on propaganda, discussed in the previous chapter.

MacLeish called America's information war a "strategy of truth." The "strategy of truth," MacLeish argued, recognized the important role of government in disseminating information about the war to the general population. The thing that distinguished this activity by the United States government from the propaganda activities of totalitarian governments, according to MacLeish, was that totalitarian countries falsified information to serve their policy objectives.

MacLeish expanded on this argument in an address to the annual luncheon of the Associated Press in 1942. He told the journalists and news executives that the American population understands direct physical attack but is not prepared for the type of psychological warfare being mounted by the enemy. Calling the cooperation of the government with the radio and the press the front line of defense against enemy propaganda, MacLeish outlined the "strategy of truth" as "appropriate to our cause and our purpose...which opposes to the frauds and the deceits by which our enemies have confused and conquered other peoples the simple and clarifying truths by which a nation such as ours must guide itself." For instance, to combat the Nazi peace offensive, MacLeish argued, the American people must be shown the "truth" that for the Nazi "the end is never peace but always conquest—and that the inevitable consequence to the Nazi victim is defeat."[17]

Obviously, the problematic part of MacLeish's argument was the concept of truth. Whether or not an enemy's actions were for peace or conquest was open to interpretation, depending on the perspective of the person viewing the events of the war. In this case, truth is relative to the beliefs of the speaker. But as MacLeish presented the issue, and as it was presented in public schools, a person could find truth in the news distributed by a free press and in the information disseminated by a democratic government. Democracies spread truth, the argument suggested, and totalitarian governments spread propaganda.

The flaw in this argument is exemplified in his reasoning that the necessity of total victory was the "truth" about the events of World War II. MacLeish told the audience at the Associated Press luncheon,

> The strategy of truth, in other words, has for the object of its strategy a truthful understanding by the people of the meaning of the war in which they fight. Specifically, the strategy of truth has for object an understanding by the free peoples of the world that this war is a war in which no outcome but their victory can be conceivable.... That is one fact which the free peoples of the world must understand—the fact that this war is the last war those who love their freedom will ever have the chance to fight for freedom—if they lose.[18]

MacLeish's speech contained some obvious problems regarding the concept of a campaign to spread truth. Is it truth or even a "fact" that this would be last war for freedom if the Axis countries won? Obviously, this was a statement designed to rally people around the flag—an exhortation to win the war. While MacLeish might have viewed the statement as truth, others might doubt the assertion.

One thing that MacLeish's rhetoric could accomplish was to create the impression that information from the U.S. government was true. The actual relativity of the truth dispensed by the OWI was exemplified by the actions of the director, Elmer Davis, a veteran newspaperman and radio newscaster. Davis worked within the guidelines of the Executive Order establishing the OWI, which stated that the organization was

> to coordinate the dissemination of war information by all federal agencies and to formulate and carry out, by means of the press, radio and motion pictures, programs to facilitate an understanding in the United States and abroad of the progress of the war effort and of the policies, activities, and aims of the government.[19]

To accomplish this purpose, Davis assigned specific individuals to control the flow of information to the press, radio, and motion pictures. In addition, the OWI monitored and directly influenced these media to assure that their actions conformed to the war program of the federal government. Obviously, since they lived with persistent fear of government intervention, the broadcasting and movie industries were very willing to cooperate with the OWI.

In a manner similar to the radio industry and public schools, Davis claimed to be objective. In a letter to Milton Eisenhower, the younger brother of General Dwight D. Eisenhower, Davis wrote, "We must maintain our policy of objectivity.... O.W.I....should continue to be thought of primarily as an information agency." Yet the lack of objectivity and the political requirements of managing information were made evident in a dispute Davis had with Secretary of the Interior Harold Ickes.

Davis objected to an article by Ickes in a 1943 issue of *Collier's* that criticized a strike by the United Mine Workers as inflationary, blaming the strike on the War Labor Board. Ickes referred to the strike, over the protests of Davis, as "a black—and stupid—chapter in the history of the home front." Davis complained to the White House that "some of the statements are at variance with the Government's policy in the coal matter."[20] In this situation it would be difficult to define "truth" in a labor dispute and difficult to be "objective" when information has to conform to government policies.

The "strategy of truth" also ran into difficulty when reporting international affairs. For instance, China faced the problem of an invasion by the Japanese and a civil war between the Kuomintang and the Communists. President Roosevelt gave his support to the Kuomintang. On the other hand, reports of representatives of the OWI contained favorable impressions of the Communists. Yet because of official U.S. government policy, the OWI steered clear of issuing any statements that might weaken support of the Kuomintang. The OWI also avoided any statements critical of Great Britain's colonial empire. In 1942, the OWI agreed to maintain a common front with British policies regarding India.[21]

Nothing more clearly demonstrates the political quality of information than the Republican attack on the OWI. In February 1943, Republican Senator Rufus Holman of Oregon attacked films and magazine articles produced by the OWI as "personal, political propaganda" for President Roosevelt's campaign for a fourth term. Representative John Ditter of Pennsylvania attacked the OWI staff as " thousands of starry-eyed zealots out to sell their particular pot of gold to a bewildered people."[22]

The concepts of truth and objectivity were another way of dividing the world. Democratic governments were portrayed as disseminators of information that was truthful and objective, while totalitarian governments were pictured as distributing falsehoods and propaganda. As discussed in the previous chapter, this image fit the image of a divided world being taught in the public schools in the late 1930s. During World War II, public schools, radio, and movies sharpened the image of a world divided between the forces of good and evil.

A WORLD DIVIDED

In any war, the enemy is portrayed as a diabolic villain that must be vanquished. While schools and radio played an important role in stirring up hatred of the enemy, it was the movies that contributed most to creating this image. Clayton Koppes and Gregory Black conclude, in *Hollywood Goes To War,* that wartime movies created the myth of "the division of the world into slave and free. They divided a world of total peril into forces of either ultimate evil or righteousness."[23]

During World War II, radio and movies provided the opportunity to bombard the population with multiple images of evil. Many of the images of the Japanese were explicitly racist. Liberals and even the staff of the OWI objected to the stereotypes being used by the media. But given the nature of the entertainment industry, radio and movie producers preferred stereotypes over subtle portrayals. Without doubt, this wartime imagery contributed to the style of anti-Communist purges that occurred after the war.

The public schools continued their prewar emphasis on the differences between democracy and totalitarianism. This instruction was often swept up in wartime rhetoric, as exemplified by the declaration of the Chancellor of the Oregon State System of Education, Frederick Hunter, to the 1942 NEA convention that, "a special wartime assignment for the schools is to undertake the all-out project of diverting the critical attitude of mind from the weaknesses and failures of our democracy to the threats to it from these subversive, fifth column assaults," the Nazi and Japanese attempts to control American opinion. Hunter gave this picture of a divided world: "It is now, and for years it will continue to be, a major responsibility of the schools to emphasize the great basic difference between free and slave-driven peoples."[24]

Early in the war, the Office of Education began to deluge the schools with pamphlets, radio scripts, and recordings. Popular radio scripts and recordings were "Democracy in Action," "I'm an American," "Freedom on the March," "Patriotic Pages in American History," and "Let Freedom Ring." Pamphlets ranged from information on national defense to "Our Democratic Heritage."[25] As U.S. Commissioner of Education Studebaker noted in 1942, schools were giving "increased emphasis to courses which help youth to understand and to appreciate our democratic heritage."[26]

Educators were quick to argue that the conflict was a war of ideas for the control of minds. It was on this basis that they demanded a role in any peace conference. The Chairman of the NEA War and Peace fund, George Strayer, argued in 1943, "that when the war ends those responsible for...the peace conference [should] be brought to realize that the shaping of the minds of men is no less important than the determination of the political and economic and military controls."[27] That same year, the report of the Educational Policies Commission called for the use of education in the reconstruction of the world. The report warned of the "degradation and the prostitution of a whole generation of youth" by the educational systems of Germany and Japan. The influence of these educational systems must be "counteracted by an equally potent influence over the minds and spirits of the youth of democracies." Within this framework, the war was being fought between educational systems competing for the domination of the minds of youth.[28]

In the battle to control minds, the meaning of democracy disseminated by the schools during World War II focused on the all-encompassing phrase, "the democratic way of life." In 1943, the National Seminar on Practicing Democracy in Our Schools defined democracy as "a way of life, a system of values which extends to every aspect of life." The treatment of democracy as a way of life was reflected by actual practice in public schools.

In 1944, Grace Storm reported her findings on the teaching of citizenship in public schools between 1941 and 1943. She examined new and supplementary courses of study for social studies used by twenty-one city and state school systems. Nineteen of these school systems emphasized the development of good citizenship through the teaching of democracy as a way of life. As one bulletin stated, "To make democracy a living force in the lives of children requires that the principles of democracy be translated into practical everyday experiences of both thinking and acting."[29]

The teaching of democracy as a way of life was backed by a strong dose of patriotism. In Storm's words, "The past few years have seen, in connection with the building of loyalty and patriotism, a growing interest in the role of the emotions and the imagination." Schools were capturing and directing children's emotions and imagination through patriotic songs and dramatization, the memorizing of patriotic poems, and the celebration of national holidays and flag ceremonies. In addition, schools were stressing the importance of good relationships between nations.[30]

Radio was another vehicle for portraying a divided world. Working quickly, the broadcasting industry introduced war themes into programs. In the episode following the bombing of Pearl Harbor, Jack Armstrong was immediately transferred from an adventure in the Philippines to another location to fight the Axis enemy. The program's announcer advised listeners that it was treasonous not to keep in shape by eating Wheaties for breakfast. Some radio portrayals of the enemies were literally larger than life-size. The cowboy hero Tom Mix chased a giant through the West only to discover it was a huge balloon manipulated by Japanese agents. War themes entered soap operas, and deaths caused by military action appeared in half-a-dozen programs in 1942.[31]

The OWI worked with radio scriptwriters. On "Front Page Farrell," the star reporter covered war stories selected by the staff of OWI.[32] The federal agency had messages appear on the "Lone Ranger" and "Terry and the Pirates." On the "Victory Parade" 1942, comedian Jack Benny included the OWI message in his jokes. In one of many routines, Benny's friend Mary Livingston related how her uncle lost thirty pounds. In reply to Benny's quip that the uncle must have a lot of willpower, Mary delivered the punch line: "No, my aunt gave his teeth to the Rubber-drive." A routine was developed for the "Fibber McGee and Molly" show, in which the couple received a government circular asking for workers for war industries. After passing jokes back and forth, Fibber declares the importance of finding skilled workers, to which Molly replies, "DON'T FORGET...IT'S YOUR SONS OF TOIL THAT'LL HELP PUT THOSE NAZIS UNDER TONS OF SOIL!"[33]

The OWI even got into the business of publishing comic books after two psychologists reported that while most comic heroes were engaged in some form of war activity, the comics only poked fun at efforts on the home front. The report stated, "The effect of the war on the civilian is only subject of humor. The home front's actions and thoughts, and the demands on the civilian, have yet to receive serious and sympathetic treatment." The OWI's efforts at producing comic books was shortlived after it made the mistake of publishing "The Life of Franklin D. Roosevelt," which was quickly condemned by a Republican congressman as political propaganda and ridiculed as a poor imitation of "Tarzan of the Apes."[34]

Pressures on Hollywood to produce movies that would aid in the war effort came from a variety of often conflicting sources. The OWI felt particularly concerned that Hollywood put the right messages into movies. But the liberal concerns of the OWI were often in conflict with the conservative attitudes and profit motives of Hollywood. For instance, in movies dealing with the Japanese, the OWI was concerned that movies emphasize the fascist qualities of the Japanese government and avoid racist overtones. The first major confrontation between Hollywood executives and OWI's Bureau of Motion Pictures was over the 1942 film, *Little Tokyo.*

The film created the image of all Japanese-Americans participating in a plot with the Japanese government to defeat the United States. From the perspective of Hollywood producers, the movie followed in the tradition of such earlier films as *Menace of the Rising Sun, Secret Agent of Japan,* and *A Prisoner of Japan.* All three of these films were overtly racist. According to Koppes and Black, the ads for *Menace of the Rising Sun* depicted "A huge Japanese figure, blood dripping from its buck-tooth fangs [rising] from the sea." Lines in the ads referred to "Japan's Double Decade of Double Dealing," and claimed "Japs repaid kindness with ruthless murder."[35]

The OWI complained that *Little Tokyo* preached hatred against all Japanese-Americans and would open a floodgate of racial prejudice. The film, according to OWI reviewers, seemed to forget that the United States was fighting for protection of the Bill of Rights. Ironically, Hollywood executives could point to the actions of the federal government in the placement of Japanese-Americans in internment camps as proof that film was in line with official government policies.[36]

An outgrowth of this confrontation was the decision by OWI to review film scripts prior to production. This meant films were censored before production not only by the industry's Production Code Administration but also by the OWI. When the domestic branch of the OWI was shut down in 1943, the international branch took over, since most Hollywood films were exported. Movies were part of America's overseas propaganda campaign to sell America to the rest of the world. Other hands were also at work shaping the content of Hollywood movies. The Office of Censorship of the federal government exercised control over international mail, the import and export of movies, as well as other printed material.

While Hollywood executives had resisted pressures from the liberal-minded domestic branch of the OWI while it existed, they willingly tried to please these government agencies. Foreign exports were an important source of profits, and therefore attention was paid to directives and proposals by the international branch of the OWI and the Office of Censorship. Many Hollywood films required the cooperation of the armed forces. Even before the war, Hollywood producers would regularly send scripts involving the military to the Army and Navy Departments for approval.[37] War movies often depended on the loan of military equipment and personnel from the different services. Therefore, producers were anxious to comply with requests and requirements from the armed forces for changes in scripts.

In *Hollywood Goes To War,* Koppes and Black provide a wealth of examples of the impact of these various political forces on the content of wartime movies. For its treatment of the home front, Koppes and Black single out the 1943 film *Since You Went Away* as a model of the type of messages the OWI wanted conveyed to the public. The agency worked closely with the producers to create an idealized depiction of American life for both domestic and foreign audiences.

Since You Went Away is filled with messages on the meaning of democracy and the importance of national unity. It begins with the caption, "This is a story of the Unconquerable Fortress: the American Home...1943." The opening scene shows the wife, Anne, returning home after bidding good-bye to her warbound husband. The viewers' attention is then focused on incidents that show the importance of sacrifice for the war effort. An affluent woman says that she can't tell the difference between butter and margarine, and a sailor uses five months' salary to buy war bonds. The delay of a passenger train becomes an opportunity for a conductor to comment on the importance of keeping supply trains moving for the war. These are only a few examples of messages interjected into the drama. Eventually, Anne goes to work as a welder and her daughter joins the Red Cross. Through the various adventures and romances in the movie there is conveyed a message of personal sacrifice and the importance of breaking down social class barriers for the war effort. When Anne takes a step down the social ladder to work as a welder she makes friends with a Czechoslovak woman. Anne comments that the woman's name was "like nothing we ever heard at the country club." The immigrant tells Anne about her trip to the Statue of Liberty, she tells Anne, "You are what I thought America was." The movie ends with the husband returning to his idyllic Midwestern home with a final caption, "Be of good courage, and He shall strengthen your heart, all ye that hope in the Lord."[38] In their conclusion about movies that depicted the home front during World War II, Koppes and Black argue that Hollywood and the OWI teamed up to create an image of "an America of infinite promise, in which the sacrifices of today bought security and prosperity for tomorrow."[39]

In summary, movies, shaped by different political pressures, showed a world divided between the forces of freedom and of slavery, and a unified domestic world where class barriers were being erased and social problems were easily solved. As part of its effort, the OWI wanted movies among other things to help solve the labor shortage by reducing prejudice against such minorities as African-Americans and against working women, discussed in the next section. These were all a product of the government's conscious attempt to use entertainment as a means of propaganda.

EDUCATION AND BUSINESS JOIN HANDS

For public schools, solution of economic problems became a primary educational objective. This set the pattern for educational developments after the war. It meant that the curriculum and content of instruction would be judged, in part, by their contribution to economic efficiency. The school served the war effort by training for industry and teaching about a world divided between democracy and totalitarianism.

Mobilization also had important consequences for public schools' images of the American family. Mobilization forced schools to adopt new attitudes toward women and the family. The need for female war workers required a sudden change in the traditional message that married women should stay at home. In addition, working mothers created a demand for day care centers. And, ironically, juvenile delinquency, the very problem that educators of the 1920s argued would result if mothers worked, did indeed increase during the war. After the war, a continuing concern about the rise in juvenile delinquency would contribute to efforts to censor comic books.

The labor needs of the war healed the breach between the educational establishment and the business community. Still feeling the financial effects of the Depression, public school officials welcomed the opportunity to cooperate with business. In contrast to the 1930s, when many business leaders complained that schools caused high taxes, business leaders during World War II supported public schools because they trained workers for war industries. After the war, many in business would continue to consider the primary objective of education to be the education of workers to serve business needs.

The rapprochement between the schools and business was heralded in the March 1941 issue of the *Nation's Business* by the Secretary of the NEA's Educational Policies Commission, William Carr. The lead for Carr's article noted, "The U.S. Chamber [of Commerce] is urging a revival of interest in education among its members." Carr recommended that business and schools cooperate in the teaching of "Americanism." In addition, Carr wrote, business and schools could develop "economic literacy," "promote efficiency in personal economics," and "prepare youth for useful work." Economic literacy meant teaching about the economic system of the United States, while personal economics meant the education of the consumer. Carr wrote, "This training...has provided a highly literate and educated population...constituting the world's greatest consuming market. It has a key value in maintaining American standards of business and of living."

The goal of training good workers and consumers, according to Carr, should be done through cooperation between business and the public schools. He stated that over three hundred sixty local Chambers of Commerce helped local schools provide programs in citizenship, economic literacy, personal finances, and work training programs. Local Chambers were now supporting increased financing for public schools. Carr praised the work of local Chambers in planning vocational education.[40] With over eighteen hundred chapters and one million members,[41] these Chambers of Commerce had a great potential for influencing local school systems.

The U.S. Chamber of Commerce's cooperation with the public schools received an added boost in 1942 with the election of Eric Johnston as president. Johnston would later play an important role in the movie industry when he replaced Will Hays as President of the M.P.P.D.A. As head of the U. S. Chamber of Commerce, Johnston called for a new era of cooperation between business and government. As explained in more detail in the next chapter, Johnston believed this cooperation would be the source of America's economic strength in the postwar period.[42]

Declaring a "new era of understanding" between business and the schools, Walter Fuller, Chairman of the National Association of Manufacturers (NAM) Board of Directors and President of Curtis Publishing, declared at the 1942 meeting of the NEA: "Just as the first responsibility of industry today is to produce the weapons of war...so the responsibility of education is to make available an increasing manpower, especially to meet the needs for skilled men and women...." This "new understanding" resulted from a series of joint conferences between the NAM and the NEA.[43]

While increased cooperation between business and public schools was occurring in local school systems and between the NAM and the NEA, the federal government also was launching a massive program to push the public schools in the direction of serving industry. In 1941, the Office of Education organized a defense vocational training program enrolling a million women and men. By 1942, the numbers had increased to three million.[44]

The U.S. Commissioner of Education hoped the close relationship established between education and employment would be carried over into peacetime. In a speech to the 1943 NEA convention, he told delegates, "Probably the most basic lesson we are learning in the schools in wartime is that boys and girls gain educationally from contact with the real world of work...." The four major contributions of the schools, according to Commissioner Studebaker, were citizenship training, vocational education, training for community service, and building national unity.[45]

The political factors shaping the content of instruction in the schools included the newly strengthened relationship between business and education, and the continued activities of patriotic groups such as the American Legion and Daughters of the American Revolution. In many local school systems, representatives of both the local Chamber of Commerce and the American Legion post participated in and monitored school activities.

Concerned about financial support for schools, national and local educational leaders paid attention to the demands of business and patriotic organizations. While the war effort increased the importance of education to business, it also increased financial hardships for the schools. Communities that sprang up around newly constructed war plants faced shortages of classrooms and teachers. Nationally, a shortage of teachers plagued the schools, and it was difficult to increase school funding because of the economic needs of the war. Consequently, the NEA, in cooperation with the American Legion, continued its campaign for federal aid for education. Throughout the war, the NEA maintained its public relations campaign to win general support for the schools.[46]

Within the context of these political pressures, the image of democracy disseminated by the schools swung sharply to the political right. The demise of the Rugg textbooks symbolized the declining influence of the progressive thinking of the 1930s. The social reconstructionist belief in cooperative economic planning was replaced with the Chamber of Commerce belief in the importance of unregulated "free enterprise."

CHANGING THE IMAGES OF AFRICAN-AMERICANS AND WOMEN

Besides bringing together business and schools, mobilization of the work force created a need to change public images of African-Americans and women. Simply stated, the labor shortage created by the war required dipping into these usually ignored sources of labor. Commissioner of Education Studebaker gave the government's position on this issue in 1941: "It seems clear that increasing employment needs will call shortly for the recruiting and training of many more women for defense jobs." To support his point, Studebaker quoted the head of Bell Aircraft to the effect that 40 percent of the work in airplane manufacturing could be successfully completed by women. Studebaker added, "Another source of manpower which must increasingly be used is the Negro worker."[47]

The OWI and other government agencies played a major role in trying to change white attitudes toward African-Americans and the attitudes of African-Americans toward the United States. Of particular concern for government officials was the apparent ambivalence of African-Americans toward the war. Officials were shocked when a 1942 survey of African-Americans in Harlem by the U. S. government Office of Facts and Figures found that 49 percent of the respondents believed that their lives would not significantly change if Japan won the war and 18 percent thought their lives would improve.[48]

In response to these findings, the OWI distributed a pamphlet, *Negroes and the War,* which stressed the stake African-Americans had in the United States' winning the war. The introductory essay by an African-American publicist, Chandler Owen, quoted Hitler's *Mein Kampf* to indicate the racism of the Nazis, and stressed the improving economic and social conditions for African-Americans in the United States. The remainder of the pamphlet used words and pictures to depict African-Americans in a variety of war work and military activities.[49]

Concerned about segregated units in the Army and the potential for racial conflict, the public relations section of the War Department decided to use radio to reduce racial prejudice. In 1942, Louis Cowan, a staff member of the public relations section and creator of several radio shows, met with Mr. and Mrs. Frank Hummert to discuss the issue of African-American soldiers.[50] In 1931, the Hummerts produced the first daytime radio soap opera, "Stolen Husband." They went on to create such major soap operas as "Our Gal Sunday," "The Romance of Helen Trent," "Backstage Wife," "Just Plain Bill," and "Ma Perkins."[51] Cowan believed that soap operas would be an ideal vehicle for reaching lower middle class whites.

The War Department became directly involved in trying to change public images of African-Americans by manipulating the content of soap operas. In 1942, the character of a young African-American in military training was introduced into "Our Gal Sunday." While his actual appearances were infrequent, he was the focus of discussion by other characters regarding the loyalty of African-Americans to the United States. On the "Romance of Helen Trent," a young African-American doctor saves the heroine after she falls into an abyss while trying to protect a truck loaded with war goods. The plot lasted several weeks with "intermittent discussion concerning 'the capabilities of the Negro, his unflagging loyalty to his country, and his patience with persecution'."[52]

Movies were the prime target for the government's attempt to improve the image of African-Americans. Since the demonstrations over *Birth of a Nation* and the creation of municipal censorship codes banning movies that might contribute to race riots, major film producers had avoided racial themes. African-Americans were primarily depicted in movies in servant or comedy roles. The liberal-minded OWI hoped that wartime would provide the opportunity for creating movies with more favorable portrayals of African-American lives.

The OWI wanted movies to build loyalty among African-Americans toward the United States, eliminate racial stereotypes, and foster a sense of racial harmony. Consequently, wartime movies avoided any suggestion of their segregation by law in Southern states and by practice in Northern states, and of segregated military units.

In its first confrontation with OWI over racial issues, the movie industry adopted a strategy of eliminating African-American parts from scripts. Ironically, one consequence was unemployment for many African-American actors. The initial conflict occurred in 1942 over a M-G-M film that praised the administration of President Andrew Johnson and attacked the character of radical Republican leader Thaddeus Stevens. The film portrayed Johnson as a President noted for his generosity toward the South and his opposition to aid to freed slaves, the right of African-Americans to vote, and his support of Black Codes. Under pressure from the OWI, M-G-M changed scenes to provide a more positive portrayal of Thaddeus Stevens, but still presented Johnson as a champion of the common person. The four African-Americans in the movie played servant roles and only four lines referred to slavery.[53]

While the OWI tried to get Hollywood producers to present a more positive view of African-Americans, the actual response, judged by later standards, was minimal. Koppes and Black write, "The easiest way for Hollywood and OWI to deal with racial problems was 'writing out'—simply eliminating a potentially troublesome character."[54] For example, when African-Americans were to appear in a Civil War movie set in Maryland, the parts were eliminated because the characters might be perceived as slaves. The staff at OWI reasoned that while slavery did exist, it was best forgotten because of its potential to create disharmony between the races. In other words, the OWI wanted positive roles for African-Americans but it also wanted to avoid controversial racial issues.

The OWI did applaud roles given to African-Americans in *Casablanca* (1943) and *The Ox-Bow Incident* (1943) because they suggested racial equality without introducing racial conflict. In *Casablanca,* an African-American played the cafe's piano player. In *The Ox-Bow Incident,* an African-American is part of a group of men who are opposed to lynching. In *Bataan* (1943), an African-American joins a group of ethnically diverse soldiers who eventually die in the face of an overwhelmingly superior Japanese force. But, as Koppes and Black argue, the character is never completely equal. He participates in discussions of strategy by making vague comments about faith in the United States and takes instruction from a white partner on setting an explosive. African-American appearances in other movies served the function of giving an appearance of racial harmony and equality without suggesting racial conflict.[55]

While national leaders worried about winning the loyalty of African-Americans, the concerns about women focused on gaining public acceptance of married women serving as war workers and on the potential dangers of that role to family life. Public schools actively recruited young girls for occupational training programs. As part of the general effort to prepare youth for war work, U. S. Commissioner of Education Studebaker reported in 1943, "Girls, too, have been given occupational information and guidance concerning the part which women can play in the war effort." Because of the teacher shortage, married women were also actively recruited into teaching.[56]

However, certain traditional images remained. For instance, in 1944 the National Education Association distributed 50,000 copies of a poster as part of its "teacher-recruiting and morale-building campaign." The poster, titled "The Teacher," depicts a female teacher with an elementary school boy and girl standing around a globe of the world. The little girl is wearing a neat dress and her hair is perfectly groomed. She is staring passively with a blank expression on her face at the globe, her empty arms dangling at her side. The teacher is seated between the two children with her head turned away from the girl and her eyes staring in approval at the boy. The boy clutches a book in one hand and with the other hand points at a place on the globe. Unlike the girl, his hair is rumpled and his face is animated. The poster clearly conveys an impression of males as active learners and intellectually superior to females, and of girls as passive and dull learners.

Yet this image was in conflict with the efforts of school officials to convince girls to enter war work. While it is difficult to determine the impact of schools on future actions, one wonders about the effect of being surrounded by images of women workers on the future lives of young girls.

The federal government engaged in an all-out attempt to attract women to wartime work. This effort changed the media image of women. The Secretary of War, Henry Stimson, issued a pamphlet with the commanding title, "You're Going to Employ Women." The pamphlet instructed businesses, "The War Department must fully utilize, immediately and effectively, the largest and potentially the finest single source of labor available today—the vast reserve of woman-power." U.S. employment offices insisted on the employment of women and the War Manpower Commission told employers to "remove all barriers to the employment of women in any occupation for which they are or can be fitted."[57]

The OWI actively engaged in a campaign to help achieve the goals of the War Manpower Commission. Portrayals of working women sprang up throughout the media. One result of the OWI's work was the rush of female characters to war work on radio soap operas. There were special week-long serials devoted to domestic war problems, which included an emphasis on female workers.[58] NBC offered the Victory Volunteers and CBS offered Victory Front. In addition, a weekly radio serial called "Commando Mary" was created to show women how to assist in the war effort.[59]

The OWI instructed Hollywood to show women taking the place of men, and sending their children to day care centers. A 1944 OWI informational manual stated that "American women are finding new expression in jobs they have assumed" and urged Hollywood to find methods for portraying these new roles on the screen.[60]

Whether or not schools, radio, and movies were responsible for changing opinions regarding working women would be difficult to determine. But a survey in 1942 did indicate a dramatic shift in attitudes. In sharp contrast to the more than 80 percent of the population opposing married women working during the Depression, only 13 percent expressed opposition in 1942. In 1942, 60 percent believed married women in fact should work.[61]

Fear that working mothers might cause the family to breakdown and increase juvenile delinquency remained a concern of some educators. In 1943, Strayer, Chair of the NEA War and Peace Committee, reported to the NEA that since the beginning of the war juvenile delinquency had increased by 40 percent. In Strayer's mind the cause of delinquency was parents who were "so fully occupied outside of the home that they find little time to provide the guidance so sorely needed by children and youth."[62]

Expressions of concern were heard from other parts of society. A 1943 pamphlet issued by the U.S. Children's Bureau entitled "Understanding Juvenile Delinquency," warned that working mothers were "a hazard to the security of the child in his family." In the same year, conservative Clare Booth Luce demanded that all mothers return to their homes.[63]

The seriousness of the problem was dramatized in a 1942 *Saturday Evening Post* article, "Eight-Hour Orphans." The article was based on research conducted by Maxine Davis, the well-known author of the book on Depression youth, *The Lost Generation*; Warner Olivier, a staff writer; and Grace Allen, a social worker. The accompanying pictures told a great deal of the story. One showed a little girl with house keys dangling from a string around her neck. The caption read: "'Door-key children,' whose parents must be away from home all day at jobs in war plants, wear their house keys on strings about their necks." A more dramatic picture showed a boy wrapped in chains with the caption reading: "In a Southern California trailer camp children were found chained to trailers while their parents worked in factories. Half a million war workers poured into the state within a few months."[64]

The researchers found some of the worst conditions in communities suddenly inundated by workers for recently built war plants. They listed many of the ways mothers coped with the problem. In one case, a mother took her baby to work with her. In another situation, a twelve-year-old was locked out of the house while her parents were at work. And children were found locked in automobiles in the parking lots of war plants.[65]

Believing that these conditions were having a negative effect on children, the authors of the article warned, "No informed American needs a psychologist to tell him that children separated from home ties and without competent care during their most impressionable age are the troublemakers, the neurotics, the spiritual and emotional cripples of a generation hence."[66]

As previously mentioned, the OWI played an important role in promoting day care centers. Also, business had a stake in day care centers because many mothers were forced to quit their jobs to take care of their children. As the title in a 1943 *Business Week* article warned, "Women Drop Out." The article lamented the serious losses in "womanpower" as women stayed home to take care of their children. It was estimated that 197 day care centers were needed to release mothers for employment.[67]

The issue of day care centers and juvenile delinquency created an ambivalent attitude toward working mothers. On the one hand, schools, radio, and movies were consciously creating positive images of working mothers and praising them for their contribution to the war effort. On the other hand, working mothers were being blamed for neglecting their children. This ambivalence was expressed by the War Manpower Commission, which, after declaring the importance of working mothers for the war effort, stated, "the first responsibility of women, in war as in peace, is to give suitable care in their homes to their children."[68]

By trying to gain public acceptance for day care centers, the OWI provided a way out of this dilemma. But in doing so, it was suggesting to the public that there could be an institutional alternative to family care of children. Therefore, the media, in trying to accomplish the goals of the OWI, projected alternatives to both the traditional role of mothers and to the organization of the family.

It would be difficult to measure the lasting impact of these wartime images of women and of African-Americans. Participation in the war effort lasted only five years. On the other hand, the manipulation of these images did occur at a time when lives were being uprooted and transformed. There is the additional problem of determining the impact on different social groups. Did African-Americans listen to soap operas like "The Romance of Helen Trent" and attend movies such as *Bataan*? The OWI's manipulated images may have reached a primarily white audience.

Of course, the actual impact could have been an unintended one. For instance, one might wonder about the projected images of loyal African-Americans living in a racially harmonious society, while in fact race riots and other racial tensions were occurring throughout the war.[69] In this context, the images appear as wishful thinking on the part of government liberals as opposed to the reality of circumstances. The tensions between reality and the projected images may have contributed to the frustration of African-Americans and increased their anger about the inequalities in American society.

On the other hand, women were presented with a set of conflicting images that might have created a sense of guilt. Women were told to be both good mothers and good Americans by contributing simultaneously to the contradictory maintenance of the home and the war industries. Consequently, working mothers became heroines of war and destroyers of family life. How much this tension and possible guilt contributed to the rush back to domesticity after the war is difficult to determine but the themes of family versus juvenile delinquency were important in the postwar period.

PROTECTING THE AMERICAN WAY OF LIFE

While the federal government assumed a major role in using schools, movies, and broadcasting to mold opinion for the war effort, various pressure groups continued their efforts to influence the dissemination of knowledge. The continued importance of these groups was reflected in comments by soap opera pioneer Irna Phillips in the closing years of the war. Among many soap opera triumphs, Irna Phillips is best remembered for her creation of "The Guiding Light" in 1937.[70] At a college conference in 1944, she listed the following groups she consulted in developing story lines:

1. American Legion
2. American Medical Association
3. Association for Family Living
4. Federal Council of Churches of Christ in America
5. National Education Association
6. Navy Department
7. Office of War Information
8. Red Cross
9. Veterans Administration
10. War Department.[71]

Her list provides an important insight into the filters affecting the content of radio broadcasting during the war. The Navy Department, the OWI, the Veterans Administration, the Red Cross, and the War Department were part of the war-related filters discussed earlier in the chapter. Consultation with the Federal Council of the Churches of Christ ensured that program material did not offend major religious groups. Logically, the National Education Association, the Association for Family Living, and the American Medical Association could be used to ensure that the program conformed to expert advice in the respective areas of education, family life, and medicine.

The major private political filter on her list was the American Legion. The war seemed to strengthen the role of the American Legion in ensuring that only ideas about "100 percent Americanism" were disseminated to the public. From this perspective, World War II set the stage for the postwar struggle by the Legion to purge schools, movies, and radio of suspected Communists and Communist ideology. During the postwar period, the American Legion would be a major leader in demonstrations against movies identified as having "subversive" actors.[72]

During the war, neverthelesss, the American Legion continued building its campaigns against subversive textbooks and its relationship with the NEA. The Legion advocated teaching in favor of continuing military buildup into the postwar period. Speaking before the NEA convention in 1943, Commander Atherton again stressed the Legion's belief in the importance of schooling in maintaining democracy, and he warned that, "weak nations have had nothing to do or to say in influencing the world toward peace. During the rather infrequent periods of peace in the world's history, the world had peace because there was a dominant, strong nation that desired the world to continue at peace."[73]

There was an unbroken thread between the Legion's struggle against subversion in the 1920s and the attacks on Rugg's textbooks just before and during World War II. This line continued into the postwar period with the continuation of an image of a world divided between freedom and slavery.

In general, the war set the stage for a new round of censorship of schools, movies, and broadcasting. This time censorship would dig deeper into the content of instruction and entertainment. The general public would receive news of the political purge of schools, movies, and broadcasting in newscasts that claimed to be free of political bias.

The crusade against Communism in public schools was accompanied by a changing curriculum designed to meet the labor needs of the business community. Claiming that the superiority of Soviet schools would result in world conquest of Communism, many national leaders called for an increased emphasis on the teaching of science and mathematics. Consequently, the knowledge disseminated by schools was influenced by the desires of the business community and the needs of the Cold War with the Soviet Union.

World War II expanded the vision of a world divided between democracy and totalitarianism into a world divided between freedom and slavery. Americans were now fighting to preserve something called the American Way of Life. While no one could provide a coherent definition of the American way of life, it did create an impression that subversion was creeping into every aspect of life in the United States.

Against the background of the 1930s vision of a world divided between good and evil, the protection of the American Way of Life became the crusade for good. An attack on any aspect of what one believed to be the American way of life was, within this imagery, the work of evil. And evil in the postwar period would mean Communism.

CHAPTER TEN

SUBVERSION AND HARMONY

"ALL AMERICANS ARE capitalist," the President of the U. S. Chamber of Commerce and future leader of the motion picture industry, Eric Johnston, declared in 1944 as he anticipated America's postwar economic expansion.[1] In the same year that Johnston was envisioning America's economic power being built on a combination of individual competition and social cooperation, President Roosevelt asked his director of the Office of Scientific Research and Development, Vannevar Bush, to prepare a report on America's future scientific needs. Completed in 1945, the report, *Science—The Endless Frontier,* prepared the way for major federal involvement in shaping the goals of American schools.[2] The report called on the schools to produce scientifically and technologically oriented citizens who would help the United States become the world's military and industrial leader.

While Bush and Johnston outlined strategies for making the United States the dominant economic and military power in the postwar epoch, others worried that political subversion was undermining the American way of life. Reminiscent of the Red Hunt after World War I, patriotic organizations tried to weed out all possible Communist contamination from the major distributors of knowledge. Movies, broadcasting, and public schools were targets for those who wanted to purge America of all possible traitorous ideas. Often portrayed as a battle to control human minds, World War II set the stage for these continuing concerns about the ideas disseminated to the American population.

The fight against racism added an extra dimension to the struggle to control the distribution of ideas. Locked into a major struggle for civil rights, African-Americans lobbied for their more positive representation in textbooks, movies, and radio and television programming. While efforts to obtain positive representation would be delayed until the 1960s, the civil rights movement did achieve a major victory in the 1954 U.S. Supreme Court ruling that school segregation was unconstitutional. Others, like Johnston, when he became movie czar, believed racial harmony was necessary for the United States to achieve economic superiority. Countering these efforts to end racism, patriotic groups considered the civil rights movement a subversive plot to destroy the American way of life.

159

CHANGING CONDITIONS
IN THE MOVIE INDUSTRY

The concerns about economic and technological superiority and racism took place against a background of changing conditions in the movie and broadcasting industries, and in the public schools. The entertainment industries changed dramatically with the rise of television and the decline of movies. In addition, major influence over national educational policy gradually shifted from the NEA to the federal government.

In 1946, movie attendance reached an all-time high of 82 million, and then quickly plummeted to 36 million by 1950. On the other hand, commercial television, which NBC demonstrated at the 1939 New York World's fair, quickly found its way into the American home. Immediately after the war, seven thousand homes were equipped with television sets. This number increased to two hundred thousand by 1948 and to fifty million sets by the middle of the 1950s.[3]

During the years of decline, the movie industry was ruled by one of the most articulate representatives of American postwar capitalism, Eric Johnston. In his study of Hollywood politics of the postwar period, Lary May writes that Johnston "tried to convince Hollywood leaders in the spring 1946 that they epitomized a new era in American history."[4] After Johnston replaced Will Hays, who resigned in 1945, he changed the name of the Motion Picture Producers and Distributors Association to the Motion Picture Association of America.

Johnston brought to Hollywood an economic vision formed during his years as businessman and as President of the U.S. Chamber of Commerce. Born in 1896 in Spokane, Washington, Johnston shifted his career to business after being injured in the Marine Corps in China shortly after World War I. During the 1920s, he organized a successful electrical supply company in Spokane and became active in local civic affairs. In 1931, he became President of the Spokane Chamber of Commerce and in 1942, President of the U.S. Chamber of Commerce.

While in this post, Johnston set forth his economic thinking in a 1944 book with the intriguing title, *America Unlimited: The Case for a People's Capitalism.* The book's title reflected Johnson's basic thesis about changing the relationship between business and the public. As discussed in Chapter 9, Johnston advocated greater cooperation between local Chambers of Commerce and school systems to assure that educational programs served the needs of American business. This cooperation reflected Johnston's belief that economic prosperity required some collaboration between business and government. Johnston wrote, "Americans will accept collective action through their government but only to achieve purposes which cannot be achieved by private capital."[5]

Johnston's general economic arguments centered around a consensus view of society. He argued, in contrast to the divisive economic trends in the 1930s and World War II, that business, labor, and agriculture shared more common interests than disagreements. In a chapter entitled "Neither Right nor Left," he rejected what he called the ultra-conservative position opposed to organized labor and government involvement in the economy, as well as the collectivist position of complete government control. Choosing a middle ground between these two political positions, he argued that there could be a balance between competition and cooperation. From his perspective, both competition for self-interest driving the economic system and cooperation for the self-interest of the community were necessary for the maintenance of a capitalist economy.

Johnston's attack on racial prejudice was part of his belief that any form of divisiveness hindered the development of the American economy. Therefore, he opposed conflict between the races, as well as between labor and capital. It also meant that he strongly opposed Communism. Under his supervision, the U.S. Chamber of Commerce issued a booklet in 1945 entitled *Communist Infiltration in the United States,* which argued that Communists were trying to gain control of the entertainment and information sectors in the United States.[6]

Therefore, Johnston brought to the leadership of the Motion Picture Association of America (M.P.A.A.) a complex prescription for making the United States a world economic leader by building cooperation and consensus values, recognizing the economic importance of the pursuit of individual self-interest, eliminating racial intolerance, and purging Communism from American institutions. In addition, he recognized the importance of ideological management for advancing his economic goals. After assuming leadership of the M.P.A.A., he wrote in a 1946 article, "Utopia is Production:" "There is not one of us who isn't aware that the motion picture industry is the most powerful medium for the influencing of people that man has ever built.... We can set new styles of living...."[7]

Historian Lary May argues that when the Communist purge that swept Hollywood is considered in the context Johnston's economic philosophy, then it does not appear to be a movement led by small-town conservatives. In May's words, the Hollywood Red Scare of the late 1940s and early 1950s was "sparked by corporate leaders who hoped to convert national values and popular imagery away from doctrines hostile to modern capitalism."[8] To May's thesis I would add that corporate concerns also resulted in some Hollywood producers' being willing to deal with racial themes.

During Johnston's leadership of the M.P.A.A., Hollywood was in a tumultuous period of red baiting, challenges to the Hays Code, and court rulings. Hollywood's control of the movie industry was curtailed in 1948, by the Supreme Court ruling in *United States v. Paramount Pictures,* that the big studios had to end their monopolistic control of movie production, distribution, and exhibition. One important consequence of this decision was that local movie theaters now had a freer hand in selecting films.[9] They no longer had to take any film forced on them by the studios. This gave theater owners, and ultimately local interest groups, greater influence on movie production.

Government censorship of movies was challenged in 1950 by the showing of the Italian film, *The Miracle,* at New York's Paris theater. The movie was about an Italian peasant girl who imagines that a wandering vagrant who seduces her is Saint Joseph. While the Vatican did not invoke sanctions against the movie being shown in Italy, New York's Cardinal Francis Spellman condemned the film as being "vile and harmful." Acting as the state's movie censor, the New York Board of Regents ruled that the movie was sacrilegious, and revoked the theater owner's license. The owner appealed through the courts, and in *Burstyn v. Wilson* the U.S. Supreme Court placed movies under the protection of the First Amendment.[10]

In its decision, the Supreme Court recognized that movies "may affect public attitudes and behavior in a variety of ways, ranging from direct espousal of a political or social doctrine to the subtle shaping of thought which characterizes all artistic expression." In reversing the original *Mutual Film* decision, the Court stated, "Expression by means of motion pictures is included within the free speech and free press guaranty of the First and Fourteenth Amendments. To the extent that language in the *Mutual Film* opinion is out of harmony with the views here set forth, we no longer adhere to it."[11]

Of course, the Supreme Court's decision occurred as movies were losing their audience to television and the Red Scare was putting a lid on the production of politically and socially controversial films. But the decision, along with declining audiences, did contribute to an atmosphere that fostered challenges to the 1934 movie code. In 1953, the Production Code Administration objected to the romantic comedy, *The Moon Is Blue,* because the dialogue included "virgin," "seduce,' and "pregnant." In addition, the film broke a major taboo in the code by suggesting that a person could be immoral and likeable at the same time. The heretical line that upset the Code's emphasis on portraying all immorality as destructive and detestable was, "You are shallow, cynical, selfish, and immoral, and I like you."[12]

The producer, Otto Preminger, rejected the Production Code Administration's ban on these words and lines, and announced that the code was "antiquated." The movie was released without Production Code Administration approval and with declarations by the Legion of Decency and some local politicians that the film was obscene and immoral. The economic success of the movie dealt a blow to the belief that movies without M.P.A.A. approval would meet with economic disaster.

In 1955, Preminger again challenged the Code with *The Man with the Golden Arm,* starring Frank Sinatra as a heroin addict. Since the Production Code forbade the mention of addictive drugs, the movie was refused a seal of approval. Playing in movie houses around the country, the film was a financial success and forced Hollywood to reconsider the rules of the Production Code. Consequently, in 1956 Johnston announced the removal of four absolute taboos from the Production Code—depictions of illicit narcotics practices, kidnapping, abortion, and prostitution. The ban on miscegenation was also dropped and racial slurs were discouraged. While these areas of the Code were liberalized, another part was given an increased emphasis.[13]

The anti-Communist atmosphere of the 1940s and 1950s raised some Americans' concern for maintaining a respect for law and order. In addition, the Catholic Church did not want Hollywood making movies such as *The Miracle*. Therefore, the word "divine" was added to the requirement that, "Law—divine, natural, or human—shall not be ridiculed, nor shall sympathy be created for its violation."[14]

While movie producers were experiencing greater freedom of expression as that audiences dwindled, just the opposite was happening to television producers, as their audiences increased in size. A pattern seemed unfolding, that the degree of attention given by government officials and private groups to controlling ideas in the different media was directly related to their apparent relative importance for influencing public opinion.

TELEVISION CENSORSHIP

"Nowhere," wrote Murray Schumach, television and movie critic and reporter for *The New York Times* on Hollywood and the movie industry in the 1950s and 1960s, "in art or show business in the United States has there been anything comparable to the censorship that afflicts television." After describing censorship demands by private interest groups, advertisers, networks, stations, and government officials, Schumach concluded, "This attrition of originality by censorship has made television writers the most frustrated hacks since man first learned to chip cuneiform characters into stone."[15]

During the 1950s, the least effective of these censorship pressures was the television industry's self-regulatory code. More strength was given to the code in the late 1950s after public outcry over quiz show scandals and a series of government investigations. In its initial phase, the television code was an extension of the radio code. Like the radio code, it was shaped by fear of government censorship and attacks by various groups on the content of programming. A major concern in the early years of television was violence, children's programming, and quantity of advertising. When the television code was created in 1951, programming included a long list of gore and mystery shows, such as "Lights Out," "Suspense," "Danger," "The Clock," "The Web," "Tales of the Black Cat," and "Man Against Crime." General variety and drama shows included "Texaco Star Theater," "Philco Playhouse," "Goodyear Playhouse,"

"Toast of the Town" hosted by Ed Sullivan, "Your Show of Shows," headlined by Sid Caesar and Imogene Coca, and "Arthur Godfrey's Talent Scouts."[16] Schumach claims that early television dramas were of a fairly high literary quality until the mid- to late 1950s. Then a combination of censorship by advertisers and pressure from outside groups stripped programming of any potentially controversial material.[17]

The 1951 television code of the National Association of Broadcasters (NAB) was adopted because of, in the words of the NAB, "a threat of government censorship." During that year, legislation was pending in Congress to create a citizens' committee to review all radio and television programming. The NAB frankly admitted that the adoption of the code was for the purpose of stopping this particular piece of legislation.[18] Members of Congress were feeling political pressure from various groups. In a pattern similar to the 1930s' response to radio, both the PTA and *Parents Magazine* wanted to "get rid of tele-violence."[19] Of course, broadcasters lived in constant fear of government intervention. Owners were particularly concerned about government anti-trust action after the FCC in 1943 forced the sale of NBC's Blue Network to the American Broadcasting System, creating a rival network to NBC and CBS, the American Broadcasting Company (ABC),[20]

Initially, the enforcement of the code depended on complaints from the public and occasional field visits from staff members of the Code Board. This method of enforcement was very limited and difficult. In 1959, the Code Board was expanded; staff members monitored television networks and stations across the country.[21] Like the earlier movie and radio codes, the original television code emphasized the importance of creating the image of a proper moral world where crime was not condoned, and law and order and the police were given respect. Marriage was to be respected and illicit sex was not to be presented as commendable. Drunkenness and narcotic use were only to be depicted as vicious habits. Horror for its own sake and lewdness were forbidden. No words were to be used that might offend any race, color, creed, or nationality, except to combat racial prejudice. The Code emphasized the need for "respect for the special needs of children, for community responsibility, for the advancement of education and culture, for the acceptability of the program materials chosen, for decency and decorum in production, and for propriety in advertising."[22]

During the early days of commercial television, as it would be throughout its history, advertisers were the greatest source of censorship. Obviously, advertisers did not want to sponsor programming that would have a negative effect on the sales of their products. Through the years, they have been particularly concerned about sexual and religious issues because of potential protests from religious groups.

In addition, business advertisers are concerned about the image of business portrayed in television programs. Plainly, business does not want television

to create a public sentiment hostile to their activities. Indeed, as described earlier, when Eric Johnston was head of the U.S. Chamber of Commerce, he considered entertainment as a vehicle for creating a postwar sentiment favorable to the
operation of American businesses. Just as important, the Cincinnati-based Procter & Gamble Corporation, television's largest advertiser, insisted that programs
project a positive image of American business.

In the 1950s, Procter & Gamble developed its own media code. This forbade shows it sponsored to contain excessive passion or morally suspect scenes.
Sponsored programs had to show that crime was evil. In keeping with the early
attempts of the movie code to protect the image of government officials, particularly those associated with law enforcement, Procter & Gamble insisted on the
protection of the image of any government agent. In its concerns for patriotism,
members of the U.S. armed forces could not be cast as villains.[23] And if a character in a program attacked "some basic conception of the American way of
life," then a rebuttal "must be completely and convincingly made someplace in
the same broadcast."[24] As I discuss later, anti-Communism made advertisers
wary of sponsoring anything that might suggest an attack on the American Way
of Life.

In its later memorandum of instructions for television programming,
Procter & Gamble insisted on the protection of the image of business and business people. As presented to the FCC in 1965 by Albert Halverson, General
Advertising Manager of Procter & Gamble, the memorandum states, "There
will be no material on any of our programs which could in any way further the
concept of business as cold, ruthless, and lacking all sentiment or spiritual motivation. If a businessman is cast in the role of villain, it must be made clear that
he is not typical but is as much despised by his fellow businessmen as he is by
other members of society."[25]

Besides wanting television programming to project a favorable image of
business, corporations were interested in shows that would sell a product. In
other words, programs should not inhibit a viewer's desire to consume. Richard
E. Forbes, in charge of advertising for the Chrysler Corporation worried that
shows "may be so exciting as to completely remove [a] normal approach to
what advertising is trying to do." The head of advertising at DuPont, J. Edward
Dean, explained to the FCC that commercials worked more effectively on the
consumer if accompanied by light entertainment, as opposed to serious drama.
The head of one advertising agency, C. Terence Clyne, Vice-President of
McCann-Erickson, told networks that his clients did not want to sponsor programs that made the audience sad. General Electric, a company noted for its frequent rejection of scripts, turned down most proposals for shows because they
were "sad, downbeat, depressing."[26]

In many cases, advertising agencies exercised censorship power for
sponsoring companies. In a 1959 investigation by the FCC of the power of

advertising agencies over programming, Nicholas Edward Keesley of the Lennen & Newell agency said, "When we are representing a client and his investment we have to bend backwards to be sure that you don't get into these [dangerous] areas...." One example of a "dangerous area," he explained, was the sponsorship by a natural gas company of a play about the Nuremberg trials. In showing the role of advertising agencies in censoring material, he told the FCC: "The script came through and this is why we get paid, going through the script. In going through the script, we noticed gas referred to in a half dozen places that had to do with the death chambers."[27] Consequently, the word "gas" was removed from the script.

In many cases, advertising agencies and networks did not have to exercise censorship because writers and producers already followed the rules of the game. Clyne, of McCann-Erickson, which spent one hundred million dollars a year for sponsors of radio and television programs, explained this form of censorship to the FCC in 1959.

> Actually there have been very few cases where it has been necessary to exercise a veto, because the producers involved and the writers involved are normally pretty well aware of what might not be acceptable.
> Q. In other words, they know already before they start writing and producing what the limitations are, the subject matter limitations, that you will accept and your client will accept—is that correct?
> A. That is correct.[28]

In summary, the forces of ideological management that had affected schools, movies, and radio were shaping the content of television. For the sponsor, a television show ideally would not offend any vocal group in the United States, it would project a positive image of American business, and it would create a climate conducive for consumption. And in a period of anti-Communism, as discussed later, television shows should not threaten the American government, justice system, or way of life.

PUBLIC SCHOOLS AND THE COLD WAR

World War II set the stage for American schools to participate in the protection of the American Way of Life through the education of the people required to win the military and technological race with the Communist countries. The growing discussion of education as part of national and foreign policy slowly shifted influence on national educational policy from the National Education Association to the federal government. The concern with weeding subversives out of the schools during World War II was a prelude to the extreme anti-Communist attack on schools to turn them into citadels for protecting of the American way of life. The combination of these factors made the schools a significant institution for transmitting the values of the Cold War.

Like the mobilization of public schools to meet the requirements of World War II, Vannevar Bush's report, *Science—The Endless Frontier,* gave the same role to public schools for the Cold War. In the report, Bush argued that the key to maintaining U.S. world leadership and national security was increasing scientific capital by funding basic research and educating more men and women for scientific research. To accomplish these two goals, Bush proposed the creation of a National Science Foundation (NSF) funded by the federal government.

Bush's proposed role for the public schools in maintaining America's global power was directly tied to the establishment of the NSF. Besides funding basic research and supporting college students studying science, Bush envisioned the NSF working with public schools in developing new courses in science and mathematics to attract more students.[29]

As the drama of international politics unfolded in the 1950s, the Cold War was sometimes presented as a competition between the educational systems of the United States and the Soviet Union. Throughout the 1950s, Admiral Hyman Rickover, often called the father of the American nuclear submarine, complained that the American school system was the weakest link in America's defense against the Soviet Union. In *Education and Freedom,* published in 1959, Rickover argued that the real military race with the Soviet Union was a race between educational systems to supply adequately trained engineers and scientists. The Soviet Union, he felt, was winning this educational battle because it was concentrating on providing a high quality education for a large number of students. After complaining about the failure of the U.S. educational system to keep up with the Soviet system, he warned, "Let us never forget that there can be no second place in a contest with Russia and that there will be no second chance if we lose. But should we lose, it would be largely by default."[30] Echoing the same sentiment, Edward Teller, the physicist who played a crucial role in the development of the atomic and hydrogen bombs, told a Congressional hearing in 1958, "One of the very important reasons why the Russians are pulling ahead of us in science is...the fact that they drive their children on toward a very solid education, particularly in science, and they drive them on in a really merciless manner."[31]

Bush's effort to establish the NSF was delayed for several years by President Truman's veto of a 1947 bill because he felt the proposed governing board of the NSF was given too much independent power. A compromise was reached with the passage of the National Science Foundation Act 1950.[32]

James Conant, President of Harvard University and first Chairman of the Board of the National Science Foundation, had built relationships with government power brokers during World War II when he acted as liaison between

Bush's Office of Scientific Research and the Manhattan Project. In 1947, he helped organize what was to become the most important testing organization and gatekeeper to colleges—the Educational Testing Service. Because of Conant's support of the Republican national presedential campaign in 1952, newly elected President Eisenhower appointed him U.S. High Commissioner for occupied Germany and later Ambassador to Germany. Upon his return to the United States in 1956, Conant was hired by the Carnegie Corporation to do a national study of the high school. His final report was published in 1959 as the highly influential book *The American High School Today*.[33]

Conant outlined his views on the relationship between the Cold War and education in 1947 at a Congressional hearing on the establishment of the NSF. Conant told the committee, "It is men that count. And today we do not have the scientific manpower requisite for the job that lies ahead."[34] Conant presented the committee with a view of the social role of the high school that would later appear in his *The American High School Today*. One of the primary roles of high school education, according to Conant, was the identification and selection of talent needed by the national economy. During the Cold War, the emphasis should be on the selection of future scientists and engineers. In *The American High School Today,* he carried this argument one step further and called for a closer alignment between the high school curriculum and labor market needs. To aid this process, he proposed that high school diplomas be reduced to wallet size so that graduates could easily carry them for presentation to prospective employers.[35]

During the 1958-59 academic year, Conant elaborated on the relationship between education and the Cold War in a series of lectures at Harvard University, Wayne State University, and Smith College. He told audiences that "many people are quite unconscious of the relation between high school education and the welfare of the United States. They are still living in imagination in a world which knew neither nuclear weapons nor Soviet imperialism." He went on to argue not only for the necessity of improved scientific education to win the Cold War, but also for increased instruction in foreign languages.[36]

As Chairman of the Board of the NSF, Conant helped organize the writing of curriculum for American high schools. This was a radical departure from previous involvement of the federal government in public schools. The goal was to directly influence the public school curriculum. By the middle of the 1950s, the NSF launched its first attempt to develop a new high school physics course. The evaluation of the new course materials was under the direction of another creature of the Cold War, the Educational Testing Service. Funded by the NSF, the project had by 1957 completed one-fourth of a new text, one experimental classroom film, teachers' guides, and examinations.[37] These initial endeavors to develop a science course were suddenly accelerated in 1958 with the passage of the National Defense Education Act.

The very title of the legislation, National Defense Education Act (NDEA), captured the spirit of Cold War educational policy. The NDEA embodied all the trends in Cold War educational policy that had been evolving since World War II. The legislation opened the door to major federal support and involvement in American public schools. But the nature of the federal support under the NDEA was completely contrary to the type of federal financing the National Education Association had campaigned for since the 1930s. The rejection of NEA proposals and the anti-NEA sentiment of proponents of the NDEA legislation reflected declining NEA and increased federal influence over national educational policy.

What sparked the push for major federal involvement in public schools was the dramatic launching by the Soviet Union of the space craft *Sputnik I* on October 4, 1957. For U.S. national leaders, *Sputnik I* seemed to represent America's failure to keep up with the Soviet Union in the international arms race. Of course, part of the blame was placed on the public schools. Shortly after the launching of the Soviet space craft, President Eisenhower outlined the U.S. response to this challenge in a speech in Oklahoma City on November 13, 1957. After sketching a defense plan based on nuclear retaliatory power, he argued that the most important problem in preparing for this new age was the production of more U.S. scientists and engineers to match the increased quantity and quality of graduates from the Soviet education system. Specifically, Eisenhower called for nationwide testing of high school students and incentives to persuade students with high ability to pursue scientific or professional studies. He urged a program "to stimulate good-quality teaching of mathematics and science" and fellowships to increase the number of qualified teachers.[38] Eisenhower's proposal of January 27, 1958, to Congress for NDEA legislation included a five-fold increase in appropriations for NSF scientific education activities.[39]

Passage of the NDEA in 1958 represented the decline of the NEA as a national force in pre-college educational policy. The organization would begin to recoup its power only in the 1960s as it became the largest teachers union in the United States. NDEA legislation began linking educational policy directly to national policy objectives. It symbolized the triumph of Cold War educational policies.

The actual NDEA legislation provided funds for hiring more local high school mathematics and science teachers and for purchasing equipment for their courses. In addition, the legislation increased by five hundred percent the amount of money allotted to the NSF for developing new mathematics and science courses. Other money was allocated for programs to fund college students. Also included were funds to support the teaching of foreign languages and for vocational guidance.[40]

Support for foreign languages and vocational guidance was considered necessary for the Cold War. Eisenhower stated, "Knowledge of foreign languages is particularly important today in the light of America's responsibilities of leadership in the free world. And yet the American people generally are deficient in foreign languages, particularly those of emerging nations in Asia, Africa, and the Near East."[41] The identification of national talent through an improved vocational guidance system was an essential part of the plan to use the schools to create the skills required to maintain America's role as a world power.

Increased NSF funding led to development of new high school mathematics and science courses. By interlocking the publishing of new materials, funding by the federal government, and the training of teachers at NSF summer institutes, most of these science and mathematics programs found their way into the public schools. Probably the most famous of these programs was the "new math," which after its development was rapidly introduced into the schools. The initial work on the New Math was begun during the summer months of 1958. As the planning evolved, it was decided to base the instruction of mathematics on set theory. This decision would cause much confusion among parents used to more traditional methods of teaching arithmetic. By 1960, the project began to publish and distribute the New Math to public schools. Consequently, commercial presses quickly followed the lead of the project and New Math swept through the schools like a firestorm.[42]

While the federal government was trying to shape the public schools to meet the needs of the Cold War, the Red Scare was purging any leftist or radical ideas from the school curriculum. Furthermore, the search for more scientific talent was occurring at the same time that the Civil Rights movement was scoring major victories in its fight for school integration. As I discuss later, both of these movements added another dimension to the image of America disseminated by the schools in the late 1940s and 1950s.

THE ANTI-COMMUNIST PURGE

The anti-Communist crusade of the postwar attempted to purge subversive ideas from movies, broadcasting, and public schools. Of course, as I discussed in previous chapters, this kind of effort was not new to the American scene. Patriotic organizations in the 1920s, 1930s, and 1940s kept close tabs on radio, films, and textbooks and teachers to assure that they did not dispense treasonous ideas. In the 1950s, these organizations still wanted to assure that no un-American ideas were implanted in American minds by schools, movies, or broadcasting.

A major result of the crusade was to make teachers, textbook publishers, movie producers, and broadcasters fearful of presenting any ideas or entertainment that might be branded "subversive." In general, the concept of subversion during this period ranged from explicit advocacy of Communist doctrines to any criticism of the American Way of Life.

While anti-Communist crusaders often included principles of Christian morality in the idea of the American Way of Life, the primary emphasis was on international and economic relations. In other words, an anti-Communist might brand as a threat to the American Way of Life any criticism of U.S. foreign policies designed to expand U.S. influence in the world and contain Soviet power. Included in the list of possible threats to the American Way of Life were criticisms of U.S. business, business people, free enterprise, economic individualism, and suggestions for government economic planning or collective action.

In 1944, writer Ayn Rand, a member of the Motion Picture Alliance for the Preservation of American Ideals, wrote a movie code that captured the economic aspects of the American Way of Life. The Alliance was organized in 1944 by a group of Hollywood actors, producers, studios heads, and writers. The leadership of the organization included such notables as, Walt Disney, Gary Cooper, Hedda Hopper, and John Wayne. The organization made quite clear its intention of trying to keep subversive ideas out of American films. The Alliance declared, "In our special field of motion pictures, we resent the growing impression that this industry is made up of, and dominated by, Communists, radicals and crackpots." The organization gave its promise to the American people "to fight, with every means at our organized command, any effort of any group or individual to divert the loyalty of the screen from the free America that gave it birth."[43]

Ayn Rand's movie code reflects the economic beliefs she stressed in her novels and other writing, and the economic beliefs anti-Communists often included in American ideals and the American Way of Life. To protect the image of free enterprise and American business people, Rand's code included the following precepts:

> Don't Smear the Free Enterprise System
> Don't Glorify the Collective
> Don't Glorify Failure
> Don't Smear Success
> Don't Smear Industrialists
>
> It is the moral (no, not just political but moral) duty of every decent man in the motion picture industry to throw into the ashcan where it belongs, every story that smears industrialists as such.[44]

While it would be difficult to determine if Rand's code had any direct impact on the content of movies, it did reflect the constant theme of protecting the image of American business that was heard throughout anti-Communist movement.

Leading the groups that claimed to be protecting these ideals of the American Way of Life was the American Legion. Looking for subversive ideas in movies and on radio and television was a natural extension of the organization's previous efforts to assure 100% Americanism in public schools. The decision by the American Legion to participate in attempts to control the ideas presented in entertainment sent chills through the movie and broadcasting industries.

The movie industry worried that the Legion would be able to stage demonstrations outside theaters. This became a particular concern after the 1947 investigations of Communism in Hollywood by the House Un-American Activities Committee (HUAC). Ten of the screen writers called by the Committee were eventually imprisoned for contempt of Congress for refusing to answer whether or not they were members of the Communist Party. The day that the Committee issued its contempt charge against the ten writers, Eric Johnston, speaking for the M.P.A.A., issued a statement that the industry would not employ the ten until they declared under oath that they were not Communists. The statement pledged, "We will not knowingly employ a Communist or a member of any party or group which advocates the overthrow of the Government of the United States by force, or by any illegal or unconstitutional method."[45]

This M.P.A.A. pledge set the stage for the infamous blacklist which made it impossible for many unsuspecting actors and actresses, writers, directors, and producers to find work. Often, a person's name appeared on the blacklist because of an association with the ten held in contempt by HUAC or with some organization that protested the activities of the Committee. A formal mechanism for enforcement was put into place when the American Legion published its list of subversives in Hollywood.

In the spring 1951, the soon-to-be elected National Commander of the American Legion, Donald Wilson, proposed that the Legion and Hollywood discuss subversion in the film industry. When the industry ignored Wilson's request, the Legion published in December 1951 an article by Joseph Matthews with the provocative title, "Did the Movies Really Clean Up?" Matthews had previously prepared a six-volume listing of subversives in Hollywood for HUAC. Senator Joseph McCarthy would later make him Executive Director of the Senate investigation into subversion. The list of supposed subversives was primarily of those associated with protests over the HUAC hearings and the jailing of what were by then called the Hollywood Ten. There was little evidence that any of them actually belonged to the Communist Party. The part of Matthew's article that caused Hollywood to fear possible Legion picketing of films was the closing line: "Only an aroused public opinion is likely to exert the necessary pressure to cleanse Hollywood of all Communist influence."[46]

Eric Johnston immediately reacted to the article by arranging a meeting between delegates from eight major studios and leaders of the American Legion. On March 31, 1952, Johnston and the eight delegates met with Commander Wilson and the person in charge of Legion publications, former National Commander James O'Neil. At the meeting, Wilson suggested that movie people and the Legion compare notes on movie personnel. Upon the request of the industry, the Legion supplied a list of 300 suspected subversives.[47]

The power of the American Legion and the fear of the anti-Communist crusade was manifest when Legion offices were swamped with requests from actors and writers for some form of security clearance.[48] It would later seem incredible that individuals actually asked the Legion to provide them with a statement to prove they were loyal Americans. This is evidence of the extent to which people feared being labeled "subversive."

Using the Legion list, studios managers confronted identified employees and asked them if they had ever been engaged in Communist activities. If they did not disavow their past activities, they were fired. Listed employees were also given a chance to explain their activities in a letter to an extra-legal body established by the industry. The person approved by the Legion to judge the letters of appeal was Hearst newspaper columnist George Sokolsky.

The American Legion also sent waves of fear through the broadcasting industry when in 1948 its Americanism Commission started a newsletter, *Summary of Trends and Developments Exposing the Communist Conspiracy*. The newsletter told readers to "organize a letter-writing group of six to ten relatives and friends to make the sentiments of Americans heard on the important issues of the day. Phone, telegraph, or write to radio and television sponsors employing entertainers with known front records." The newsletter suggested that mere suspicion of subversion was enough to warrant removal from a show when it advised readers: "DON'T LET THE SPONSORS PASS THE BUCK BACK TO YOU BY DEMANDING 'PROOF' OF COMMUNIST FRONTING BY SOME CHARACTER ABOUT WHOM YOU HAVE COMPLAINED. YOU DON'T HAVE TO PROVE ANYTHING.... YOU SIMPLY DO NOT LIKE SO-AND-SO ON THEIR PROGRAMS."[49]

Local Legion posts also joined a supermarket campaign to convince sponsors not to employ entertainers listed in the book, *Red Channels: The Report of Communist Influence in Radio and Television*. The introduction to the book warned that "Cominform and the Communist Party USA now rely more on radio and TV than on the press and motion pictures as 'belts' to transmit pro-Sovietism to the American public." The book was issued in 1950 as the work of the "American Business Consultants, publishers of *Counterattack, the Newsletter of Facts to Combat Communism*." *Counterattack* was started in 1947 by three former agents of the Federal Bureau of Investigation. Besides warning of a Communist conspiracy, the newsletter listed names found in articles in the Communist newspaper, *The Daily Worker*. Of course, this was guilt by association. A mention in the *Daily Worker* did not mean that a person was a Communist or even sympathetic to Communism. Eventually, the newsletter focused on entertainers from the broadcasting industry.[50]

A reader of *Red Channels* and *Counterattack,* Eleanor Buchanan of Syracuse, New York, enlisted her father, Laurence Johnson, who owned four supermarkets, in a campaign to exclude Communism on radio and television. In

1951, they began discussions with members of their local American Legion post. The nature of these discussions are captured in the letter Eleanor Buchanan wrote to the Legionnaires:

> Dad and I were pleased that you agree manufacturers can be persuaded to remove Communist sympathizers from their advertising programs on radio and television. As you gentlemen pointed out in our meeting last Friday, the task is too great for me alone. I am grateful for your aid.[51]

Besides owning four supermarkets, Laurance Johnson was an official in the National Association of Supermarkets. This created the impression that he could influence stores around the country and, because of the cooperation of the local Legion post, that he had power in the national organization of the American Legion, as well. Consequently, the sponsor, Amm-i-dent Toothpaste, took his action seriously when he protested the use of actors listed in *Counterattack* in the television drama "Danger."

The method proposed for his protest must have sent shivers up and down the sponsor's spine. He wrote the company that he planned to create two displays in his supermarkets. One display would be for Amm-i-dent's competitor Chlorodent Toothpaste. The sign on this display would thank Chlorodent for sponsoring programs with pro-American artists. The other display would be for Amm-i-dent, with a sign, to be written by the company, explaining why the sponsor selected subversives as actors. A copy of the letter was sent to CBS.[52]

This and later letters of Johnson sent sponsors and broadcasters scurrying to review copies of *Red Channels*. Thank-you notes were sent to Johnson from such sponsors as Bordon Milk Company, Kraft Foods, and General Ice Cream Corporation.[53] The Red Scare sent a pall of fear over the broadcast industry.

The American Legion was joined by a whole host of other patriotic organizations in purging schools. The Guardians of American Education, one many organizations in the 1950s to search for subversive thinking in textbooks, had played a role in the campaign against Harold Rugg's books in the early 1940s. In fact, Rugg's chief enemy, Augustin Rudd, served as chairman of the Guardians of American Education. Formed in 1940, the Guardians of American Education stated as its purpose the preserving in public schools of faith in American institutions. The association urged parents to: "Examine your child's textbooks. Demand to see the teacher's guides.... Look for subversive material in...books or courses."[54]

During the 1950s, the Guardians of American Education distributed American Legion articles dealing with subversion in public schools. They also distributed an article by Kitty Jones entitled, "How 'Progressive' Is Your School?" In 1952, Jones began her career looking for subversion in the Tenafly, New Jersey, public schools. After taking a public relations workshop at

Columbia's Teachers College, she was convinced that progressive education and the professors at Teachers College were undermining the American Way of Life. In her attack on the Tenafly schools, she distributed materials that argued there was subversive infiltration of school materials, a growing illiteracy among public school graduates, and that educational improvements were being blocked by the education profession. Besides charging the Tenafly schools with creating juvenile delinquency by teaching progressive education, she produced a list of nine textbooks in the school system which she claimed, "favor the Welfare State and Socialism,...follow the Communist line, and...are written by Communist sympathizers and...members." While the Tenafly school system eventually rejected her charges, the episode propelled Jones into the national spotlight and created an audience for her 1956 book, *Progressive Education Is REDucation,* coauthored with Robert Olivier. The book contained such descriptive chapter titles as, "Making Little Socialists."[55]

America's Future, Inc., located in New Rochelle, New York, was a distributor of Jones's book and articles. During the 1950s, America's Future was a leader in combing through textbooks for evidence of subversion. According to historian Mary Anne Raywid, America's Future was created to maintain the tax-exempt status of the Committee for Constitutional Government. It was one of four organizations created for this purpose. Included in this web of organizations was America's Future, the Free Enterprise Foundation, Fighters for Freedom, Features for America, and the original Committee for Constitutional Government. According to Raywid, the goals of all five organizations are characterized in the following platform of Fighters for Freedom:

1. Pitilessly expose communism...and stop the march to fascism or socialism.
2. Restore the American incentives to work, own, and save.
3. Protect every individual's right to work where he will....
4. Safeguard our system of free, untrammeled, competitive markets.
5. Stop using taxpayers' money to compete against private enterprise.[56]

These goals are similar to those found in the publications of Eric Johnston, the screen code of Ayn Rand, and in such blacklists as *Red Channels.* The goals are a combination of resistance to an assumed Communist conspiracy to take over the United States and a desire to maintain an economic system that operates with a minimum of government interference.

These goals are different from those commonly expressed by public schools in the late 1930s and early 1940s. During that earlier period, schools emphasized that the important difference between the United States and totalitarian countries was its political rights and freedom of speech. For the patriotic organizations of the late 1940s and the 1950s, however, the focus was on economic freedom, and not political rights and freedom of speech. Of course, the very campaigns conducted by these organizations seemed to have little regard for either.

Two newspaper reporters, Jack Nelson and Gene Roberts, who visited the America's Future's offices in 1961 and 1962, found the organization emphasizing economic freedom in its attempt to censor textbooks. The reporters were investigating censorship in public schools as part of their Niemann Fellowships for newspapermen at Harvard University. The President of America's Future, Rudolf Scott, explained that the organization was not interested in destroying textbooks but in forcing publishers to make changes by documenting supposed "errors." Scott stated that the issue was not subversion by textbook publishers but the inclusion in books of a steadily expanding form of economic liberalism. "The whole thing of liberalism in the textbooks," Scott told the reporters, "has been an evolution, taking place over the past decade or two. But we are going to change that."[57]

Using committees of educators and business people, America's Future reviewed textbooks with an eye for liberalism and "left-wing" philosophies. Typical of these reviews was one by Hans Sennholz, Chairman of the Department of Economics at Grove City College, in Grove City, Pennsylvania. Sennholz complained that an economics text, *American Capitalism,* made, "no mention...of the minimum wage legislation that keeps millions of Americans unemployed, or ever-rising unemployment compensation that destroys the incentive to work."[58]

Russell Kirk's reviews for America's Future exemplifies the lack of concern by the organization for political rights and freedoms. Kirk, a professor of political science at Long Island University, objected to textbooks' mention of what he called the "god-term 'democracy'." He warned that a "besetting vice of democracies is their tendency to submerge the individual in the mass; aristocratic republics are far more concerned for individuals."[59]

America's Future was one of the largest of many organizations in the 1950s worrying about the content of textbooks. Raywid identified about a thousand groups highly critical of public schools in the 1950s. She mailed out three hundred questionnaires, of which eighty-three were returned, half from patriotic organizations. She found that the criticisms of the schools focused on the teaching of subversive ideas, lack of traditional emphasis on basic subjects, and the high cost of education.[60]

In addition to America's Future, the quarterly newsletter, *Educational Reviewer,* inundated publishers with accusations, such as the charge that Frank Magruder's high school text, *American Government,* attacked the free enterprise system and presented a view of democracy which led "straight from Rousseau, through Marx, to totalitarianism." National radio commentator Fulton Lewis, Jr., using portions of this review of Magruder's book on a coast-to-coast broadcast, added the statement, "That's the book that has been in use in high schools all over the nation, possibly by your youngster." Attacks on the textbook occurred throughout the country; the book was eventually banned in Richland,

Washington, Houston, Texas, Little Rock, Arkansas, Lafayette, Indiana, and the entire state of Georgia.[61]

When suggestions were made that textbook writers join teachers in taking loyalty oaths, the American Textbook Publishers Institute issued a warning that such a requirement would lower the quality of textbook authorship. The Institute claimed that the highly individualistic and competitive system in the textbook industry provided adequate safeguards against 'the deliberate introduction of harmful or subversive material.'[62]

The reaction of the textbook industry to the attempted purge of "Communism" paralleled those of the movie and broadcasting industries. The primary concern was protection of the economic interests of the industries. However the effect of the anti-Communist crusade on publishers was, as in previous decades, to make them wary of publishing anything that sounded controversial. William E. Spaulding, President of the Houghton Mifflin publishing house, told reporters Nelson and Roberts, "Many a superintendent of schools has quite naturally said to himself, if not to a bookman, 'I don't want a book that has been under fire. It may get me into trouble and I don't need to look for trouble these days'."[63]

Nelson and Roberts found most publishers aware that an attack by patriotic groups caused sales of textbooks to dramatically decline. Consequently, sales people were often relied upon to determine what should not be mentioned in texts. Writer Martin Mayer stated, "Every publisher knows what he [the sales person] can't sell, and will insist that such things be kept out of his satchel." Besides loosing sales on controversial textbooks, publishers found certain novels suddenly banned from schools. During the 1950s the following novels were banned from schools scattered through out the country: J. D. Salinger's *The Catcher in the Rye*; Ernest Hemingway's *The Sun Also Rises*; Aldous Huxley's *Brave New World*; Thomas Wolfe's *Look Homeward, Angel*; and William Saroyan's *Human Comedy.*[64]

The American Textbook Publishers Institute issued a pamphlet in the 1950s entitled, *Textbooks Are Indispensable,* which suggested that publishers "avoid statements that might prove offensive to economic, religious, racial or social groups, or any civic, fraternal, patriotic or philanthropic societies in the whole United States." The general climate for textbooks was summarized in 1960 by the Deputy Superintendent of the District of Columbia school system, Lawson Cantrell: "We try to make sure that the books we select are not objectionable to anyone."[65]

In the movies and broadcasting, this was usually accomplished by firing anyone who might be open to criticism and carefully going over scripts and textbooks to assure that nothing in them would offend patriotic organizations. Obviously, this created a major filter for the ideas disseminated by these media in the 1950s.

CREATING A CLIMATE
SAFE FOR BUSINESS

In reality, there were very few, if any, textbooks, radio and television programs, or movies that openly or covertly advocated Communism. Consequently, the major effect of this filter was on what patriotic organizations considered dangerous economic ideas. Anything that smacked of government interference in the economic system was condemned as subversive. When effective, this "anti-Communist" filter only let through to the public ideas that supported "free enterprise," the role of business in society, and individualism. And it filtered out ideas supportive of unionism, collective action, and government programs such as minimum wage and social security, and criticism of the profit motive and business organizations.

The filter primarily worked indirectly to cause studio owners, broadcast executives, script writers, producers, teachers, school administrators, and textbook publishers to avoid issues that might provoke a reaction from the very vocal patriotic organizations. In fact, movie historian Robert Sklar argues that the Hollywood red purge killed the movie industry. Sklar writes, "In the Cold War atmosphere of the late 1940s and 1950s...the studios tried to avoid making movies that would offend any vocal minority. As a result they lost touch both with their own past styles and with the changes and movements in the dominant culture at large." As a result, Sklar concludes, "Let it not be said that television killed the movie industry: The movie industry must take that responsibility itself."[66]

Of course, Hollywood did make movies between 1947 and 1954 which were supportive of the anti-Communist crusade. Some of these movies bore such descriptive titles as, *The Iron Curtain, The Red Menace, The Red Danube,* and *I Married a Communist.* The theme of individualism was forcefully presented in the film version of Ayn Rand's novel, *Fountainhead* (1949). A film produced to please HUAC was *Big Jim McLain* (1952) starred John Wayne as a House Un-American Activities Committee (HUAC) agent ridding Hawaii of Communism. The most famous of these anti-Communist films, *My Son John* (1952), was about an all-American family in which the father belongs to the American Legion and the mother is a devout Catholic. The son, John, returns from college espousing liberal ideas and ridicules the American Legion. The FBI visits the family which causes the mother to investigate her son's activities. She discovers that he is a Communist spy and reports him to the FBI. After escaping, he decides to turn himself in anyway and consequently is killed by Communists. He leaves behind a tape-recorded confession which is played for students at his alma mater.[67]

The filter also worked directly to destroy many careers. In his Fund for the Republic study of blacklisting, John Cogley traced the history of many writers and actors who found themselves unable to get work because their names appeared on the blacklist. In one case, Cogley found a writer who for many years was unable to get work, until it was discovered that people were confusing his name with another name on the blacklist which, except for one letter, was spelled the same. The most famous case recorded by Cogley was that of actress Anne Revere. Now largely forgotten except by film buffs, her star rose rapidly in Hollywood in the 1940s. She won an Academy Award for her role in the movie *National Velvet* and between 1940 and 1950 had major parts in 40 movies. But in 1949, she worked only eight days because she was placed on the blacklist for signing an *amicus curiae* brief submitted to the U.S.Supreme Court on behalf of the Hollywood Ten. In 1950, her name was listed in *Red Channels* because of her signature on the brief and, as a result, she worked only three weeks. In 1951, her career ended after she invoked the First and Fifth Amendments at a hearing held by HUAC. Her name was never directly linked to any Communist organization.[68]

Radio and television were similarly affected. Writers and actors listed in *Red Channels* could not find work and scripts were censored for any material that might cause patriotic groups to charge subversion. Of particular importance was protecting the image of business people. The word "peace" was considered subversive, which caused the deletion of a peace-pipe scene in a production of *Hiawatha*. After 1950, the famous commentator on China, Pearl Buck, could no longer find work doing radio documentaries. She wrote, "Today it is dangerous even to declare belief in the brotherhood of peoples, in the equality of the races, in the necessity for human understanding, in the common sense of peace."[69]

In the public schools, suspect teachers and administrators were fired and textbooks were purged of anything that sounded like liberalism or Communism. The most famous firing of a school administrator—one that put most schools administrators in a state of apprehension about attacks from patriotic groups— was that of Superintendent Willard Goslin of Pasadena, California, in 1950. Goslin was a national figure in professional education circles. In 1948, the same year he accepted the superintendent position in Pasadena, he was installed as President of the American Association of School Administrators. The problems for Goslin began when some parents read a right-wing National Council of American Education pamphlet, *Progressive Education Increases Juvenile Delinquency*. The author of the pamphlet, Allen Zoll, also wrote the widely read pamphlet, *The Commies Are After Your Kids*. In the context of the time, Goslin's error was in inviting the progressive educator, William Heard Kilpatrick, to a teacher-training workshop. As a Professor of Education from Columbia's Teachers College, Kilpatrick represented the enemy for most patriotic organizations. The local parents' organization immediately reacted to the invitation by asking the school board if the workshop was "part of a campaign to 'sell' our children on the collapse of our Way of Life and substitution of collectivism." The final blow to Goslin's tenure in Pasadena occurred when the parents' group organized an investigation into written materials used in the Pasadena schools. To Goslin's amazement, the school system was charged with promoting un-American ideas in the school system's handbook "Audio-Visual Education," because of a passing reference to Rome as a democracy and the supposed use of "The Star-Spangled Banner" as a war-mongering song.[67] School administrators around the country watched in dismay while the President of their organization was dragged through the wringer of an anti-Communist crusade.[70]

Like the movies, and radio and television programs, there was little that could be found in public school curricula and textbooks that explicitly advocated Communism. Consequently, the primary concern was with material that suggested any form of collective economic action, criticized American business, demeaned individualism and individual action, or suggested any criticism of American individualism. From this standpoint, the image of America that emerged from this filtering process in movies, broadcasting, and public schools was one that primarily emphasized free market economics. Missing from this image was the emphasis given in the late 1930s and early 1940s on the political distinctions between democracy and totalitarianism. Lost in the swirl of the anti-Communist purge was the idea that the primary distinction between totalitarianism and democracy was free speech. In the image of the American Way of Life in the 1950s, the primary distinction between America and Communism was economic individualism, freedom in the marketplace, and freedom to consume.

IN SEARCH OF RACIAL HARMONY

The American Way of Life disseminated by schools, movies, and broadcasting was primarily that of a white world. But challenging this image was a rapidly expanding civil rights movement. For some, the Civil Rights Movement of the 1940s and 1950s threatened the American Way of Life, while for others the resolution of the problem of racism was essential in the battle against Communism. In terms of competition with the Soviet Union for global domination, the existence of racism in the U.S. made it difficult to project a positive image of the American Way of Life to Third World countries. In addition, some industrial leaders, such as Eric Johnston, believed the elimination of racism was necessary before the United States could achieve world economic supremacy.

The contradiction between the image of the democratic Way of Life and the existence of racism was not lost on U.S. Cold War leaders. The attitudes and actions of President Eisenhower suggest the ambivalence of white American political leaders regarding the Civil Rights Movement. On the one hand, he claimed, "The Communist Party of the United States, doing its best to twist this movement for its own purposes, was urging it members to infiltrate the NAACP...and had launched a program to drive a wedge between the administration and its friends in the South in the election year 1956."[72] On the other hand, when he finally took action to support civil rights by sending troops to Little Rock, Arkansas, in 1957 to assure school desegregation, he justified his action in terms of the international image of the United States. He wrote, "Overseas, the mouthpieces of Soviet propaganda in Russia and Europe were blaring out that 'anti-Negro violence' in Little Rock was being 'committed with the clear connivance of the United States government'."[73] On radio and television, he told the nation that troops were sent to Little Rock to demonstrate "to the world that we are a nation in which laws, not men, are supreme." The broadcast ended on the note that the restoration of peace in Little Rock would remove "a blot upon the fair name and high honor of our nation in the world.... Thus will be restored the image of America and of all its parts as one nation, indivisible, with liberty and justice for all."[74]

Besides concern for the international image of the American Way of Life, people like Eric Johnston made the ending of racism an important part of their economic vision for the United States As a member of the NAACP, he believed that racism was a destructive economic force because it divided society and kept business from adequately using human resources. In the closing pages of *America Unlimited: The Case for a People's Capitalism,* he used the image of blending metals to describe the importance of developing racial and cultural tolerance in American society. He wrote,

> It is thus with the American, who fuses in his blood and his spirit the virtues and vitalities of many races, creeds, and cultures—giving us an amalgam that is new, unique, and immeasurably strong. That is why tolerance is necessarily and rightly a supreme American characteristic.[75]

For Johnston, racism limited the ability of American business to select the best workers. Within this framework, equality of opportunity meant giving all races an equal chance to compete for jobs. This would promote industrial and corporate efficiency, because employers would be able to select the best workers regardless of race. For Johnston, it was only "crackpots and psychopaths...who teach race hatreds."[76]

Johnston tied the theme of intolerance to ideological management in a 1945 speech to the Writers' War Board. Here, too, he argued that prejudice and intolerance hurt the American economy and produced no wealth. He called upon the gathered writers and their colleagues in the movies, theater, radio, and the press to use their influence to fight racism in American society. "You are the people with direct access to the mind," he told the writers, "and what is more important, to the heart and emotions of the American people."[77]

Arguing from the belief that economic development required the cooperation of all elements of society, Johnston called upon artists to work cooperatively to eliminate racism. He equated the attacks on ethnic and racial groups with attacks on business, agriculture, and labor. "Surely," he told the writers, "the businessman and the artist share responsibility in eradicating the myth of group or class superiority." To the gathered writers, he again stressed the importance of eliminating intolerance for economic development: "Wherever we erect barriers on the grounds of race and religion, or of occupational or professional status, we hamper the fullest expansion of our economic society. Intolerance is destructive. Prejudice produces no wealth. Discrimination is a fool's economy."[78]

During Johnston's early years in Hollywood, major studios for the first time since *Birth of a Nation* were willing to tackle racial themes. Two important films produced by Darryl Zanuck, *Gentleman's Agreement* (1947) and *Pinky* (1949), dealt with the issue of prejudice. *Pinky* created a stir in Southern states because it showed the problems encountered by a white-skinned but partly African-American nurse who travels from the North to Mississippi.

Portraying the problems of a African-American physician who passes as white, *Lost Boundaries* was banned in Memphis, Tennessee because it dealt "with social equality between whites and Negroes in a way that we do not have in the South."[80] In 1949, the Supreme Court of Tennessee upheld the right of the Memphis censorship board to ban the movie *Curley* because it showed, according to the chair of the censorship board, "little negroes [mixed with whites in a classroom], as the South does not permit negroes in white schools nor recognize social equality between the races even in children." Eric Johnston reacted to the *Curley* decision with the vow that the M.P.A.A. "intends to meet the issue of political censorship head-on in the highest court."[81]

But it was the banning of *Pinky* by censors in some Southern cities that resolved the legal issue of the power of municipal and state censorship boards to prohibit the showing of films dealing with racial issues. In an important decision regarding the showing of such movies, the United States Supreme Court in 1952 overturned the conviction of a Texas theater owner for showing *Pinky*. The *Pinky* case limited the ability of Southern censors to ban movies containing racial themes. The 1952 decision of the United States Supreme Court dealt with the denial by the censors of Marshall, Texas, of a license to show *Pinky* because the film was "of such character to be prejudicial to the best interests of the people of said City." The theater owner who ignored the ban was convicted in a jury trial held in the local county court. Using the *Miracle* decision explained in Chapter Nine, the United States Supreme Court dismissed the conviction as a violation of the First Amendment.[79]

On another front, the Supreme Court declared school segregation unconstitutional in 1954, although it was not until the 1960s that the federal government took significant steps to start integrating public schools.[82] The 1950s was marked by dramatic events such as, the integration of the Little Rock High School. But the actual restructuring of the racial images dissemination by the school curricula would only take place in the 1960s as a result of political pressure.

In the 1950s, textbook publishers still worried about Southern markets. Many publishers adopted policies of printing two editions, one for Southern and one for Northern schools. For instance, Rand-McNally published a Northern version of a social studies text that included some Puerto Rican students in a chemistry class, while the Southern version showed an all-white class. In most situations, publishers avoided any pictures showing races together. Reporters Nelson and Roberts gave the following example: "A Macmillan civics text got into final proof with a picture of an integrated playground; a salesman spotted it and screamed; and Macmillan, with a gesture of rebuke to the editor responsible, remade the book with a different picture."[83] Like public schools, such integrated pictures in text books would have to wait until the political pressures of the late 1960s forced publishers down a different path. Therefore, the rising Civil Rights Movement of the 1950s paved the way for significant changes in the 1960s in the dissemination in movies, broadcasting, and public schools of new ideas about race and race relations.

THE AMERICAN WAY OF LIFE DEFINED

In the postwar period, the United States desire for international economic and military superiority and the anti-Communist movement directly affected the images of America disseminated by the schools, movies, and broadcasting. In most cases, this image was contrasted with an image of Communist subversion at home and abroad.

In the late 1930s and early 1940s, the image of the American Way of Life emphasized the importance of political rights, particularly free speech. By the 1950s, those who advocated free speech and constitutional rights in movies, broadcasting, and schools tended to be suspected of Communist subversion. This phenomenon is best exemplified by the blacklists circulated after the HUAC investigations of Hollywood and the publication of *Red Channels*. Consequently, political rights tended to fade from images of Americanism.

By the 1950s, the central core of the image of Americanism was economic. Both economic leaders, such as Eric Johnston, and patriotic organizations stressed that the key to economic prosperity was the free market and rugged individualism. In addition, these individuals and organizations promoted the importance of business and business people to the fulfillment of the American dream. Of course, the promotion of this positive image of business was aided by the censorship exercised by sponsors over television programs. Within the context of this image, consumption was the fulfillment of the American dream.

The lack of controversy in the ideas distributed by schools, movies, and broadcasting created a false sense of calm and harmony. In the 1950s, movie and television producers, textbook publishers, school administrators, and teachers lived in fear that some unintentional action or idea might cause an eruption of controversy and bring done the wrath of the anti-Communist crusade. The image of Americanism distributed by these media was one of harmony and consensus about ideas and values.

While the schools, movies, and broadcasting would be forced by political pressures in the 1960s to project a more racially integrated image of America, during the 1950s the image was of a white, techno-scientific culture that was economically prosperous and harmonious. Pressure groups from the right favored individualism and free enterprise accompanied by an image of America that was free of conflict and held together by a consensus of values. Movie producers, school people, and broadcasters worried that discussions of free speech, free thinking, collective economic action, government regulation of the economy, and corrupt business practices would bring out an army of Legionnaires chanting "Subversion." But not all pressure came from patriotic organizations. Corporations also wanted the schools, movies, and broadcasting to create a favorable climate for domestic and international business expansion. From this perspective, corporate America and the patriotic organizations joined arms to assure that their version of Americanism reached the people. It was through a filter of fear and protection of business that the 1950s image of the American Way of Life was dispensed to the population.

CHAPTER ELEVEN

DELINQUENCY, TELEVISION, AND COMIC BOOKS

"TELEVISION IS PERHAPS the most powerful force man has yet devised for planting and spreading ideas," declared Senator Robert Hendrickson, chair of the Senate Subcommittee to Investigate Juvenile Delinquency, at the opening of the 1954 hearings on the effects of television on juvenile delinquency. Outlining their goals, Senator Hendrickson stated, "We are only interested in ideas that spring into the living room for the entertainment of the youth of America, which have to do with crime and with horror, sadism, and sex." Network executives indicated during their testimony to the committee that they were practicing political censorship of scripts, along with censorship of violence and sex.[1]

The Senate investigation was prompted by an apparent increase in juvenile delinquency. While divorce and poor home life were most often identified as causes of delinquency, television and comic books were blamed for putting criminal and violent ideas in children's minds. One critic went so far as to call comic books "the marijuana of the nursery."[2] Such criticisms caused the television and comic book industries to practice a self-censorship similar to that under the early movie code. A 1954 article in *Christian Century* pointed out the parallels between the development of industry regulation of comic books and in the movies and broadcasting. "Like movie magnates and radio station operators before them," the article states, "24 of the 27 leading publishers of these often lurid picture-pulps [comic books] are trying to still cries for censorship by promising to censor themselves."[3]

How bad was the juvenile delinquency that prompted calls to censor television and comic books? As indicated in Chapter 9, juvenile delinquency increased during World War II, and it was often blamed on unstable family conditions then. After World War II, the numbers and percentage of arrests of youth under twenty-one declined rapidly. In 1945, 21 percent of the total of all arrests were of youths under twenty-one. By 1948 this figure declined to 15.3 percent and by 1951 it reached 14.4 percent. The arrests of those under eighteen followed a similar course. In 1945, 9.1 percent of the total of all arrests were of those under eighteen. By 1951, the percentage declined to 4.5.[4]

The declining rates of juvenile delinquency was reversed in 1953, however. Beginning in 1952, the popular press began reporting alarming jumps in delinquency, and portraying a generation engaging in violent crime. *Newsweek* opened a 1953 article on delinquency with a description of teenagers in Texas forcing motorists off the road and beating them with chains, and in Massachusetts storming a reformatory to free a girl.[5] In the same year, *Cosmopolitan* warned readers of a 19 percent increase in crime by youngsters. A picture accompanying the article showed a weeping fifteen-year-old boy who had killed his younger brother after watching a Western on television.[6]

A vivid portrayal of juvenile crime appeared in a 1955 series of articles in the *Saturday Evening Post,* by the Executive Director of the Senate Investigation of Juvenile Delinquency, Richard Clendenen, and the Chief Counsel to the Investigation, Herbert Beaser. Entitled "The Shame of America," the five-part series summarized the varieties of juvenile crime the investigation had found as it traveled across the country. The first article opened with a picture of two policemen with drawn pistols pointing at four white teenagers lying on the ground. In the background was a souped-up roadster. The picture's caption reads, "Berkeley, Cal., cops captured these teen-agers after a wild gun battle. 'The delinquent may be any child you know, including your own,' say the authors."[7]

In the series, the two Senate investigators warned of a 45 percent increase in juvenile crime from 1950 to 1955. The opening lead warned, "Gangster rackets thrive in schools, kids from 'good families' become killers and dope addicts."[8] Page after page of the series showed pictures of juveniles being hauled off to jail for crimes ranging from burglary to murder.

During the 1950s a frequent explanation for the rise in crime was the coming of age of children raised during World War II. A police officer in the movie *Blackboard Jungle* (1955) tells teachers in an urban school plagued with delinquency: "Five or six years old in the last war. Father in army. Mother in defense plant. No home life. No church life. No place to go. They formed street gangs.... Gang leaders have taken the place of parents."

Blackboard Jungle opens with a recently certified teacher and veteran of World War II, Mr. Dadier (Glenn Ford) on his first teaching assignment, entering a schoolyard filled with teenagers dancing to "Rock Around the Clock" by Bill Haley and His Comets. The allegation that Rock-n-Roll was associated with delinquency was common in the 1950s. The audience for the movie is told in a printed introduction that,

> We, in the United States, are fortunate to have a school system that is a tribute to our communities and to our faith in American youth.
>
> Today we are concerned with juvenile delinquency—its causes—and its effects. We are especially concerned when this delinquency boils over into our schools.

The scenes and incidents depicted here are fictional. However, we believe that public awareness is a first step toward a remedy for any problem.

It is in this spirit and with this faith that BLACKBOARD JUNGLE was produced.

Like *Blackboard Jungle,* most popular articles traced the causes of delinquency to malfunctioning of the family. The most frequently cited study was by Sheldon and Eleanor Glueck, who compared 500 delinquent boys with an equal number of nondelinquents. Their analysis of the data revealed that delinquency was not linked to social class or geographical location. The main factor determining delinquency, according to the Gluecks, was the quality of home life. From their analysis, a delinquent was formed by a family having such problems as alcoholism, emotional disturbance, criminal behavior, separation, and divorce. This was the theme that ran through most of the popular literature of the time.[9]

No one could find any hard evidence to link television and comic books to delinquency. Even Richard Clendenen, Director of the Senate subcommittee investigating delinquency, while trying to prove that crime shows on television caused delinquency, admitted that there was no evidence even of a one-to-one relationship between delinquency and television.[10] Yet there were still widespread attempts to establish a causal relationship.

Most attempts to establish a causal relationship focused primarily on the content of television programs and comic books. In other words, it was assumed by many that portrayals of crime and violence taught children how to be criminal and violent. For instance, a 1953 *Cosmopolitan* article linking delinquency to television opened: "Would you like to live in a place where in one week your family would be exposed to 852 major crimes, including 167 murders, assorted robberies, jail breaks, lynchings, dynamitings, saloon brawls, and sluggings?" These crimes, the reader was informed, were beamed into households in Los Angeles during one week in 1952.[11] The National Council of Churches stated in 1955 that its survey found parents objecting to the large number of Westerns, the violence on other programs, and the lack of educational and religious programs. The Rev. Everett Parker, director of the survey by the National Council of Churches, declared that television programs were undermining the authority of law enforcement agencies. A similar opinion was expressed by the head of the American Association of University Women, Mrs. Milton Wiltman, who told the Senate subcommittee that television was undercutting the power of law enforcement and that her group "discovered what has been said here before, that there is a steady diet [on television] of crime and violence."[12]

While general complaints were being lodged about the alleged effect of television content on children, psychiatrist Fredric Wertham, at the Lafargue Clinic in New York City, was documenting the effect of comic books on juvenile criminal behavior. Sometimes Wertham linked both television and comic books as sources of crime. In 1953, he declared, "There is no doubt that crimes of violence among young people are increasing. Crime stories on radio and in the comics and now on television are adding fuel to the fire."[13] As the leading crusader for the censorship of comic books, he published his arguments in popular magazines and in his widely read 1954 book, *Seduction of the Innocent.* Wertham complained of child psychologists who considered the relationship between violent crime and comic books as trivial. "I thought that once, too," he wrote. "But the more children I studied, the more comic books I read, and the more I analyzed the arguments of comic book defenders, the more I learned that what may appear as 'trivia' to adults are not trivia in the lives of many children."[14] Wertham's campaign for the censorship of comic books was joined by a host of local organizations who forced "objectionable" comic books off the shelves of local stores and campaigned for censorship laws. For both television and comic books, the attempts to establish a relationship with juvenile delinquency resulted in greater attention to industry codes.

TELEVISION

The ongoing fears of increased government regulation and interference caused the industry to react sharply to suggestions that television programs caused delinquency. Representatives from CBS, NBC, and the National Association of Radio and Television Broadcasters (NARTB) appeared at the 1954 Senate hearings on television and juvenile delinquency armed with proof of careful censoring of their television scripts. But prior to the industry's presentations, the subcommittee was presented with a list of statistical findings on television viewing.

While none of these statistical reports demonstrated a direct relationship between television viewing and criminal acts, they did show that the first generation of viewers were hooked on television and exposed to a high level of violence. These findings included a 1953 survey of 4,000 Chicago elementary school students, which revealed that 80 percent watched television. A study by the United States Parent's Association found that elementary school children were spending as much time watching television as they were attending school. And a 1953 survey of programs shown on seven New York television stations found that there was an average of 6.2 acts of violence per hour, and on the children's programs between 5 and 7 p.m. there was an average of 15.2 acts of violence per hour.

The networks probably were pleased with the statistics on the amount of television viewing. On the other hand, the issue of violence and crime in programming created problems. First, violence, crime, and sex in programming attracted many viewers. Second, it was their prevalence in programming that created the greatest threat of government intervention and censorship. Therefore, the networks were faced with the problem of using these issues in a manner that appeared safe for viewers. The best tactic, and the one used by network executives during the Senate hearings, was to claim that these topics were made safe by the application of the NARTB code and each network's own code.

Merle S. Jones, Vice-President of CBS, described to the subcommittee how his network enforced the NARTB and CBS code. All scripts were reviewed by the CBS editing department. If any material was found in violation of the codes, the producer was contacted and changes were made in the script. In addition, the lyrics of all songs were carefully scrutinized by the editing department. The director of editing had a personal conference with the producers of any new programs for the purpose of outlining code standards and how they would be enforced.[15]

After describing CBS procedures, Jones turned to the issue of crime programs. As with the movie code, Jones stressed that material was removed from scripts that might teach viewers how to commit crimes or create disrespect for law enforcement agencies. And, of course, in "every mystery program the criminal must be brought to justice and some constructive element implied in the overall dramatic presentation."[16]

These practices were illustrated by the CBS editorial department's schedule for program and advertising material for the week of October 4, 1954. These examples reveal that the editing department went far beyond the requirements of the codes to make decisions based on current political conditions. These provide good examples of ideological management in the early television industry. For instance, the script for "You Are There: Liberation of Paris," to be broadcast on October 27, 1954, was revised "in accordance with discussion with the producer because of inadvisability of dramatizing, at this critical stage in the German rearmament negotiations, material which tends to foster and inflame hatred of the French for the Germans." In addition, the script under went the following revisions:

(ii) Substituted word "venom" for "vomit" in sentence: "It is the pent-up venom of 4 years pouring from the suppressed people * * *."
(iii) Deleted an unnecessary reference...[to] prisoners from Spanish concentration camps which was open to pro-Communist interpretation.
(iv) Deleted word "Boche" and substituted "Nazi" in referring to German soldiers.[17]

Political issues crept into other script revisions. For instance, it was decided that a script for the October 5, 1954, production of "On Your Account," dealing with a New York City area with a high crime rate "could not be considered criticism of the present city administration but rather would point out the responsibility of individual citizens to eliminate factors that breed and sustain crime in New York City."[18]

Other types of editing involved issues of family standards, morality, and crime. A divorce situation in "The Seeking Heart" for October 9, 1954, required assurances that this "situation will be handled in accordance with CBS television and NARTB policy, which is, in brief, that divorce is never treated casually or justifiably."[19] The following were typical lines removed from scripts because of moral considerations.

Do you remember the first time you made love to me?

And I think about all the wicked things I have done, and about you and me.

She swears she'll be discreet. She doesn't know the meaning of the word.[20]

In an example of the importance of teaching that crime never pays, the editing department told the producer of the October 10, 1954, production for "G.E. Theater" to "indicate that actual killers are apprehended in Los Angeles and charged with murder."[21]

Jones also explained that motion pictures were edited by the network before being shown on television. This meant that motion pictures shown on CBS television in the 1950s were first censored in Hollywood and then in television editing departments. In fact, Jones stated that forty movies had been wholly rejected over the last year and a half.

In defending violence in Westerns, Jones alluded to the importance of instructing children in American virtues and moral values. Primarily viewed by children, Westerns were a popular part of television programming in the 1950s. Jones's defense reveals how television networks justified violence if it was related to a popular and, therefore, lucrative part of programming. Jones referred to Westerns as 'standard American entertainment' and explained to the Senate subcommittee, "Since fighting and gunplay were a part of the conflict which existed in early Western America, we believe that it would be unrealistic to delete such scenes. Westerns invariably feature the triumph of good over evil, and emphasize the traditional American virtues." In fact, Jones seemed to indicate that complaints about the number of Westerns on television were un-American. "Furthermore," he stated, "the place of the Western is so well established in every form of American entertainment that we believe it needs no special justification."[22]

An example of what television producers regarded as "safe" violence was given by Al Hodge who played Captain Video on children's television. The subcommittee asked Hodge to testify because he portrayed a character that was often violent. Hodge told the subcommittee that the program was carefully monitored to conform to the requirements of the code. "When I say we try to go over and beyond the television code," Hodge explained to the subcommittee, "we have been meticulous to the point of not using the word 'kill' in the program."[23]

Even with this editing, Hodge argued, the program still had to contain violence. "Of necessity," Hodge stated, "we have to have violence. Otherwise, there is no excuse for a heroic character existing. He has to go after somebody."[24] But Hodge argued that while violence was necessary for heroism, the villain was never subjected to any form of capital punishment.

Hodge justified violence as necessary not only for heroism, but also for ideological management. The program consciously attempted to teach moral values. Hodge gave as an example an episode dealing with three rangers at the fictional Ranger Academy. Hodge explained,

> One we said was a liar, one was a braggart, one was a coward. We attempted to show how teen-agers working together as a group on a mission realized the value of working together and as a result the liar was no longer a liar, the braggart was no longer a braggart, and the coward found himself.[25]

The testimony of Joseph Heffernan, vice President of NBC, also blended defense of the code's application to assure broadcast standards with a justification of violence on some programming. Heffernan presented the NBC code to the subcommittee: Children's's shows would be designed "to convey the commonly accepted moral, social, and ethical ideals characteristic of American life; to reflect respect for parents, good morals, and honorable behavior; to foster healthy personality development; and to provide opportunities for cultural growth as well as entertainment." Like CBS, the NBC code required that programs not teach criminal behavior; that they treat law enforcement with respect; and that criminals "are always punished, specifically or by implication."[26]

After presenting the network's code, Heffernan launched into a discussion of two Western films, *Borderland* and *Devil Riders,* shown earlier to the subcommittee as examples of violence. Heffernan explained that when NBC was requested by the subcommittee for copies of the films, network editors put back parts that they had originally edited out while cutting the films from 60 minutes to 38 minutes. Heffernan told the subcommittee that NBC editors removed two scenes from *Borderland,* one involving the shooting of a Texas Ranger and the other involving the shooting of an outlaw by the film's main character, Hopalong Cassidy.

Under cross examination by the subcommittee's chief counsel, Herbert Beaser, Joseph Heffernan expressed the network's justification for the violence in Westerns and the tensions they generated in young viewers. To Beaser's question about a dance scene in *Devil Riders,* Heffernan responded that some people might be finding tension where it did not exist. In fact, Heffernan suggested, children could relax during Westerns because they knew that all the problems in the program would be satisfactorily resolved by the end of the story. "I am not sure," Heffernan stated, "that these Westerns are not one of the most relaxing programs on the air, because if there is one thing certain about a Western, everything is going to come out all right in the end, and the children are completely aware of that." Beaser reacted by claiming that pictures taken in the dark of children watching Westerns showed definite signs of tension. Beaser asked about scenes of Hopalong Cassidy apparently in danger of bleeding to death. But Heffernan said he could not believe that everyone did not know that Westerns all ended in favor of the hero and justice. In Beaser's words, "I would doubt Hopalong Cassidy bleeding to death because the man never dies."[27]

The subcommittee's executive director, Richard Clendenen, asked Heffernan why Westerns were not classified as crime programs, since they contained crime and violence. Heffernan's response was that Westerns were not crime programs but rather children's folklore programs. In fact, Heffernen argued, it was wrong to use the term "crime" too literally, because under a broad definition of crime the television series about World War II, "Victory at Sea," could be classified as a crime program. "War certainly is violence," Heffernan said, "and we had a war crimes trial. So it was about crime. Now is 'Victory at Sea' to be classified as a crime program?"

Heffernan's comment sparked an interchange that highlights the subjective nature of the meaning of "crime" and "violence" in issues of censorship.

Mr. Clendenen.	Excuse me for interrupting, but we did cover that this morning by saying that these were matters that involved individual lawlessness. In other words, we excluded "Victory at Sea."
Mr. Heffernan.	We had a war crimes trial.
Mr. Clendenen.	That is a national type of lawlessness.
Mr. Heffernan.	The late Mr. Justice Jackson was the prosecutor, and a former Attorney General of the United States was one of the judges. History of World War II is taught. Is that teaching crime in the schools when war is taught?

After a quick exchange over the classification of the television series, "Justice," as a crime program, Clendenen continued his questioning.

Mr. Clendenen.	However, my question here was to the effect: Do Western pictures involve crime? And I think you agree that Western pictures do involve crime, do they not?
Mr. Heffernan.	Western pictures involve crime in the sense that "Victory at Sea" involves crime.[28]

While network executives defended Westerns as "American folklore" programs and critics attacked them for exposing children to violence and crime, no evidence was presented to the Senate subcommittee of a one-to-one relationship between television viewing and delinquency. But the defense of Westerns presented by Heffernan did raise legitimate questions about what was acceptable violence. Obviously, the presentation of programs about World War II did entail the telecasting of extreme violence. The bombing and shelling of ships and land targets showed violence and destruction on a scale far beyond an ordinary television mystery tale. But, except for Heffernen's comments under cross-examination, I could find no condemnation of this type of violence in government documents, newspapers, or popular magazines.

Of course, as discussed in the previous chapter, this was a period of anti-Communist witch hunts and any suggestion of pacifism or condemnation of war could easily lead to the American Legion or other patriotic organization's branding an individual or group as un-American or pro-Communist. Therefore, it was safe for television networks to broadcast scenes of war. Besides, studio networks defended Westerns in the framework of Americanism. By calling Westerns "American entertainment" and "folklore programs," network executives appeared to be placing these programs under the protection of Americanism.

On other types of programs, violence was allowed if it was sanitized by editing according to the code. The Television Code of the NARTB specifically stated that, "The use of horror for its own sake will be eliminated; the use of visual or aural effects which would shock or alarm the viewer, and the detailed presentation of brutality or physical agony by sight or by sound are not permissible."[29] This meant that people could be killed, tortured, and maimed on television programs as long as the actual process was not shown.

Therefore, television created a sanitized image of violence. Violence occurred in a variety of television programs, but the viewer never saw the actual act of violence. It is difficult to determine what effect the presentation of violence that was abstracted from the actual physical details of the violent act might have had on the viewer. One could speculate that viewers might become callous about violence since they were never confronted with the actual physical results. This could have led viewers to accept violence as a natural part of life.

The sanitized presentation of violence on television included the moral requirement that good always win out over evil. In the context of Cold War images discussed in the previous chapter, the viewer of the 1950s might have been educated by television programs to separate the violence of war from the actual physical harm it caused. A television viewer might have thought about war without feeling the fear of potential death and bodily harm. In a strange way, television may have made war safe for the viewer. In addition, since good always won out over evil, the viewer could expect the United States to triumph over Communism. Therefore, not only would war appear to be safe, but it would seem to lead to an inevitable victory for the United States.

The Senate hearings did not quiet complaints about violence and the quality of television programming for children. In the 1960s, as I will discuss later, one answer to the problem of children's programming was the production of "Sesame Street."[30] But during the 1950s, many people agreed with the statement of J. Joseph Foley, Commissioner of Police, Schenectady, New York that, "It is my opinion that the many recent TV crime programs available at hours when children are listening, the great influx of crime comic books, and the ever-present crime movies are all contributing to a very serious degree to the recent increase in juvenile crimes."[31]

COMIC BOOKS

The attacks on television as a source of juvenile delinquency were mild compared to the outcry over comic books. The attacks on comic books resulted in the imposition of an industry code, similar to self-censorship in movies, radio, and television. Like television, comic books under their code offered readers a sanitized picture of violence.

From their early development in the 1930s up to the early 1950s, comic books were a major part of the American publishing industry. In 1940, there were one hundred fifty comic book titles generating an annual revenue of $20 million. By 1950, there were three hundred comic book titles, with annual revenues of $41 million. Then in the early 1950s the industry rapidly expanded: Between 1950 and 1953, the number of titles jumped to over six hundred fifty and revenues leaped to 90 million dollars a year.[32]

What set off the hue and cry about comic books was the appearance of crime and horror comics between 1945 and 1954. Adding to the public shock at the appearance of these types of comic books was the flippant attitude of the publishers. In 1954, when the Senate subcommittee on Juvenile Delinquency opened hearings on comic books, Senator Estes Kefauver confronted William Gaines, President of the Entertaining Comics Group, with a cover of one of his company's comic books, *Shock SuspenStories,* depicting an ax-wielding man holding the severed head of a blonde woman. Gaines responded by saying that the cover would only be in bad taste if the head were held "a little high so the neck would show with the blood dripping from it." Kefauver shot back, "You've got blood dripping from the mouth."[33]

The horror and crime comic books of the early 1950s depicted many criminal acts, maimed and tortured individuals, and suggestive sexual scenes. At the New York City hearings of the Senate subcommittee on Juvenile Delinquency, a variety of comic books were introduced to illustrate possible harmful effects on children. In one example, "Bottoms Up," from *Story Comics,* an alcoholic father is responsible for the accidental death of his son while obtaining liquor from a bootlegger. The mother is shown taking revenge in the final four panels of the story by proceeding to kill and hack her spouse to pieces with an ax. The first panel show her swing-ing the ax, burying the blade in her husband's skull. Blood spurts from the open wound and the husband is shown with an expression of agony.... She then cuts his body into smaller pieces and disposes of it by placing the various pieces in the bottles of liquor her husband had purchased. She then returns the liquor to the bootlegger and obtains a refund.

Another example provided by the subcommittee was from "Frisco Mary" from *Ace Comics*. One scene in this story showed Mary standing over a police officer pouring machine gun bullets into his back while other gang mem-bers urge her to stop shooting and flee. In "With Knife in Hand" from *Atlas Comics*, a young surgeon ruins his career by being forced by the spendthrift habits of his wife to treat criminals. In the final scenes of this story, a criminal brings in his wounded girl friend to be treated by the doctor. The doctor discov-ers that the girl is his own wife. The next panel shows

the doctor committing suicide by plunging a scalpel into his own abdomen. His wife, gasping for help, also dies on the operating table for lack of medical atten-tion. The last scene shows her staring into space, arms dangling over the sides of the operating table. The doctor is sprawled on the floor, his hand still clutching the knife handle protruding from his bloody abdomen. There is a leer on his face and he is winking at the reader, connoting satisfaction at having wrought revenge upon his unfaithful spouse.

Other illustrations presented to the subcommittee contained similar scenes of blood and gore. One comic book is described as ending with the victim "lying dead on the bed with a gaping hole in his chest, a rib protruding, blood flowing over the bed onto the floor, his face fixed in a death mask as he stares at the reader."[34]

Although many discounted the importance of comic books in fostering juvenile delinquency, nevertheless local community groups and some individu-als considered comic books the cause for the rapid increase in juvenile crime in the early 1950s. Foremost among the individuals claiming that comic books caused crime was psychiatrist Fredric Wertham. Besides objecting to scenes of crime and violence, Wertham was upset by the sexual themes in comic books. In *Seduction of the Innocent*, Wertham provided what he called a typical exam-ple of "brutal near-rape scenes." Opening with a lone girl on a street late at night, the panels show:

1) The girl walking along with a dark figure, his arm stretched out toward her, lurking behind. 2) The girl falling over, her breast prominent, her skirt thrown up to reveal black net panties, the 'attacker' a black, shadowed figure leaning over

her. 3) He 'drags her into the gloom,' holding his hand over her mouth and tearing off her coat. 4) He has her on the ground behind some bushes. 5) A girl, murdered, and presumably raped, is shown on the ground with her clothes disordered and torn.[35]

Wertham argued that comic books were worse then ordinary pornography because they often contained forms of brutality. In comparing pornographic comics to ordinary violent comic books, he wrote, "In the ordinary children's comic books, the would-be raper grabs the half-nude girl violently and says: 'You have your choice—come as my prisoner or I'll choke the life out of you!'; in the little pornographic comics, everything is done voluntarily." Wertham made a similar argument at a U.S. Post Office hearing on obscenity in the mails. While defending nudity in art, Wertham condemned sexuality in comic books. "I pointed out," he wrote, "that the picture of a nude girl per se may be the opposite of obscene, as compared to one [in a comic book] of a girl in brassiere and panties about to be tied up, gagged, tortured, set on fire, sold as a slave, chained, whipped, choked, raped, thrown to wild animals or crocodiles, forced to her knees, strangled, torn apart and so on."[36]

Wertham also objected to advertisements appearing in comic books. He reported signing a child's name to an order blank and receiving a switchblade knife in the mail. Also available to children in the early 1950s through advertisements in comic books were rifles, an assortment of knives, and whips. From Wertham's perspective, comic books not only tempted children to commit crimes and taught them how to be criminals, but they also provided the implements of crime.

From newspaper files and records at the Lafargue clinic, Wertham drew many examples of children re-enacting criminal scenes from comic books:

1. Three boys, six to eight years old, took a boy of seven, hanged him nude from a tree, his hands tied behind him, then burned him with matches. Probation officers investigating found that they were re-enacting a comic-book plot....

3. A boy of eleven killed a woman in a holdup. When arrested, he was found surrounded by comic books. His twenty-year-old brother said, "If you want the cause of all this, here it is: It's those rotten comic books. Cut them out, and things like this wouldn't happen...."

7. A boy of thirteen committed a "lust murder" of a girl of six. After his arrest, in jail, he asked for comic books. "I refused, of course," said the sheriff....

11. A fourteen-year-old crime-comics addict killed a fourteen-year-old girl by stabbing her thirteen times with a knife....

19. In one city within a few months there were five separate instances where

very young children were tortured by boys from five to eight years old in comic-book fashion....[37]

Other students of juvenile delinquency disputed Wertham's claim that comic books were a major factor in delinquency. One of Wertham's major critics was famed sociologist Fredric M. Thrasher, a specialist in urban youth gangs. Writing in the December 1949 issue of the *Journal of Educational Sociology*, Thrasher criticized Wertham for only providing impressionistic proof of a relationship between comics and delinquency. Thrasher argued that there did not exist any scientific proof that comic books caused crime. The only thing that did exist, Thrasher claimed, were complaints about comic books from parents, psychiatrists, lawyers, and judges.[38] Other experts agreed with Thrasher. Carl Rush, executive assistant at the American Psychological Association, declared that comic books were an insignificant contributor to juvenile delinquency.[39] Writing in the *Journal of Criminal Law,* John Cavanagh, Associate Clinical Professor of Medicine at Georgetown University, stated that he could find no evidence of a harmful effect of comic books on children.[40]

While most social scientists dismissed the idea of a causal relation between comics and crime, parents' organization and community groups leveled a barrage of complaints about the alleged effect of comic books on children. *Parents' Magazine* assumed an early role in criticizing the contents of comic books. As I discussed in Chapter 7, *Parents' Magazine* had led public attacks on children's radio in the 1930s. As early as 1941, *Parents' Magazine* announced the publication of its own comic book, *True Comics,* as a substitute for ordinary comic books. The magazine's editor, Clara Savage Littledale, wrote that most comic books were "lurid, fantastic, cheap, terrifically time-wasting and over-stimulating." Rather than parents prohibiting their children from reading comic books, they were supposed to give their children *True Comics,* which contained stories of real heroes, such as Winston Churchill and Simon Bolivar.[41]Beginning in 1952, *Parents' Magazine* published an annual rating of comic books by the Cincinnati Committee on the Evaluation of Comic Books.[42]

The Cincinnati Committee, however, was only one of several community groups focusing on the issue of comic books. *Publishers Weekly* reported in 1948 the existence of many local groups trying to enforce censorship of comic books through ordinances and pressure on sellers of magazines.[43] In the summer 1948, Mayor Don E. Satterlee of Bellingham, Washington, asked the city's Censorship Board to investigate the content of comic books being distributed in the community. It appointed a Special Investigative Committee composed of a minister, a teacher, a housewife, and a representative from the Women's Christian Temperance Union who created a community comic book code. Reviewing 278 comic books according to the code, the committee found 67 objectionable, and local magazine distributors agreed not to sell them.[44] In 1949, school children in Spencer, West Virginia and Binghamton, New York, participated in comic book bonfires.[45]

In December 1948, the President of the National Congress of Parents and Teachers, Mabel Hughes, announced with regard to comic books that, "The time has come when direct attack is in order." A resolution passed by the organization called for the establishment of local and state groups to evaluate comic books and investigate local and state laws regarding objectionable literature.[46] These sentiments were followed up in 1949 by the local St. Paul, Minnesota, PTA, which teamed up with the local council of churches, the Legion of Decency, and other community groups to create a list of 136 approved comic books. The group used the list in its attempts to place pressure on local magazine distributors to remove objectionable comic books from newsstands. The guidelines of the St. Paul committee for comic book censorship stated "that acceptable comic books should emphasize the principles of democracy, show respect for the moral laws of God, and portray characters who if imitated as heroes would contribute to wholesome personality development."[47]

The code of the Cincinnati Committee on the Evaluation of Comic Books was widely known because of its annual publication by *Parent's Magazine*. The Cincinnati Committee was formed in 1948 by the Cincinnati Council of Churches under the leadership of the Rev. Jesse Murrell, a minister in the Methodist Church. Working with Murrell were representatives from the local PTA, the Cincinnati Board of Education, a Women's Page editor from the local newspaper, and psychologists from local universities. The committee opposed censorship laws and hoped instead that its review of comic books would influence parents, publishers, and magazine distributors.

The Cincinnati Committee issued its first rating of comic books in 1949. It used the following rating scale:

A—No Objection
B—Some Objection
C—Objectionable
D—Very Objectionable

While the Committee gave most horror and crime comics a C or D rating, they also targeted American Indian and Western comic books because "the 11 magazines dealing with the American Indian and many of the 45 Western comics put the Indian in a bad light. This was considered undesirable and unfair to the many American Indians who are law-abiding citizens. The criteria of the Cincinnati Committee condemn all acts, words, and deeds that tend to belittle or misrepresent any such group."[48]

Other communities tried different tactics to combat what was believed to be the bad influence of comic books. In the early 1950s, protests by the local PTA in Santa Barbara, California, resulted in the elimination from local newsstands of all crime and horror magazines. In 1954, the Santa Barbara PTA established lending libraries in elementary schools "to combat the influence of objectionable comic books."[49]

In 1954 many local women's clubs removed comic books they objected to from newsstands after their national organization, the General Federation of Women's Clubs, urged them to vigilantly "watch the newsstands in your neighborhoods to see that the objectionable comic books...are not there." In Kokomo, Indiana, the local women's club teamed up with the PTA to force magazine distributors to remove such comic books. In Arlington, Massachusetts, a committee of parents went from store to store checking comic books. These actions were typical of women across the country who believed it was their duty to rid the country of the scourge of horror and crime comic books.[50]

Efforts were made to establish government censorship laws. In 1949, a special committee was established by the New York State Legislature to study the comic book issue. Governor Thomas Dewey of New York vetoed a bill that would have required publishers to obtain a permit from the State Education Department before distributing comic books. In the same year, similar bills were defeated in the Massachusetts state legislature. In 1950, the Canadian House of Commons passed a bill making crime comic books illegal. In 1952, Governor Dewey again vetoed a bill designed to censor comic books. Another such bill was proposed in the New York state legislature in 1955, forbidding the sale of comics dealing with crime, horror, sex, or brutality to anyone under 18 years of age.[51]

Following the pattern with movies and broadcasting, the comic book industry was forced to act because of the combination of threats from federal, state, and local governments, and local and national organizations. Wanting to avoid continued community protest and the threat of censorship laws, comic book publishers organized to create and impose their own standards. Their first attempt was the 1948 formation of the Association of Comics Magazine Publishers and its adoption of a six-point code. A seal was to be attached to comic books to indicate conformity to the code.[52] Like other codes, there was an emphasis on issues involving sex, crime, language, the family, and attacks on religious and racial groups. These rules stipulated that:

1. Sexy, wanton comics should not be published.
2. Crime should not be presented in such a way as to throw sympathy against law and justice or to inspire others with the desire for imitation. No comics should show the details and methods of a crime committed by a youth. Policemen, judges, government officials, and respected institutions should not be portrayed as stupid or ineffective, or represented in such a way as to weaken respect for established authority.
3. No scenes of sadistic torture should be shown.

4. Vulgar and obscene language should never be used.
5. Divorce should not be treated humorously or represented as glamorous or alluring.
6. Ridicule of or attack on any religious or racial group is never permissible.[53]

This early code proved ineffective, because only 12 of the 34 major publishers of comic books belonged to the comic book association.[54] In 1950, the attorney for the association, Henry Schultz, described the reasons for the failure of the code: "The defections became so bad we could not afford to continue...[the] precensorship arrangement and that has been discarded. Today we do no self-regulation at all except as it may exist in the minds of the editors as they proceed in their daily work...."[55]

With increased pressure from government and private organizations, a new organization, Comics Magazine Association of America, was formed in 1954 with a membership of 28 of the by then 31 major publishers of comic books. This association appointed New York City magistrate Charles Murphy to enforce a comic book code.

The code was similar to the earlier one. The words "horror" and "terror" were not allowed in titles. Crime comics were to be screened to exclude methods of committing crimes. No sympathy was to be given for criminals and nothing should "create disrespect for established authority." In addition, the code banned "profanity, obscenity, smut, vulgarity, ridicule of racial or religious groups." The "sanctity of marriage" and the "value of the home" were to be upheld, and "divorce was not to be shown as desirable."[56]

A budget of $100,000 was agreed upon to pay a staff to review comic book manuscripts. Like the previous attempt to enforce the code, comic books approved by Judge Murphy's staff were to display a special seal of approval on the front cover. On December 28, 1954, Judge Murphy announced that by February 1955 all approved comics published by member firms would have such a seal. Murphy's office estimated that the code would be enforced on 75 percent of the estimated 60 million comic books published each month in the United States.[57]

Dell Comics, one of the three publishers that did not belong to the Comics Magazine Association of America, and publisher of approximately twenty percent of the comic books in the United States, did not join the association because it already had its own code of ethics. In any case, Dell primarily published comics based on adventure stories and Walt Disney characters. It was known in the trade as having a "wholesome approach." One of the other non-members was Classics Illustrated, which adapted classic novels, such as Charles Dickens' Oliver Twist, to a comic book format. William Gaines, the originator of horror comics and another nonmember, announced that he would cease publishing all horror and terror magazines. Thus comic books joined movies, broadcasting, and public schools in distributing a sanitized image of the world.[58]

CONCLUSION

As discussed in Chapter 10, the public schools, broadcasting, and movies during the 1950s disseminated an image of America that focused on the value of free enterprise and rugged individualism. The portrayal of sanitized violence added another dimension to the image of America disseminated during the 1950s. During the Cold War, the possibility of nuclear destruction was always present. One wonders what the possibility meant to television viewers and readers of approved comic books who were inundated by acts of violence that had been edited to remove any portrayal of the actual physical consequences of violence. Surrounded by images of sanitized violence and of a world where good always won out over evil, an individual might have imagined a war without physical consequences and with a guaranteed victory.

An interesting question in retrospect is whether or not sanitized violence did contribute to juvenile delinquency and increased crime rates. Commentators in the 1950s might have been right that, surrounded by images of crime and violence, people more readily committed criminal acts. And if those acts are stripped of their physical consequences, then the individual might be more willing to exhibit those behaviors.

In any event images of family harmony and the avoidance of positive portrayal of divorce fit into the more general theme that a good America was a harmonious America. Many public leaders in the 1950s traced the origins of juvenile delinquency to the broken family. Therefore, the image of harmony was associated the American Way of Life and individuals. This was an image of an America of economic prosperity and individualism, sanitized violence, consensus values, harmonious families, patriotism, and triumphant justice.

CHAPTER TWELVE

MANAGING IMAGES:
CIVIL RIGHTS AND THE ANTI-WAR MOVEMENT

"AS RALPH ELLISON'S novel, *Invisible Man,* demonstrates," states a 1964 California State Department of Education report on "The Negro in American History Textbooks," "whites frequently do not 'see' Negroes. But Negroes are Americans…. They need to be 'seen' in textbooks."[1] During the same period, African-American students in an elementary school class in New York City drew white faces when asked to complete self-portraits. Of them broadcasting historian Eric Barnouw wrote, "Accepting the world's verdict, they denied themselves…. It is perhaps not a coincidence that the beginnings of the Negro revolt—the rise of the 'invisible man'—coincided with the spread and penetration of television."[2]

Amid fears of Communism and juvenile delinquency, the civil rights movement precipitated a conflict over the image of African-Americans in textbooks and television programming. On the one hand, Southern communities resisted adoption of multiracial textbooks and television programming with positive African-American images. Of particular concern for Southern communities were television newscasts and programs about civil rights demonstrations. On the other hand, federal legislation and civil rights' protests persuaded publishers to create textbooks reflecting a multiracial society and presenting positive images of African-Americans. Television broadcasts of civil rights demonstrations not only made African-Americans "visible," but also contributed to the pressure for desegregation of public schools and other institutions. During the 1960s, civil rights activities increased the visibility of African-Americans in television programming.

These changes in racial images took many subtle twists and turns. For instance, television news brought the civil rights movement directly into American homes and forced viewers to confront issues of discrimination and segregation. In this context, television became a political tool for the civil rights movement. A successful demonstration could be measured by the amount of television coverage. William Paley, founder and chairman of CBS, wrote in his memoirs, "Some of the civil rights protests and marches seemed to be planned with one eye on the TV camera." Paley quoted the President of CBS, Frank Stanton: "There seems to be a tendency on the part of persons who are setting up demonstrations to accommodate the networks to reap the most publicity and exposure."[3]

After complaints about the political power of television, networks tried to modify their coverage of demonstrations. Paley received complaints from city officials in Toledo and Newark that television provoked racial riots. The governor of Tennessee, Buford Ellington, charged in 1960 that "the sit-in demonstration by Negro students in downtown Nashville today was instigated and planned by, and staged for, the convenience of the Columbia Broadcasting System." Paley recounted how CBS answered these complaints by "using unmarked cars, avoiding the use of bright lights, and declining to promise TV coverage of future protests."[4]

Television coverage also changed the political direction of various organizations. As I will discuss in more detail later in this chapter, television coverage had a dramatic impact on the goals and organization of the Students for a Democratic Society (SDS). In *The Whole World Is Watching: Mass Media in the Making & Unmaking of the New Left,* Todd Gitlin traces television's effect in transforming SDS from a loosely structured organization promoting the goals of participatory democracy to a major national leader of anti-war demonstrations.[5]

While television had a political impact on the civil rights and anti-war movements, the Civil Rights Movement battled to gain equal access to public schools and television programming, and to change the nature of ideas distributed by these ways. The struggle to integrate public schools reflected a belief that knowledge can provide political and economic power. Furthermore, both whites and African-Americans in the integration struggle recognized that the social organization for the distribution of knowledge determines the exercise of that power. Central to the debate over school segregation was the argument that the social relationships established in schools were as important as the quality of instruction.

Most segregated schools did not provide African-American students with an education equal to that of white students. Compared to white students in segregated Southern school systems, African-American students attended schools with poorer facilities, textbooks, curriculum, and teachers. Under segregation, there was an unequal distribution of knowledge to African-Americans. In addition, the very nature of segregation conveyed a message of their inferiority to African-American students. The 1954 United States Supreme Court decision declaring school segregation unconstitutional was based on the argument that segregation was inherently unequal.[6]

Of course, changing the ideas disseminated by schools was just as important as gaining equal access. Most textbooks contained only pictures of whites and excluded African-Americans in stories and examples. In addition, textbooks tended to stereotype the role of African-Americans in United States history. During the 1960s, a complex set of political circumstances partially rectified this situation.

The issues in education were similar to those in broadcasting. African-American actors, writers, and producers wanted equal employment opportunities in the broadcasting industry. In addition, civil rights organizations wanted to end the casting of African-Americans only in stereotyped roles on television programs.

Paralleling civil rights gains in the public schools, television programming in 1960s began to include more African-Americans in realistic roles. In addition, television broadcasts of civil rights demonstrations presented white audiences with images of strong and heroic African-Americans, while at the same time aiding the civil rights movement by showing the brutality of white opponents. Pressured by a variety of political forces, executives of television networks in the 1960s tried to assure that African-Americans received equal access to employment and equal treatment on television programs.

Changes in public schooling and television were the result of the same political events. Civil rights organizations, particularly the National Association for the Advancement of Colored People (NAACP), provided leadership for legal challenges to segregation and for grassroots political movements. These organizations played a similar role in television. As a result of these grassroots political efforts, national politicians responded in the 1960s with legislation and government pressure that changed the public school curricula and textbooks, and helped to integrate American broadcasting.

Changes in public school textbooks and television occurred most rapidly between the volatile years 1963 and 1968. Civil rights activities in the 1950s focused primarily on gaining equal rights in the South. The "March on Washington" in the summer 1963 sent a message to the nation that the civil rights movement was turning into a national Poor People's Crusade for Economic Justice. Northern urban riots increased fears that the United States was on the verge of class warfare. After riots in Harlem in 1964 and Los Angeles in 1965, racial rebellion spread rapidly across the country. In 1966 riots broke out in San Francisco, followed by major rebellions in 1967 in Milwaukee, Detroit, Cincinnati, Minneapolis, Tampa, Newark, and Rochester. In 1968, Chicago, Washington, D.C., and Memphis erupted in racial violence.

But concerned about the role of television in publicizing demonstrations against the Viet Nam war, President Richard Nixon became a vocal critic of the television industry. The Nixon administration accused the media of provoking and increasing the intensity of anti-war and civil rights demonstrations, and it tried to reduce the role of television in bringing about social change.

CHANGING TEXTBOOK IMAGES OF AMERICA

An analysis of white-dominated textbooks appeared in 1954, the year of the Supreme Court's school desegregation decision, in an article in *Progressive*

Education by educator Abraham Tannenbaum entitled "Family Living in Textbook Town." Tannenbaum surveyed ten years of primers and first-, second-, and third-grade reading texts to determine the cultural images being imparted to students. He called this cultural image, "Textbook Town."[7]

Tannenbaum noted that Textbook Town was *not* a composite of different neighborhood environments. All the texts had the same type of neighborhood. Tannenbaum described this neighborhood as,

> rows of brightly polished little cottages, fronted by neatly manicured lawns, all suggesting an atmosphere of order and cheerfulness. In this sunny neighborhood setting, children have lots of room for out-of-doors play, and families are able to enjoy their living space with the kind of "elbowroom" that is not possible in the more thickly populated cities. The reader gets to know these picturesque surroundings quite intimately, for much of the action in the stories takes place there.

Typically, the family home in Textbook Town was comfortably furnished, the father having his favorite easy chair and workshop, and the mother, a well-equipped kitchen. The father was usually slim and handsome, often depicted arriving home from work dressed in a neat suit in the family car. Fathers in Textbook Town were all businessmen or professionals. Only when making minor home repairs was the father shown in work clothes.

The mother had no occupation outside of housework, devoting her time to caring for her family. She was usually young, attractive, and well-dressed. The only time she was seen outside of the house was shopping and on family recreation trips .

The children in Textbook Town were all happy and well-adjusted. They spent their time in play and in doing minor chores with their parents. They were well-behaved and never fought with their siblings or parents. In Tannenbaum's words, "Nothing is ever allowed to interfere seriously with the spirit of joy, security, and cooperativeness that dominates family living in Textbook Town."[8]

Everyone in Textbook Town was white. No people of color or distinctive ethnic characteristics lived in Textbook Town. And, no one in Textbook Town was poor. Tannenbaum complained that the unrealistic social composition of Textbook Town provided little motivation for reading among lower class children, and they were of little interest to the middle class child,

> for Textbook Town, with its bland style of living, is nothing more than an idealized middle-class community where characters are mere shadows, and where nothing exciting or of real importance ever happens. To the lower-class child it looms as a "never-never world" that may excite in him vague dreams for attainment, but which will probably elude him forever.[9]

The report on "The Negro in American History Textbooks" also criticized the unrealistic view of American life presented in school books. This study was initiated in 1963 by the Berkeley, California, chapter of the Congress on Racial Equality (CORE). CORE played a major role in civil rights activities in the 1950s and 1960s, and it was one of the first advocates of nonviolent methods for social change.[10]

Politically, CORE's investigation of textbooks in California was very important. The California State Board of Education was mandated to select textbooks that could be adopted by local school systems in the state. Given the large number of sales involved, the textbook industry was very attuned to the desires of the California State Board of Education.[11]

CORE organized a distinguished panel of University of California historians headed by Kenneth Stampp to analyze American history textbooks adopted for use in grades five and eight and two textbooks used in the state's high schools in 1964. The report was presented to the State Board of Education, whose members directed the California Department of Education to distribute it to interested groups, including textbook publishers. In 1966, the report was used by a committee of the U.S. House of Representatives investigating the treatment of minority groups in textbooks and reprinted in the proceedings of the committee.[12]

The panel of academic historians were amazed by the almost total neglect of African-Americans' history. One textbook did not mention African-Americans in any connection. One did not refer to slavery during the colonial period, while others did not discuss anything about African-Americans after the Civil War. The report complained, "The greatest defect in the textbooks we have examined is the virtual omission of the Negro."[13]

The panel criticized the unrealistic treatment of the relationships between whites and African-Americans. When discussed at all in the textbooks, interracial contacts were portrayed as harmonious. There was little if anything mentioned in the textbooks about the long history of violence between African-Americans and whites. "In their blandness and amoral optimism," the analysis concluded, "these books deny the obvious deprivations suffered by Negroes. In several places they go further, implying approval for the repression of Negroes or patronizing them as being unqualified for life in a free society."[14]

The report recommended full treatment of African-American history. The historians on the panel suggested that books begin with the early importation and treatment of slaves and conclude with the recent history of the civil rights movement. And, the report urged, the "Gains that have been made should be described realistically and not as an ode to the inevitable justice and progress of the democratic system."[15]

The NAACP, too, was interested in the content of textbooks. Since the NAACP's demonstrations against the movie *Birth of a Nation* in 1915, the organization had paid vigilant attention to public images of African-Americans (As discussed later, the NAACP was a leading critic of the television version of "Amos 'n' Andy." In 1966, the organization issued a guide to integrated textbooks with the statement that "in the crucial effort to guarantee to all our children, white and black, a curriculum that makes sense in a multi-racial society, such a listing is long overdue."[16]

The editors of *Ebony Magazine* also expressed concern about history textbooks. The Senior Editor of *Ebony* and its specialist in historical articles, Lerone Bennett, spent five years studying textbooks and concluded that, "The use of textbooks filled with half-truths, evasions and distortions is disastrous to both white and black Americans...[and] white-oriented textbooks tend to inoculate white Americans with the virus of racism...." Bennett called on the federal government to provide the resources and power to solve the textbook problem.[17]

While the March on Washington and urban riots added urgency to the issue of making "visible" the "invisible" African-American, the 1965 Elementary and Secondary Education Act (ESEA) provided the economic incentives for publishers to produce multiracial textbooks. As a central piece in President Johnson's War on Poverty program, the legislation's premise was that education could offer escape from poverty by providing equality of opportunity.[18]

By providing money for research and for purchase of textbooks, like the National Defense Education Act discussed in Chapter 10, ESEA influenced the content of textbooks. The difference was in objectives. Whereas the National Defense Education Act was primarily for winning the Cold War with the Soviet Union by helping "excellent students" in the sciences and engineering, the ESEA was concerned with aiding "culturally deprived" students as a means of ending racial tension and the possibilities of class warfare. In both cases, the federal government took an active role in shaping the goals and practices of public schools by providing funds for the development and purchase of educational materials.[19]

Like the argument of movie czar Eric Johnston in the 1940s, ESEA's premise was that racism was a destructive economic force because it divided society and hindered economic development by not allowing equal economic opportunity for all people.[20] The same argument for integrating textbooks was made by Charles F. Bound, Vice-President of Morgan Guaranty Trust Co., and banker for many leading publishers. Speaking before a joint conference on "Education in a Changing Society" held by the American Textbook Publishers Institute and the Urban League in April 1965, Bound stated, "At the heart of the poverty problem and of the urban problem is the Negro problem. Unless we successfully solve the Negro problem, we will not solve the other two."[21]

Integrating texts was also considered a means of ending racial rebellion. Against a background of rising urban riots, Lerone Bennett warned the 1966 House subcommittee investigating the treatment of minorities in textbooks that "segregated textbooks...are as dangerous to the internal peace of America as segregated schools and residential areas." In fact, he argued that if all schools and neighborhoods were immediately integrated without integrating textbooks, then all schools and neighborhoods would soon become segregated again. Bennett found it ironic that one of the largest race riots had occurred in Chicago which was originally founded by the African-American Jean Baptiste Pointe Du Sable. "And it seems to me," he declared, "that a solution to our current crisis depends to a great extent on the opening of our minds and our textbooks to all the Du Sables and the excluded range of American life and culture that they personified."[22]

The American Textbook Publishers Institute (ATPI), the trade association representing 110 publishers of textbooks and other educational materials, acted as mediator between publishers and civil rights organizations in the development of multiracial textbooks. The organization played an important role in making publishing companies aware of educational trends and new research. One of the problems for textbook publishers is that although they must do market research on what types of textbooks are wanted by school systems, they do not often conduct their own research and therefore have to rely on outside research organizations. By bringing together publishers, researchers, and educational leaders, the ATPI attempted to make textbooks more responsive to market demands. Speaking before the 1966 House subcommittee investigating the treatment of minorities in textbooks, Austin J. McCaffrey, Executive Director of ATPI, explained the role of his organization in the early 1960s.

> Educational publishers, through the institute, have become increasingly aware of the changing trends in education and the dramatic challenges which are facing the schools of today. The curriculum studies of the National Science Foundation and the United States Office of Education, the research projects of private educational organizations, and reports of leading educational spokesmen all tended to emphasize the cross currents in American life which were giving rise to innovative thinking in all areas of education.[23]

"But in the profitable field of textbooks, altruism is rarely a motivating factor," as a 1966 article in *Newsweek* pointed out. The article quoted a textbook salesman, "We're in business to sell books, not to make sociological decisions."[24] The ATPI pursued the economic interests of publishers by working closely with the United States Office of Education and state departments of education in what could be characterized as a classic example of the relationship between government and private industry. On the one hand, the government provided money for research and development of a product, and then provided funds for its purchase. On the other hand, the industry received free research advice paid for out of public funds and then received a profit for selling the developed product back to government.

For example, the ATPI organized its first conference in 1964 in cooperation with the office's Adult Education Branch of the United States Office of Education. In fact, Dr. Edward Brice of the Adult Education Branch assumed leadership in organizing the conference. Participants in the conference included private educational agencies, schools systems, universities, public libraries, state departments of education, and publishers. The focus of the conference was the development of instructional materials for adult education. The obvious economic beneficiaries of the conference were the publishers.[25]

Cooperating with another government agency, the ATPI held a 1964 conference with the New York State Department of Education on instructional materials for disadvantaged students. A featured topic of the conference was "the role of the textbook and the role of the publisher." The Associate Commissioner of the New York State Department of Education, Walter Crewson, declared that "a historic step has been taken, although just a first step in eliminating that which is...discriminatory in our curriculum and in our textbooks with respect to minority groups."[26]

In 1965, the publishers scheduled a joint conference with the Urban League to determine "the needs of the Negro child and the kinds of materials which would help him relate to the total American society."[27] The Executive Director of the National Urban League, Whitney Young, Jr., told the meeting, "You publishers want the respect of generations born and generations yet unborn. We live together as brothers, or we die together as fools." Another member of the Urban League, Edwin Berry, insisted that publishers do more than just integrate textbooks with pictures of differing ethnic groups. They should also, he argued, provide a realistic view of society by including "tall people, short people, fat and slim people, people with glasses, balding men and pregnant women."[28]

By establishing relations with the Great Cities Research Council, the ATPI provided publishers with another source of free research and influential contacts. Organized in 1956, the Council was composed of educators from the fifteen largest American cities. At their first joint meeting in 1965, the Council and the ATPI agreed to collect urban-oriented educational materials in cooperation with the Educational Materials Center in the United States Office of Education. The ATPI organized itself as a clearinghouse for new research. To further aid the objectives of publishers, the joint conference arranged visits by teams of publishers to meet with educators in all of the member school systems.[29]

In addition, the ATPI lobbied for federal funds to purchase textbooks. In explaining to Congressional investigators that ESEA provided funds for increased purchases of textbooks, ATPI Executive Director McCaffrey claimed: "After conferring with educators, the institute has reached the conclusion that the per pupil expenditures for instructional materials would have to at least double in order to properly equip a student today." While presented in the language of helping students, the proposed increase in purchases of textbooks would also have at least doubled the profits of publishers.

The ATPI also tried to influence textbook purchases by distributing to local schools a booklet entitled, "Planning Your Purchases of Educational Materials," which provided guidelines for the basic minimum of educational materials for each grade level and recommendations for the amount to spend.[30]

Before the Congressional investigators, McCaffrey argued that publishers were already being pressured by local school systems to produce multiracial textbooks. McCaffrey told the House subcommittee that: "I think 2 or 3 years ago a number of principal cities in the country passed resolutions in their boards of education that it was the policy of these cities to purchase only books that had a fair representation of minorities.... We had no pressures outside of resolutions passed by government bodies at the local level."[31]

Some publishers directly linked the availability of federal funds to the production of multiracial texts. A Senior Vice-President of McGraw-Hill, Robert W. Locke, testified that the publication of the new urban and multiracial books were a result of the profits that could be made with the passage of the ESEA. Locke told the House Subcommittee, "Purchases of new textbooks and other instructional materials have risen sharply this year because of ESEA, and part of the gap has been closed between what should be done for schoolchildren and what is being done." In fact, Locke indicated that federal money was the most important element in the expansion of the textbook publishing industry in the early 1960s; he told the subcommittee: "My guess is that something like 30 or 40 percent of our increase in sales this year at the elementary and secondary level will be a result of NDEA funds or ESEA funds."[32]

In response to ESEA, McGraw-Hill published texts depicting multiethnic urban settings. In 1965, the company issued the *Skyline* reading series for grades two through four, which contained stories about people living in multiethnic cities. For example, a story in the series, "The Hidden Lookout," is about Rosita's search for a place of her own in a city with millions of people. Eventually, she builds a box house on an apartment roof.[33]

The *Skyline* series was only one of several related series published by McGraw-Hill in 1965. It also published that year a series *Americans All,* with specific titles on "The American Negro," "Our Oriental Americans," "Our Citizens From the Caribbean," and "Latin Americans of the Southwest." In addition, in 1965 it published a high school textbook focusing on civil liberties, *Heritage of Liberty.*[34]

The President of ATPI and Scott, Foresman & Co., Darrel Peterson, made a special plea to the subcommittee for more federal money for textbooks: "I would like to offer strong endorsement for the Government's efforts to improve the quantity and quality of educational materials available to students in our schools.... These Federal investments in libraries and instructional materials in general are eminently worthwhile."[35] Loading his statement with altruistic appeals to helping inner city children, he argued that federal money for improving textbooks was essential for improving society.

A major issue for the subcommittee was Southern resistance to multiracial texts and publishers issuing special editions for Southern schools. Harcourt, Brace & World, Inc., was being pressured by Southern states to issue a special edition that eliminated multiracial pictures. In 1966, the company distributed a new edition of a series of elementary school grammar and composition texts. In 1965, Southern states approved sight-unseen the purchase of the new edition. But when one state saw the new edition in 1966 with illustrations of white and African-American children playing together, they sent an immediate protest to the publishers. The vice-president of the publishing company, Cameron S. Moseley, explained, "There was an unofficial, implied threat to cancel all our contracts in the state, not just for that series." Publishers were interested in profit and not social causes. Consequently, Harcourt, Brace & World printed a special version of the text which "de-integrated" the illustrations by showing only white children.[36]

In 1965, Scott, Foresman published three new multiethnic series in reading, health, and social studies. "These books," Peterson stated, "which are multiethnic in character, present all kinds of children in natural situations and, where appropriate, contribute to the positive imagery of the diversified composition of American society."[37]

But Scott, Foresman continued printing its 1962 all-white edition of the reading series. When questioned by members of the subcommittee on the continued publication of the all-white series, Peterson claimed that the company was not producing a series just for the South. He stated that both series were being sold throughout the country. In other words, all school districts in the country had a choice between the multiethnic and all-white versions. The increased cost of publishing two editions, he explained, was balanced by the bigger volume of business.[38]

The major differences between the all-white and multiethnic editions in the Scott, Foresman series were in the illustrations. Besides the texts specifically written for urban areas, most of the changes made by other publishers were also in the illustrations. Holt, Rinehart & Winston applied this principle to a new program that used 100 magnetized multiethnic cutout characters. In describing its new urban social studies program, the Executive Vice-President of the company, Ross Sackett, emphasized that, "Dramatic photographs capture the interaction between individuals and groups in an actual multicultural, multiracial community."[39]

In fact, publishers described their books according to the number of illustrations that included minority groups. For example, Craig Senft, President of Silver Burdett Co., proudly described his company's new first grade textbook, *Families and Their Needs,* as identifying "facts that determine just how the needs of families from a variety of physical environments and cultures are met. It so happens that of the 54 photographs illustrating some aspect of American families, 18 show minority group families or individuals." He emphasized, "We intentionally chose photographs that included minority groups to show as many ethnic and socioeconomic strains as were needed to portray the differences that give our society its variety and richness."[40]

The harmony in Textbook Town did not decline with integrated illustrations, however. Now African-Americans and whites in textbook pictures were portrayed as working or playing together, while discrimination and racial violence actually continued in society. No longer invisible in textbooks, African-Americans were catapulted to equality in their illustrations. The process of adding African-Americans to pictures was sometimes referred to as giving textbook characters a "sunburn."[41]

There were several techniques involved in this process. One created "integrated" drawings by using different mechanical color separations or simply two colors. Simple black and white line drawings showed ethnically vague features that could be filled in by the reader's imagination. Photographs of integrated groups were frequently used in popular settings such as stores, playgrounds, neighborhood streets, and homes.[42]

Relying upon changes in illustrations, textbook publishers could claim integration of a wide variety of texts, including those in science and mathematics. Locke, of McGraw-Hill, considered an elementary school science program, "Experiences in Science," as integrated because, in his words to the House subcommittee, "we have taken great care to include minority-group children in the illustrations." He also included an arithmetic filmstrip because its frames included both white and nonwhite groups.[43]

Integrated stories appearing in textbooks also conveyed a message of racial harmony. While illustrations were the easiest and most popular method for publishers to integrate textbooks, multiracial and multiethnic stories were placed in readers. Typical of these additions to readers was the series published by Houghton Mifflin. "Galumph," the opening story of its second grade reader, is about a cat who divided its time between an African-American child, an Italian baker, a Hispanic girl, and a sick white child. Another story, "Traffic Policeman," is about a white child cooperating with an African-American policeman. And "A Penny for a Jack Rabbit" is the unlikely tale—given the racial tension and housing discrimination in the society at that time—of suburban African-American and white children playing together at a party.[44]

Therefore, the setting and population of Textbook Town was transformed without disturbing the basic message of harmony and happiness. Political pressures and government funding added an urban dimension and a multiracial and multiethnic population to Textbook Town. Textbook Town now included apartment buildings as well as suburban bungalows, where happy groups of multiracial children played together. History textbooks contained sections on slavery and the civil rights movement.

These changes were an important victory by civil rights groups in the struggle for ideological management. African-Americans were no longer invisible in American textbooks. On the other hand, textbooks still skimmed the surface of reality. Dick and Jane lived in the Textbook Town of the 1950s in a harmonious and happy relationship with their parents, friends, and neighbors. Nothing controversial disturbed the placid living of Textbook Town. The same thing was true when Textbook Town became integrated. But an integrated Textbook Town still seemed out of touch with the reality of racial violence and discrimination.

PUBLIC PARTICIPATION IN THE CONTROL OF TELEVISION IMAGES

When "Amos 'n' Andy" made its debut on CBS television in 1951 with an all–African-American cast, the NAACP launched an immediate campaign to get it off the air. William Paley recalls, "Five days after the first broadcast, the National Association for the Advancement of Colored People denounced the show as insulting to blacks.... The television show, under attack by black leaders for its entire life, left the network after two seasons."[45]

Historian Thomas Cripps argues that the protest primarily came from the African-American middle class, because the program conveyed the impression that all African-Americans were ignorant and rowdy. The image projected by the program threatened African-American middle class pretensions. According to Cripps, the African-American community was divided over the program. Many African-American actors saw the program as opening the door to employment, and many African-Americans enjoyed the program and questioned the charge of racism. The sponsor of the program, Blatz Beer, released a poll showing that 77 percent of African-American New Yorkers liked the program.[46]

Joined by the middle class African-American magazine *Ebony,* the NAACP, according to Cripps, led "the black middle class in challeng[ing] what they took to be a parody of their historical struggle for social mobility in a hostile society."[47] In fact, Cripps argues that the NAACP was not successful in convincing all African-Americans that the show was their enemy. He also argues that Blatz withdrew its sponsorship because of its desire to sponsor a more prestigious show, the "Four Star Playhouse," and not because of the protests by the NAACP.[48] In the light of Cripps' argument, it would be difficult to claim a major victory for the NAACP, but one could assume that the organization's protest played some role in Blatz's decision to end its sponsorship.

As civil rights activities increased, many advertisers refused to sponsor programs that might create the impression that they supported the civil rights movement. Advertisers feared antagonizing Southern audiences and losing sales. One of the first victims of these fears was a 1957–1958 miniseries on the Civil War. Called "The Gray Ghost," it was a romantic portrayal of Confederate Colonel John Singleton Mosby and his band of raiders. The series premiered in September 1957 at the same time as the civil rights confrontations at Central High School in Little Rock. Fearing entanglement in civil rights issues, advertisers withdrew support from the program. Another source of problems were television broadcasts of movies. In 1957, many Southern stations refused to air the African-American musical *Cabin in the Sky*. Broadcasts of the movies *Go, Man, Go,* about the Harlem Globetrotters, and *The Jackie Robinson Story* met with Southern resistance. And in the early 1960s, Monitor South was organized to coordinate rejection of network programming.[49]

To counter protests against the lack of African-Americans on television, NBC in the 1950s adopted a policy of "integration without identification." This meant the avoidance of racial themes on television but the use of African-American actors in minor parts. In 1957, a NBC official stated:

> It is so easy, really, in casting for sympathetically portrayed roles to hire actors whose racial derivation is apparent.... I hope you have noticed here and there everything from taxi-drivers to newspapermen, from doctors to social workers, played by competent Negro actors or actors of other racial minority derivation.[50]

Pressure from civil rights organizations continued to force broadcasters to take a stand. In the spring 1962, CBS announced its adherence to a policy of "no discrimination because of race, creed, religion, or national origin." In 1963, the American Federation of Television and Radio Artists issued a declaration of non-bias. But these pronouncements seemed to have little effect on the actual images in television programming. A survey in 1963 found that a viewer in New York City on an average evening would see a total of three African-Americans, only one of these for longer than a minute. An editorial in the June 11, 1963, issue of the *Daily Defender* complained that "the TV industry as a whole is still perpetuating a picture of lily-white America on video in keeping with the "boob tube" concept.[51]

In the early 1960s, African-Americans did appear in newscasts and documentaries. The March on Washington in the summer 1963 set the stage for a number of TV documentaries. ABC produced a five-part series, "Crucial Summer" presenting African-Americans in a heroic struggle to overcome segregation and prejudice. Featured on the series were Roy Wilkins and Martin Luther King, Jr. An NBC special, "The American Revolution of '63," devoted five and one-half hours over a period of five weeks to examining the civil rights movement. The pressure of political events was forcing a revolution in African-American images on television.[52]

Things changed when the issue of white Southern resistance reached the United States Court of Appeals in 1966. The case involved television station WLBT in Jackson, Mississippi. Complaints against the station to the Federal Communications Commission (FCC) were first made in 1955 when a network program on race relations featuring the General Counsel of the NAACP was cut off and replaced by a sign flashing "Sorry, Cable Trouble." Complaints were again lodged in 1957 for the broadcast of a program urging racial segregation, and the subsequent refusals by the station to broadcast opposing viewpoints. Similar charges regarding the presentation of only one viewpoint were lodged in 1962 after the outbreak of civil rights demonstrations at the University of Mississippi. In 1964, Dr. Henry, President of the Mississippi NAACP, filed a petition with the FCC to deny the renewal of WLBT's broadcast license. The petition claimed that the station did not give fair and balanced treatment of controversial issues, especially those concerning African-Americans. It also claimed that the station discriminated against the Catholic Church.[53]

Dr. Henry claimed in his petition that he represented organizations that represented nearly half of "WLBT's potential listening audience who were denied an opportunity to have their side of controversial issues presented." He also claimed to represent the total WLBT audience because, he asserted, of "the right of all listeners, regardless of race or religion, to hear and see balanced programming on significant public questions."[54]

The case was considered by the United States Court of Appeals after the FCC granted a one-year renewal of license over the protests of the petitioners. The FCC claimed that the license was granted so that the station could "carry out its stated willingness to serve fully and fairly the needs and interests of its entire area-so that it can, in short, meet and resolve the questions raised." In its decision, the Court of Appeals compared this argument to assigning the wolf to guard the sheep as a means of determining if the wolf could mend its ways. The Court ruled that the issuance of the license was erroneous and that new hearings should be held.[55]

The most important part of the Court's decision was its criticism of the FCC for limiting the participation of public groups in license renewal hearings. The FCC claimed that opening the doors to public groups would clog their dockets and make hearings unworkable. In addition, the FCC was primarily concerned with hearing complaints from those who felt they received a direct economic injury from a broadcast.

The Court rejected these arguments. It was particularly critical of the FCC for limiting general public participation to letters written to the Commission, its inspection of records, and nonparticipation appearance at hearings. The Court ruled that FCC hearings should be opened to public participation. The Court also rendered an opinion as to what general types of groups should be recognized as reflecting the public interest. In the words of the Court:

The responsible and representative groups eligible to intervene cannot here be enumerated or categorized specifically; such community organizations as civic associations, professional societies, unions, churches, and educational institutions or associations might well be helpful to the Commission. These groups are found in every community; they usually concern themselves with a wide range of community problems and tend to be representatives of broad as distinguished from narrow interests, public as distinguished from private or commercial interests.[56]

This decision made it possible for organized groups to directly influence the broadcasting industry. Five years after the decision, the journal *Broadcasting* summarized the impact of the decision:

> The case did more than establish the right of the public to participate in a station's license-renewal hearing. It did even more than encourage minority groups around the country to assert themselves in broadcast matters at a time when unrest was growing and blacks were becoming more activist. It provided practical lessons in how pressure could be brought, in how the broadcast establishment could be challenged.[57]

Opening the doors to public participation in broadcasting launched a major series of battles over the images disseminated by television. Media advocacy groups were formed representing African-Americans, women, homosexuals, and other minorities. The television industry now confronted a variety of organizations concerned about the image of their constituents on television. Besides the NAACP and CORE, groups such as, the National Organization of Women (NOW) set up special media task forces. In 1970, NOW announced its intention to change "the derogatory, demeaning and stereotyped images of women presented by broadcast programming and advertising." Other groups that organized to protect their image on television included the National Black Media Coalition, the Italian-American League to Combat Defamation, the German-American Anti-Defamation League, the Polish-American Guardian Society, the Tribal Indian Land Rights Association, and the Gay Media Task Force.[58]

The development of these advocacy groups and their new power to influence license renewals created real economic threats to the networks. Tom Kersey, an ABC vice-president, estimated at the time that "any challenge to a station would be an enormous threat. [And] one of our stations was worth between $35 and $40 million."[59] This meant that the networks were forced to manage advocacy groups. This created an interplay between the desires of advocacy groups to manage television images and the needs of the television industry to control the power of the advocacy groups.

In *Target: Prime Time: Advocacy Groups and the Struggle over Entertainment Television*, Kathryn Montgomery traces the history of strategies developed by the networks for controlling advocacy groups. Her example was Mexican-American protests about television characters presenting an image of Mexican-Americans as meek and hat-in-hand. The advocacy group Justicia demanded television networks put aside $10 million for shows portraying Chicano characters in a positive manner. In 1971, Justicia launched challenges to all California television licenses. Justicia was joined by the Mexican-American Anti-Defamation Committee, the League of United Latino Citizens, and the National Latino Media Coalition to drive two well-known Chicano characters off the television screen. One was the "Frito Bandito" used in commercials for Frito Corn Chips. The cartoon character was charged with creating a racist image of Mexican-Americans as sneaky thieves. Another was "José Jimenez" who, it was charged, created the image of Mexican-Americans being happy-go-lucky and not very bright.[60]

In response to these pressures, ABC began using "technical consultants" from the advocacy groups to avoid any potential problems. For instance, ABC invited leaders from Justicia to review scripts containing Mexican-American characters. This was similar to the traditional use of professionals to review scripts. For example, a rotating panel of teachers from the NEA reviewed scripts for the program "Mr. Novak." But this policy did not stop criticism of situations where networks neglected to include Mexican-American characters in programs. In addition, advocacy groups were invited to prescreen programs. And, networks began to hire minorities into their departments of standards and practices to be more sure to reflect the pluralistic quality of American society.

The use of technical consultants from advocacy groups created the problem of identifying which group should represent a particular community. For instance, should Mexican-Americans be represented by Justicia or the Mexican-American Anti-Defamation Committee? This question was answered by the "one voice concept," which meant that networks identified a single organization to represent a whole group. Of course, the networks were interested in working with the most moderate organizations. In the case of Mexican-Americans, the networks finally decided to work closely with the Nosotros, an advocacy group for Hispanic actors, which acted in a moderate fashion toward the networks. Summarizing the evolution of network management of advocacy groups, Montgomery writes that while the court decision in 1966 gave advocacy groups access to the networks, "the networks had found ways to set the terms for continuing access." In the late 1970s and 1980s, she states, advocacy groups "would encounter a team of experts within the networks, equipped with a sophisticated set of skills and strategies designed to minimize disruption and maximize friendly, cooperative relationships."[61]

According to Montgomery, gay activists groups were one of the most effective in changing network policies. One reason was the large number of gays employed by the industry. Many of these insiders would supply outside organizations with information. For instance, a script for an upcoming episode of "Marcus Welby, M.D." was smuggled out of ABC in 1973 and given to the Gay Activist Alliance (GAA). In the episode, Marcus Welby advises a married man concerned about his homosexual tendencies that he would not fail as a husband and father if he suppressed his gay tendencies. The smuggled script caused angry members of the GAA to descend on network offices. Following the pattern described by Montgomery, after this protest networks began to consult regularly with gay activists about any scripts dealing with homosexuality.[62]

The combined forces of the civil rights movement and the development of television advocacy groups changed images on television at the same time that they were being changed in Textbook Town. During what media historian J. Fred MacDonald calls "The Golden Age of Blacks in Television: The Late 1960s," there were over two dozen programs featuring African-Americans as leading characters. In addition, there were nineteen television series with supporting African-American characters.[63]

The programs with African-Americans in leading roles ranged from "I Spy" and "Mission Impossible" to "The Bill Cosby Show" and "The Young Lawyers." MacDonald argues that "I Spy" had the greatest effect on the position of African-Americans on television. The show was the first network dramatic series to feature an African-American actor, Bill Cosby. Cosby's character projected a new image of African-Americans to white television audiences. He was equal to white characters in his encounters with foreign spies, women, government leaders, and criminals. In an early episode he committed the revolutionary act, at least for television, of kissing a Japanese woman. Cosby's character broke the unspoken television taboo against showing African-Americans kissing and demonstrating affection.[64]

As in Textbook Town, the images on television were integrated without any major changes in content. After all, Cosby's part on "I Spy" could have been played by a white without any noticeable change in the character. Certainly, Cosby was not playing a part that would have required an African-American. No major African-American themes or issues were raised by the program. In fact, "The Bill Cosby Show," which by the 1990s was the most popular program on television, featured an African-American family that could have been easily interchanged with any white upper middle class family.

Where television went beyond the happy life of Textbook Town was in the satire of a white racist and bigot, Archie Bunker, in the program "All in the Family." American public school textbooks would never contain the racial epitaphs that spewed forth from the mouth of Archie Bunker. Norman Lear, the program's producer, consciously sought to fight racism and bigotry by having Archie use words such as "spades, spics, spooks, schwartzes, coons, coloreds, and chinks." The program broke all the traditional television taboos by dealing with issues such as homosexuality, race, female equality, and birth control. A spin off of the program, "Maude," caused a storm of protest the following year when it dealt with the issue of abortion. *Time* magazine noted in 1972 that in the wake of "All in the Family" there were twenty new series dealing with controversial themes.[65]

The fact that CBS was willing to experiment with such a controversial program as "All in the Family" was a reflection of the economics of broadcasting. This, of course, is a distinctive difference between public schools and broadcasting. Because of the political power of single interest groups, public schools could not afford controversy. On the other hand, after many years of following the same pattern of avoiding controversy, television broadcasters decided that controversy could be useful in attracting viewers and thus advertisers.

As William Paley describes the events leading up to the decision to broadcast "All in the Family," advertisers in the 1960s began to use audience demographic data to make decisions about buying time on television. Advertisers were primarily concerned about reaching audiences between the ages of eighteen and forty-nine. It was decided that while CBS was the number-one network during the 1960s, its audience was getting older the longer top rated series lasted. Paley wrote that the "statistics were saying to us, in effect: The percentage of older people in your audience is too large.... You are not building a base in the new and younger audience.... You need to attract a larger proportion of younger people."[66] In addition, the statistics suggested the need for building a larger urban audience.

It was decided that CBS should abandon fantasy and rural settings for realism and urban settings as a method of attracting a younger audience. During the 1970–71 season, CBS began the transition by introducing programs reflecting the concepts of "realism and relevance." It was decided to group older rural-type programs on Tuesday night and present newer programs for younger audiences on Wednesday and Saturday night. In Paley's words, "The biggest break with the past came in the middle of the 1970–71 season, when we put on "All in the Family'." Paley recalls how "all of us realized the tremendous risk involved in putting such a different kind of program on the air.... For the first time, we allowed an entertainment program to deal in a real way with ordinary subjects, using the kind of conversations that one might hear in any household—ethnic attitudes and all."[67]

Therefore, "All in the Family" was a break with the traditional avoidance of controversy, a product of a new marketing strategy. This strategy would have a tremendous impact on television programming. Now programs were to be produced that would appeal to the most affluent audiences. Restating Paley's argument in critical language, media critic Ben Bagdikian writes, "Broadcasters cannot keep the nonaffluent and elderly from watching or listening to their programs, but they design the content to attract younger, affluent viewers.... The 'unwanted American population' that is systematically discouraged by advertising-supported media is not small." Using 1984 statistics, Bagdikian estimated that these policies excluded families with less than median income (or 50 percent of American families) and the 54 percent of the American population younger than 18 and older than 49. Those over 50 years of age constituted 26 percent of the population.[68]

This explains why television was willing to adopt a more critical tone than the public schools were. For textbook publishers. sales depended, in part, on avoiding controversy. For broadcasters, controversy was a path into a lucrative market. While an integrated Textbook Town avoided realism, the broadcasting industry tried to make realism profitable.

THE VIET NAM WAR

Viet Nam tested the outer limits of TV's willingness to deal with controversy. It also demonstrated the political power of television, as broadcasting transformed the Students for a Democratic Society (SDS) from a small organization to a major leader of the anti-war movement. The spread of the anti-war movement into the nation's schools caused the Nixon administration to make major changes in educational policies and to attack the political power of television.

Besides providing graphic news coverage of the Viet Nam war and anti-war demonstrations, television programming began to reflect the increasing divisions among the U.S. population over continued pursuit of the war. This is vividly demonstrated by the abrupt cancellation near the end of the 1968–69 television season by CBS of the very popular "Smothers Brothers Comedy Hour." The show started its meteoric rise in popularity shortly after its debut in 1966. The comedy team quickly infused their program with political jokes about the Viet Nam war. This created a running battle with CBS censors. For instance, when Joan Baez appeared on the program and dedicated her song to her husband who was in jail for resisting the military draft, CBS censors cut the reference to the draft. Also cut was a seven-and-a-half minute segment of Harry Belafonte singing against a backdrop of film clips of riots at the 1968 Democratic convention.[69]

The major controversy that erupted between the comedy team and CBS censors was over the appearance of folk singer Pete Seeger. Seeger was named in the infamous "Red Channels" and was blacklisted from television until his appearance on the "Smothers Brothers Comedy Hour" in September 1967. During his blacklisting years, Seeger performed with the successful singing group the Weavers and sang at many anti-war demonstrations. In his first Smothers Brothers appearance, CBS censors cut from the final tape his performance of the song "Waist Deep in the Big Muddy." The final stanza of the song was a direct attack on President Johnson's continued pursuit of the Viet Nam war. The song told of a platoon during World War II that was ordered by its captain to cross a river that no one knew was dangerous. The captain was swept away and the platoon was almost drowned. The final stanza advised listeners to read the newspapers again to discover that they are once again "Waist Deep in Big Muddy."[70]

Dick and Tom Smothers were furious at the censorship. In February 1968, Pete Seeger was invited back and included in his performance "Waist Deep in the Big Muddy." This time CBS officials relented and did not censor the final tape. But the battles did not stop. As the popularity of the show increased, CBS continued to battle the Smothers brothers over the political content of their program. Finally, even though the show continued to be very popular, CBS axed the show in April 1969 when a tape of a program containing an appearance of anti-war activist Dr. Benjamin Spock arrived too late at CBS headquarters for network editing.[71]

On the surface, there was no economic reason for CBS to cut the show. It fit neatly into the network's goal of attracting young and urban audiences. And it was popular. Given these facts, one might conclude that the program was cut because of its political content. In this regard, it is important to distinguish the content of the "Smothers Brothers Comedy Hour" from that of "All in the Family." "All in the Family" was controversial because of the social issues, raised such as racism, homosexuality, and birth control. Of course, these issues have a political dimension. But they are not as directly political as the issues raised in the "Smothers Brothers Comedy Hour." On that program, American foreign policy and political leaders were directly criticized.

After the program was removed from the air, Tom Smothers accused CBS chairman William Paley of eliminating the program because of his friendship with President Nixon and his desire to be appointed by Nixon to be ambassador to England. The show, which often contained criticisms of President Nixon, was cancelled only three months after Nixon's inauguration.[72]

Interestingly, Paley, in his autobiography, is completely silent on the affair. In fact, Paley never mentions the program. But Paley does admit to his close relationship to the Republican Party. Paley wrote about Nixon, "I knew him from his days as Vice-President under Eisenhower. I even made a contribution to his 1960 campaign for President, for I was raised as a Republican, although I often crossed party lines in my voting." At the 1968 Republican Convention, Paley supported Nelson Rockefeller for the nomination. In Paley's words, "I went to the Republican Convention with Nelson Rockefeller as my personal choice. But Nelson failed to take the convention by storm and Nixon had the delegates lined up behind him."[73]

Paley claims that he had little to do with the Nixon Administration until Vice President Spiro Agnew launched his attack on the networks in a speech in Des Moines on November 13, 1969. Seven months after the "Smothers Brothers Comedy Show" cancellation and ten months after Nixon's inauguration, Agnew attacked news organizations in all the networks, and particularly industry leaders such as William Paley. In the speech, Agnew asked, "Is it not fair and relevant to question its [the broadcast industry's] concentration in the hands of a tiny, enclosed fraternity of privileged men elected by no one and enjoying a monopoly sanctioned and licensed by government."[74]

The attacks by the Nixon Administration made networks leery of sponsoring programs that made direct attacks on political leaders and policies. The Nixon Administration was particularly concerned with network handling of news items dealing with the Administration's policies and the war. It is important to understand that the Nixon Administration's criticism of the broadcast industry was also tied to the Administration's criticism of public schools and colleges. Besides the major demonstrations at the 1968 Chicago Democratic Convention, most anti-war demonstrations took place on college campuses. Therefore, as discussed later, the Nixon Administration was concerned with the actions of the two major disseminators of information—schools and television.

TELEVISION AND ANTI-WAR DEMONSTRATIONS

The complex linkages between politics, educational institutions, television, and the anti-war movement are explored in Todd Gitlin's study of the SDS. Gitlin's basic framework of analysis emphasizes what he calls the "struggle over images." He argues that television and the anti-war movement needed each other. Television news needed stories, and the anti-war movement needed publicity. In this symbiotic relationship, there was a struggle between the anti-war groups, the media, and government leaders over the image of the "movement" to be projected to the public. Gitlin identifies five stages in the evolution of this symbiotic relationship.[75]

Focusing on the SDS's leadership of the anti-war movement, Gitlin argues that the SDS did not seek any news coverage during its first stage between 1960 and 1965. In turn, news media showed little interest in covering the actions of this small and decentralized organization which was dedicated to visiting college campuses. But suddenly, during Gitlin's second phase, the media discovered the SDS during the Free Speech Movement at the University of California. Because of the publicity surrounding the Free Speech Movement, the media searched for more material to highlight student radicalism. At this point, SDS leadership was still not interested in publicity.[76]

Dramatic changes began after the 1965 SDS March on Washington to protest the war. Suddenly, the SDS became big news as a leader of the anti-war movement. After this third phase, members of the SDS were divided over how to deal with the attention from the media. Some members of the organization remained committed to face-to-face relationships through campus organizing. Other members began the fourth phase of holding anti-war demonstrations for the purpose of attracting media coverage. In the fifth and final phase, media coverage helped to attract new members to the SDS. These new members were primarily interested in anti-war activity. By 1966, Gitlin argues, the new generation of anti-war activist held key positions of leadership in the organization.

Gitlin stresses that the media had conflicting effects on the anti-war movement and the SDS. On the one hand, it gave the organization and movement wide publicity and helped to recruit many to the anti-war effort. On the other hand, the media created negative images of the movement by the way it framed news reports. According to Gitlin, the media used the following devices:

- *trivialization* (making light of movement language, dress, age, style, and goals);
- *polarization* (emphasizing counterdemonstrations, and balancing the anti-war movement with ultra-Right and neo-Nazi groups as equivalent 'extremists');
- *emphasis on internal dissension*;
- *marginalization* (showing demonstrators to be deviant or unrepresentative);
- *disparagement by numbers* (under-counting);
- *disparagement of the movement's effectiveness.*[77]

Gitlin provides several examples of how the media framed these particular images of SDS and the anti-war movement. In 1965, for CBS Arthur Barron produced "The Berkeley Rebels" a documentary on the New Left. After its completion and initial editing by Fred Friendly, the vice President in charge of documentaries, William Paley and Frank Stanton ordered the cutting of a sequence of a fraternity party designed to contrast the average college student with political activists. Paley and Stanton thought that the sequence was "a slander against nice kids." They told Barron to interview Berkeley professors to say things like, "The kids are immature and impatient. It will all blow over...." One sequence of the original film showed a political discussion without any narrative commentary. Barron was ordered to add a voice-over statement to this sequence, according to Gitlin, along the lines: "The bull session—an old and true ritual of young people, wherein much heat but little light is shed."[78]

While early television coverage trivialized and marginalized anti-war demonstrators, television broadcasters after the 1968 Democratic Convention were ordered to reduce coverage of actual events. When Richard Nixon was inaugurated in 1969, NBC gave strict orders to its staff not to broadcast demonstrations against the inauguration. CBS apologized to its viewers for a brief broadcast of the demonstrations.[79]

MANAGING SCHOOLS AND TELEVISION

The conservative reaction that set in after Nixon's inauguration extended to education.[80] The strategy of the Nixon Administration was to change the national goals of education, and to apply political pressure on the media. This two-pronged effort was explicitly designed as ideological management. With regard to education, emphasis was placed on tying educational goals to economic goals. As for television, the emphasis was on public attacks and threats of cancelling licenses.

Educational policy shifted from an emphasis on eliminating poverty to creating a closer link between public schools and the needs of the labor market. Of course, Textbook Town remained integrated. But now the emphasis was on careers and an integrated labor force. Underlying these changes was a belief that emphasizing career education would reduce and control student unrest.

Appointed by President Nixon, United States Commissioner of Education Sidney Marland began to campaign in 1971 for career education. Marland believed career education was the answer to student rebellion, delinquency, and unemployment. In his first annual report to Congress in 1971, he argued that disenchantment among youth existed because education did not lead to career opportunities. For Marland, the villain was general education programs that lacked specific goals and were not linked to the job market. Marland argued that education should be meaningful, and by "meaningful" he meant related to a career objective. He stated, "When we use the word 'meaningful,' we imply a strong obligation that our young people complete the first 12 grades in such a fashion that they are ready either to enter into some form of higher education or to proceed immediately into satisfying and appropriate employment."[81]

The fundamental concept of career education was that all elements of education had to be justified by their contribution to career development. Marland's Associate Commissioner stated, "The fundamental concept of career education is that all educational experiences, curriculum, instruction, and counseling should be geared to preparing each individual for a life of economic independence, personal fulfillment, and an appreciation for the dignity of work."[82]

Marland believed career education would be one solution "to some of our more serious social and economic problems, including high unemployment and the attendant problems of disaffection and drug excess among the young."[83] To accomplish this goal, career education was to permeate the curriculum. What distinguished career education from vocational guidance was that career education was to become part of the academic program beginning in the elementary school years. During elementary and junior high school years, career education, as an academic subject, would acquaint students with the world of work and the varieties of occupations available. In high school, students would be studying to prepare either for entry directly into an occupational career or into higher education.

Financial support for career education began with the 1972 amendments to the Elementary and Secondary Education Act (ESEA). The original 1965 legislation had undergone a number of changes by the 1970s, primarily the addition of programs for specific groups labeled as "disadvantaged." In 1966, ESEA was amended to include special programs for Native American children, migratory agricultural workers, delinquents, and the handicapped. Bilingual education programs directed primarily at aiding Hispanic and Native American children were added in 1967. The 1972 amendments called for the development of career education programs that would be treated as academic subjects and be given equal status with other educational programs.[84]

The 1972 amendments also broadened the support for instructional materials. As I discussed earlier in the chapter, the original ESEA provided funds for the purchase of instructional materials for educational programs for the disadvantaged. Wanting to take advantage of federal money, textbook publishers rushed in with textbooks reflecting a multiracial population. A 1972 amendment called for "equal consideration...to the needs of elementary and secondary schools for library resources, textbooks, and other printed and published material utilized for instruction, orientation, or guidance and counseling in occupational education."[85]

The focus on career education occurred in an atmosphere of declining expectations for the ability of education to solve the problem of poverty and provide social mobility for the children of the poor. A number of reports issued in the late 1960s concluded the compensatory education could do little to improve the achievement levels of disadvantaged students. In addition, the Nixon Administration opposed the emphasis on equality of educational opportunity. The emphasis, the administration argued, should be on high-quality education. It was this argument that Nixon used to oppose busing for the purposes of integration. He argued that the original intention of integration was providing a good education for all students. Therefore, he argued, the goal of education should not be integration but high-quality education for all. Of course, high-quality education in this context meant education related to career goals.[86]

These educational changes did not turn back the clock on images of a multiracial, multiethnic America. But the changes did reduce the hope for many students of rising above the economic conditions of their parents. Career education and the expansion of vocational schools during the 1970s conveyed the message to students that the primary goal of education was preparation for ordinary work. Therefore, the image of America being conveyed to students in the 1970s was of a multiracial society, with a career as life's most important objective.

As Nixon tried to put the breaks on student radicalism and the social upheavals of the 1960s, he became more and more embroiled in a war with the media. The result made newscasters apprehensive about covering civil rights and anti-war demonstrations and making critical comments about the Nixon Administration. About the pressure on the media from the Nixon Administration, CBS news commentator Walter Cronkite stated: "I think the industry as a whole has been intimidated."[87]

In October 1969, shortly before Vice President Agnew's opening salvo against the media, the White House Chief of Staff, H. R. Haldeman, prepared a memo for President Nixon on methods for controlling television news broadcasts. Titled "The Shot-Gun versus the Rifle," the memo recommended that the White House "should begin concentrated efforts in a number of major areas that will have much impact on the media and other anti-administration spokesman and will do more good in the long run."[88]

The memo is important because it outlines the methods that government leaders can use to control the networks. First were threats of cancelling licenses of broadcasters through the FCC. The second was one that went back to the 1920s and 1930s. This was to threaten anti-trust action against the broadcast industry. And lastly, Haldeman proposed to use Internal Revenue Service investigations as a method of intimidating broadcasters. The Haldeman memo suggested,

1. Begin an official monitoring system through the FCC as soon as Dean Burch is officially on board as Chairman. If the monitoring system proves our point, we have then legitimate and legal rights to go to the networks, etc., and make official complaints from the FCC....

2. Utilize the anti-trust division to investigate various media relating to anti-trust violations. *Even the possible threat of anti-trust action I think would be effective* [emphasis added] in changing their views in the above matter.

3. Utilizing the Internal Revenue Service as a method to look into the various organizations that we are most concerned about. Just a threat of an IRS investigation will probably turn their approach.[89]

The White House was particularly concerned about the news commentaries after Nixon's speeches. After a major speech by Nixon on Viet Nam, the FCC Chairman Dean Burch telephoned all three networks for transcripts of commentators' remarks. This was just another method of letting the networks know that they were being watched.[90]

Relations between the White House and the networks became very strained as the story of Watergate unfolded. The administration was particularly concerned about CBS coverage. On September 15, 1972, just prior to the presidential election, White House aide Charles Colson called Frank Stanton, the former President and now Vice-Chairman of CBS, to his office to complain that CBS had an anti-Nixon bias. Colson produced a chart prepared by the White House which purported to show that during the two weeks ending September 8, CBS gave Nixon's opponent George McGovern 64 minutes and 32 seconds of positive network time and Nixon only 23 minutes and 26 seconds of positive air time.[91]

On October 27, CBS further incensed the White House when their newscaster Walter Cronkite did a special evening report on the Watergate affair. Earlier in the day, Colson had called Frank Stanton to accuse Conkrite of trying to "zing" Nixon by not interviewing him. After seeing the evening report, Colson called William Paley. Former CBS newscaster Daniel Shorr reported that Colson told Paley,

> President Nixon was getting tired of trying to make peace with CBS. Nixon, in case Paley hadn't heard it, was going to be reelected overwhelmingly, and CBS should not expect any friendly hand from the President after the election. Colson says that Paley, apologetic, contrite, promised to "get into" the question of Part II [a proposed second part to the Watergate report].[92]

Paley also recounts the same conversation. In Paley's words, "Colson put in a barb, saying that if the President were re-elected, which he thought very likely, it would be difficult for them to establish good relations with us."[93] White House pressure resulted in "Watergate: Part II" being cut from fourteen minutes to seven minutes and its broadcast delayed by one day.[94] But even the reduced coverage did not satisfy the White House. After its broadcast, Colson called Stanton with a new list of threats, which Stanton recorded. These included government support of cable television, a limitation on the number of times a movie could be rerun on television, challenges to the licenses on network affiliates, a proposal to license the networks, and a threat to force the networks to divest themselves of their affiliates. Stanton recorded Colson's final comment: "Even if we don't succeed, we'll hurt them [CBS]—bring them to their knees in the market-place: Wall Street and Madison Avenue."[95]

Nixon's ability to intimidate extended even to coverage of his resignation. Richard Salant, President of CBS News, recounted to Daniel Shorr his decision to defuse the impact of Nixon's resignation. In part, this decision was a result "of the fear—later allayed—of a Nixon attack on television." The method was to frame the resignation so as to defuse its political impact. The framing was almost the opposite of that described by Todd Gitlin in television's treatment of the SDS. Salant gave orders that the coverage "emphasize continuity in government, not jump up and down in glee on Nixon's body, but concentrate on the transition."[96] Consequently, CBS news coverage of the resignation included comments such as those by newscaster Dan Rather: "I think it may very well go down, when history takes a look at it, as one of Richard Nixon's, if not his finest, hour.... He did give...this moment a touch of class."[97] In a broader perspective, these are strange comments when a President is resigning because of criminal activity. Certainly, the story could have been framed in an entirely different manner. But this reflects the power of government leaders to influence television news.

SOFTENING THE IMAGE OF AMERICA

CBS's treatment of the Nixon resignation illustrates television's transition from the 1960s to the 1970s. America was no longer being presented as a nation engrossed in active social change and political unrest. It was now presented as a nation of passive citizens. Unlike the 1960s, networks avoided playing up political dissension. Nixon had cooled off the media.

While television avoided political controversy in the 1970s, it was willing to deal with explosive social issues like those in "All in the Family." It was also willing to present an image of a multiracial country without resorting to racial and ethnic stereotypes. In this regard, advocacy groups and new marketing techniques had won the day.

Aided by government funding, Textbook Town changed from a happy little white community to a multiracial city. In the 1970s, government funding made work a central focus in Textbook Town. The workplace in Textbook Town was racially integrated with happy employees. In the 1970s, students were taught that the most important reason for going to school was getting a job. The Nixon Administration appeared to be as successful in cooling off schools as it had been in cooling off television. Schools and television combined to present an image of passive workers and citizens.

As they had with television, racial and ethnic advocacy groups forced publishers and public schools to make them more visible. United States history textbooks attempted to be histories of a multiracial and multiethnic society. But like television, they did not have the sharp political edge that seemed promised by the civil rights and anti-war movements of the 1960s. The images of a dynamic and politically interested society of the 1960s were replaced with images of a hard-working multiracial society.

CHAPTER THIRTEEN

PUBLIC BROADCASTING AND BIG BIRD: FOUNDATIONS AND GOVERNMENT MANAGING KNOWLEDGE

"ITS ATTITUDE WILL be neither fearful nor vulgar," states the Carnegie Commission on Educational Television 1967 proposal for the establishment of the Corporation for Public Broadcasting. "It will be, in short," the proposal continues, "a civilized voice in a civilized community."[1] The proposal echoed the 1930s, when educators claimed that commercial radio was destroying national culture. The difference in the 1960s was the Carnegie Commission's acceptance of commercial television's role in determining mass culture. The purpose of public television, according to the proposal, was to serve special audiences by adding diversity to program selection. It was not suppose to displace commercial television. "Television," the Commission's report states, "should serve more fully both the mass audience and the many separate audiences that constitute in their aggregate our American society."[2]

Children's programming by the Corporation for Public Broadcasting was designed to make television the third educator, along with family and school. The most famous of these programs, "Sesame Street," was inspired by a belief that television could be both an educator and a social reformer. It was hoped that "Sesame Street" would break the cycle of poverty among children of the poor. Also, it was argued, television was a better educator than the public schools and that it might be the savior of the educational system.

Given the fact that many of the advocates of the Corporation for Public Broadcasting were cultural liberals, as Ellen Condliffe Lagemann calls them in her history of the Carnegie Corporation, there was an element of elitism in the establishment of public television.[3] Commercial television was to serve the masses, while public television was to serve special audiences, which, in reality, seemed to be upper socioeconomic audiences. According to Willard Rowland, the Chief Research Associate of the Public Broadcasting System, in 1976, "public broadcasting audiences continue to come disproportionately from the higher socio-economic brackets."[4] Other data suggested that except for the absence of blue collar workers, the characteristics of Public Broadcasting System's audience were similar to the total adult population.[5]

There was another strikingly different feature of the advocacy for public television in the 1960s. In the 1930s, the issue of educational radio was fought out between organizations representing educators, along with others interested in educational radio, and the owners of commercial broadcasting. The final decision then was in the hands of the Federal Communications Commission (FCC).

In the 1960s, plans for public television were developed through cooperation between private foundations and the White House. The final action in creating the Corporation for Public Broadcasting was made by Congress. The role of private foundations represents an important change in the management of knowledge after World War II. From the 1950s to the 1990s, foundations have had an important effect on the creation and distribution of knowledge in the United States, by supporting research and educational programs, and by the easy movement of personnel between foundations and government. The Carnegie Corporation and the Ford Foundation were leaders in the evolution of educational television, the creation of the Corporation for Public Broadcasting, and the creation of the Children's Television Workshop and its production of "Sesame Street."

Fears about commercial television's effect on national culture and about the effect of poverty and urban riots on American capitalism influenced the decisions of the Carnegie Corporation leaders. In proposing to add a "civilized voice in a civilized community," the Carnegie Commission on Educational Television was influenced by criticism in the 1950s and 1960s that commercial television was a "wasteland." As colorfully stated by one FCC commissioner, Lee Loevinger, commercial television was "the literature of the illiterate; the culture of the low-brow; the wealth of the poor; the privilege of the underprivileged; the exclusive club of the excluded masses...a golden goose that lays scrambled eggs."[6]

Cultural liberals criticized television in the same way as they did public schools. In the 1950s and 1960s, American intellectuals expressed a feeling of their rejection by popular culture. They credited public schools and television with creating an anti-intellectual atmosphere in the United States. An important expression of this viewpoint was Richard Hofstadter's 1962 volume, *Anti-Intellectualism in American Life*. Hofstadter argued that anti-intellectualism became a national issue during the 1952 presidential election, which pitted the intellectual Adlai Stevenson against the Western-novel-reading Dwight D. Eisenhower. In Hofstadter's words, Adlai Stevenson was "a politician of uncommon mind and style, whose appeal to intellectuals overshadowed anything in recent history." The election, according to Hofstadter, was portrayed as being between "eggheads" and the people of common sense. When Stevenson lost, *Time Magazine* claimed that it disclosed "an alarming fact long suspected: there is a wide and unhealthy gap between the American intellectuals and the people." In addition, anti-Communist attacks were directed at intellectuals. These right-wing attacks, Hofstadter wrote, referred to Harvard professors as "twisted thinking intellectuals" who, while "burdened with Phi Beta Kappa keys," were not equally loaded with honesty and common sense." One of the root causes of anti-intellectualism, Hofstadter believed, was the American public school. Like many academics of the 1950s and 1960s, he criticized schools for breeding a disrespect for the life of the mind by spoonfeeding a curriculum that consisted of intellectual pabulum.[7]

Television was also identified as a source of intellectual pap for the masses. Arthur Schlesinger, Jr., historian and advisor to Adlai Stevenson and John F. Kennedy, worried that television was breeding disrespect for the intellectual and destroying the quality of American life. "I cannot repress my feelings," he wrote, "that in the main, television has been a great bust." He argued that government had to act to improve the quality of television "because there seems no other way to rescue television from the downward spiral of competitive debasement."[8]

Others joined the attack on television. Child care advocate Dr. Benjamin Spock wrote President Kennedy that instead of television instilling virtue in the citizen, "there is the constant search for the commonest level of taste in passive entertainment…used, in turn, to sell goods, in a manner which breeds insincerity and cynicism, and which appeals always to more gratification." Writing in the *Saturday Review*, critic Robert Lewis Shayon expressed disgust at a 1958 episode of "Leave It to Beaver" where the main character was upset at a school IQ text that accidentally classified him as a genius. "Beaver" was portrayed at not wanting to be a genius. For Shayon, this was another example of television appealing to the masses by deprecating the intellect.[9]

Critics of the intellectual and cultural quality of television found a spokesman in President John F. Kennedy's appointee to head the FCC, Newton Minow. A young lawyer from Chicago, Minow decided to launch his attack on the quality of television in a speech to the National Association of Broadcasters at its 1961 national convention in Washington, D.C., Minow opened the speech with praise for the potential of television and a denial that he intended to use government powers to censor broadcasting. After soothing his audience with these words, Minow launched his attack. He invited the broadcasters to sit with their eyes glued to their television sets from the time stations went on the air until the stations signed off. "I can assure that you will observe," he told them in words that were to be echoed around the country, "a vast wasteland." This wasteland is, he stated,

> a procession of game shows, violence, audience participation shows, formula
> comedies about totally unbelievable families, blood and thunder, mayhem, vio-

lence, sadism, murder, Western bad men, Western good men, private eyes, gangsters, more violence, screaming , cajoling, and offending. And most of all, boredom. True, you will see a few things you will enjoy. But they will be very, very few.[10]

Minow's speech rallied the intellectuals who were critical of the cultural quality of commercial television. When President Johnson accepted the 1967 recommendations of the Carnegie Commission of Educational Television, he was, according to historian James Baughman, making a political maneuver designed to "please that group of liberals and intellectuals once the champions of Newton Minow."[11]

Fears of anti-intellectualism and of the effect of television's wasteland helped to focus the attention of the Carnegie Corporation on the establishment of public television. Apprehension about poverty and urban riots provided impetus to fund public television programs for children. When Alan Pifer was made acting President of the Carnegie Corporation in 1965, he brought to the post a concern about poverty and urban conditions. Under his leadership, the Carnegie Corporation sponsored a Task Force on the Disadvantaged, which issued its report in 1967—the same year that Pifer was appointed full president of the Carnegie Corporation.

Pifer believed that foundations had an important role in improving social conditions and fighting for social justice. He stated that the Carnegie Corporation should support the "four basic principles: the right to a job for anyone who needs to or wants to work; equal opportunity and fair rewards for everyone in all sectors of employment; development and utilization of the abilities of every citizen; and maximum flexibility for each person in the organization of his or her own pattern of life."[12]

Pifer believed that providing social justice was necessary for the survival of capitalism. As he stated in his last report in 1982, the Carnegie Corporation's involvement in social issues in the 1960s was designed to ease social tension as a means of protecting capitalism. Without a program of social justice and welfare, he warned in his last report, "there lies nothing but increasing hardship for ever-growing numbers, a mounting possibility of severe social unrest, and the consequent development among the upper classes and the business community of...fear for the survival of our capitalist economic system...." And, reflecting on the past, he predicted that, "Just as we built the general welfare state in the 1930s and expanded it in the 1960s as a safety valve for the easing of social tension, so will we do it again in the 1980s. Any other path is simply too risky."[13]

Pifer's concern with social justice spilled over into considerations of the public role of television. The Carnegie Corporation was interested in sponsoring preschool television programs for disadvantaged children through the Corporation for Public Broadcasting. As I discuss later, it was this interest that led to the creation of the Children's Television Workshop and "Sesame Street."

The involvement of foundations in television and education added a new dimension to decisions about the distribution of knowledge. As discussed in previous chapters, the federal government in the 1950s and 1960s was increasingly involved in decisions about what should be taught in schools and in the content of textbooks. During this same period, foundations became more active in influencing educational policy. In the 1950s, the Carnegie Corporation had sponsored James Conant in an influential study of the American high school, *The American High School Today*.[14] In the 1970s, the foundation sponsored the important studies *All Our Children: The American Family under Pressure* and *Small Futures: Children, Inequality and the Limits of Liberal Reform*. In addition, there was a host of other studies that had a significant impact on thinking about educational institutions and practices.[15]

The influence of foundations was enhanced by their connections with the federal government. The federal government provided financial support for some foundation projects and personnel moved from foundations to the federal government and back. For instance, Alan Pifer became acting President of the Carnegie Corporation in 1965, because the current president, John Gardner, was appointed Secretary of Health, Education, and Welfare by President Johnson. "Sesame Street" was supported by a mix of private and government funds from the Carnegie Corporation, the Ford Foundation, the U.S. Office of Education, and the Corporation for Public Broadcasting.[16] The initial involvement of the federal government in "Sesame Street" occurred when Barbara Fineberg, a program officer for the Carnegie Corporation, went to Washington in 1967 to discuss the program with the United States Commissioner of Education, Harold Howe II. Howe, who knew many of the people at the Carnegie Corporation, was immediately attracted to the project and became one of its major proponents.[17]

Out of these interconnections there developed a complex relationship between the private foundations, the federal government, public schools, and public television. Often working in cooperation, the federal government and foundations were the source of funds and policies affecting both public schools and public television. In addition, the Children's Television Workshop was considered part of the educational system. Public television was often referred to as the third educational institution along with the family and public schools.[18] "Sesame Street" was planned as a program to prepare children for public schools.[19] And, of course, workers in public schools and public television influenced policy decisions by government and foundations.

From the perspective of foundation leaders like, Alan Pifer, these interconnections could produce policies and programs that would stabilize the social system, protect capitalism, and save American culture from the vulgarity of commercial television.

Of course, this was an elitist view of social control. The protected wealth of private foundations was to provide social justice to all people. Son of an executive in a New England paper manufacturing company and a graduate of Groton School, Harvard College, and Emmanual College, Cambridge, Alan Pifer wanted to help the poor through the administration of the protected wealth of the Carnegie Corporation.[20] It was this noblesse oblige of foundation leaders and the interconnections between foundations and government that created the Corporation for Public Broadcasting and the Children's Television Workshop.

THE CORPORATION FOR PUBLIC BROADCASTING

The creation of the Carnegie Commission on Educational Television illustrates the interconnections between government and private foundations. President Lyndon Johnson wanted to distance himself from policy recommendations regarding broadcasting because of the potential conflict of interest resulting from his family's ownership of radio and television stations. Consequently, he asked his Secretary of Health, Education, and Welfare, and former President of the Carnegie Corporation, Gardner, to seek the financial support of the Carnegie Corporation for a commission to investigate educational television. The members of the commission were selected by the Carnegie Corporation and approved by President Johnson. Johnson added to the original list J. C. Kellam, the manager of his wife's television and radio stations, and a trusted friend, Oveta Culp Hobby, chairman of the board of the Houston Post Company. Except for its tax proposal, President Johnson sent on unchanged the commission's recommendations to Congress. These recommendations provided the basic structure and purpose for the Corporation for Public Broadcasting.[21]

The membership list seemed to contradict the commission's basic policy position that public television serve diversity in American life. "Our varying regions," the commission report states, "our varying religious and national and racial groups, our varying needs and social and intellectual interests are the fabric of the American tradition." Yet absent from its membership were any members of middle- or lower-income groups. The closest representative of blue collar workers on the commission was Leonard Woodcock, Vice-President of the United Automobile Workers of America. On the other hand, university presidents and corporate leaders were well represented. Five of the fifteen members of the commission were heads or former heads of universities, five were from the business community, and rounding off the list were a performing artist, one author, a former Ambassador to Switzerland, and the former governor of North Carolina, Oveta Culp Hobby.[22]

The lack of diversity in its membership seemed to affect the ability of the commission members to spell out the meaning of diversity and special audiences. Writing in the middle of the 1970s, Steve Millard, the director of publications of the Corporation for Public Broadcasting, complained, "Public broadcasting has always suffered from a chronic inability to name its own mission." A major part of the problem, he felt, were the vague references in the commissions report to serving diversity and special audiences. In Millard's words, "The spirit behind 'serving specialized audiences' is that public broadcasting—beginning at the local level—will devote its attention to establishing...what true specialized audiences are; that it will try to ascertain in detail what the audiences need and want; and that its programming will be tailored to meet those expressed needs." Millard argued that it is difficult to clearly define the meaning of "specialized audiences." For some people, it meant special programming for children, women, minorities, and those with special interests in music, drama, yoga, cooking, and other activities. But Millard argued that this definition excluded news and public affairs programming, which are intended for any audience.[23]

Faced with the difficulty of defining programming for specialized audiences, Millard proposed that the true meaning had to do with programming for a particular type of person. Millard wrote, "Specialized audiences? It would be more accurate to say that public broadcasting was meant to address a special quality in every person. The individual who notices, who questions...public broadcasting was intended to address us in those moments."[24]

According to the leadership of the Corporation for Public Broadcasting, a "surprising" number were low-income viewers. Willard Rowland, Chief Research Associate for the Public Broadcasting Service, while noting that a disproportionate number of public television viewers were from "higher socio-economic brackets," wrote that "the amount of viewing and listening by Americans in low-income, low-education and blue-collar categories is larger than is *popularly known* [emphasis added]."[25]

From another standpoint, serving specialized audiences was part of the argument that public television should be an addition to television programming and not a replacement for commercial television. During the 1930s, advocates of public radio wanted a greater share of radio licenses. This would have replaced many commercial with nonprofit stations. But in the 1960s, the role of commercial television in serving mass culture was not challenged, and the emphasis was on creating more options for the television viewer and more competition. This was the position taken by Newton Minow.

After his famous 1961 description of television as a vast wasteland, Minow campaigned for expansion of the number of UHF stations as a means of increasing variety and competition. At the time, very few television sets were being manufactured that could receive stations in the UHF band. All the network programs were broadcast in the VHF band. Another option for increasing competition was cable television. Minow rejected cable television and advocated requiring manufacturers to produce sets that could receive both VHF and UHF channels.

In addition to creating more competition, the production of more television sets capable of receiving UHF signals was essential for educational television. During the early history of television, education groups, as with radio, campaigned for channels to be set aside for educational purposes. In 1950, the Joint Committee of Educational Broadcasters was formed under the leadership of Richard Hull, President of the National Association of Educational Broadcasters, and Franklin Dunham, chief of Radio-Television, U.S. Office of Education. The membership of the Joint Committee included many of the same groups that had struggled for increased licenses for educational radio in the 1930s.[26]

As they had in the 1930s, educational leaders faced a difficult task in competing with commercial broadcasters for licenses. In 1950, they presented the FCC with a plan that one VHF educational channel be set aside in every metropolitan area and that at least 20 percent of all UHF channels would be devoted to education. The setting aside of VHF channels was important because no television sets were being manufactured in 1950 that could receive UHF signals.

At the 1950 FCC hearings, the educators were bitter in their attack on the decisions made in the 1930s. They claimed that commercial broadcasters had never lived up to their promise of providing more educational programming. In addition, educators complained that they were unable to compete with commercial broadcasting for licenses. They needed to have channels specifically reserved for nonprofit broadcasting. For example, the leaders of the Joint Committee on Educational Television related to the FCC the story of the University of Wisconsin application for a 1933 clear-channel radio license. According to the educators, after the application was filed, NBC advised the Governor of Wisconsin that it planned to spend a million dollars campaigning against the license. The governor was intimidated and "he advised withdrawal of the application, and it was never pressed."[27]

Apparently convinced by the educators' arguments, the FCC did not take the position it had with regard to radio. On March 22, 1951, the FCC proposed reserving 209 noncommercial educational channels. Unfortunately, the majority of these channels were in the UHF band which could not be received by most television sets in use at that time. By 1952, 66 percent of the educational television stations in the United States were in the UHF band.[28]

Like the Carnegie Corporation's support of the Corporation for Public Broadcasting, the Ford Foundation was the champion of educational television in the 1950s. In 1948, the Ford Foundation established a study committee to decide what to do with a large donation of stock from the Ford Motor Company. In 1950, the trustees of the Foundation formally accepted the study committee's five objectives—strengthening democracy, strengthening the economy, improving education, and increasing knowledge in the behavioral sciences. In 1951, the Foundation created a subsidiary foundation called the Fund for Adult Education, whose directors decided that "a program of liberal adult education must employ the mass media of communications as well as the traditional channels of adult education."[29]

Since the Fund for Adult Education had decided to enter the arena of broadcasting during the period of extreme anti-Communism, it was a potential target of readers of *Red Channels* and members of the American Legion. Like commercial broadcasters, the Fund for Adult Education assured these groups that educational television was not subversive. Robert Blakely, the Vice-President of the Fund for Adult Education, received an invitation from the Executive Committee of the American Legion to explain the Fund's activities. It is important to note that Blakely accepted the invitation. This acceptance indicated the power of the American Legion and the willingness of the Fund to appease anti-Communist groups. Blakely recounted, "I spent a full day in Indianapolis answering its [the American Legion] questions. The committee asked about the entire range of the Fund's activities, but its focus was on support to ETV [educational television]. My answers apparently satisfied the committee."[30]

After the 1951 allocation of channels, the Fund for Adult Education played a major role in establishing local education stations through matching grants and building a network between stations. In 1952, the Fund supported the establishment of the Educational Television and Radio Center, which produced and distributed programs between educational stations. Of particular concern were programs in "the four subject areas...international affairs, national or political affairs, economic affairs, and the humanities."

Support of these four subject areas changed the basic premise of educational television. In the first place, support for the four subject areas meant that educational television did not focus on school age children. Educational television was also to serve adults. Second, three of the subject areas dealt with issues in citizenship education. At least for the adult viewer, the Educational Television and Radio Center's intention was to emphasize citizenship education through programming in international, national, and economic issues.[31]

Providing adult education set the stage for the later emergence of the Corporation for Public Broadcasting. Adult programming involved an important policy issue. Educational television could be geared to providing programs that would be used in classrooms at all levels of education or it could provide programs that adults and children out of school could freely choose to watch. The Ford Foundation was interested in both types. Beginning in 1955, the Foundation directly supported educational television for general audiences, while through a subsidiary foundation, The Fund for the Advancement of Education, it also supported programming for direct instruction.[32] It was this early work in providing education programs for general audiences that established the framework for the general programming of the Corporation for Public Broadcasting.

In 1958, the federal government joined the Ford Foundation and educators in supporting educational television. Title VII of the National Defense Education Act (NDEA) provided money for "Research and Experimentation in More Effective Utilization of Television, Radio, Motion Pictures, and Related Media for Educational Purposes." NDEA funds were used to sponsor a study of the feasibility of state and regional educational television networks. The study played an influential role in the House of Representative's approval of the Educational Television Facilities Act 1962, which provided grants for the establishment of more educational stations.[33]

The Educational Television Facilities Act 1962 is another example of the interconnections in policy developments between foundations and the federal government. Essentially, Ford Foundation policies regarding educational television were turned into law and received funding from the government. The 1962 law also exemplifies the far-ranging effects of the NDEA. As discussed in previous chapters, the NDEA had a direct impact on public school curricula and textbooks. But in addition, the NDEA influenced the dissemination of ideas through educational television.

Educational television needed both funding for stations and a solution to the problem of broadcasting on the UHF band. Throughout the 1950s, advocates of educational television campaigned for a law requiring that all television sets be manufactured to receive UHF stations. Commercial broadcasters opposed this law because of the potential for increased competition and manufacturers resisted the law because of additional production costs.

On this issue, promoters of educational television found a friend in Newton Minow. For Minow, UHF offered the path out of the vast wasteland of television. A requirement that all sets be equipped with the capability of receiving UHF channels would improve the general quality of programming, Minow argued, by providing increased competition and variety, and decreased regulation by the FCC. In what became known as "Minow's Law," he stated that increased competition would reduce the necessity of federal regulation. In 1962 he wrote, "If we gradually replace VHF sets, we will also act to loosen, rather than tighten, the bands of regulation, because we will move toward a promised land with many television services and choices."[34]

Commercial broadcasters countered with the argument that increased competition would fragment the audience and create a lower level of programming. Minow responded by stressing the value of diversity and programming for special audiences. Comparing television to the magazine industry, which supplies magazines for both the mass audience and special audiences, Minow stated, "so, in television, we could also have such diversity: stations serving smaller, special groups—but groups that are, in toto, significant both in numbers and taste."[35]

Minow's arguments for support of the All-Channel Television Receiver Act 1962 anticipated the arguments for creating the Corporation for Public Broadcasting. The legislation required that television sets be built to receive both VHF and UHF channels. With that hurdle past, the Ford Foundation in 1963 began providing annual grants to the National Educational Television and Radio Center to produce five hours of television per week to be distributed to educational stations. After dropping its involvement in radio and instructional television, the Center changed its name to National Educational Television (NET).[36]

The Ford Foundation's funding of NET and the decision to drop instructional programming for schools meant that the primary purpose of a national network would be the production of programs for out-of-school audiences. This was the objective that eventually led to the Corporation for Public Television. Therefore, the Carnegie Commission's plan reflected Minow's advocacy of diversity and programming for special audiences, and the Ford Foundation and NET emphasis on educational television for out-of-school audiences.

The final recommendations of the Carnegie Commission on Educational Television included a tax plan, which President Johnson deleted when he sent the plan to Congress. This would have provided some independence of the Corporation for Public Broadcasting from the influence of government and from corporate, foundation, and individual donors. "The goal we seek," the recommendation states, "is an instrument for the free communication of ideas in a free society."[37] The proposal was for a 2 percent manufacturer's excise tax on television sets. The Carnegie Commission expressed its concern that without financing from this type of tax the Corporation would have to worry about the political pressures generated in the annual governmental budgeting and appropriation procedures. What the Commission did not foresee when it made the tax proposal was that this might also have protected the Corporation from the influence of corporate, foundation, and individual donors.

Another recommendation was to increase local programming. An emphasis on localism would help achieve the goal of diversity. The Commission believed that local programming would "deepen a sense of community in local life." The Commission envisioned local meetings being brought into the home which "would provide a voice for groups in the community that may otherwise be unheard."[38]

In addition, the Commission wanted public television to project an image of a multicultural America. In this regard, the Commission was reflecting the same emphasis on disseminating an image of a multiracial and multicultural society that was occurring in public school textbooks and in commercial programming. In the words of the Commission, "Public Television should be the mirror of the American style.... [It] should help us know what it is to be many in one, to have growing maturity in our sense of ourselves as a people."[39]

"SESAME STREET" AND THE CHILDREN'S TELEVISION WORKSHOP

The Carnegie Commission's recommendation for children's television included the use of television as a means of social reform. The Carnegie Commission's proposal for children's programming contained two revolutionary ideas about the educational use of television. First was the idea that television could be used as an informal means of education. This proposal harkened back to the debates during the early days of movies when, as pointed out in Chapter 1, censorship was proposed to turn entertainment movies into a form of public education. In the words of the Carnegie Commission, "Important as this can be for adults, the informal educational potential of Public Television is greatest of all for children."[40]

Second, the Commission proposed that television should focus on preparing preschool children for formal education. This proposal was very much in line with the development of Head Start programs in the 1960s, to prepare "disadvantaged" children for kindergarten or the first grade. In the proposal, television would informally educate preschool children, focusing on the education of the "disadvantaged." "Public Television programs," the report states, "should give great attention to the informal educational needs of preschool children, particularly to interest and help children whose intellectual and cultural preparation might otherwise be less than adequate."[41]

Essentially, the proposal was a call to enlist television in President Johnson's War on Poverty. It was based on an idea gaining popularity in the 1960s, that preschool education significantly improved the achievement of children in school and that it could break the cycle of poverty. In March 1966, one of the supervisors of the Carnegie Corporation's grants, Lloyd Morrisett, at a dinner party proposed to television producer Joan Cooney the idea of television as a form of preschool education. Funded by the Corporation, in October 1966 Cooney completed a feasibility study on the use of television to educate preschool children.[42]

Lloyd Morrisett hoped that television could solve the problem of the slow spread of kindergarten and nursery schools around the United States. Believing that preschool education was important for the cognitive development of children, he worried that preschool programs "would slowly, if at all, reach many of the children who needed them, particularly underprivileged children for whom preschool facilities might not be available." The answer to this problem, he felt, lay in the ability of television to reach enormous numbers of preschool children.[43]

As Morrisett conceptualized the project, television should become a partner in the general education of children. Within this framework, television was the third educator along with the family and the school. "The real answer to problems of early education," Morrisett wrote, "is for the total culture of childhood, including television as an important element, to work in harmony with the family and later the school."[44]

Like others, this proposal of the Carnegie Corporation received federal money. During the two years between the feasibility study and the establishment of the Children's Television Workshop, 48.8 percent of the 8 million dollars spent on the project came from federal sources. The majority came through the United States Office of Education. The importance of informal relationships between the government and foundations is illustrated by a story told in Lagemann's history of the Carnegie Corporation. Lagemann describes a trip by Joan Cooney, now an employee of the Corporation, and Barbara Finberg, a Corporation program officer concentrating on early childhood education, to Washington to see the United States Commissioner of Education. According to Lagemann, Commissioner Howe was "well acquainted with many people at the Carnegie Corporation, including Morrisett...[and he was] quickly interested in the idea of a children's series. 'Let's do it,' Cooney remembered him saying at the end of their meeting."[45] Commissioner Howe became a major proponent of preschool education through television. In 1968, the Children's Television Workshop was organized, and on November 10, 1969, the first production of "Sesame Street" was broadcast.

The organization of the Children's Television Workshop required cooperation between the educators and television producers. As Cooney described the process, the informal network of the Carnegie Corporation was used to select an educational advisor for the Workshop. Cooney had met many academics selected by the Corporation while doing the feasibility study. In addition, Morrisett, in Cooney's words, "through his position at Carnegie, knew personally most of the leading people in the field of educational psychology." As their first choice, they decided to ask Gerald Lesser, Bigelow Professor of Education and Developmental Psychology at Harvard, to be their chief advisor and Chairman of the Board of Advisors.[46]

Lesser was the guiding hand in developing the educational goals for "Sesame Street," the first major production of the Children's Television Workshop. Lesser rejected the attitude of many educators that education could solve most of the world's problems. He wrote that, "Educators cannot remedy the injustices to minorities in our society or create new life styles or new communities to replace deteriorating ones. Yet they sometimes act as if they think they can."[47] The belief that education could only have a limited role in social reform tempered the original focus on helping children of the poor.

While Lesser saw a limited role for education in social reform, he did believe that something drastic had to be done about educational problems in the United States. Writing about the "fifty billion dollars" that was spent on a "massive educational superstructure which holds captive over fifty million children," he complained that "we are failing to educate our children, either disastrously or to a degree no worse than the failures of other social and political institutions, is almost beyond dispute."[48]

Lesser believed that television could be a means of rescuing the entire educational system. In fact, he argued that television had certain ingredients that made it somewhat superior to the public schools. Public schooling, he maintained, depended on control of the student by others, public humiliation, and the continuous threat of failure. Television learning contained none of these elements. In front of the television, Lesser argued, the child learns without fear of a public or teacher, there is no threat of humiliation, and the child can control the learning process by the flip of a switch.

Therefore, Lesser believed that television was an ideal educator. It was nonpunitive and it provided a shelter from the emotional stress of society. "We may regret the conditions in our society that make sanctuaries necessary and must guard against a child's permanent retreat into them," Lesser wrote, "but sanctuaries are needed, and television is one of the few shelters children have."[49]

Lesser also believed that television was a superior educator because it could be entertaining. He argued that traditionalist thinkers had separated entertainment from education. In fact, many believed that entertainment would contaminate education. Lesser referred to this as a "lunatic" view of education. Like the early censors who wanted entertainment movies to be "educational," Lesser believed that television would be an ideal vehicle for educating through entertainment.[50]

Besides lauding the potential educational value of television, Lesser was impressed by the statistics on television viewing. Using calculations made in 1967, Lesser estimated that in homes with preschool children the television set was on fifty-four hours per week. On the average, a high school graduate had spent twelve thousand hours in school and fifteen thousand hours watching television. In fact, the high school graduate had spent more time watching television than was spent at any other activity.[51]

Given all of these factors, Lesser believed that television could be the savior of the entire educational system, although at the same time he doubted the ability of education to achieve massive social reform. Consequently, he felt the Children's Television Workshop should not limit its focus to the education of children of the poor. In addition, his desire for the Workshop's success influenced his proposal to create a program for all children. In Lesser's words, "To succeed, a national television series must attract as large a national audience as possible, including children from all social classes and cultural groups and from all geographic regions."[52]

Producing a program for all children raised a dilemma for the goal of reducing the educational gap between the children of the rich and the poor. Obviously, the attempt to reach all children restricted the ability of the program to narrow these differences; in fact, as Lesser admitted, the program might increase them. Lesser wrote, "We hoped that poor children would learn as much and that the gap would not be widened, despite the fact that almost all comparisons of educational progress show middle-class children proceeding more rapidly."[53] The solution he offered was to make the series appealing to children of the poor and to encourage viewing in poor families.

Therefore, while "Sesame Street" was to suppose to appeal to a national audience, concerns with educating the children of the poor directly influenced the overall goals of the program. Even though Lesser felt negatively about public schooling, he argued that the only realistic goal was to emphasize an education that would prepare children to enter school. This approach tied the program directly to the needs of formal schooling.

Lesser added a somewhat cynical note as to how the program could prepare children. "Since one major premise was the preparation of disadvantaged children for school," Lesser argued, "the most useful ammunition we could give the child was the ability to 'read' the teacher, to pick up the small covert clues in the teacher's behavior that would allow him to guess what the teacher wants to hear."[54] Therefore, from Lesser's perspective, "Sesame Street" could help children by teaching them the implicit rules of schooling so that the child could conform to teachers' behavioral expectations. Lesser's proposal, however, was overruled by the staff of the Children's Television Workshop.

The emphasis on preparation for school and concerns about children of the poor determined the basic shape of "Sesame Street." The staff believed that poor parents wanted their children to achieve in the basic subjects of reading, writing, and arithmetic. The major complaint of these parents, the staff understood, was the failure of the school to teach these subjects. Therefore, the staff concluded that the program should focus on preparation for learning these subjects in school.

According to Lesser, teaching the alphabet was the most controversial decision on preparation for school. This created "howls of repugnance... over...use of the new technology to teach what appears to be an arbitrary and useless skill."[55] But, it was argued, the alphabet was essential for early reading. What television could accomplish, in the framework of Lesser's belief that learning can be entertaining, was to make memorizing of the alphabet a form of entertainment.

During its early years, "Sesame Street" scored a major success in reaching children of the poor. During its first year, almost fifty percent of the potential preschool audience were estimated to have watched the program, including children in day-care and other prekindergarten programs serving children of the poor. The program was watched by ninety-one percent of the at-home children in low-income Bedford-Stuyvesant and Harlem sections of New York City. Eighty-eight percent of low-income families interviewed in Chicago tuned their sets to "Sesame Street."[56]

One reason for the success of the program was the campaign, particularly in low-income urban areas, to create awareness of the program. To do this, "Sesame Street" Clubs were established, people went door-to-door to alert families to the program, a *Sesame Street Magazine* was distributed, and announcements were made through libraries, schools, and community organizations. In Chicago, 120 mothers in low-income areas conducted "Sesame Street" viewing sessions. A similar project was conducted in the Mexican-American section of Los Angeles. The Children's Television Workshop ran a Neighborhood Youth Corps Project that involved adolescents from poor families in teaching preschool children and focused on viewing "Sesame Street." During the first year, 240 adolescents worked in viewing centers with fifteen hundred children. The following year the numbers increased to twelve hundred adolescents helping fifteen thousand children of the poor in thirteen different cities. By 1972, there were ten thousand tutors helping one hundred thousand preschool children in viewing centers.[57]

More broadly, the publicity campaign helped to legitimize television as the third educator considered equal to the role of formal schooling and the family. Again, it is important to note that the "Sesame Street" concept was different from instructional television designed for the classroom. Now education moved into the home in the format of an entertainment program. In addition, it truly nationalized the educational process. From coast-to-coast, children were watching the same program. The program created a mass culture among preschool children.

The use of television as an educator seemed to contradict all the charges that television viewing was a passive and mind-numbing experiencing. Lesser argued that a great deal of learning takes place through modeling. Children do not need to interact to learn, according to Lesser; they can model themselves after television characters. In fact, modeling fit Lesser's concept of a nonpunitive form of education. "The child," Lesser wrote, "imitates the model without being induced or compelled to do so.... By watching televised models, children learn both socially desirable and undesirable behaviors."[58] Television, Lesser argued, can provide models that show what behaviors are possible and what consequences might occur from a action.

In addition to modeling behavior, Lesser believed television could create myths to guide children's actions. In this context, television was suppose to educate the public in the same manner as movies censored by their 1930 code. In Lesser's words, television could provide "a vision of the world as it might be." These myths were to be created by the presentation of what Lesser called "simple goodness." He believed that children did not learn from preaching. Considering television's role in presenting life's tensions and deprivations, Lesser reasoned, "Surely it can create others that help them toward a more humane vision of life."[59]

The argument for creating myths made ideological management dependent on creating unrealistic images of goodness. As in previous movie and broadcasting codes, good had to win out over evil. This reasoning spilled over into decisions about portraying normal urban life on "Sesame Street." In the end, the decision was made to present urban life as "a vision of the world as it might be" and not in its reality.

Therefore, "Sesame Street" joined Textbook Town in presenting scenes of a harmonious world. Lesser wrote that this issue was debated by members of the Children's Television Workshop. He believed that little could be gained in showing to the child living in an urban ghetto the harsh realities of life. As planning of the program evolved, there was a drift toward presenting the sweeter side of life. In giving only the positive side, they realized that they might be accused of presenting a sugar-coated world.[60]

The decision to present a distorted view of urban living is exemplified by Lesser's description of a program designed to show children how an urban bus driver and passengers act on a trip around the city. "Now, we all know that a bus driver is often not our best example of someone who is courteous and civil," Lesser wrote. "But on the 'Sesame Street' bus trip, the driver responds to his passengers' hellos and thank-yous, tells a child who cannot locate his money, 'That's all right, you can pay me tomorrow,' and upon seeing a young woman running after his bus just as it has left the curb, actually stops to let her on."[61]

This depiction of an urban bus trip Lesser referred to as an "outrageous misrepresentation" of most urban transportation systems. But he justified it as presenting a model of behavior that would guide children to a better world. In justifying the presentation of an urban transportation system in this idealized fashion, Lesser stated, "We wanted to show the child what the world is like when people treat each other with decency and consideration. Our act of faith...was that young children will learn such attitudes if we take the trouble to show them some examples, even if *we stretch familiar reality a bit in order to do so* [emphasis added]."[62]

The desire to create positive myths and to help children of the poor influenced the decision to present strong male role models. The staff reasoned that poor children lacked positive male figures in their lives and that public schooling was dominated by female role models. Therefore they decided to "show men on "Sesame Street" in warm, nurturing relationships with young children." This led to attacks on the program for its lack of strong female characters. Newspaper columnist Ellen Goodman complained that, "The females that do live on 'Sesame Street' can be divided into three groups: teacher, simp, and mother.... Oh yes, a cow." As time went on, the program introduced more positive female roles. But the early emphasis was on strong male roles.[63]

Like the new Textbook Town of the late 1960s, "Sesame Street" was harmoniously and racially integrated. Of course, this presentation sugar-coated the harsh realities of racial conflict in American society. Lesser noted that one of the charges made against the program was that it taught "minority-group children to accept quietly middle-class America's corrupt demands to subjugate themselves." Like the new Textbook Town, multiracial groups worked and played harmoniously on "Sesame Street" while whites and African-Americans clashed on the streets.[64]

The production of "Sesame Street" opened the door to a new era in public education and to the influence of national educational policy on the world of television. "Sesame Street" extended organized education to out-of-school children while joining the government's War on Poverty. This new era in television was highlighted by the Children's Television Workshop's production of "The Electric Company" and "3–2–1 Contact."

Edward Palmer, the Director of Research for the Children's Television Workshop, called "The Electric Company" and "3–2–1 Contact" "home-and-school hybrids." Like "Sesame Street," they were expected to attract out-of-school viewers. In addition, they could be viewed in school. Consequently, these programs brought together the world of home television viewing with formal classroom instruction. Also like "Sesame Street," the programs reflected federal educational policy. In the words of Palmer, "Both series further illustrate how television can be tied to needs of children in which our whole society has a stake."[65]

The production of "The Electric Company" was directly tied to the Nixon Administration's concern with teaching of basic skills. Its first broadcast in 1971 was intended to reach 7-to-10-year-olds who might be having difficulty reading. It was also used in first grade classrooms as an introduction to reading. Half the viewers were estimated to be in school settings. After one year, 34 percent of the nation's elementary schools used the program. Using closed circuit television systems, some elementary schools made the program available to teachers throughout the school day. Nixon's Commissioner of Education, Sidney Marland, called "Sesame Street" and "The Electric Company" "the best educational investment ever made."[66]

"3–2–1 Contact" was directly related to career education. In addition, pressure continued for educating more scientists and technical workers. As Palmer indicates, the program was a direct reflection of these national policy objectives. Palmer wrote, "The series was created in the late 1970s because the United States had fallen behind as a nation in preparing large enough numbers of children well enough to fill the demand for specialists in science and technology in the workplace." The program was designed to attract children to science and technology before they entered the ninth and tenth grades.[67]

The argument that television should be used to influence career choices continued into the 1980s. Ernest Boyer, President of the Carnegie Foundation for the Advancement of Teaching, argued in 1983 that teenagers were confused about life's choices. "Public television," he stated, "better than the high school vocational counseling programs, could show teenagers what it is like to work at various occupations." Boyer's statement reflected the fact that the productions of the Children's Television Workshop and the Corporation for Public Broadcasting had convinced educational leaders that television could be the third educator.

CONCLUSION

The government officials, educators, and foundation leaders responsible for developing the Corporation for Public Broadcasting and the Children's Television Workshop conceded to commercial television the determination of mass culture. In contrast to the 1930s, little was said in the 1960s about audiences' choices turning commercial broadcasting into a form of democratic culture. There seemed to be a general acceptance of the fact that commercial programming was shaped by a combination of influences from advocacy groups, government officials, advertisers, industry standards, and the production process. If commercial television shaped mass culture, then mass culture was indirectly shaped by these influences on commercial broadcasting. From this perspective, public television was given influence over high culture, while commercial television was allotted low culture.

The division of influence on national culture was made primarily by an interconnected set of ideological managers. Among these managers, of major importance were private foundations, whose influence expanded after World War II through the funding of research, policy commissions, and educational and broadcasting programs themselves.

This web of educators, foundations, and intellectuals extended into the federal government. Funds, policies, and personnel moved along the threads of this web between government bureaucracies, foundations, educational institutions, and the Corporation for Public Broadcasting. It is difficult to determine the boundaries of influence of the different parts of the web.

The Children's Television Workshop is an example of the web's interconnections. The Workshop received funding from foundations, the United States Office of Education, and the Corporation for Public Broadcasting. Its advisors and staff were drawn from educational institutions, foundations, the U.S. Office of Education, and the world of broadcasting. The result of this web was to make the Children's Television Workshop an instrument of federal educational policies.

The Children's Television Workshop continued the pattern of trying to shape public morality by presenting the world as harmonious and good. Like the movie and broadcasting codes of the 1930s, the comic book code of the 1950s, and Textbook Town, programs such as "Sesame Street" created a tension between reality and the projected image of the world. On the one hand, this tension might have created a cynical feeling toward these images. This cynicism might have led to a rejection of these forms of projected morality. On the other hand, these images might actually have provided a standard as to what the world should be like.

The images projected in the adult programming of public television are more difficult to determine. The failure to pass a tax measure to support the Corporation for Public Broadcasting opened the door to influence from private donors. In contrast to commercial television's influence on mass culture, private donors to public television are interested in influencing high culture.

Therefore, the creation of the Corporation for Public Broadcasting and the Children's Television Workshop added a new dimension to ideological management in the United States. Corporations, foundations, educators, and government officials joined hands to make television an instrument of federal educational policies and a molder of high culture. Along with the family and the school, public television, by instructing out-of-school children, became the third great educational institution. While commercial television was given influence over mass culture, public television assumed leadership of high culture.

CHAPTER FOURTEEN

CONCLUSION AND EPILOGUE

IDEOLOGICAL MANAGEMENT IN the United States involves the interaction of government, private enterprise, advocacy groups, and, in more recent years, philanthropic foundations. With the easy movement of their personnel between government and educational institutions, foundations are gaining increasing power over the dissemination of ideas. For instance, the Carnegie Corporation continues to shape educational policy in the 1980s and 1990s through its sponsorship of policy reports and its provision of seed money for new educational projects.[1] The influence of foundations illustrates the intersection of private and government power in shaping the distribution of ideas. Both foundations and advocacy groups are able to use their organizational power because of the economic and political mix of free enterprise and government in the United States.

As discussed throughout this book, the movie, broadcasting, and textbook industries and the public schools fear attacks by advocacy groups because of the potential damage to their sources of revenue. Advocacy groups are powerful because they can organize a concerted effort to influence politicians and government officials, and, in the case of broadcasting, sponsors. But advocacy groups are not necessarily representative of the majority of the population. Rather, members of these groups tend to be the most active and vocal citizens in a community. Throughout the twentieth century, religious and patriotic organizations wielded the greatest influence. Joining their ranks in recent years are organizations representing various racial and ethnic groups.

The broadcasting industries constantly fear that complaints from advocacy groups will result in government censorship or loss of licenses. In addition, broadcasters worry that, as patriotic and religious organizations were able to do in the past, advocacy groups will drive away sponsors. Throughout the century, public school officials feared that offending any organized group might cost them their jobs or a loss of tax support. Few school officials relish the idea of being attacked by any of the groups discussed in this volume. In its pursuit of profit, the textbook industry fears criticism from the same groups that public school officials fear. Consequently, the images in textbooks are shaped in a similar manner as those in the public school curriculum. And, of course, the movie

251

industry has always feared a reduction in its profits caused by government censorship of popular subjects, boycotts by advocacy groups, and, in earlier years, government anti-trust action.

Of course, the influence of advocacy groups varies over time. While the possibility of criticism from the American Legion sent chills through school officials and executives in the broadcasting and movie industries throughout much of the century, it took the struggles of the civil rights movement in recent decades to give the same power to the National Association for the Advancement of Colored People. On the other hand, the potential threats of the Religious Right have been an important concern of these industries throughout the twentieth century.

Schools and the broadcasting and movie industries find that the easiest way to protect revenue is through self-censorship. The movie, textbook, and broadcasting industries find direct government censorship expensive. Self-regulatory codes allow changes at the time of production and consequently avoid the greater expense of changing a completed product. This is why movie, broadcasting, comic book, and recording codes are created. Textbook publishers and public school officials follow a similar practice by avoiding topics that might offend some vocal organization. And, as argued throughout this volume, this self-regulation in each of the movie and broadcasting industries and in public education is often a reaction to pressure from the same or similar groups. One of the best illustrations of the effect of an advocacy group on all media is the unbroken thread of influence by the American Legion on public schools, textbooks, movies, radio, and television from the 1920s through the 1950s.

ENTERTAINMENT AS A FORM OF PUBLIC EDUCATION

These patterns of ideological management continued into the late 1980s and the 1990s. Of particular interest is the persistent belief throughout the twentieth century that entertainment should serve as a form of public education. For example, in 1988, Jay A. Winsten, the Assistant Dean of the Harvard School of Public Health and founder of the Harvard Alcohol Project, announced a cooperative effort with television networks "to model a new social norm by reaching 240 to 250 million Americans, working through news organizations, public-service announcements and the entertainment media." The principal thrust of the project is the use of entertainment television to shape behavior regarding the use of alcohol. This effort reflected the continued efforts of public leaders throughout the twentieth century to use entertainment as a form of public education.[2]

In this example, the use of entertainment for public education is designed to encourage the use of designated drivers who will not drink and who will assume responsibility for taking home friends who have been drinking.

Harris Katleman, President of the television division of 20th Century–Fox Film Corporation, announced that any party or tavern scene in programs produced by his studio would include a mention of designated drivers: "If you're doing a scene in 'L.A. Law' where the characters are in a bar and one of them says, 'Have a drink,' another will respond, 'No, I'm the designated driver'." Grant Tinker, former Chairman of NBC and now President of GTG Entertainment, Inc., described the importance of entertainment as a form of public education. As one of the leaders of the Alcohol Project, Tinker is reported as saying, "You couldn't have enough billboards or skywriting or newspapers to equal the impact of a star like Michael J. Fox talking about designated drivers on one episode of 'Family Ties,' a popular NBC series."[3]

Interestingly, the use of entertainment programs to change the public's behavior was labeled a success by Jay A. Winsten. One year after the beginning of the Alcohol Project, Winsten reported a 1989 Gallup poll in which 72 percent of respondents reported using a designated driver. This figure was compared to 62 percent who answered the same way in 1988 when the campaign used only public service advertisements. Supposedly, the difference between the two figures proved the superiority of changing behavior by sneaking social messages into entertainment as opposed to straightforward advertising. *New York Times* television reporter Bill Carter wrote, "The sweeping nature of the designated-driver campaign raises questions about how easily the power of such underlying television messages could be abused."[4]

SHAPING NATIONAL CULTURE

Also continuing into the 1990s is the conflict over of broadcasting and public schools' role in shaping national culture. The movement toward cultural pluralism from the 1970s into the 1990s differs not only from the integration goals of the 1950s and 1960s, but also from public schools' traditional goal of creating a common culture. The debate between educators and broadcasters in the 1930s over who should control "the" national culture seems meaningless in the 1990s as advocacy groups push for a wholly multicultural society. Indeed, the diverse programming available, especially on cable television, might be contributing to the breakdown of a common culture.

Exemplifying the issues surrounding the development of a multicultural society is Richard Bernstein's September 2, 1990, *New York Times* article, "Who Controls Art? Artists or Social Goals?," on an art world torn apart by cultural differences. Placing the blame on deviation from the goals of the civil rights movement of the 1950s and 1960s, Bernstein claimed that the multiculturalism of movies, television, and theater—he could have added to his list the public schools—is reinforcing ethnic and racial violence in the United States. Bernstein wrote,

Twenty-five years ago, the civil rights movement began to erase differences imposed by race and ethnic origin. Now the cult of otherness asserts that the differences are unbridgeable.... The tendency now is for individuals, particularly members of minority groups, to identify primarily with their groups rather than with the common culture—often pushed into it by the radicalism of militant leaders."[5]

The racial and ethnic advocacy groups that helped to integrate Textbook Town and television in the 1960s began to splinter society in the 1980s. By then, the emphasis began to shift from integration to the promotion of a multi-cultural society. One reason was the increasing number of immigrants entering the United States. For instance, immigration from Asia jumped from a little over one hundred thousand in 1971 to over three hundred thousand in 1989. During the 1980s, the overall Asian population of the United States grew by 70 percent, from 3.8 million in 1980 to 6.5 million in 1988. Another major source of immigrants is Latin America. During the 1980s, Mexico continued to lead the list of sources of immigration.[6]

By 1990, one of the major arguments for increasing immigration was the need to improve the American labor force. A Senate bill in 1990 provided for a substantial increase in the number of skilled immigrants brought into the United States by corporations. "The question is, should immigration be encouraged or should national policy encourage training to allow those here, including blacks, to take those jobs?" asked Arthur F. Brimmer, a former member of the Board of Governors of the Federal Reserve System. "My own view is that we should do both." On the other hand, Hazel Dukes, New York State President of the N.A.A.C.P., said, "Why let foreigners or newcomers have these jobs, while blacks, who have been here for hundreds of years, can't support themselves or their families?"[7]

Increased immigration created the specter not only of heightened tensions over employment between African-Americans and the new immigrants, but also of new problems in discrimination in education. During the 1980s, Asian advocacy groups began to protest discrimination in the American educational system. The Asian-American Task Force on University Admissions charged the University of California with discrimination against Asians. The cochair of the advocacy group, Alameda County Superior Court Judge Ken Kawaichi, declared that university administrators envisioned a campus that "is mostly white, mostly upper class, with limited numbers of African-Americans, Hispanics, and Asians. One day they looked around and said, 'My goodness, look at this campus. What are all these Asian people doing here?' Then they started tinkering with the system."[8]

During the late 1960s and the 1970s, Hispanic groups pushed for establishment of bilingual education programs in public schools. In part, bilingual education programs were to serve the purpose of maintaining Hispanic culture within the walls of American schools. Such bilingual education teaches subject-matter courses in Spanish while teaching English language proficiency. Integrated into this kind of bilingual education is an emphasis on Hispanic culture.

Some members of the Republican Party joined a movement opposing bilingual education and supporting the adoption of English as the official language of the United States. The movement for making English the official language is led by an organization called United States English, founded in 1983 by former Republican Senator S. I. Hayakawa. A leaflet distributed by the organization in California warns, "Some spokesmen for ethnic groups reject the 'melting pot' ideal; they label assimilation a betrayal of their native cultures and demand government funding to maintain separate ethnic institutions."[9]

In reaction to the activities of United States English and to President Reagan's opposition to bilingual education, the National Association of Bilingual Education announced at a 1986 meeting that it would engage in increased political activities and intensified public relations efforts for bilingual education. Gene T. Chavez, the retiring President of the Association, warned referring to the U.S. English supporters, that "those who think this country can only tolerate one language" were more motivated by political than educational concerns. At the same meeting, the incoming President of the organization, Chicago school administrator Jose Gonzalez, attacked the Reagan Administration and the U.S. Department of Education for entering an "unholy alliance" with right-wing groups opposing bilingual education, such as U.S. English, Save Our Schools, and the Heritage Foundation.[10]

In 1990, some African-American groups were demanding segregation of schools as a means of providing an Afro-centric curriculum. For example, in Milwaukee, Wisconsin, a group of African-American educators and parents prodded the school board into creating two schools specifically designed for African-American boys. Joyce Mallory, a black School Board member, said "African-American males are doing dismally in our schools. We need to do something drastically different. And we need to do it quickly."[11] Like the original "Sesame Street," these two schools were to provide positive male models. In addition, the schools were to stress an Afro-centric curriculum. Across the country, Afro-centric schools and curricula are being introduced into school systems.[12]

Cultural separatism spread to the arts. In the previously cited article by Richard Bernstein, he points out how the arts in the United States reflect its cultural pluralism. Of particular concern to Bernstein is the anti-Semitism that he finds in movies by African-American director and producer Spike Lee. He believes that these movies increase friction among racial and ethnic groups. In providing an opposing argument, Bernstein quotes a Professor of African-American studies at Temple University, Molefi Kete Asante, "Whenever black people want to move off the plantation, white people see it as a threat. Nobody gets upset over Chinatown, but if blacks created a Nigeria-town, they would be called separatist, rather than people trying to reinforce cultural roots that are significant for them."[13]

The development of cable television might be another factor in creating an image of a multicultural society. The variety and specialized quality of the programming on cable television allows the projection of multiple images of society. The block that had been placed in the way of the development of cable television was removed in 1972, when the FCC issued its Cable Television Report and Order. Opening the door to cable television sparked several decades of controversy over which companies should be granted municipal franchises and what provisions should be made for community and political access. While these problems were being argued, new cable networks sprouted up providing a variety of specialized programming, from movies and news to sports and children's programming.[14]

The effect of specialized programming on national culture is difficult to determine. Certainly, the concern of educators in the 1930s that radio would take over the role of the school in determining national culture takes on a different meaning with the specialized programming of cable television. Rather than broadcasting's creating a unified national culture, cable television might be joining the schools in creating a multicultural society.

ADVOCACY GROUPS AND THE RELIGIOUS RIGHT

By influencing the dissemination of ideas, some advocacy groups work to develop a multicultural society, while other groups continue their efforts to shape specific public beliefs. The Religious Right persists in its campaign to expunge "immorality" from textbooks and the media. With claims that public schools are teaching an anti-religious philosophy of secular humanism, Christian fundamentalists attack textbook publishers and school officials. Conservative organizations, such as Phyllis Schafly's Eagle Forum, are organizing parents to monitor local school systems for any sign of "secular humanism." The Eagle Forum issued a form letter to parents which they could send to their local school district. The form letter objects to such school activities as values clarification, death education, discussion and testing of interpersonal relations, sex education, drug and alcohol education, and "anti-nationalistic, one-world government, or globalism curricula."[15]

Across the country, textbook controversies continue to erupt. Two new groups have emerged that focus on the content of textbooks. One group is led by a husband-and-wife team from Texas, the Gablers. They try to weed out of textbooks anything they consider attacks on Americanism and free-enterprise economics, and any suggestion that federal controls might be needed to protect the environment. On the other end of the political spectrum, People for the American Way states that a specific purpose of the group is to limit the influence of the Religious Right on the public schools.[16]

Exemplifying the tensions over charges of "secular humanism" in textbooks, a group of parents in West Virginia's Hawkins County School System charged that the 1983 edition of the Holt, Rinehart & Winston reading series created the possibility that after reading the books "a child might adopt the views of a feminist, a humanist, a pacifist, an anti-Christian, a vegetarian, or an advocate of a 'one-world government'." The protest resulted in violence and a series of court cases.[17]

In 1990, Holt, Rinehart & Winston was attacked for its four-year-old reading series called *Impressions*. The series is designed to add realism to Textbook Town and higher-quality literature to reading books. The books contain stories by outstanding writers, including Lewis Carroll, A. A. Milne, Laura Ingalls Wilder, and C. S. Lewis. Leading the attack were the Religious Right organizations Focus on Family, Christians for Educational Excellence, the National Association of Christian Educators, and the Western Center for Law and Religious Freedom. These groups object to both the realism and fantasy in the stories. The realism in the books is criticized for being depressing and violent, while the fantasy is criticized for Satanic references.[18]

Controversy over the reading books erupted in late September 1990, when the *Citizen,* a publication of Focus on Family, issued a list of objections to the series. The controversy spread to North Carolina and Georgia where state textbook advisory committees recommended against adopting the series. Testifying about the books before the Georgia textbook advisory committee, Karen LaBarr, a parent, said, "The issue is a pervasive negativeness and pervasive weirdness that just doesn't need to be there." On the other side, Donald Fowler, Issues Director for People for the American Way, warned that controversies would increase when you give "kids...real literature that might expose them to potentially controversial topics in contrast to the pablum of 'See Spot run'...."[19]

During the 1980s, President Ronald Reagan gained most of his support on educational issues from the Religious Right. Working with the conservative Heritage Foundation and Moral Majority, Reagan appointed members of the Religious Right to the Department of Education. When Reagan selected William Bennett to be Secretary of Education in 1985, the Moral Majority report proudly announced in its headlines, "Finally a Friend in Education."[20] Reflecting the influence of the Religious Right on Reagan's administration, in 1985, Thomas Tancredo, the Department of Education's representative in Denver, distributed at government expense a speech written five years previously by the then–Executive Director of the Moral Majority, Robert Billings. The speech declared that "godlessness has taken over America." President Reagan had subsequently appointed Billings to direct the Department of Education's ten regional offices.[21]

The Religious Right continues to campaign against "immorality" in television programming, as well as in public education. Leading the charge is Christian Leaders for Responsible Television or, as it is also called, Clear-TV. In 1989, the group announced its intentions of monitoring prime time television and, using the methods of similar groups in the 1950s, leading boycotts against any programs containing objectionable sex, violence, profanity, or anti-Christian stereotyping. Of particular concern are new programs such as "Married… With Children."[22] In fact, a Michigan woman, Terry Rakolta, is responsible for Procter and Gamble, McDonalds, and Kimberley-Clark dropping their sponsorship of the program. She sent letters to the company complaining about feeding "kids a steady diet of gratuitous sex and violence."[23]

But unlike their predecessors, many sponsors today are not concerned about complaints regarding sexual and violent themes. In the advertising field, many sponsors are known as "tonnage" sponsors.[24] These sponsors are interested in getting the largest audiences for their advertising. In general, they don't care about the level of sex or violence as long as programs continue to attract large numbers of viewers.

Still, some advertisers remain apprehensive about program content. Many advertising agencies rely on a screening service called Advertising Information Services, which employs twenty people to watch tapes of upcoming programs. Others use their own screening offices. An advertiser that employs its own screeners, Paul Schulman, head of the Paul Schulman Company, described one innocuous situation: "We had a problem with an episode of 'Little House on the Prairie' because wild dogs were chasing a girl and we had a Puppy-Chow ad. We have to pull cat food commercials out of 'Alf' because Alf is constantly trying to eat the cat."[25]

Proctor and Gamble, the nation's largest television advertiser, continues its tradition of rejecting programming that it finds politically and morally offensive. The consumer giant withdrew ads from two television stations in Massachusetts because the stations broadcast 30-second commercials by a peace advocacy group, Neighbor-to-Neighbor, which were critical of Proctor and Gamble's purchase of coffee from El Salvador. One of the stations in the dispute said that the loss of revenue from the advertising of Proctor and Gamble products such as Head and Shoulders Shampoo, Spic 'n Span Cleanser, Bold Detergent, White Cloud Toilet Tissue, Citrus Hill Orange Juice, and Folgers Coffee could mean financial ruin. Senator Edward Kennedy and three other congressmen issued a statement that argued, "At stake in Procter & Gamble's decision is the concept of a free exchange of ideas upon which our democracy works." The statement by the lawmakers warned, "The fact that numerous other television stations have elected not to broadcast the Neighbor-to-Neighbor commercial highlights the economic weight P&G...can wield in its effort to silence another advertiser with whom it disagrees."[26]

Parents groups, similar to those that influenced radio and comic books in the 1930s and 1950s, continue to pressure television broadcasters. Leading the group is Action for Children's Television (ACT). ACT was organized in 1968 by a group of mothers in Newton, Massachusetts, who, like the mothers in the 1930s, were concerned about the effects of violence and commercials in broadcasting. One of the first concerns was the number of commercials shown on the children's program "Romper Room."[27]

ACT perseveres in its efforts to limit children's exposure to commercials. It was the major organization lobbying for 1990 federal legislation requiring broadcasters to provide more educational programming for children and to limit commercials on children's programs to ten and a half minutes per hour. Echoing the arguments of Newton Minow in the 1960s, Peggy Charren, President of ACT, said about the legislation: "It's an issue of choice. For parents who do not want their children to see violent cartoons or 'Looney Tunes,' there should be a choice."[28]

SELF-CENSORSHIP AS A FORM OF IDEOLOGICAL CONTROL

Exemplifying the continuing importance of self-censorship as a form of ideological management resulting from fears of government control and threats to profits is the recent adoption by the recording industry of a self-censorship code. In addition, the movie and television industries in 1990 revised their self-censorship codes to meet new economic conditions.

Of major importance in the development of a code in the record industry were government actions and public protests regarding the rap music of groups such as 2 Live Crew. In early 1990, Jack Thompson, a fundamentalist Christian, began a campaign in Florida to ban the 2 Live Crew album, "As Nasty as They Wanna Be." Conducting his crusade from a two-bedroom house in Coral Gables, Thompson transcribes objectionable lyrics from music albums and sends them to reporters, law enforcement officials, politicians, and the record companies themselves. In addition, his crusade against obscene lyrics has been carried to 35 campuses, via a college lecture tour. He sent copies of the lyrics of "As Nasty as They Wanna Be" to Florida's Governor Bob Martinez and to sheriffs in 65 counties. After receiving the lyrics from Thompson, Governor Martinez denounced the album as obscene. Along with 2 Live Crew, Thompson's list of objectionable rap music groups includes Geto Boys and Too Short.[29]

Because of complaints about obscene lyrics, local law enforcement officers began arresting record store owners. In 1989, a record store owner in Alabama was arrested for selling 2 Live Crew's album, "Move Something."

Similar arrests were made in Texas. On June 8, 1990, sheriffs in Broward County, Florida, motivated in part by Thompson's campaign, arrested record store owner Charles Freeman for selling a copy of "As Nasty as They Wanna Be" to an undercover officer. In July 1990, Anchorage Mayor Tom Fink announced that 2 Live Crew would be barred from using the local convention center. During the same period, sales of "As Nasty as They Wanna Be" were banned in Chapel Hill, North Carolina. But on July 25, Louisiana Governor Buddy Roemer vetoed a bill that would have required warning labels on recordings that deal with drug abuse, sex, or violence, and prohibited their sale to people under seventeen years of age.[30]

The recording industry reacted to these censorship pressures by adopting an industry code. In 1986, the Recording Industry Association of America, a trade association representing ninety percent of the industry, under pressure from the Parents' Music Resource Center, agreed to place warning labels on potentially objectionable records. The Parents' Music Resource Center was organized by Elizabeth "Tipper" Gore, wife of U.S. Senator Albert Gore, to direct attention to recordings that might be considered violent or sexually explicit. In 1990, Jennifer Norwood, Executive Director of the parents' group, said, "Part of our problem is our culture tends to look at children as miniature adults. We expect them to handle things they're not ready to handle yet at their age."[31]

It wasn't until 1990, when attacks against rap music started in earnest, that members of the Recording Industry Association of America began placing warning labels on records that read, "Explicit Lyrics—Parental Advisory." Immediately, these labels were placed on the popular rap album "Fear of a Black Planet," by the political music group Public Enemy. Of course, they also ended up on albums by 2 Live Crew. Some record stores began moving records with the stickers into sections that are off-limits to children; others removed such albums completely from their stores. In St. Louis, record stores began to require customers to produce proof that they were over eighteen years of age before they are allowed to purchase labeled albums. The second largest record store chain in the country, Camelot Music, checked identifications for several months before changing to a money-back guarantee for dissatisfied parents.[32]

While the recording industry was adopting a code, the movie industry was revising its. The code adopted by the movie industry in 1990 is a variation on the one adopted in the 1960s. During the 1960s, as television continued to replace movies as America's favorite form of entertainment, film producers tried to boost attendance by adding increasing levels of sex and violence. This changing film content required a new type of code. In 1966, the Motion Picture Producers Association selected Jack Valenti as its leader to fill the vacancy left by Eric Johnston's death in 1964. One of Valenti's first tasks was to create a code that could accommodate the new type of films. He decided to junk the original code and replace it with one based on the maturity of the viewer. The rating G was given to movies for general audiences, PG for movies requiring parental guidance, R for movies restricted to people over 17 unless accompanied by an adult, and X for films to which those under 18 could not be admitted. Later a PG–13 category was added to caution parents that some material be might not be suitable for pre-teenagers.[33]

Valenti justified the new code as a means of freeing the creative energies of the film community. Writing in 1990, Valenti recalls, "When I became President of the Motion Picture Association of America, one of my first decisions was to collapse the old Hays Office Code, with its 'do's and don't's' and its seal of approval, both of which choked the creative reach of filmmakers." The primary purpose of the code, Valenti argues, is to protect children and not to force changes on films. The new method of applying the code, according to Valenti, assures that producers will be able to practice artistic freedom. Regarding the code, Valenti states, "My objective was to free the creative community, so its members could tell any story they chose."[34]

The rating code adopted in the 1960s was no longer intended to turn movies into a form of public education. The code was a form of censorship designed to restrict audiences according to age. Unlike the 1930 code, the new code did not require film producers to make changes based on a concept of consensus on public morality. "Moreover," Valenti writes, "under the rating system no movie maker need cut one millimeter of his story to go to the marketplace. No one could force him to alter his movie one jot. For the first time in more than fifty years, the screen was free."[35]

Of course, this freedom was immediately compromised by local censorship of X-rated movies. Pressure was placed on newspapers not to advertise X-rated movies, and some municipalities passed laws banning X-rated films. Since the X-rating was one part of the code that was not copyrighted, pornographic films were given the X as a means of advertising them. By the 1970s, pornographic theaters were popping up around the country with billboards advertising their films as "X-rated."

Therefore if film makers wanted wider distribution of their films, they had to keep the content within the boundaries of the R rating. In the late 1980s, some film producers refused to submit their films for rating because of the possibility of an X-rating. Consequently in 1990, the X-rating was abolished in favor of a new rating category. Jack Valenti announced, "We are taking the name 'X' and discarding it, not adding a new adults-only category." The new category, NC-17, was immediately given to *Henry and June,* a film story of the sexual relations between writers Henry Miller and Anais Nin.[36]

Of course, *Henry and June* and the new rating category were immediately attacked by local censors. Following in the footsteps of the social purity movement of the early twentieth century, the National Council of Churches and the United States Catholic Conference issued a joint statement accusing the

Motion Picture Association of America of "caving in to the commercial interests of those who are attempting to get sexually exploitive material into general theatrical release." The largest newspaper in Birmingham, Alabama, *The Birmingham News,* announced that it would not carry advertisements for films rated NC-17. Across the country, protesters appeared outside theaters showing *Henry and June.*[37]

In the television industry, self-censorship continued to be a means of protecting profits and holding off government censorship. Competing with the new cable television networks, the traditional networks tried to maintain their grip on the market by introducing more violence and more sexually oriented programming. The networks felt free to experiment with new programming in the 1980s, because of the emphasis on deregulation during the Reagan Administration. After this period of deregulation and a hands-off attitude, the FCC in 1990 announced its intention of more closely monitoring radio and network television. On July 13, 1990, the FCC declared a twenty-four-hour-a-day ban on 'indecent' broadcasts. The agency indicated that it would be looking closely at programs such as "L.A. Law" and "Thirtysomething." The FCC gave as examples of what it considered "indecent": a prime time movie about a housekeeper's seduction of a 15-year-old boy, shown on a Kansas City station, and broadcasts by four radio stations of songs and skits about homosexual sex acts, penises, and masturbation. FCC Chairman Albert Sikes said, "The purpose of this is to protect children from indecency on the airwaves. It would be wrong to define this as some sort of knee-jerk reaction to the Religious Right."[38]

Timothy Dyk, an attorney representing a coalition of the three major networks, warned that investigation by the FCC would have a chilling effect on the networks. In other words, the investigation would pressure networks to increase self-censorship. "Broadcasters have been saying to themselves, 'when in doubt, leave it out'," said Dyk. "There are large areas of doubt [in the application of the ban]. The effect has been self-censorship. No one wants to be fined by the FCC."[39]

Admitting that it represented the interests of broadcasters, an editorial in the *Washington Post* asked, "Is government a good judge of what people should be allowed to see and hear?" Calling government censorship an "extreme response," the editorial's solution was the same one given by radio broadcasters in the 1930s. Let the public apply pressure by giving "a firm poke of the 'OFF' button."[40]

As it had in the past, the broadcasting industry opted for self-censorship. In August 1990, the U.S. Senate and House of Representatives approved legislation that would free the networks of threats of anti-trust legislation and would require them to work cooperatively to established standards to limit the amount of violence on television. As *New York Times* reporter Bill Carter notes, there is a paradoxical twist to this legislation. In Carter's words, "any recent loosening of television standards can be traced to the push for industry deregulation under President Ronald Reagan, who was ardently backed by many of the conservative elements that support tighter controls on television." In other words, conservatives in the Reagan Administration wanted freedom for broadcasters to pursue profits, but not freedom to broadcast any material regardless of its content. The legislation passed by the House and Senate protects the economic freedom of broadcasters, but it does not protect freedom to disseminated unpopular ideas.[41]

THE EFFECT OF IDEOLOGICAL MANAGEMENT

These patterns of ideological management raise the issue of the effect on the American population of the images disseminated by schools, movies, and broadcasting. This question is difficult to answer with any certainty. Many of the images disseminated to the public are the result of a desire by individuals and groups to change the moral, political, and social attitudes of the population. The differences between projected images and the actual beliefs held by the population may result in some form of compromise belief.

On the other hand, the sexual revolution of the twentieth century was not stopped by the guardians of morality. The conservative political control of the 1920s did not stop the growth of radicalism in the 1930s. The harmonious family and societal images in the anti-Communism of the late 1940s and the 1950s did not stop the political unrest of the 1960s. The multiracial harmony of Textbook Town and "Sesame Street" did not stop racial and ethnic violence in the 1960s, 1970s, 1980s, and 1990s.

Maybe, these images have an apparently contradictory effect because of their lack of realism. Most of the images are of a world that should be. They are not images of what is. It could be that images of what should be result in a disillusionment that heightens the level of anger. During World War I, the Committee of Public Information disseminated through public schools, posters, and four-minute speeches an image of democracy as a social system providing equality of opportunity, and needing service and cooperation. The image of democracy as a superior economic system requiring loyal citizens was reinforced in the 1920s by the business community, by the activities of patriotic organizations such as the American Legion, and by the public schools and textbooks. Certainly the general population was not prepared for the economic collapse of the 1930s.

Standing amid the economic rubble of the 1930s, the American who had imbibed those images of the 1920s might have felt frustration, confusion, and anger, particularly, since the next set of images about democracy shifted from economic to political ideas. Now democracy was superior to Communism and fascism because it guarantees freedom of speech and political rights. These were the very rights that were trampled on during the surge of anti-Communism in the 1920s. This image of human rights was reinforced during World War II by the presentation of a world divided between freedom and slavery. Americans were told that the world struggle protected the American Way of Life.

After World War II, anti-Communism again reared its head to trample on free speech and political rights. The image of America shifted again, from an emphasis on political rights to economics. America was presented as a harmonious land of rugged individualism, a working free market, and happy consumers. Any deviation from this image was quickly branded as pro-Communist. But the image did not fit a world soon torn apart by the civil rights movement. Suddenly, images began to shift in the 1960s to an America where democracy meant social and political activism. The conservative and liberal reaction quickly tempered this image with an image of what should be. Amid racial violence and poverty, the new image was of a harmonious multiracial society working to end poverty. Bitterness, anger, and disillusionment might have been felt by many people in the 1980s and 1990s as this image rubbed against the reality of homeless people and racial violence.

Anger might have been compounded by the persistent image of the inevitable triumph of good over evil. The movie and radio codes of the 1930s, the television codes after World War II, the textbook self-censorship, and the comic book code created images of superheroes, patriotic leaders, and protectors of law and order who would assure the ultimate triumph of good. Of course, these images were constantly stained by the reality of corrupt public leaders. No super hero has led Americans to the promised land. In fact, these images did little to help Americans analyze their political and economic problems. Besides not providing the tools of analysis, these images might have created a spirit of not caring, since they taught the inevitable triumph of good.

Apathy, disillusionment, cynicism, or anger could all be the result of the tension between reality and the images disseminated by schools, movies, and broadcasting. On the other hand, these images could also achieve their desired outcomes. In fact, people might live as if they are in a world made by schools, movies, and television. While it remains difficult to answer the questions raised by the differences between projected morality and the morality held by the majority of the population, and the effect of manipulated images, there are persistent, on-going efforts by advocacy groups, the business community, and politicians and government officials to manipulate the images disseminated to the general population.

NOTES

INTRODUCTION

1. I emphasize the competition over differing purposes of public schooling and the use of schooling as an instrument of power in Joel Spring, *The American School, 1642–1985* (White Plains, N.Y.: Longman, 1986).
2. Joel Spring, *Conflict of Interests: The Politics of American Education* (White Plains, N.Y.: Longman, 1988).
3. Edward S. Herman and Noam Chomsky, *Manufacturing Consent: The Political Economy of the Mass Media* (New York: Pantheon, 1988).
4. Ibid., p. 29.
5. Kathryn C. Montgomery, *Target: Prime Time—Advocacy Groups and the Struggle over Entertainment Television* (New York: Oxford University Press, 1989).
6. Todd Gitlin, *Inside Prime Time: How the Networks Decide About the Shows That Rise and Fall in the Real World Behind the TV Screen* (New York: Pantheon, 1985).

CHAPTER 1. CENSORING MOVIES AND TEACHING KIDS TO LOVE WORLD WAR I

1. Quoted in Lewis Todd, *Wartime Relations of the Federal Government and the Public Schools, 1917–1918* (New York: Teachers College Press, 1945), pp. 64–65.
2. Chapter 2, "The War for the American Mind, " in David M. Kennedy, *Over Here: The First World War and American Society* (New York: Oxford University Press, 1980).
3. See Stephen L. Vaughn, *Holding Fast the Inner Lines: Democracy, Nationalism, and the Committee on Public Information* (Chapel Hill: The University of North Carolina Press, 1980).
4. William Graebner, in *The Engineering of Consent: Democracy and Authority in Twentieth-Century Life* (Madison: University of Wisconsin Press, 1987), makes a strong case for the concept of democracy's not becoming important in American thought and discourse until World War I. This was the first war fought by the United States to protect something called "democracy."
5. Will Hays, "Improvement of Moving Pictures, " *Annual Proceedings of the National Education Association, 1922*, vol. 60 (Washington, D.C.: NPA, 1922), pp. 252–257.
6. Ibid., p. 255. A history of the M.P.P.D.A. can be found in Raymond Moley, *The Hays Office* (Indianapolis, Ind.: Bobbs-Merrill, 1945).

7. The M.P.P.D.A. public relations campaign is analyzed in a report by the Department of Research and Education, Federal Council of the Churches of Christ in America, *The Public Relations of the Motion Picture Industry* (New York: Federal Council of Churches, 1931).

8. Richard Randall, *Censorship of the Movies: The Social and Political Control of a Mass Medium* (Madison: University of Wisconsin Press, 1968), p. 11.

9. A standard history of the early development of films is Lewis Jacobs, *The Rise of the American Film: A Critical History* (New York: Teachers College Press, 1967). Figures on movie attendance and description of early audiences can be found in Lary May, *Screening Out the Past: The Birth of Mass Culture and the Motion Picture Industry* (New York: Oxford University Press, 1980), pp. 35–42.

10. "Cheap Theaters, " *The Social Evil in Chicago* (Chicago: Chicago Vice Commission, 1911), reprinted in *The Movies in Our Midst*, ed. Gerald Mast (Chicago: University of Chicago Press, 1982), pp. 61–63.

11. May, pp. 35–42.

12. Walter Prichard Eaton, "Class-Consciousness and the Movies, " *Atlantic Monthly*, vol. 115, January, 1915, pp. 48–56.

13. May, p. 37.

14. Terry Christensen, *Reel Politics: American Political Movies from* Birth of a Nation *to* Platoon (New York: Basil Blackwell, 1987), p. 15.

15. Ibid.

16. Randall, pp. 12–13.

17. Will H. Hays, "Motion Pictures and Their Censors, " *The American Review of Reviews*, vol. 75 (April 1927), pp. 393–398.

18. *Mutual Film Corporation v. Industrial Commission of Ohio* (1915) reprinted in Mast, pp. 136–143.

19. Ellis Oberholtzer, "What Are the 'Movies' Making of Our Children?" *World's Work*, vol. 4 (January 1921), pp. 249–263.

20. Ellis Oberholtzer, "The Censor and the Movie 'Menace', " *The North American Review*, vol. 212, no. 780 (November 1920), pp. 641–647.

21. Thomas Cripps, *Slow Fade to Black: The Negro in American Film, 1900–1942* (New York: Oxford University Press, 1977), pp. 41–69.

22. Ibid., pp. 90–114.

23. John Collier, "Censorship in Action, " *The Survey*, vol. 34 (August 1915), p. 423.

24. May, pp. 53–55.

25. John Collier, "Censorship and the National Board, " *The Survey*, vol. 35, October 1915, pp. 9–14.

26. Ibid., p. 31.

27. John Collier, "A Film Library, " *The Survey*, vol. 35 (March 1916), p. 668.

28. Collier, "Censorship and the National Board, " p. 12.

29. Kennedy, p. 24.

30. As quoted in Vaughn, p. 2.

31. Ibid., pp. 27–28, 39–42, 98–99.

32. The historian who first recognized the importance of the concept of social efficiency in proposals for educational changes, and how it permeated all aspects of discus-

sions about education in the late nineteenth and early twentieth centuries was Edward Krug. See his *The Shaping of the American High School*, vol. 1 (New York: Harper & Row, 1964).

33. As a research assistant to Edward Krug, I used the concept of social efficiency and the image of the modern corporation in examining educational ideas and changes in the late nineteenth and early twentieth centuries in my dissertation, published as *Education and the Rise of the Corporate State*. Since then, much historical writing has been focused on this period. David Tyack's *The One Best System: A History of Urban Education* in part emphasizes the role of the corporate model in shaping the methods of control and administrative organization of schools during this period. Julia Wrigley, *Class Politics and Public Schools: Chicago, 1900–1950* (New Brunswick, N.J.: Rutgers University Press, 1982) examines the evolution of educational policy as the interplay among different social class interests. Herbert Kliebard's *The Struggle for the American Curriculum* (Boston: Routledge and Kegan Paul, 1986) is a history of school curriculum in the twentieth century that stresses the conflict between social efficiency advocates, humanists, social meliorists, and developmentalists.

34. William C. Bagley, "Some Handicaps to Education in a Democracy, " *School and Society*, vol. 3 (June 3, 1916): 807–816.

35. Vaughn, p.115.

36. William C. Bagley, "Education and Our Democracy, " *Proceedings of the National Education Association, 1918*, vol. 56 (Washington, D.C.: NEA, 1918), pp. 55–58.

37. Ibid., p. 57.

38. Commission on the Reorganization of Secondary Education, *Cardinal Principles of Secondary Education* (Washington, D.C.: U.S. Bureau of Education Bulletin, 1918), p. 110.

39. Ibid.

40. Ibid.

41. Vaughn, p. 52.

42. Ibid., p.45.

43. Ibid., pp. 45–48.

44. Ibid., p. 59.

45. For a study of social efficiency educators' belief in government by experts, see Joel Spring, *The American School: 1642–1985* (White Plains, N.Y.: Longman, 1986), pp. 222–256.

46. Todd, pp. 64–65.

47. Ibid.

48. Ibid., pp. 49–50.

49. Ibid., pp. 55–59.

50. Ibid., p. 60.

51. Ibid.

52. As quoted in Howard K. Beales, *Are American Teachers Free?* (New York: Scribner's, 1936), p. 103.

53. Ibid., p.41.

54. Vaughn, pp. 116–140.

55. Vaughn reprints a whole series of World War I posters on pp. 131–188.
56. Ibid., pp. 204–213.
57. As quoted in Beales, p. 295.
58. See Joel Spring, *The Sorting Machine Revisited: National Educational Policy Since 1945* (White Plains, N.Y.: Longman, 1988).
59. Walter Lippmann, *Public Opinion* (1921;/reprint New York: Free Press, 1965), p. 31.
60. Ibid., p. 158.
61. Ibid., p. 132.

CHAPTER 2. AMERICANISM AND CORPORATE SPIRIT IN THE 1920s

1. "Report of the Committee on Character Education of the National Education Association, " *U.S. Department of the Interior Bureau of Education Bulletin, 1926, no. 7: Character Education* (Washington, D. C.: U.S. Government Printing Office, 1926), p. 6.
2. William Gellerman, *The American Legion as Educator* (New York: Teachers College, Columbia University, 1938), p. 88.
3. Howard K. Beales, *Are American Teachers Free?* (New York: Scribner's, 1936), pp. 108–109.
4. Ibid., p. 126.
5. Howard K. Beales, *A History of Freedom of Teaching in American School* (New York: Scribner's, 1941), p. 247.
6. David Kennedy, *Over Here: The First World War and American Society* (New York: Oxford University Press, 1980), pp. 287–292.
7. T. W. Galloway, *Sex and Social Health: A Manual for the Study of Social Hygiene* (New York: Social Hygiene Association, 1924), p. 96.
8. Edward A. Ross, *Social Control* (New York: Macmillan, 1906), pp. 164–175.
9. A good guide to character education, relied on in this research, is Stephen Yulish's *The Search for a Civic Religion: A History of the Character Education Movement in America, 1890–1935* (Lanham, Md: University Press of America, 1980).
10. For the organization of the National Institution for Moral Instruction, see "Interstate Character Education Methods Research, " in *Character Education Methods: The Iowa Plan $20, 000 Award 1922* (Washington, D.C.: Character Education Institution, 1922), p.vii.
11. Ibid., pp. iii–v, and Milton Fairchild, "Character Education, " *Proceedings of the Annual Meeting of the National Education Association, 1918*, vol. 56 (Ann Arbor, Mich.: NEA, 1918), pp. 120–121, for a description of the contest. Also see Yulish, pp. 60–63. Examples of later reprinting and use of the code can be found in W.W. Charters, *The Teaching of Ideals* (New York: Macmillan, 1927), pp. 51–53, and Frank Sharp, *Education for Character* (Indianapolis, Ind.: Bobbs-Merrill, 1927), pp. 402–409.
12. "Interstate Character Education, " p. v.
13. Ibid., pp. v–vii.

14. Fairchild, "Character Education, " p. 120.
15. Ibid., pp. 120–121.
16. Sharp, p.409.
17. The code is reprinted in ibid., pp. 403–409.
18. *Character Education Methods*, p. 11.
19. Commission on the Reorganization of Secondary Education, *Cardinal Principles of Secondary Education* (Washington, D.C.: U.S. Bureau of Education Bulletin, 1918) (hereafter cited as *Cardinal Principles*).
20. *Ibid., p. 111.*
21. *Milton Bennion, "Report of the Committee on Citizenship and Character Education, "* School and Society, vol. 14 no. 351 (September 17, 1921), pp. 190–191.
22. "Report of the Committee on Character Education."
23. Ibid., pp. 5–7.
24. Ibid., p. 6.
25. Ibid., p.8.
26. Ernest Smith, "Compulsory Character Education, " *Proceedings of the Annual Meeting of the National Education Association, 1920,* vol. 58 (Ann Arbor, Mich.: NEA, 1920), pp. 471–474.
27. F. M. Gregg, "Symposium on Citizenship Training—The Nebraska Plan, " *Proceedings of the Annual Meeting of the National Education Association, 1928,* vol 66 (Washington, D.C.: NEA, 1928), pp. 67–73.
28. Charters, pp. 202–203.
29. *Cardinal Principles*, p. 20.
30. "Report on Character Education" pp. 28–30.
31. Charles R. Foster, *Extra-Curricular Activities in the High School* (Richmond, Va., 1925), pp. 108–109.
32. Eileen H. Galvin and M. Eugenia Walker, *Assemblies for Junior and Senior High Schools* (New York, 1929), p. 1.
33. Russell Cook, "American Legion, " *Proceedings of the Annual Meeting of the National Education Association, 1934,* vol. 72 (Washington, D.C.: NEA, 1934), pp. 111–116.
34. Ibid., p. 111.
35. Gellerman, p. 20.
36. Ibid., pp. 21–39.
37. As quoted in ibid., p. 68.
38. As quoted in ibid.
39. As quoted in ibid, pp. 70–71.
40. As quoted in ibid., pp. 90–91.
41. As quoted in ibid., pp. 203–204.
42. As quoted in ibid., p. 206.
43. Mrs. Russell William Magna, "Daughters of the American Revolution, " *Proceedings of the NEA, 1934*, pp. 116–121.
44. Gellerman, pp. 206–207.
45. Ibid., pp. 208–214.

46. Ibid., p. 25.
47. Beales, *Are American Teachers Free?* p. 317.
48. These laws are reviewed by Bessie Louise Pierce, *Civic Attitudes in American Schools* (Chicago: University of Chicago Press, 1930), pp. 231–235.
49. A. Duncan Yocum, "Report of the Committee on the Teaching of Democracy, " *Proceedings of the Annual Meeting of the National Education Association, 1923,* vol. 61 (Washington, D.C.: NEA, 1923), p. 451.
50. Beales, *Are American Teachers Free,* pp. 317–318.
51. Ibid., p. 295.
52. Ibid., pp. 298–299.
53. As quoted in ibid., p. 278.
54. Pierce, pp. 246–248.
55. Ibid., p. 139.
56. Edward S. Herman and Noam Chomsky, *Manufacturing Consent: The Political Economy of the Mass Media* (New York: Pantheon, 1988), p. 29.
57. A.B. Hollingshead, *Elmtown's Youth* (New York: Wiley, 1949).

CHAPTER 3. EDUCATORS AND THE MOVIES IN THE 1920s AND 1930s

1. As quoted in Neal Gabler, *An Empire of Their Own: How the Jews Invented Hollywood* (New York: Crown, 1988), p.277.
2. Norman Zierold, *The Moguls* (New York: Coward-McCann, 1969), p. 287.
3. Ibid., p.24.
4. Raymond Moley, *The Hays Office* (Indianapolis, Ind.: Bobbs-Merrill, 1945), pp. 32–33.
5. May, pp. 169–177.
6. For a more complete description of the immigrant Jewish background of the founders of Hollywood, see Gabler.
7. Ibid., pp. 164–165.
8. Moley, p. 41.
9. Moley, p. 135–137.
10. Gabler, pp. 277–278.
11. David Kennedy, *Over Here: The First World War and American Society* (New York: Oxford University Press, 1980), pp. 281–284.
12. Randall provides a chart categorizing the various censorship laws of state and city governments. See Randall, pp. 88–89.
13. "Film Censors and Other Morons, " *The Nation,* vol. 117, no. 3049 (December 12, 1923), pp. 678–679.
14. Randall, p. 24.
15. For surveys of state and municipal censorship boards, see Thomas Leary and J. Roger Noall, "Note: Entertainment: Public Pressures and the Law—Official and Unofficial Control of the Content and Distribution of Motion Pictures and Magazines, " *Harvard Law Review,* vol. 71 (1957), pp. 326–367, and Randall, pp. 15–18, 88–89.

16. Jacobs, p. 23.

17. Amy Woods, "Boston and the Movie Censorship, " *The Survey,* vol. 44 (April 17, 1920), pp. 108–109.

18. W. D. McGuire, "Freedom of the Screen vs. Censorship, " *The Survey,* vol. 44 (April 24, 1920), pp. 181–182.

19. Randall, p. 16.

20. Alfred H. Saunders, "Motion Pictures as an Aid to Education, " *Annual Proceedings of the National Education Association, 1914,* vol. 52 (Ann Arbor, Mich.: NEA, 1914), pp. 743–745; quote from p. 744.

21. "Discussion, " *Annual Proceedings of the NEA, 1914,* p. 747.

22. Ibid., p. 746.

23. "Education and the Movies, " *The Elementary School Journal,* vol. 23 (February 1923), pp. 406–408.

24. This financial support is recounted in Charles Judd, "Report of Committee to Cooperate with the Motion Picture Producers, " *Annual Proceedings of the National Education Association, 1923,* vol. 61 (Washington, D.C.: NEA, 1923), pp. 243–244.

25. Ibid., p. 245.

26. Col. Jason Joy, "Motion Pictures in Their Relation to the School Child, " *Proceedings of the National Education Association, 1927,* vol. 65 (Washington, D.C.: NEA, 1927), pp. 964–969.

27. Ibid., p. 967.

28. Ibid., pp. 968–969

29. Moley, pp. 77–78.

30. See W. W. Charters' "Chairman's Preface" in *Motion Pictures and Youth: A Summary* (New York: Macmillan, 1933), pp. v–vii.

31. The following is a list of the authors and their research titles. Many of the researchers sponsored by the Payne Fund were in their own disciplines and consequently added to the prestige of the studies.

    1. P. W. Holaday, Indianapolis Public Schools, and George Stoddard, Director, Iowa Child Welfare Research Station: "Getting Ideas from the Movies."

    2. Ruth C. Peterson and L.L. Thurstone, Department of Psychology, University of Chicago: "Motion Pictures and the Social Attitudes of Children."

    3. Frank Shuttleworth and Mark May, Institute of Human Relations, Yale University: "The Social Conduct and Attitudes of Movie Fans."

    4. W. S. Dysinger and Christian Ruckmick, Department of Psychology, State University of Iowa: "The Emotional Responses of Children to the Motion Picture Situation."

    5. Charles Peters, Professor of Education, Pennsylvania State College: "Motion Pictures and Standards of Morality."

    6. Samuel Renshaw, Vernon L. Miller, and Dorothy Marquis, Department of Psychology, Ohio State University: "Children's Sleep."

    7. Herbert Blumer, Department of Sociology, University of Chicago: "Movies and Conduct."

    8. 9., and 12   Edgar Dale, Research Associate, Bureau of Educational Research, Ohio State University: "The Content of Motion Pictures, " "Children's Attendance at Motion Pictures, " and "How to Appreciate Motion Pictures, " respectively.

    10. Herbert Blumer and Philip Hauser, Department of Sociology, University of Chicago: "Movies, Delinquency, and Crime."

    11. Paul Cressey and Frederick Thrasher, New York University: "Boys, Movies, and City Streets."

32. Henry James Forman, *Our Movie-Made Children* (New York: Macmillan, 1933).

33. Charters, 12.

34. Ibid., p. 13.

35. Ibid., p. 13.

36. Forman, pp. 280–282.

37. Edgar Dale, *How to Appreciate Motion Pictures: A Manual of Motion-Picture Criticism Prepared for High School Students* (New York: Macmillan, 1933).

38. Carl Milliken, "How the Movies Will Enrich Life, " *Proceedings of the Annual Meeting of the National Education Association, 1931,* vol. 69 (Washington, D.C.: NEA, 1931), pp. 73–77.

39. Ibid., p.74.

40. Ibid., p. 76.

41. Dale, p. vii.

42. William Lewin, *Photoplay Appreciation in American High Schools* (New York: Appleton-Century, 1934), pp. v–vii, 69.

43. Dale, p. 22.

44. Ibid., p. 22.

45. Ibid., p. 231.

46. Ibid., p. 227.

47. Lewin, pp. v–vii, 69.

48. Ibid., p. xiii.

49. Ibid., p. 4.

50. Ibid., p.xiv.

51. Ibid., pp. 30–33.

52. Ibid., p. 51.

53. Ibid., pp. 94–95.

54. Moley, pp. 148–149.

55. Ibid.

56. The article is quoted in ibid., pp. 151–153.

57. Ibid., pp. 154–155.

58. Will H. Hays, "The Motion Picture in Education, " *National Education Association, 1939,* vol. 77 (Washington, D.C.: NEA, 1939), pp. 80–86.

CHAPTER 4.
CONTROLLING SEXUALITY

1. John D'Emilio and Estelle Freedman, *Intimate Affairs: A History of Sexuality in America* (New York: Harper and Row, 1988), pp. 256–257.

2. Cited in Lary May, *Screening Out the Past: The Birth of Mass Culture and the Motion Picture Industry* (New York: Oxford University Press, 1980), p. 203.

3. D'Emilio and Freedman, pp. 256, 268.

4. Footnote 12 in William H. Chafe, *The American Woman: Her Changing Social,*

Economic, and Political Roles, 1920–1970 (New York: Oxford University Press, 1972), p. 279.

5. Herbert Blumer, *Movies and Conduct,* (New York: Macmillan, 1933), p. 50.

6. Ibid., pp. 45–49.

7. Charles Peters, *Motion Pictures and Standards of Morality* (New York: Macmillan, 1933).

8. Robert Sklar, *Movie-Made America: A Cultural History of American Movies* (New York: Random House, 1975), pp. 81–82.

9. Ibid., pp. 86–96.

10. Ibid., pp. 97–103.

11. Carl N. Degler, *At Odds: Women and the Family in America from the Revolution to the Present* (New York: Oxford University Press, 1980), p. 350.

12. Ibid., p. 356; Chafe, pp. 25–48.

13. "The Case Against the Younger Generation, " *Literary Digest,* June 17, 1922, p. 40.

14. Ibid., p. 42.

15. Mather A. Abbott, "The New Generation, " *The Nation,* December 8, 1926, p. 587.

16. Anne Temple, "Reaping the Whirlwind, " *Forum,* vol. 74, July 1926, pp. 21–26.

17. Regina Malone, "The Fabulous Monster, " *Forum,* vol. 74, July 1926, pp. 26–30.

18. Temple, p. 22.

19. G. Stanley Hall, *Adolescence,* vol. 1 (New York: Appleton, 1904), p. xv.

20. Degler, pp. 279–297; D'Emilio and Freedman, pp. 139–171.

21. Degler, pp. 249–282.

22. D'Emilio and Freedman, p. 175.

23. G. Stanley Hall, "Childhood and Adolescence, " reprinted in *Health, Growth, and Heredity,* ed. Charles Strickland and Charles Burgess (New York: Teachers College Press, 1965).

24. Hall, *Adolescence,* vol. 2, p. 125.

25. Ibid., p. 432.

26. "Tentative Report of the Committee on a System of Teaching Morals in Public Schools, " *Proceedings of the National Education Association, 1911,* vol. 49 (Ann Arbor, Mich.: NEA, 1911), p.360.

27. Irving King, *The High-School Age* (Indianapolis, Ind.: Bobbs-Merrill, 1914), p. 80.

28. Michael V. O'Shea, *The Trend of the Teens* (Chicago: Drake, 1920), p. 13.

29. William Bagley, "The Crucial Problem of the Next Decade, " *National Education Association Journal,* vol. 18, April 1929, p. 107.

30. John J. Tigert, "Character Education from the Standpoint of the Philosophy of Education, " *Proceedings of the National Education Association, 1929,* vol. 69 (Washington, D.C.: NEA, 1929), p. 770.

31. Frank Eversull, "Character Education, " *Journal of Education,* vol. 111, January 6, 1930, p. 12.

32. "Report of the Committee on Character Education of the National Education Association, " *Department of the Interior Bureau of Education Bulletin, 1926, no. 7: Character Education* (Washington, D.C.: U.S. Government Printing Office, 1926), pp. 57–65.

33. Walter May, "Character Training as a High School Problem, " *Proceedings of the National Education Association, 1927,* vol. 69, pp. 609–615.

34. "Report of the Committee on Character Education, " p. 15.

35. D'Emilio and Freedman, pp. 203–208.

36. Thomas W. Galloway, *Sex and Social Health: A Manual for the Study of Social Hygiene* (New York: Social Hygiene Association, 1924), pp. i–vii.

37. Ibid., p. 51.

38. Ibid., p.9.

39. Ibid., p. 73.

40. Ibid., p.71.

41. Ibid., p. 51.

42. Ibid., p.134.

43. Ibid., p. 33–34.

44. Ibid., p. 35.

45. Ibid., pp. 286–287.

46. Ibid., p. 228.

47. The poster is reprinted in D'Emilio and Freedman between 274 and 275.

48. Ibid., p. 65.

49. Ibid., p. 96.

CHAPTER 5. MOVIES AS A FORM OF PUBLIC EDUCATION

1. Will H. Hays, "The Motion Picture in Education, " *Proceedings of the Annual Meeting of the National Education Association, 1939,* vol. 77 (Washington, D.C.: NEA, 1939), p.80.

2. Moley, pp. 57–58.

3. Ibid., pp. 87–88.

4. William Berchtold, "The Hollywood Purge, " *The North American Review,* vol. 238 (December 1934), pp. 503–512.

5. Martin Quigley, *Decency in Motion Pictures* (New York : Macmillan, 1937).

6. The 1930 movie code can be found in Moley, pp. 241–248, and Mast, pp. 321–333.

7. The 1927 code can be found in Moley, pp. 240–241.

8. Edward Angly, "Boycott Threat Is Forcing Movie Clean-Up, " *The Literary Digest,* vol. 118, July 7, 1934, p. 34.

9. "The Legion of Decency, " *The Commonweal,* vol. 20, May 18, 1934, p. 58.

10. Ibid.

11. The pledge can be found in ibid.

12. "Catholics Attack Obscenity on the Screen, " *The Literary Digest,* vol. 117, May 5, 1934, p. 22.

13. Moley, pp. 77–79.

14. Angly, p. 34.

15. Moley, pp. 81–83.

16. Reprinted in Gerald Gardner, *The Censorship Papers: Movie Censorship Letters from the Hays Office 1934–1968* (New York: Dodd, Mead, 1987), pp. 2–3.
17. Moley, pp. 101–102.
18. Gardner, pp. 38–39.
19. Moley, p. 115.
20. Gardner, pp. 122–127.
21. Moley, pp. 124–125.
22. Winchell Taylor, "Secret Movie Censors, " *The Nation,* July 9, 1938, pp. 38–39.
23. Douglas Fairbanks, Jr., "Address, " *Proceedings of the NEA, 1939,* pp. 466–470.
24. Christensen, p. 212.
25. Ibid., pp. 45–48; quote on p. 46.
26. Moley, p. 117.
27. Christensen, p. 39.
28. Ibid., pp. 48–53.
29. Moley, p. 112.
30. Gardner, pp. 5–6.
31. Ibid., p. 77.

CHAPTER 6. EDUCATORS VERSUS COMMERCIAL RADIO

1. "British Vs. American Radio Slant, Debate Theme in 40, 000 Schools, " *Variety,* vol. 111, no. 12, August 29, 1933, p. 1.
2. See Philip T. Rosen, *The Modern Stentors: Radio Broadcasters and the Federal Government, 1920–1934* (Westport, Conn.: Greenwood Press, 1980), pp. 128–133, and Erik Barnouw *A Tower in Babel: A History of Broadcasting in the United States to 1933* (New York: Oxford University Press, 1966), pp. 172–179.
3. S. E. Frost, *Education's Own Stations: The History of Broadcast Licenses Issued to Educational Institutions* (Chicago: University of Chicago Press, 1937), pp. 1–5.
4. Susan J Douglas, *Inventing American Broadcasting 1899–1922* (Baltimore: Johns Hopkins Press, 1987), provides a good social history of the early evolution of American broadcasting. The standard history of radio is Erik Barnouw's two volumes, *A Tower in Babel* and *The Golden Web: A History of Broadcasting in the United States, 1933–1953* (New York: Oxford University Press, 1968).
5. Ibid.
6. "Virtues, Vices of Radio: Debate Teams Point 'Em Out, " *Variety,* vol. 113, no. 4, January 9, 1934, p. 29.
7. The other members were the National University Extension Association, the Jesuit Educational Association, The Association of Land-Grant Colleges and Universities, and the Association of College and University Broadcasting Stations.
8. "Virtues, Vices, " pp. 3–10.
9. Joy Elmer Morgan, "A National Culture—By-Product or Objective of National Planning?" ibid., p. 29.
10. Ibid., p. 30.

11. Ibid., p. 27.
12. Ibid., p. 30.
13. Ibid., p. 32.
14. Ibid., p. 33.
15. Ibid., p. 34.
16. Ibid., p. 35.
17. Ibid., p. 36.
18. "Fight Pedagogs' 25% Raid: Radio Answers Uplift Group, " *Variety,* vol. 115, no. 9, August 14, 1934, p. 31.
19. Merlin H. Aylesworth, "Radio as a Means of Public Enlightenment, " *Proceedings of the National Education Association, 1934,* vol. 72, pp. 99–102.
20. Ibid., p. 101.
21. "A.F.L. Intent on Corralling 11 more Radio Assignments for Educational Use, " *Variety,* vol. 116, no. 1, September 18, 1934, p. 37.
22. "Pastors, Pedagogs Attack Radio: Father Deeney Blames Radio for Part in Recent California Lynching, " *Variety,* vol. 116, no. 4, October 9, 1934, p. 41.
23. "Educational Groups Marshall at Washington for Radio Onslaught, " *Variety,* vol. 116, no. 3, October 2, 1934, pp. 57, 66.
24. "Radio Industry Presents United Front Against Educational Leaders Claims, " *Variety* vol. 116, no. 5, October 16, 1934.
25. "FCC Hears NBC, CBS and N.A.B. Pile Up Anti-Pedagogy Evidence, " *Variety,* vol. 116, no. 6, Oct. 23, 1934, pp. 34, 38. Mencken is quoted on p. 38.
26. William Paley, "Radio as a Cultural Force, CBS Reference Library, New York City. These notes on the economic and social philosophy of America's radio industry, as represented by the policies and practices of the Columbia Broadcasting System, Inc., were embodied in a talk on October 17, 1934, before the Federal Communications Commission, in its inquiry into proposals to allot fixed percentages of the nation's radio facilities to non-commercial broadcasting, " pp. 8–9.
27. Ibid., p. 13.
28. Ibid., pp. 13–14.
29. Barnouw, *The Golden Web,* p. 26.
30. Ibid., pp. 14.
31. Ibid., p. 18.
32. Ibid.
33. These activities were described by John W. Studebaker in "Radio in the Service of Education, " a paper given at the First National Conference on Educational Broadcasting in 1936. The speech was reprinted in *Educational Broadcasting 1936,* ed. C. S. Marsh (Chicago: University of Chicago Press, 1937), pp. 21–34.
34. Referred to in Marsh, pp. ix–x.
35. Anning S. Prall, "American Radio, " ibid., pp. 15–21.
36. Ibid., p. 20.
37. Ibid.
38. Studebaker, pp. 22–23.
39. Marsh.

CHAPTER 7. CRIME AND GORE IN CHILDREN'S RADIO

1. *Variety*, vol. 117, no. 1, December 18, 1934, p. 34.

2. "St. Paul Meet on Kid Programs Calls Radio Villains Likeable; Suggest Boycott, Probation" *Variety*, vol. 117, no. 2, December 25, 1934, p. 29.

3. "Air Reformers After Coin, " *Variety*, vol. 117, no. 7, January 29, 1935, pp. 1, 66.

4. Raymond Stedman, *The Serials: Suspense and Drama by Installment* (Norman: University of Oklahoma Press, 1977), pp. 143–191, and Erik Barnouw, *The Golden Web: A History of Broadcasting in the United States, 1933–1953* (New York: Oxford University Press, 1968), pp. 89–108.

5. Stedman, p. 192.

6. Ibid., pp. 194–195.

7. *Radio's Golden Years* (tape recording) (Minneapolis: Cassettes, Inc., 1972).

8. Clara Savage Littledale, "Better Radio Programs for Children, " *Parents Magazine*, vol. 18, no. 13 (May 8, 1933).

9. "Boycott MDSE in Air Protest?" *Variety*, vol. 109, no. 12, February 28, 1933, p. 47.

10. "Cal. Teachers List 'Bad' Programs, " *Variety*, vol. 110, no. 8, May 2, 1933, p. 34.

11. "Squawks Force NBC Move for Less Horror, " *Variety*, vol. 109, no. 12, February 26, 1933, p. 45.

12. "Now Agree Too Much Horror for Kids, Junior Programs Turning to Fantasy, " *Variety* vol. 111, no. 8, August 1, 1933, p. 41.

13. "Mrs. Harold Milligan, " *Educational Broadcasting 1937*, ed. C. S. Marsh (Chicago: University of Chicago Press, 1938), pp. 258–261.

14. "Radio: Mothers Chasing the Ether Bogeyman, " *News-Week*, March 11, 1933, p. 30.

15. "Clubwomen Launch Westchester Cowboys, " *Variety* vol. 117, no. 10, February 20, 1935, p. 39.

16. "Women's Radio Committee Clarifies, " *Variety*, vol. 118, no. 10, May 22, 1935, p. 36.

17. "Mrs. Harold Milligan, " p. 259.

18. Ibid., pp. 258–259.

19. Ibid., p. 261.

20. "Radio Wants Clubwoman Good Will: Offer Transmitters to Gals with Messages—Will Hays Started It, " *Variety*, vol. 112, no. 6, October 17, 1933, p. 37.

21. "Dime Novel Air Stuff Out: Protests Chafe FCC Into Action, " *Variety*, vol. 118, no. 3, April 3, 1935, pp. 1, 58.

22. "Stations Must Be Mind-Readers; FCC Will Not Divulge Policies, " *Variety*, vol. 118, no. 8. May 8, 1935, p. 51.

23. "Radio's 10 Commandments, " *Variety*, vol. 118, no. 12, June 5, 1935, p. 31.

24. "Radio Should Fight Back, " *Variety*, vol. 118, no. 9, May 15, 1935, p. 39.

25. "Air Decency League's Letter, " *Variety*, p. 38.

26. "Radio Should Fight Back, " p. 39.

27. "Talk of Radio 'Hays Org.', " *Variety*, vol. 118, no. 13, June 12, 1935, p. 43.

28. "CBS' Clean-up Pledges, " *Variety*, vol. 118, no. 10, May 22, 1935, p. 37.

29. "Paley in Annual Report Deprecates 'Straightjacket' for Broadcasting; Air Voluntarily Censors Programs, " *Variety,* vol. 113, no. 12, March 6, 1934, p. 44.

30. "Summary of CBS Policies Relating to Program Material and Advertising Copy" (CBS Research Department, October 1940), CBS Reference Library, New York City.

31. "NBC Slant on CBS Policy, " CBS Reference Library, p. 37.

32. "Sponsor Rights Defined, " *Variety,* vol. 134, no. 4, April 5, 1939, p. 23.

33. "Statement by William S. Paley over the Columbia Network, Tuesday, May 14, 1935, " CBS Reference Library.

34. Arthur Jersild and Frances Holmes, *Children's Fears* (New York: Teachers College, 1935), pp. 318–335.

35. "For Immediate Release: Columbia Announces Advisory Committee on Children's Programs (July 10, 1935), " CBS Reference Library; Newell W. Edson, "Discussion Outlines on Love, Courtship and Marriage, " *Journal of Social Hygiene,* vol. 21, no. 7–8–9 (October–November–December 1935), pp. 346–360. The titles of pamphlets written for the Social Hygiene Association were "From Boy to Man" and "Choosing a Home Partner."

36. "New Policies: A Statement to the Public, to Advertisers, and to Advertising Agencies (May 15, 1935), " CBS Reference Library, p. 2.

37. Ibid., p. 3.

38. Ibid.

39. Ibid., p. 4.

40. Ibid., p. 5.

41. Ibid., p. 6.

42. "For Immediate Release: Announcement of New Policies on CBS Brings Wide Response (May 15, 1935)" CBS Reference Library, p. 1.

43. Ibid., p. 3.

44. From Henry Smith, President of the National Education Association, to William Paley, President of CBS, May 16, 1935, CBS Reference Library. This letter was included in a large group of similar letters labelled "Have You Heard This One?"

45. "NBC's Tentative Program Code, " *Variety,* vol. 134, no. 4, April 5, 1934, p. 24.

46. Ibid.

47. Ibid.

48. Stedman, pp. 211–224.

49. Ibid., p. 206.

50. Ibid., p. 201.

51. Thomas Andrae, "From Menace to Messiah: The History and Historicity of Superman, " in *American Media and Mass Culture—Left Perspectives,* ed. Donald Lazere (Berkeley and Los Angeles: University of California Press, 1987) p. 131.

52. Ibid., 157. The rest of the creed is,

   Never will I enter into any jingoistic proposition, but will devote my entire life to protection of my Country. The whole purpose of my life is that of promoting Peace—not War. I will work in the interests of Peace and will promote the fulfillment of all things that are clean, wholesome and upright. Join me not alone in observing this creed, but likewise be patriotic.

53. Ibid., p. 205.

CHAPTER 8. PROGRESSIVISM AND SUBVERSION IN THE 1930S

1. Commission on Character Education, *Tenth Yearbook: Character Education* (Washington, D. C.: Department of Superintendence of the National Education Association, 1932), p. 15.
2. Educational Policies Commission, *Learning the Ways of Democracy: A Case Book of Civic Education* (Washington, D.C.: NEA, 1940), p. 54.
3. Educational Policies Commission, p. 66.
4. Ibid., pp. 63–64.
5. Ibid., p.65.
6. Ibid., p. 109.
7. Ibid., p. 110.
8. Ibid., p.171.
9. Ibid.
10. David H. Culbert, *News for Everyman: Radio and Foreign Affairs in the Thirties* (Westport, Conn.: Greenwood Press, 1976), p.24.
11. All quotes are from William Gellerman, *The American Legion as Educator* (New York: Teachers College, Columbia University, 1938), pp. 221–222.
12. David Tyack, Robert Lowe, and Elisabeth Hansot, *Public Schools in Hard Times: The Great Depression and Recent Years* (Cambridge, Mass.: Harvard University Press, 1984), pp. 22, 58.
13. See Jeffrey Mirel, "The Politics of Educational Retrenchment in Detroit, 1929–1935, " *History of Education Quarterly* vol. 24 (Fall 1984), pp. 325–350.
14. Charles F. Dienst, "The American Legion and Other Service Organizations, " *Proceedings of the National Education Association, 1939,* vol. 77 (Washington, D.C.: NEA, 1939), pp. 874–875.
15. Charles F. Dienst, "American Legion Cooperation, " *Proceedings of the National Education Association, 1940,* vol. 78 (Washington, D.C.: NEA), p. 881.
16. Ibid., p. 222.
17. Ibid., pp. 222–223.
18. Ibid., p. 223.
19. Ibid., pp. 225–227.
20. Gellerman, p. 93.
21. Ibid., p. 131.
22. "Joint Committee of the National Education Association and the American Legion, " *Proceedings of the National Education Association, 1941,* vol. 79 (Washington, D.C.: NEA, 1941), p.927.
23. Ibid., p. 928.
24. "Joint Committee of the National Education Association and the American Legion, " *Proceedings of the National Education Association, 1943,* vol. 81 (Washington, D.C.: NEA, 1943), p. 325.
25. "Joint Committee of the National Education Association and the American Legion, " *Proceedings of the National Education Association, 1944,* vol. 82 (Washington, D.C.: NEA, 1944), p. 363.

26. "Joint Committee of the National Education Association and the American Legion, " *Proceedings of the National Education Association, 1945–1946*, vol. 83–84 (Washington, D.C.: NEA, 1946), p. 443.

27. Gellerman, p. 122; Harold Hyman, *To Try Men's Souls: Loyalty Tests in American History* (Berkeley and Los Angeles: University of California Press, 1959), pp. 323–326.

28. Edward A. Krug, *The Shaping of the American High School, 1920–1941* (Madison: University of Wisconsin Press, 1972), pp. 231–232.

29. Russell Cook, "American Legion, " *Proceedings of the National Education Association, 1934*, vol. 72 (Washington, D.C.: NEA, 1934), pp. 111–116.

30. C. A. Bowers, *The Progressive Educator and the Depression: The Radical Years* (New York: Random House, 1969), p.15.

31. As quoted in ibid., p. 19.

32. As quoted in ibid., p. 23.

33. As quoted in Mary Anne Raywid, *The Ax-Grinders: Critics of Our Public Schools* (New York: Macmillan, 1963), p. 51.

34. Augustin G. Rudd, *Bending the Twig: The Revolution in Education and Its Effect on Our Children* (New York: New York Chapter of the Sons of the American Revolution, 1957), pp. 24–25.

35. Ibid., p. 24.

36. Ibid., pp. 26–27.

37. Ibid., p. 27.

38. Harold Rugg, *That Men May Understand: An American in the Long Armistice* (New York: Doubleday, Doran, 1941), pp. 10–11.

39. Frances Fitzgerald, *America Revised: History Schoolbooks in the Twentieth Century* (Boston: Little, Brown, 1979), p.37.

40. Rugg, p.44.

41. Ibid., p.37.

42. Rugg, pp. 36–44.

43. Reprinted in ibid, pp. 54–69.

44. Rugg, p. 25.

45. Ibid., pp. 29–30.

46. Rudd, p.85.

47. "Advertising Groups Pursuing Professor Rugg's Books, " *Publishers Weekly*, vol. 138 (September 28, 1940), pp. 1322–1323.

48. Ibid., p. 1323.

49. Rudd, p. 65.

50. "Book Burnings: Rugg Texts, " *Time*, vol. 36, September 9, 1940, pp. 64–65.

51. Rugg, p.3.

52. Ibid., p. 4.

53. Ibid., p.8.

54. Ibid., p. 12.

55. For a discussion of the current politics of the textbook publishing industry, see Joel Spring, *Conflict of Interests: The Politics of American Education* (White Plains, N.Y.: Longman, 1988), pp. 125–149.

CHAPTER 9. A WORLD DIVIDED

1. Quoted in Clayton Koppes and Gregory Black, *Hollywood Goes to War: How Politics, Profits & Propaganda Shaped World War II Movies* (New York: Free Press, 1987), p. 64.

2. Kyle Crichton, "Hollywood Gets Its Teeth Kicked In, " *Collier's,* vol. 11, January 9, 1943, p. 35.

3. Blum, John M., *V Was For Victory: Politics and American Culture During World War II* (New York: Harcourt Brace Jovanovich, 1976), p. 39.

4. John W. Studebaker, "Contribution of Education to the War Effort, " *Proceedings of the National Education Association, 1943,* vol. 81 (Washington, D.C.: NEA, 1943), p. 72.

5. David H. Culbert, *News for Everyman: Radio and Foreign Affairs in Thirties America* (Westport, Conn.: Greenwood Press, 1976), p. 24.

6. Quincy Howe, "Policing the Commentator: A News Analysis, " *Atlantic Monthly,* vol. 172, November, 1943, p. 48.

7. Ibid., p. 47.

8. Ibid., p. 46.

9. Ibid., p.47.

10. "Chatter Checked, " *Newsweek,* vol. 21, February 22, 1943, pp. 92–94.

11. Culbert, pp. 5–7.

12. Lucas Powe, *American Broadcasting and the First Amendment* (Berkeley and Los Angeles: The University of California Press, 1987), p. 71.

13. Ibid., pp. 109–110.

14. A copy of the *Mayflower* decision is reprinted in Frank J. Kahn, ed., *Documents of American Broadcasting* 2nd ed. (Englewood Cliffs, N.J.: Prentice-Hall, 1973), pp. 367–369.

15. Paul Lazarsfeld, *The People Look at Radio* (Chapel Hill: University of North Carolina Press, 1946), pp. 5–6, 78.

16. See Allan Winkler, *The Politics of Propaganda: The Office of War Information, 1942–1945* (New Haven, Conn.: Yale University Press, 1978), pp. 8–37.

17. Archibald MacLeish, "The Strategy of Truth, " *A Time to Act: Selected Addresses* (Boston: Houghton Mifflin, 1943), pp. 24–25, 28.

18. Ibid., pp. 29–30.

19. As quoted in Blum, p. 31.

20. Ibid., p.35.

21. Winkler, pp. 82–83.

22. Blum, pp. 39–40.

23. Koppes and Black, p. 325.

24. Frederick Hunter, "A War Policy for American Schools, " *Proceedings of the National Education Association, 1942,* vol. 80 (Washington, D.C.: NEA, 1942), pp. 102.

25. John Studebaker, "Our Country's Training Program, " *Proceedings of the National Education Association, 1941,* vol. 79 (Washington, D. C.: NEA, 1941), p. 120.

26. John Studebaker, "Seventy-Five Years of American Education, " *Proceedings of the NEA, 1942,* p.47.

27. George Strayer, "Education in a Time of Crisis, " *Proceedings of the NEA, 1943*, p.42.

28. Frederick Hunter, "Report of the Educational Policies Commission, " *Proceedings of the NEA, 1943*, pp. 46–47.

29. Grace E. Storm, "Recent Trends in the Teaching of Citizenship, " *The Elementary School Journal*, vol. 21, February, 1944, pp. 327–330.

30. Ibid., pp. 331–335.

31. Raymond Stedman, *The Serials: Suspense and Drama by Installment* (Norman: University of Oklahoma Press, 1977), pp. 331–333.

32. Ibid., p.334.

33. Winkler, pp. 60–61.

34. Blum, pp. 36–37.

35. Koppes and Black, p. 60.

36. Ibid., pp. 72–78.

37. Ibid., pp. 59, 113–124.

38. Ibid., pp. 156–160.

39. Ibid., p.184.

40. William G. Carr, "An Educator Bids for Partners, " *Nation's Business*, March, 1941), pp. 19–20, 96–97.

41. This was the size of the nationwide Chambers of Commerce membership at the time of Eric Johnston's election in 1942 as President of the U.S. Chamber of Commerce. Eric Johnston, *America Unlimited: The Case for a People's Capitalism* (Garden City, N.Y.: Doubleday, Doran, 1944), p. 22.

42. Ibid. Johnston provides a very clear statement of the consensus philosophy that would come to dominate postwar American society.

43. Walter Fuller, "Industry and the War, " *Proceedings of the NEA, 1942*, pp. 111–114.

44. Reported by Studebaker, "Our Country's Training Program, " pp. 115–122, and "Seventy-five Years of American Education, " pp. 42–51.

45. Studebaker, "Contribution of Education."

46. A great deal of the public relations campaign was conducted by the National Commission for the Defense of Democracy Through Education. See "Report of the National Commission for the Defense of Democracy Through Education, " in *Proceedings of the NEA, 1943*, pp. 50–55, and *Proceedings of the National Education Association, 1944* vol. 82 (Washington, D.C.: NEA, 1944), pp. 371–373. For a discussion of the campaign for federal aid, see C. O. Wright, "Organizing a State for Federal Aid Campaign" and R. E. Jaggers, "Nationwide Organization for Federal Aid, " *Proceedings of the NEA, 1942*, pp. 96–98.

47. Studebaker, "Our Country's Training Program, " p.119.

48. Koppes and Black, p. 86.

49. Winkler, pp. 56–57.

50. Erik Barnouw, *Golden Web: A History of Broadcasting in the United States, 1933–1953* (New York: Oxford University Press, 1968), p. 161.

51. Muriel Cantor and Suzanne Pingree, *The Soap Opera* (Beverly Hills, Cal.: Sage, 1983), pp. 40–41.

52. Barnouw, p.162.
53. Koppes and Black, pp. 84–89.
54. Ibid., p.179.
55. Ibid., p.184.
56. Studebaker, "Contribution of Education, " pp. 70–73.
57. William Chafe, *The American Woman: Her Changing Social, Economic, and Political Roles 1920–1970* (New York: Oxford University Press, 1972), pp. 147–148.
58. Stedman, p. 335.
59. Chafe, pp. 146–147.
60. Koppes and Black, p.145.
61. Chafe, p. 148.
62. Strayer, p. 41.
63. Chafe, p.150.
64. "Eight-Hour Orphans, " *Saturday Evening Post,* October 10, 1942, pp. 20–21.
65. Ibid., pp. 21–22.
66. Ibid., p.106.
67. "Women Drop Out, " *Business Week,* August 21, 1943, p. 88.
68. Virginia Kerr, "One Step Forward—Two Steps Back: Child Care's Long American History, " in *Child Care—Who Cares?* ed. Pamela Roby (New York: Basic Books, 1973), p. 163.
69. For a discussion of racial issues during World War II, see Blum, pp. 182–220.
70. Cantor and Pingree, pp. 42–44.
71. Stedman, pp. 335–336.
72. The American Legion leadership's position after the war in claiming the existence of subversive elements in schools, movies, and broadcasting contained a strong element of anti-Semitism. See Neal Gabler's *An Empire of Their Own: How the Jews Invented Hollywood* (New York: Crown, 1988), pp. 384–385.
73. Commander Atherton, "Greetings from the American Legion, " *Proceedings of the NEA, 1944,* p. 76.

CHAPTER 10.
SUBVERSION AND HARMONY

1. Eric Johnston, *American Unlimited: The Case for a People's Capitalism* (Garden City, N.Y.: Doubleday, Doran, 1944), p.13.
2. Vannevar Bush, *Science—The Endless Frontier: A Report to the President* (Washington, D.C.: U.S. Government Printing Office, 1945).
3. For a discussion of the early introduction of television, see Erik Barnouw, *The Golden Web: A History of Broadcasting in the United States, 1933–1953* (New York: Oxford University Press, 1968), pp. 125–140. For a discussion of the decline in movie attendance and rise of television, see Robert Sklar, *Movie-Made American: A Cultural History of American Movies* (New York: Random House, 1975), pp. 269–279, and Edward de Grazia and Roger Newman, *Banned Films: Movies, Censors & The First Amendment* (New York: Bowker, 1982), p. 69.

4. Lary May, "Movie Star Politics: The Screen Actors' Guild, Cultural Conversion, and the Hollywood Red Scare, " in *Recasting America: Culture and Politics in the Age of the Cold War,* ed. Lary May (Chicago: University of Chicago Press, 1988), p. 125.

5. Johnston, p. 37.

6. De Grazia and Newman, p. 64.

7. As quoted in May, p. 126.

8. Ibid., p. 127.

9. De Grazia and Newman, pp. 68–70.

10. Richard S. Randall, *Censorship of the Movies: The Social and Political Control of a Mass Medium* (Madison: University of Wisconsin Press, 1970), pp. 28–32; De Grazia and Newman, pp. 78–86.

11. De Grazia and Newman, pp. 81–82.

12. Ibid., pp. 86–89.

13. Ibid., pp. 91–93.

14. Ibid., p.92.

15. Murray Schumach, *The Face on the Cutting Room Floor: The Story of Movie and Television Censorship* (New York: Morrow, 1964), p. 242.

16. Barnouw, pp. 295–296.

17. Schumach, pp. 241–252.

18. "Background Material: The Television Code of the National Association of Broadcasters, December 15, 1958, " NAB code file, Television Information Office Library, New York City.

19. Kathryn C. Montgomery, *Target: Prime Time—Advocacy Groups and the Struggle over Entertainment Television* (New York: Oxford University Press, 1989), pp. 16–17.

20. Barnouw, pp. 179–181, 187–190.

21. Edward H. Bronson, "Background Material: The Television Code of the National Association of Broadcasters, October 1st, 1960, " NAB code file, Television Information Office Library. New York City.

22. As quoted in Schumach, p. 229. The code can be found in *Documents of American Broadcasting,* ed. Frank Kahn (Englewood Cliffs, N.J.: Prentice-Hall, 1973), pp. 340–355.

23. Schumach, p. 246.

24. As quoted in Ben H. Bagdikian, *The Media Monopoly,* 2nd ed. (Boston: Beacon, 1987), p. 157.

25. Ibid.

26. All quotes in Schumach, p. 246.

27. As quoted in Erik Barnouw, *The Sponsor: Notes on a Modern Potentate* (New York: Oxford University Press, 1978), pp. 53–54.

28. Ibid., p. 54.

29. See Bush, *Science—The Endless Frontier,* and his *Pieces of the Action* (New York: Morrow, 1970), pp. 1–66.

30. Hyman G. Rickover, *Education and Freedom* (New York: Dutton, 1959), p. 45.

31. "Statement of Edward Teller, Physicist at the Radiation Laboratory, University of

California, " *Science and Education for National Defense: Hearings Before the Committee on Labor and Public Welfare, United States Senate, 85th Congress, 2nd Session* (Washington, D.C.: U.S. Government Printing Office, 1958), 130–139.

32. Bush, *Pieces of the Action*, pp. 65–66.

33. James B. Conant, *The American High School Today* (New York: McGraw-Hill, 1959), and *My Several Lives: Memoirs of a Social Inventor* (New York: Harper & Row, 1970).

34. *Hearings Before the Committee on Interstate and Foreign Commerce, 80th Congress, 1st Session, on Bills Relating to the National Science Foundation, March 6 and 7, 1947* (Washington, D.C.: U.S. Government Printing Office, 1947), p. 147.

35. Conant, *American High School*, p.50.

36. James B. Conant, *The Child, The Parent and the States* (Cambridge, Mass.: Harvard University Press, 1959), pp. 39–43.

37. A history of the development of PSSC can be found in Jerrold R. Zacharias and Stephen White, "The Requirements for Major Curriculum Revision, " in *New Curricula*, ed. Robert W. Heath (New York: Harper & Row, 1964).

38. Dwight D. Eisenhower, "Our Future Security, " reprinted in *Science and Education for National Defense*, pp. 1357–1359. Quote on p. 1357.

39. Dwight D. Eisenhower, "Message from the President of the United States Transmitting Recommendations Relative to Our Educational System, " ibid., pp. 195–196.

40. A reprint of the 1958 NDEA can be found in Raymond F. McCoy, *American School Administration* (New York: McGraw-Hill, 1961), pp. 421–452.

41. Eisenhower, "Message from the President, " pp. 195–197. Quote on p. 196.

42. A history of the New Math can be found in William Wooton, *SMSG: The Making of a Curriculum* (New Haven, Conn.: Yale University Press, 1965).

43. Larry Ceplair and Steven Englund, *The Inquisition in Hollywood: Politics in the Film Community, 1930–1960* (Berkeley and Los Angeles: University of California Press, 1983), p. 211.

44. John Cogley, *Report on Blacklisting* (Fund for the Republic, 1956), p.11.

45. Sklar, p. 265, and Cogley, pp. 22–23.

46. Cogley, pp. 119–124.

47. Ibid., pp. 124–125.

48. Ibid., p. 126.

49. As quoted in Barnouw, p. 257 (capitalization in original).

50. Ibid., pp. 253–257, 265.

51. As quoted in ibid., p. 273.

52. Ibid., pp. 273–274.

53. Ibid., p. 275.

54. As quoted in Mary Anne Raywid, *The Ax-Grinders: Critics of Our Public Schools* (New York: Macmillan, 1963), p. 51.

55. Ibid., pp. 35–49.

56. Ibid., pp. 59–63.

57. Jack Nelson and Gene Roberts, Jr., *The Censors and the Schools* (Westport, Conn.: Greenwood Press, 1963), pp. 99–100.

58. Ibid., p. 109.

59. Ibid., pp. 109–110.
60. Raywid, p.5.
61. Joel Spring, *The Sorting Machine Revisited: National Educational Policy Since 1945* (White Plains, N.Y.: Longman, 1989), p.9.
62. Ibid., p. 10.
63. For a general description of this anti-communist crusade against public schools, see Spring, pp. 1–35.
64. Nelson and Roberts, p. 179.
65. Ibid., pp. 180–183.
66. Sklar, p. 268.
67. Terry Christensen, *Reel Politics: American Political Movies from Birth of a Nation to Platoon* (New York: Basil Blackwell, 1987), pp. 89–92.
68. Cogley, p. 79.
69. As quoted in Barnouw, p.282.
70. David Hulburd, *This Happened in Pasadena* (New York: Macmillan, 1951); James Boyle, "Pasadena, Calif., " *Saturday Review of Literature,* September 8, 1951, pp. 7–8.
71. As quoted in Nelson and Roberts, pp. 178, 181.
72. Dwight D. Eisenhower, *Waging Peace, 1956–1961* (New York: Doubleday, 1965), p. 152.
73. Ibid., p.168.
74. "Eisenhower's Address on the Situation in Little Rock, September 24, 1957, " reprinted in *Civil Rights and the American Negro,* ed. Albert Blaustein and Robert Zangrando (New York: Trident Press, 1968), pp. 456–458.
75. Johnston, p.343.
76. Ibid.
77. Eric Johnston, *Intolerance* (New York: U.S. Chamber of Commerce, 1945), p.7.
78. Ibid., pp. 3, 5.
79. De Grazia and Newman, pp. 238–240.
80. Ibid., pp. 70–71.
81. Ibid., pp. 230–31.
82. For a history of these changes, see Spring, pp. 93–151.
83. Nelson and Roberts, p. 181.

CHAPTER 11. DELINQUENCY, TELEVISION, AND COMIC BOOKS

1. *Juvenile Delinquency (Television Programs), Hearings Before the Subcommittee to Investigate Juvenile Delinquency of the Committee on the Judiciary, U.S. Senate, Eighty-Third Congress, Second Session, June 5, October 19 & 20, 1954* (Washington, D.C.: U.S. Government Printing Office, 1955), p. 1.
2. "Code for Comics, " *Time Magazine* vol. 52, July 12, 1948, p. 62.
3. "Comic Book Publishers Promise Reforms, " *Christian Century,* vol. 71, November 10, 1954, p. 1357.

4. William Brickman, "Causes and Cures of Juvenile Delinquency, " *School and Society*, vol. 75, June 28, 1952, pp. 405–411. Brickman's figures on juvenile delinquency were compiled by the FBI. His article also reviews the major publications on delinquency in the late 1940s and early 1950s.

5. "Youth: All Our Children, " *Newsweek*, vol. 42, November 9, 1953, pp. 28–30.

6. Evan M. Wylie, "Violence on TV—Entertainment or Menace?" *Cosmopolitan*, vol. 134, February 1953, pp. 34–39.

7. Richard Clendenen and Herbert Beaser, "The Shame of America, " *Saturday Evening Post*, vol. 227, January 8, 1955, p. 17.

8. Ibid.

9. See Robert Goldenson, "Why Boys and Girls Go Wrong or Right, " *Parents' Magazine*, vol. 26, May 1951, pp. 81–84; Brickman; Albert Deutsch, "Our Rejected Children, " *Women's Home Companion*, vol. 75, July, 1948, pp. 36–37, 47, 50; Croswell Bowen, "Why They Go Wrong, " *Saturday Review*, vol. 37, February 27, 1954, pp. 13, 42; Jack Harrison Pollack, "What Are We Really Doing About Boys and Girls Who Go Wrong?" *Parents' Magazine*, vol. 28, October 1953, pp. 36–37, 127–136.

10. *Juvenile Delinquency*, p. 8.

11. Wylie, p.34.

12. *Juvenile Delinquency*, pp. 11–12, 36–38.

13. As quoted in Wylie, p. 37.

14. Fredric Wertham, *Seduction of the Innocent* (New York: Rinehart, 1954), p. 16.

15. *Juvenile Delinquency*, , p.86.

16. Ibid.

17. Ibid., p. 89.

18. Ibid.

19. Ibid., p. 88.

20. Ibid., p.92.

21. Ibid., p.90.

22. Ibid., p. 93.

23. Ibid., p.132.

24. Ibid.

25. Ibid.

26. Ibid., pp. 168–169.

27. Ibid., p. 188.

28. Ibid., p. 192.

29. Ibid., p. 47.

30. For a discussion of the development of "Sesame Street" in the context of the politics of knowledge, see Ellen Condliffe Lagemann, *The Politics of Knowledge: The Carnegie Corporation, Philanthropy, and Public Policy* (Middletown, Conn.: Wesleyan University Press, 1989), pp. 230–237.

31. Wylie, p. 37.

32. *Comic Books and Juvenile Delinquency: A Part of the Investigation of Juvenile Delinquency in the United States: Interim Report of the Subcommittee to Investigate Juvenile Delinquency to the Committee on the Judiciary Pursuant to S. Res. 89 and S. Res. 190* (Washington, D.C.: U.S. Government Printing Office, 1955), p. 3.

33. "Senate Sub-Committee Holds Hearings on 'Comics', " *Publishers Weekly,* vol. 165, May 1, 1954, p. 1903.
34. *Comic Books and Juvenile Delinquency,* pp. 8–9.
35. Wertham, p. 20.
36. Ibid., pp. 297–298, 314.
37. Ibid., pp. 151–153.
38. Frederic M. Thrasher, "The Comics and Delinquency: Cause or Scapegoat, " *The Journal of Educational Sociology,* vol. 23, December 1949, pp. 195–205.
39. "Cause of Delinquency, " *Science News Letter,* vol. 65, May 1, 1954, p. 275.
40. John Cavanagh, "The Comics War, " *Journal of Criminal Law,* vol. 40, May 1949, pp. 28–35.
41. Clara Savage Littledale, "What to Do About the 'Comics', " *Parents' Magazine,* vol. 16, March 1941, pp. 26–27.
42. Jesse L. Murrell, "Annual Rating of Comic Magazines, " *Parents' Magazine,* vol. 27, November 1952, pp. 48, 134–135.
43. F. G. Melcher, "The Comics Under Fire, " *Publishers Weekly,* vol. 154, December 18, 1948, p. 2413.
44. Thomas A. Allport, "Comic Book Control Can Be a Success, " *The American City,* January 1949, p. 100.
45. John Vosburgh, "How the Comic Book Started, " *The Commonweal,* vol. 50, May 20, 1949, pp. 146–148.
46. "Attack on Juvenile Delinquency, " *National Education Association Journal,* vol. 37, December 1948, pp. 632–633.
47. "What Comic Books Pass Muster? A Report on the St.Paul and Cincinnati Investigations, " *Christian Century,* vol. 66, December 28, 1949, pp. 1540–1541.
48. Murrell, p. 134.
49. "Santa Barbara Schools Fight Comics with Paperbounds, " *Publishers' Weekly,* vol. 166, December 18, 1954, p. 2321.
50. Margaret Hickey, "Mothers Enforce Cleanup of Comics…North Plate, Nebraska, " *Ladies Home Journal,* vol. 74, January 1957, pp. 19–20, 122.
51. "Comics Censorship Bills Killed in Two States, " *Publishers' Weekly,* vol. 155, April 30, 1949, p. 1805; "State Laws to Censor Comics Protested by Publishers, " *Publishers' Weekly,* vol. 155, March 12, 1949, p. 1243; "New Canadian Law Declares 'Crime Comics' Illegal, " *Publishers' Weekly,* vol. 157, January 7, 1950, p. 45; "Dewey Vetoes 'Objectionable' Comic Book Ban Measure, " *Publishers' Weekly,* vol. 161, April 26, 1952, p. 1766; "Anti-Comics Law Proposed in N.Y.; Industry Code Debated, " *Publishers' Weekly,* vol. 167, March 5, 1955, p. 1388.
52. *Comic Books and Juvenile Delinquency,* pp. 30–31.
53. "Purified Comics, " *Newsweek,* vol. 32, July 12, 1948, p. 56.
54. "Better Than Censorship, " *Christian Century,* vol. 65, July 28, 1948, p. 750.
55. *Comic Books and Juvenile Delinquency,* p. 31.
56. "Comics' Publishers Institute Code, Appoint 'Czar', " *Publishers' Weekly,* vol. 166, September 25, 1954, p. 1386; "Progress in Comic Book Cleanup, " *America,* October 30, 1954, p.114; "Code for Comics, " *Time,* November 8, 1954, p. 60.
57. "First 'Seal of Approval' Comics Out This Month, " *Publishers' Weekly,* vol. 167, January 15, 1955, p. 211.

58. "'Comics' Publishers Institute Code, " p. 1386; "Correspondence: Comic-Book Code, " *America,* November 13, 1954, p. 196.

CHAPTER 12. MANAGING IMAGES

1. "The Negro in American History Textbooks: A Report of a Study of the Treatment of Negroes in American History Textbooks Used in Grades Five and Eight and in the High Schools of California's Public Schools" (Sacramento: California State Department of Education, 1964), p. 2.

2. Erik Barnouw, *The Golden Web: A History of Broadcasting in the United States, 1933–1953* (New York: Oxford University Press, 1968), p. 297.

3. William S. Paley, *As It Happened: A Memoir* (Garden City, N.Y.: Doubleday, 1979), p. 304.

4. Ibid.

5. Todd Gitlin, *The Whole World Is Watching: Mass Media in the Making and Unmaking of the New Left* (Berkeley and Los Angeles: University of California Press, 1980).

6. *Brown et al. v. Board of Education of Topeka et al.,* reprinted in Albert P. Blaustein and Clarence Clyde Ferguson, Jr., eds., *Desegregation and the Law: The Meaning and Effect of the School Segregation Cases* (New Brunswick, N.J.: Rutgers University Press, 1957), pp. 95–113.

7. Abraham Tannenbaum, "Family Living in Textbook Town, " *Progressive Education,* March 1954, reprinted in *Hearings Before the Ad Hoc Subcommittee on De Facto School Segregation,* of the Committee on Education and Labor, House of Representatives, 89th Congress, 2nd Session, on Books for Schools and the Treatment of Minorities, August 23, 24, 30, 31, and September 1, 1966 (Washington, D.C.: U.S. Government Printing Office, 1966), pp. 806–816.

8. Ibid., p. 814.

9. Ibid., p. 813.

10. August Meier and Elliot Rudwick, *CORE: A Study in the Civil Rights Movement, 1942–1968* (New York: Oxford University Press, 1973), pp. 3–39.

11. For a study of the politics of textbook publishing, see Joel Spring, *Conflict of Interests: The Politics of American Education* (White Plains, N.Y.: Longman, 1988), pp. 125–149.

12. "The Negro in American History Textbooks, " reprinted in *Hearings Before the Ad Hoc Subcommittee on De Facto School Segregation,* p. 767.

13. Ibid., p. 770.

14. Ibid., pp. 770–771.

15. Ibid., p. 772.

16. Roy Wilkins, "Books for Schools and Treatment of Minorities: Introduction" (National Association for the Advancement of Colored People, 1966), p.1.

17. "Statement of Lerone Bennett, " ibid., pp. 214–215.

18. For a discussion of ESEA, see Joel Spring, *The Sorting Machine Revisited: National Educational Policy Since 1945* (White Plains, N.Y.: Longman, 1989), pp. 123–151.

19. Ibid.

20. Ibid.

21. Joel Roth, "Dick and Jane Make Some New Friends, " *Book Production Industry*, June, 1965, reprinted in *Hearings Before the Ad Hoc Subcommittee on De Facto School Segregation, p. 818.*

22. *"Statement of Lerone Bennett, " pp. 213–214.*

23. *"Statement of Austin J. McCaffrey, Executive Director, American Textbook Publishers Institute, "* Hearings Before the Ad Hoc Subcommittee on De Facto School Segregation, p. 106.

24. "Integrating the Texts, " *Newsweek*, March 7, 1966, reprinted in *Hearings Before the Ad Hoc Subcommittee on De Facto Segregation, p. 828.*

25. Ibid., p. 106.

26. Ibid., p. 107.

27. Ibid.

28. Roth, p. 816.

29. "Statement of Austin McCaffrey, " pp. 107–108.

30. Ibid., p. 109.

31. Ibid., p. 114.

32. Ibid., pp. 196, 205.

33. "Integrating the Texts, " p. 826–827.

34. "Statement of Robert W. Locke, Senior Vice President, McGraw-Hill Book Co.; Accompanied by Dr. Richard Smith, Senior Editor, Text-Film Division, McGraw-Hill Book Co., " *Hearings Before the Ad Hoc Subcommittee on De Facto Segregation*, pp. 190–191.

35. "Statement of Darrel E. Peterson, President, Scott, Foresman & Co., " *Hearings Before the Ad Hoc Subcommittee on De Facto Segregation*, pp. 122–123.

36. A. Kent MacDougall, "Integrated Books—School Texts Stressing Negroes' Role in United States Arouse the South's Ire—Primers Show Mixed Scenes; Some Publishers Turn Out Special Editions for Dixie, " *Wall Street Journal*, March 24, 1966, reprinted in *Hearings Before the Ad Hoc Subcommittee on De Facto School Segregation, p. 804.*

37. Ibid., p. 122.

38. Ibid., pp. 124–125.

39. "Statement of Ross Sackett, Executive Vice President, Holt Rinehart & Winston, Inc., " *Hearings Before the Ad Hoc Subcommittee on De Facto Segregation*, pp. 217–273.

40. "Statement of Craig T. Senft, President, Silver Burdett Co., a Division of General Learning Corporation, " *Hearings Before the Ad Hoc Subcommittee on De Facto School Segregation*, pp. 115–117.

41. "Integrating the Texts, " p. 287.

42. "Dick and Jane Make Some New Friends, " p. 816.

43. "Statement of Robert Locke, " p. 191.

44. "Statement of G.M. Fenollosa, Vice President and Director, Houghton Mifflin Co., Boston, Mass., " *Hearings Before the Ad Hoc Subcommittee on De Facto School Segregation, p. 129.*

45. Paley, p. 232.

46. Thomas Cripps, "Amos 'n' Andy and the Debate over American Racial Integration, " in *American History/American Television: Interpreting the Video Past,* ed. John E. O'Conner (New York: Frederick Ungar, 1983), pp. 33–54.

47. Ibid., p. 41.

48. Ibid., p. 49.

49. J. Fred MacDonald, *Blacks and White TV: Afro-Americans in Television since 1948* (Chicago: Nelson-Hall, 1983), pp. 68–69, 72–73.

50. As quoted in ibid., p.16.

51. Ibid., pp. 81–82; quote from p. 101.

52. Ibid., pp. 93–95.

53. *Office of Communication of the United Church of Christ v. Federal Communications Commission,* reprinted in *Documents of American Broadcasting,* ed. Frank J. Kahn (Englewood Cliffs, N.J.: Prentice-Hall, 1973), pp. 639–681.

54. Ibid., p. 641.

55. Ibid., pp. 653–654.

56. Ibid., p.650.

57. As quoted in Kathryn C. Montgomery, *Target: Prime Time Advocacy Groups and the Struggle over Entertainment Television* (New York: Oxford University Press, 1989), pp. 23–24.

58. Ibid., pp. 24–26.

59. Ibid., p. 58.

60. Ibid., pp. 51–58.

61. Ibid., p. 73.

62. Ibid., pp. 75–80.

63. MacDonald, pp. 108–109.

64. Ibid., pp. 109–111.

65. Cited in Montgomery, pp. 28–30.

66. Paley, p. 264.

67. Ibid., pp. 265–267.

68. Ben H. Bagdikian, *The Media Monopoly 2nd ed.* (Boston: Beacon, 1987), pp. 199–200.

69. Bert Spector, "A Clash of Cultures: The Smothers Brothers vs. CBS Television, " in *American History/American Television,* pp. 159–183.

70. Ibid., pp. 160–61, 179–180.

71. Ibid., 180.

72. Ibid., pp. 180–181.

73. Paley, pp. 312–313.

74. Ibid., p. 313.

75. Gitlin, pp. 24–25.

76. Ibid., pp. 25–27.

77. Ibid., pp. 27–28.

78. Ibid., pp. 64–65.

79. Ibid., p. 214.

292 IMAGES OF AMERICAN LIFE

80. See Spring, *The Sorting Machine*, pp. 151–171.

81. Sidney P. Marland, Jr., "The Condition of Education in the Nation, " *American Education*, vol. 7, no. 2, April 1971, p. 4.

82. Robert M. Worthington, "A Home–Community-Based Career Education Model, " *Educational Leadership*, vol. 30, no.3, December 1972, p. 213.

83. Sidney P. Marland, Jr., "The School's Role in Career Development, " *Educational Leadership*, vol. 30, no. 3, December 1972, pp. 203–205.

84. "Education Amendments of 1972, " *Public Law 318–June 23, 1972*.

85. Ibid.

86. Spring, *The Sorting Machine*, pp. 155–159.

87. Quoted in Gitlin, p. 278.

88. Paley, p. 314.

89. Daniel Schorr, *Clearing The Air* (Boston: Houghton Mifflin, 1977), pp. 38–39.

90. Paley, p. 314; Gitlin, p. 277–78.

91. Shorr, p. 52.

92. Ibid., p. 54.

93. Paley, p. 320.

94. Paley, p. 322; Shorr, pp. 55–56.

95. Schorr, p. 57.

96. Ibid., p. 119.

97. Ibid., p. 114.

CHAPTER 13. PUBLIC BROADCASTING AND BIG BIRD

1. Carnegie Commission on Educational Television, *Public Television: A Program for Action* (New York: Harper & Row, 1967), p. 18.

2. Ibid., p. 14.

3. Ellen Condliffe Lagemann, *The Politics of Knowledge: The Carnegie Corporation, Philanthropy, and Public Policy* (Middletown, Conn.: Wesleyan University Press, 1989), pp. 222–223.

4. Willard Rowland, "Public Involvement: The Anatomy of a Myth, " in *The Future of Public Broadcasting*, ed. Douglass Cater and Michael Nyhan (New York: Praeger, 1976), p. 111.

5. Timothy Brennan, "Masterpiece Theatre and the Uses of Tradition, " in *American Media and Mass Culture*, ed. Donald Lazere (Berkeley and Los Angeles: University of California Press, 1987), p. 376.

6. As quoted by Lagemann, pp. 222–223.

7. Richard Hofstadter, *Anti-Intellectualism in American Life* (New York: Random House, 1962), pp. 3–55.

8. As quoted in James L. Baughman, *Television's Guardians: The FCC and the Politics of Programming, 1958–1967* (Knoxville: University of Tennessee Press, 1985), pp. 34–35.

9. Ibid., p. 33.

10. As quoted in ibid., p. 61.

11. Ibid., p. 160.

12. As quoted in Lagemann, p. 220.

13. Alan Pifer, "When Fashionable Rhetoric Fails, " *Education Week,* vol. 23, February 1983, p. 24.

14. James B. Conant, *The American High School Today* (New York: McGraw-Hill, 1959).

15. Lagemann, pp. 238–244.

16. Gerald S. Lesser, *Children and Television: Lessons from "Sesame Street"* (New York: Vintage, 1975), p. xxiv.

17. Lagemann, p.233.

18. Edward L. Palmer, *Television & America's Children: A Crisis of Neglect* (New York: Oxford University Press, 1988), p. 13.

19. Lesser, p. 47.

20. Lagemann, p. 218.

21. See Baughman, pp. 160–161, and Lagemann, pp. 224–225.

22. Other members of the commission included Lee DuBridge, President, California Institute of Technology; Ralph Ellison, author; John Hayes, former U.S. Ambassador to Switzerland; David Henry, President, University of Illinois; Joseph McConnell, President, Reynolds Metals Company; Franklin Patterson, President, Hampshire College; Terry Sanford, former Governor of North Carolina; Robert Saudek, Robert Saudek Associates, Inc.; and James Killian, Chairman of the Corporation, Massachusetts Institute of Technology.

23. Steve Millard, "Specialized Audiences: A Scaled-Down Dream?" in Cater and Nyhan, p. 185, 187–188.

24. Ibid., pp. 193–194.

25. Rowland, p. 111.

26. Membership of the joint committee included representatives from the American Council on Education, the Association for Education by Radio, the Association of Land-Grant Colleges and Universities, the National Council of Chief State School Officers, the National Association of Educational Broadcasters, the National Association of State Universities, and the National Education Association.

27. Robert J. Blakely, *To Serve the Public Interest: Educational Broadcasting in the United States* (Syracuse: Syracuse University Press, 1979), p. 18.

28. Baughman, p. 90.

29. Blakely, p. 84.

30. Ibid., p. 86.

31. Ibid., pp. 102–110.

32. Ibid., p.116.

33. Ibid., pp. 135, 143–145.

34. As quoted in Baughman, p. 94.

35. As quoted in ibid.

36. Blakely, p. 147.

37. Carnegie Commission on Educational Television, p. 8.

38. Ibid., p. 92.

39. Ibid., p. 92–93.
40. Ibid., p.95.
41. Ibid.
42. Lagemann, p. 232.
43. Lloyd Morrisett, "Introduction" in Lesser, p.xxi.
44. Ibid., p. xxvi.
45. Lagemann, p. 233.
46. Joan Cooney, "Foreword, " in Lesser, p.xvii.
47. Lesser, p. 7.
48. Ibid., pp. 8–9.
49. Ibid., p. 23.
50. Ibid., pp. 89–90.
51. Ibid., p. 19.
52. Ibid., p. 80.
53. Ibid., pp. 80–81.
54. Ibid., p. 60.
55. Ibid., p. 47.
56. Ibid., p. 204.
57. Ibid., pp. 208–211.
58. Ibid., pp. 24–25.
59. Ibid., pp. 254–255.
60. Ibid., p. 95.
61. Ibid.
62. Ibid.
63. Ibid., pp. 199.
64. Ibid., p. 200.
65. Palmer, p. 103.
66. Ibid., p. 104.
67. Ibid., pp. 106–108; quote from p. 107.

CHAPTER 14. CONCLUSION AND EPILOGUE

1. See Joel Spring, *American Education, 5th ed.* (White Plains, N.Y.: Longman, 1991), pp. 203–210.
2. Randall Rothenberg, "TV Industry to Fight Against Drinking and Driving, " *New York Times,* August 31, 1988, pp. A1, D17.
3. Ibid.
4. Bill Carter, "Television: A Message on Drinking Is Seen and Heard, " *New York Times,* September 11, 1989, p. D11.
5. Richard Bernstein, "The Arts Catch Up with a Society in Disarray, " *New York Times,* September 2, 1990, Section 2, pp. H1, H12, H13.
6. Felicity Barringer, "A Land of Immigrants Gets Uneasy About Immigration, " *New York Times,* October 14, 1990, p. E4.

7. As quoted in ibid.

8. As quoted in David Brand, "The New Whiz Kids, " *Time,* vol. 130, no. 1, August 31, 1987.

9. As quoted in Judith Lessow-Hurley, *The Foundations of Dual Language Instruction* (White Plains, N.Y.: Longman, 1990), pp. 138–139.

10. James Crawford, "Bilingual Educators Seeking Strategies to Counter Attacks, " *Education Week,* vol. 5, no. 28, April 9, 1986, pp. 1, 9.

11. Dirk Johnson, "Milwaukee Creating 2 Schools for Black Boys, " *New York Times,* September 30, 1990, pp. 1, 26.

12. Suzanne Daley, "Inspirational Black History Draws Academic Fire, " *New York Times,* October 10, 1990, pp. A1, B6.

13. Bernstein, p. H13.

14. Stuart M. DeLuca, *Television's Transformation: The Next 25 Years* (New York: A. S. Barnes, 1980), pp. 179–205.

15. Phyllis Schlafly's letter was reprinted as "Please Excuse My Child from..." in *School & Community,* vol. 72, no. 1 (Fall 1985), p. 8.

16. Spring, pp. 126–131.

17. "The Ruling in *Mozert v. Hawkins County Public Schools,*" *Education Week,* vol. 6, no. 9, November 5, 1986, p. 18.

18. Debar Viadero, "Panels in Ga., N.C., Reject Controversial Textbooks, " *Education Week,* vol. 10, no. 6, October 10, 1990, pp. 13–14.

19. Ibid., p. 13.

20. As quoted by Senator Lowell Weicker in U.S. Senate, Committee on Labor and Human Resources, *Hearing on William J. Bennett, of North Carolina, to be Secretary of the Department of Education, 97th Congress, 1st Session* (January 28, 1985), p. 61.

21. Ibid., pp. 173–174.

22. N. R. Kleinfield, "Ad Scene: Television That Makes Advertisers Dive for Cover, " *New York Times,* March 6, 1989, p. D12.

23. "A Mother Is Heard as Sponsors Abandon a TV Hit, " *New York Times,* March 2, 1989, pp. A1, D20.

24. Kleinfield, p. D12.

25. Ibid.

26. "Lawmakers Criticize Proctor & Gamble over Ads, " United Press International, March 22, 1990, no. 0427, and "Boston Ad, " Associated Press, March 21, 1990, no. 1858, *Executive News Service, Compuserve.*

27. Edward L. Palmer, *Children in the Cradle of Television* (Lexington, Mass.: Lexington Books, 1987), pp. 25–26.

28. Nathaniel Nash, "White House Gets Bill Reducing Ads on Children's TV Programs, " *New York Times,* October 2, 1990, pp. A1, D21; Barbara Gamarekian, "Ads Aimed at Children Restricted, " *New York Times,* October 18, 1990, pp. D1, D22.

29. Sara Rimer, "Obscenity or Art? Trial on Rap Lyrics Opens, " *New York Times,* October 17, 1990, pp. 1, 22.

30. Jon Pareles, "Store Owner Convicted of Obscenity in Album Sale, " *New York Times,* October 4, 1990, p. A18; Jeff Berliner, "Mayor Says 'No' to 2 Live Crew

Music, " United Press International, July 13, 1990, no. 1639, *Executive News Service, Compuserve;* Guy Coates, "Record Labeling, " Associated Press, July 7, 1990, no. 1434, *Executive News Service, Compuserve.*

31. Karen Haywood, "Record Labeling, " Associated Press, July 10, 1990, no. 0336, *Executive News Service, Compuserve.*

32. Ibid.; R. B. Fallstrom, "Music Minors, " Associated Press, June 5, 1990, no. 0202, *Executive News Service, Compuserve.*

33. Robert Sklar, *Movie-Made America: A Cultural History of American Movies* (New York: Random House, 1975), pp. 296–297.

34. Jack Valenti, "We Don't Need a New Category Between R and X, " *Washington Post,* May 6, 1990, *Executive News Service, Compuserve.*

35. Ibid.

36. Larry Rohter, "A 'No Children' Category to Replace the 'X' Rating, " *New York Times,* September 27, 1990, pp. A1, C18.

37. Larry Rohter, "Resistance to NC–17 Rating Develops, " *New York Times,* October 13, 1990, p. 13.

38. Paul Farhi, "FCC Bans All 'Indecent' Broadcasts; Move Taken to Protect Children, " *Washington Post,* July 13, 1990, *Executive News Service, Compuserve.*

39. Ibid.

40. "Editorial: 24-Hour Censorship, However disgusting…, " *Washington Post,* July 15, 1990, *Executive News Service, Compuserve.*

41. Bill Carter, "Congress Frees Broadcasters to Restrain Themselves, " *New York Times,* August 6, 1990, p. E5.

INDEX

A
Action for Children's Television (ACT), 259
Adolescence, sexuality and, 72–76
Advertising, 165, 173–74
Advertising Federation of America, 133
Advocacy groups, 7–8, 256–59. *See also* specific groups, e.g., NAACP.
African-Americans. *See also* Civil rights *and* Racism.
changing image of, 151–53
ideological management by, 159
racial harmony and, 180–83
in textbooks, 203, 207
World War II and, 138
Agnew, Spiro, 222
Alcohol, 75–76, 252–53
"All in the Family," 219–20, 222
American Broadcasting Company (ABC), 99–109, 164
American Civil Liberties Union, 102
American Federation of Labor, 104
American Legion, 39–43
anti-Communism and, 157
blacklisting by, 172–73
National Education Association and, 126–27
schools and, 150
structure of, 40
American Medical Association, 7
American Social Hygiene Association, 33, 77
American Telephone and Telegraph, 99
American Textbook Publishers Institute (ATPI), 177, 209
American Way, People for, 257
Americanism, 28, 32–39, 156–58

American Legion and, 39–43
during Cold War, 166–70
commission on, 40–41
definition of, 183–84
purges for, 170–77
racism and, 161
textbooks and, 43–46
America's Answer, 27
America's Future, Inc., 175
"Amos 'n' Andy," 105, 208, 214
Andrae, Thomas, 121
Anna Karenina, 91–92
Anti-Communism, 3, 6. *See also* Cold War.
American Legion and, 157
pledge of, 172
in public schools, 126–31
purges of, 170–77
in textbooks, 131–35
Anti-intellectualism, 232–33
Anti-Semitism, 51–52
Anti-war movement, 221–24, 226–28
"Archie Bunker," 219–20
Armstrong, Jack, 146
"As Nasty as They Wanna Be," 259–60
ATPI. *See* American Textbook Publishers Institute.
Aylesworth, Merlin H., 103–4

B
Babbitt, 37
Baez, Joan, 221
Bagley, William, 20–21, 24, 75
Barnes, Walter, 62–63
Barron, Arthur, 224
Bataan, 153
Beales, Howard, 26, 31–32, 43, 45